W9-AAA-331

FOR THE GREATEST ACHIEVEMENT

A History of the Aero Club of America
and the National Aeronautic Association

THE COLLIER TROPHY

DONATED BY ROBERT COLLIER

AWARDED ANNUALLY BY THE NATIONAL AERONAUTIC ASSOCIATION
FOR THE GREATEST ACHIEVEMENT IN AVIATION IN AMERICA
THE VALUE OF WHICH HAS BEEN THOROUGHLY DEMONSTRATED
BY ACTUAL USE DURING THE PRECEDING YEAR

FOR THE GREATEST ACHIEVEMENT

A History of the Aero Club of
America and the National
Aeronautic Association

Bill Robie

Foreword by Chuck Yeager

SMITHSONIAN INSTITUTION PRESS
Washington and London

Editor and typesetter: Peter Strupp/Princeton Editorial Associates
Designer: Janice Wheeler

Cover and frontispiece: The Collier Trophy. Presented annually for the greatest achievement in aeronautics (since 1962, expanded to include space development), the Collier Trophy has remained America's most prestigious aviation award since 1911. Courtesy NAA.

Library of Congress Cataloging-in-Publication Data

Robie, William A., Jr.
    For the greatest achievement : a history of the Aero Club of America and the
  National Aeronautic Association / Bill Robie
      p.   cm.
  Includes bibliographical references and index.
  ISBN 1-56098-187-3
    1. National Aeronautic Association (U.S.)—History. 2. Aeronautics—United
  States—Societies, etc.—History. 3. Aeronautics—United States—History.
  I. National Aeronautic Association (U.S.)   II. Title.
  TL521.R56 1993
  629.13'006073—dc20   92-31823
                                                                              CIP

British Library Cataloguing-in-Publication Data is available.

99 98 97 96 95 94 93   5 4 3 2 1

∞ The paper used in this publication meets the minimum requirements of the American National Standard for Permanence of Paper for Printed Library Materials Z39.48-1984.

Publication of this volume was made possible by the National Aeronautic Association.

FOR AMY

CONTENTS

FOREWORD

The National Aeronautic Association (NAA) is the oldest national aviation organization in the United States. Its roots date back to 1905, when
members of the Automobile Club of America formed the Aero Club of
America. From that date, first the Aero Club and later its successor, the
NAA, have been at the center of aviation developments in this country.

So central to aviation was the Aero Club that it issued all pilot licenses
in the United States until 1926, when, at its urging, Congress enacted
legislation establishing federal responsibility over aviation, including licensing of both pilots and aircraft. It was the Aero Club—dismayed at the
lack of interest in aircraft expressed by our military—that, in the days
before World War I, spearheaded the public call to Congress to appropriate money to develop an air force. The Aero Club then established the
National Aeroplane Fund, which raised large sums from public donations
for pilot training and aircraft acquisition.

In the early 1920s, the leaders of the Aero Club believed that
America's aviation interests would be better served if a successor organization was established, that would bring together several aviation organizations with a national scope. The NAA was thus born in 1922, and all
of the assets of the former Aero Club were transferred to it.

In 1910, Robert J. Collier, son of Collier's Weekly publisher P. F.
Collier, established a trophy to be presented by the Aero Club annually
"for the greatest achievement in aviation in America, the value of which
has been thoroughly demonstrated by use during the preceding year."

This 525-pound trophy was first presented in 1911 to Glenn Curtiss, and has been presented every year since then, with the exception of the war years 1917–1920. It has become known as the Collier Trophy and is rightly considered the most prized of all aviation honors in the United States. A review of the winners, and the reasons they were awarded this trophy, provides a fascinating insight into the history of aviation as viewed from the insightful vantage point of those who made the selection each year over this long period of time. But this book does more than merely relate historical highlights. The appendixes offer interesting and useful information about many of America's earliest pilots—information that complements and enriches the text. Nowhere before has a list of names of the early Aero Club license holders ever been published. Bill Robie has performed a real service by painstakingly going through the early card record of the Aero Club and abstracting the names and license numbers of all these early pioneers.

Robie has also provided analysis of and insight into a number of the historical events he recounts. For example, he notes that the first five licenses issued by the Aero Club were as follows:

License number   1—Glenn H. Curtiss
                    2—Lt. Frank P. Lahm
                    3—Louis Paulhan
                    4—Orville Wright
                    5—Wilbur Wright

In the years since these first U.S. airplane pilots' licenses were issued, it has become an accepted piece of aviation folklore that the Wrights were intentionally assigned license numbers higher than Curtiss because the American aviation community wished to show its disapproval of the brothers' patent litigation efforts. Robie dispells that myth with an argument based on historical records. He shows that the Aero Club fully supported the Wrights but that, when it began issuing U.S. airplane licenses, it presented the first ones in alphabetical order to those five pilots whose flying abilities had already been demonstrated. Thus, the Wrights appear to have really been victims of the alphabet, and not of intentional malice.

Robie accurately describes the changing mission of the NAA over the years, and the evolutionary reasons for these changes. He also ably describes the importance of the NAA today as it approaches the end of its first century of service to American aviation.

The Aero Club was a founding member—also in 1905—of the Fédération Aeronautique Internationale (FAI). The FAI has since evolved into an eighty-nation organization that coordinates sport aviation and conducts world championships in much the same manner as the International Olympic Committee. The FAI is also the world's record keeper for all aviation (and now space) records, and the NAA, as the representative of the FAI in the United States, oversees all records set by Americans. The NAA ably represents U.S. sport aviation in the FAI, and is one of the leaders of this prestigious organization.

For the Greatest Achievement tells the story of a unique aviation organization; one that has made a significant contribution to aviation in this country and, through the FAI, the world. It is a story that deserves to be told because it is the story of the development of American aviation. It is a story of our heritage—of the men and women who came before us and made aviation what it is today.

Chuck Yeager

PREFACE

My first meeting with Mal Gross, president of the National Aeronautic Association, was an appropriate, if somewhat unnerving, introduction to the modern NAA. Each time we began anew to discuss my writing this book, the phone rang and I was left on the sidelines in Mal's office, trying to act as if I was not overhearing the various conversations between him and members of the world press. But I did overhear the conversations, and what I heard had special meaning for me. For Mal and I had happened to schedule our first meeting on the day after a group of California Polytechnic State University students and their advisor became the first team in history to fly a human-powered helicopter. His phone stayed tied up that morning by reporters anxious to learn the details of the first record flight in a brand new world aviation category.

The students' record was not, in terms of altitude gained and duration of flight, an impressive one. The few centimeters of height and 6.8 seconds of hover time that the crew achieved seemed trifling compared to records already set by mechanically powered helicopters. But put into the perspective of history, and seen in context with the first feeble airplane flights the Wright Brothers had made at Kitty Hawk in 1903, it is an event of incredible magnitude. It reminds us that there are still flight frontiers to be conquered, and promises that the future of aviation will be as exciting as its past. And that was the reason that I was in the NAA offices in the first place—because of the excitement that I had always found in learning about the development of American aviation.

Most institutional histories tend to be of importance only to a narrow audience—usually those affiliated with the subject organization—and, as such, they are often lightly regarded by scholars. The history of the Aero Club of America and the National Aeronautic Association is different. Since its inception in 1922, the NAA has played an important role in nearly every event that made American aviation history. It, in turn, grew out of the Aero Club of America, which was the focal point of American flying activities throughout the early days of airplane, balloon, glider, and dirigible development. The Aero Club and the NAA are institutions to which every pilot of every category of flying machine can trace his or her heritage, and the NAA and its associated air sports organizations still represent all of American aviation—from aeromodeling to aerospace. In a sense, every pilot and aviation enthusiast in the United States has a bond with this organization, and so I felt that its history should interest anyone with a love of flight and a curiosity about its origins. What I soon discovered was that there was far more to the history of the NAA and the Aero Club than "flying stories." The two organizations have had profound and long-lasting influences on the technological, political, and legislative advances of both sport and commercial aviation in this country, from the days before the Wrights unveiled their wonderful flying machine on through our exploration of space. Here was an opportunity to contribute my mite to the growing body of knowledge about the field that has been both my avocation and my occupation for many years—aviation.

I think there were a number of reasons why Tom Crouch, Chairman of the Aeronautics Department, and Peter Jakab, Curator, at the National Air & Space Museum asked if I would be interested in talking with the NAA about writing its history. They knew that I shared their interest in the early days of aviation, and that I had spent several years researching the men, women, and machines that pioneered flight in America. They also knew that I had, over the years, participated in many of the air sports that fall under the umbrella of the NAA. As the son of a career military officer, there were few times in my early life that I had not lived within sight of a military airport. My earliest (not always successful) experiments with flight were with model airplanes and, later, model rockets. A Boy Scout field trip in 1960 to see the U.S. Army's Golden Knights parachute team brought about a resolve that I, too, would someday experience the thrill of skydiving, but it would be eleven more years before I was old enough to make my first jump. From that day on, I was addicted to flight, and, over the next two decades, pursued a pilot's license, was an "early" ultralight instructor, traveled the country for a while demonstrating ultralight aircraft for a subsidiary of Piedmont Airlines (in much the same manner as the early exhibition pilots), and learned the art of antique aircraft restoration. Along the way, the generosity of pilots and aircraft owners allowed me to fly more than fifty types of civilian aircraft, from ultralights to the Cessna Citation II business jet. My heart, though, will always be in the cockpit of an antique airplane—preferably one with "stick 'n' rudder" controls and a tailwheel, unfettered by the complications of modern avionics.

The reader will soon discover that the Aero Club and the NAA represent far more than associations of hobbyists whose common interest is flying. From the very beginning, their membership included some of the most talented and influential persons in the country. Since the birth of the Aero Club in 1905, they have been the U.S. representatives to the Fédération Aeronautique Internationale (FAI) and have supervised competitions; certified flight records; presented awards for achievement (including the Collier Trophy, America's oldest and most prestigious annual aviation award); issued flying licenses for more than twenty years before the U.S. government assumed responsibility for certifying pilots; lobbied for legislation to make flying safe and practical; and created the environment into which the sport, military, and commercial aviation industries of today were born. It would, in fact, be difficult for one to find a single name among the heroes of aviation and the giants of aircraft manufacturing who did not, in some way, participate in the Aero Club, the NAA, or both.

An essential facet of the history of these two organizations is the annual presentation of the Collier Trophy. Since 1911, when Aero Club president Robert J. Collier introduced the trophy as the "Aero Club Trophy," the two organizations have been the stewards of this, America's highest aviation honor. Awarded annually for the greatest achievement in aviation as demonstrated in the previous year, the Collier Trophy counts among its recipients a "Who's Who" of flight: Wright, Curtiss, Hughes, Martin, Boeing, Yeager, Lear, Armstrong, and a myriad of other women and men who pioneered flight and flight technology. Throughout this book the winners of the Collier Trophy, and their achievements, are described in sidebars intended to highlight milestones in American aviation history. They reflect the changes in technology, industrial development, public opinion, and the political climate that so greatly influenced American aviation—from Kitty Hawk to Cape Canaveral.

Although this book surveys many of the key events in aviation history from the perspective of an organization born about the same time as the airplane, it does not pretend to be a comprehensive survey of American aviation history. Indeed, it gives some of the more popular eras of aviation—such as the wartime periods—only superficial treatment. There are so many excellent works already available on aviation during these years that it would be pointless to try to duplicate them, and the reader is encouraged to consult them for additional information. Many fine sources are cited within this book. Likewise, only the highlights of the NAA's most recent years are discussed. Like any organization with comparable longevity and scope, the NAA is constantly adapting to the ever-changing needs of aviation in the United States, and I feel that the current progress of the NAA will be accurately viewed only through the perspective of time.

What the reader will find in this book are explanations of how so much of what we know of modern aviation came to be—from the earliest days of flight through the evolution of the various associations that support and encourage gliding, parachuting, aerobatic flying, experimental aircraft flight and construction, rotorcraft, hang gliders, ultralights, aeromodeling, and other forms of sport aviation. He or she will also glimpse some of the background to many of the record-breaking flights of pioneers from before the Wrights to beyond the first space explorations.

Finally, this book is intended to be a source of information for those who are students of aviation and U.S. history. Included in the appendixes, for example, is a never before published list of all American aviation licenses, for all categories of aircraft, issued by the Aero Club through the end of World War I. As the reader looks through these names, he or she will see women and men from all parts of the United States, and many foreign countries as well. Although many of these names are familiar to people the world over, I hope that some will be recognized because of closer ties. Perhaps they were linked to flight achievements in a form of flying that is of particular interest, or they were famed fliers from one's own part of the world. A few readers may even recognize the names of persons they were privileged to know personally, or to whom they are related. I would like to think that one function of this book will be to help perpetuate fond, and respectful, memories of such pilots. They showed America how to fly—it was they who gave us our wings.

Bill Robie

ACKNOWLEDGMENTS

The image that most of us have of writers is that they are rather solitary individuals who spend countless hours alone, nurturing a manuscript from conception to birth. Although that perception is partly accurate, the process of developing the manuscript from a rough document into a finished book is unquestionably a team effort. The following persons and organizations were part of the team that made my all too imperfect manuscript into this book.

I wish first to thank Drs. William N. Still and Donald Parkerson of East Carolina University for their comments during the early stages of the manuscript's development. I owe a similar debt of gratitude to University of Maryland, Baltimore County Campus, faculty members James C. Mohr, John W. Jeffries, and Hugh D. Graham (now at Vanderbilt University) for taking the time, on countless occasions, to give me advice and encouragement. I hope that readers of this book will be the beneficiaries of the years all of them spent trying to teach me the craft of the historian.

Most sincere thanks must also be extended to Dr. Tom D. Crouch, Chairman of the Aeronautics Department, and Dr. Peter L. Jakab, Curator, at the National Air & Space Museum for having enough confidence in my abilities to recommend me for this job. They, and Aeronautics Department Deputy Chairman Dominick Pisano, always had a friendly word and the solution to a seemingly unsolvable problem when they were most needed.

Others to whom I am deeply indebted are the librarians, archivists, and curatorial staff members of the various institutions where I sought material about the Collier Trophy, the Aero Club of America, and the NAA. These women and men have repeatedly confirmed my faith that human beings are, by nature, concerned, cooperative, and helpful. Although I cannot thank each individual, I would particularly like to recognize the staffs of the National Air & Space Museum Archives; the NASM Library; the Johns Hopkins University Library; the Enoch Pratt Free Library, Baltimore; the Thayer County, Nebraska, Museum of Local History; and the Rutherford B. Hayes Presidential Center, Fremont, Ohio, for all their help.

Also richly deserving of recognition are the officers, staff, and members of the various air sports organizations in the U.S. that, together, have long succeeded in making an early NAA slogan a reality by "keeping America first in the air." The value of the assistance they provided throughout this project cannot be adequately stated.

My thanks must also go to editors Ruth Spiegel and Felix Lowe of the Smithsonian Institution Press, and especially to Peter Strupp of Princeton Editorial Associates, with whom I worked directly on the manuscript revisions. Their mixture of patience, persistence, and professionalism combined to make this one of the most rewarding learning experiences of a lifetime.

The present staff of the NAA has remained involved with this book since its inception. From the time that Malvern J. Gross, Jr. (then new to the office of NAA president) determined that the history of America's oldest extant national aviation organization needed to be recorded, until the final editing of the finished manuscript was completed, the NAA has made every effort to assure that its full resources were always available to me. In addition to the numerous instances when Mal Gross volunteered his time to confirm the accuracy and completeness of the book's contents, Arthur W. Greenfield, Secretary of the Contest and Records Board, and Linda M. Palmer, office manager, provided invaluable information and assistance throughout the project.

When the idea for this book was first conceived, the NAA was on an unstable financial footing and was unable to afford the funding for an undertaking of this magnitude. Mal Gross's appeal to the NAA membership for assistance was met with selfless enthusiasm. More than half of the funds were provided through the generosity of balloonists Jacques Soukup and Kirk Thomas. Without their encouragement, support, and knowledge the project would not have been possible. In addition, substantial resources were also provided by J. Leland Atwood, Anne Baddour,

Walter Boyne, Dean Edmonds, John Henebry, Donald Hetterman, Barron Hilton, Edward Lesher, Russell Meyer, Jr., Jim Nields, James Pyle, Jack Real, and Jack Schweibold. If this book contributes something worthwhile to the base of knowledge about U.S. aviation history, then it is they who deserve much of the credit for making it happen.

Finally, my greatest thanks go to Amy Arthur Robie, who went from new acquaintance at the beginning of the project to new bride as it approached its conclusion—all the while remaining my best friend and a constant source of inspiration. The many sacrifices that she made in order that this book could be written will take a lifetime to repay.

MEN OF WEALTH, INFLUENCE, AND ABILITY

Founders of the Aero Club and Flight before the Wrights

1

John Jacob Astor. William K. Vanderbilt, Jr. Charles J. Glidden. Phillip T. Dodge. Names to reckon with in the America of the early 1900s. These were the new American aristocrats—men of vision who had seen their dreams take tangible form on a scale hitherto unimagined in a young land. Yet still they dreamed. Although tied to the everyday reality of commerce, they possessed the wherewithal to foster new technology, the confidence to embrace it, and the foresight to plan for its orderly development.

On a desolate beach in North Carolina, two brothers toiled in anonymity. At a glance, the pair had little in common with the aristocrats. Their first venture together had been a small newspaper, and now they manufactured bicycles. Their dream was as yet elusive. But its time would soon come. When it did, their fate would be linked forever with that of their more prestigious contemporaries. In time, this confluence of lives would promote the growth of a remarkable assembly of men and women— one that would oversee a nation's reach for the sky.

On the evening of December 13, 1904, New York City Magistrate Leroy B. Crane stood before the members of the Automobile Club of America. In the audience sat men like Astor, Vanderbilt, Glidden, and Dodge. Theirs was an exclusive organization and they were among the most powerful individuals in America.

Judge Crane believed that automobiles showed some promise for benefiting humanity, but that, as long as the public perceived them to be merely dangerous toys of the irresponsible rich, they would force increasingly restrictive legislative control over the machines. The magistrate knew the men of the Automobile Club could help overcome the public's antagonistic attitude toward motorists. If he could persuade this group of gentlemen to set a clear example, other wealthy automobile owners would begin to obey the newly created laws. If the members of the club would express concern over problems like operating machines at dangerously high speeds and driving under the influence of alcohol, perhaps outrages such as the recent hit-and-run death of a Pelham, New York, farmer could be avoided, and motoring could be permitted to develop in an environment free of excessive regulation. These, he thought, are the men I need to convince. They can make the difference. The power of their opinion is more effective than any law.

Judge Crane began his speech: "You have men of wealth, influence, and ability in your club, and you can get anything you want from the legislature if you go about it in the right way." The judge encouraged these men to use their wealth for a good cause by posting substantial cash awards to promote safe automobile operations. Their club, he correctly stated, counted in its ranks men "who could give $1,000 [as a reward for locating the persons responsible for injuring the farmer] and not feel it."[1]

With these words he succinctly assessed a group that, within a year, would create another society—one so powerful that it would regulate and promote American aviation for decades. Certain of the more progressive members of the Automobile Club, in attendance that night, had already passionately seized on the concept of using their wealth and status not merely to foster safe motoring, but to reward and promote the safe, scientific development of tomorrow's technology. This motive became the cornerstone on which they were to build the Aero Club of America, an organization that later evolved into the National Aeronautic Association. From the day their charter was adopted until the present, these two associations—among many other roles—have served as the guardians of the most prestigious national and international awards ever given for aviation achievement.

At the close of 1904, the members of the Automobile Club were already showing an interest in aviation. Three weeks before Judge Crane's speech, the 461 active members had awarded their first honorary membership to Alberto Santos-Dumont, a Brazilian whose dirigible experiments over Paris constituted the first true examples of motorized flight. Throughout

1905 their interest increased as reliable sources reported that two Ohio brothers were making flights in a machine that relied on wings, rather than a gas bag, to raise it into the air. They wanted to know more about flying.[2]

In 1905 a core group of Automobile Club members decided to form an organization to promote aviation in America. In mid-October they opened their rolls with the intention of recruiting one hundred men as founding members. By November 15, they were only four short of reaching their goal—most of the recuits coming from within the ranks of the automobile club itself.[3] Although it is certainly remarkable that so powerful an organization could form in such a short time, even more amazing is the fact that some of the most influential men in America now sanctioned activities that, only a short time before, had been considered to be in the realm of dreamers, circus performers, and lunatics.

The Automobile Club's fascination with aviation appears to have grown out of the new-found European interest in ballooning. Long-distance automobile touring had for some time been a popular sport for the wealthy on both continents. In America, Charles Glidden was the master promoter, sponsoring auto rallies hundreds of miles in length and drawing enthusiasts from around the country. For some club members, however, the domestic tours were not enough. They traveled abroad to compete and to explore new territory. During such visits they were always on the lookout for the latest foreign developments in technology, and it was thus that members of the Automobile Club discovered the growing European passion for long-distance balloon racing.[4] Such activity would have been less practical in nineteenth-century America, but now it seemed possible for this country to share the new sport of the genteel.

Of course, balloon flying was not new to America. On January 9, 1793, all of Philadelphia and the surrounding countryside had turned out into the streets and lined the rooftops to witness an exciting spectacle. Most prominent among the crowd were President George Washington and Pennsylvania Governor Thomas Mifflin. As a band played, cannon boomed, and the multitudes cheered, Jean Pierre Blanchard and a small black dog took to the air from the enclosed yard of Walnut Street Prison. It was the Frenchman's forty-fifth ascension, and the first balloon flight in America.

Blanchard conducted the flight in the name of science. He performed experiments for Dr. Benjamin Rush by exposing previously sealed bottles of various liquids to the elevated atmosphere and by observing his canine companion's reactions to flying. The fifteen-mile trip, which lasted forty-six minutes and terminated near Woodbury, New Jersey, had the highest sanction in the land. Blanchard carried a letter from the President, appealing to any citizen of the United States who should encounter the balloon as it descended to "aid him with that humanity and good will, which may render honor to their country." The letter George Washington handed to Blanchard could be considered the first air mail sent in this country.[5]

When the novelty of seeing a balloon flight wore off, however, American interest in the sport proved to be somewhat limited. The huge devices were expensive to operate. They also required a large apparatus to generate lifting gas and several people to attend them during the filling process.

Over the decades that followed, various "philosophers" proposed alternative methods of flying without using large balloons, believing man to be inherently capable of (if not necessarily learned in) the art of flying. One such believer, a Frenchman, reasoned that man, more than the flying fish and flying squirrel, had "in his muscles a prodigious intuitive source of motion, [which] ought to render himself more capable of flying than any of those animals." A man, he proposed, only needed a set of wings thirty feet long with an eight-foot tail as a "helm," the whole apparatus weighing no more than fourteen or fifteen pounds, to achieve flight. The New York magazine that published this general concept in 1833 introduced it with a bit of their own philosophy:

> The noble darings of the human mind,
> Inspired by science should be unconfined,
> Nor suffer men, like groveling worms, to lie
> Supine on earth, but boldly wing the sky.[6]

In a subsequent issue of the same magazine, a correspondent countered that smaller, more personal, balloons with oars and self-contained gas-generating equipment would be the German answer to the problem that the Frenchman proposed to solve with wings. Such a device would be small enough to be manageable and would allow the wearer to cover great distances in long, floating hops. Again the magazine interjected its own philosophy of flight:

> The Frenchman, volatile and light,
> Aspires to wing the air in flight;
> The German, heavy and profound,
> With nimble feet would trip the ground:

Philosophers! do what ye will;
But—"Nature will be nature still."[7]

Although there is no evidence that the personal balloon concept was ever tested, its proposal reflected some of the shortcomings of gas bag transportation, particularly in the United States. Once airborne, balloons were at the mercy of the winds, and, in America as elsewhere, the prevailing winds tended to blow from west to east. Balloon voyages begun in the largest cities—those on the east coast—thus risked termination in the Atlantic Ocean. Attempts at longer-distance voyages starting from western population centers involved flying over sparsely populated areas with rough terrain. Only a few professional aeronauts were brave enough to attempt such flights, and those who did risked being lost forever. It was not uncommon for these brave souls to land in areas so remote that it could take days or even weeks for them to find their way back to civilization. With these hazards, long-distance ballooning held little appeal as a sport.

And so for decades American ballooning survived primarily as a means by which a few enterprising operators made a modest living roaming from town to town. They carried aloft those who were curious enough to pay, made exhibition ascents of an unusual nature (such as performing airborne wedding ceremonies), or made parachute descents from short-duration hot air balloons. These were called "smoke balloons" because they were inflated by using hot air from an open fire. As they ascended, the balloon discharged a plume of smoke.[8] Because the public was skeptical about their ability to fly, these pilots often assumed sobriquets and titles, such as "Professor" or "Captain," to give themselves a more credible image.

During the late nineteenth century, American aviation joined the circus. In 1874, master promoter P. T. Barnum used a balloon to draw record crowds to his Great Roman Hippodrome in New York. A trapeze-artist-cum-aviator named Washington H. Donaldson made daily ascents for Barnum. One observer described Donaldson's performances thus:

[the aviator ascended] . . . with naught but a trapeze swinging beneath the concentrator ring of his balloon, himself in tights perched easily upon the bar of the trapeze. And when at a height to suit his fancy, of a thousand feet or more, time and again I have seen him do every difficult feat of trapeze work ever done above the certain security of a net.[9]

Donaldson's aerial trapeze work was but a preamble to the promotional coup Barnum planned for the public. After weeks of pre-event publicity, he unveiled the world's largest balloon (not surprisingly christened the *Barnum*). Paying customers packed the Hippodrome to see this enormity of the air launched on a voyage that attempted to set world records for flight endurance and distance—and succeeded.

Pilot Donaldson carried five passengers, all reporters from New York's major newspapers. To augment the publicity for Barnum's enterprises further, the craft carried thousands of multicolored tissue paper fliers labeled "News from the Clouds," advertising Barnum's Hippodrome. The balloon crew rained these down upon awestruck spectators along the flight path. This flight of the *Barnum* terminated in Saratoga, New York, having shown that cross-country travel in America was possible. However, on a flight from Chicago the next year, aviator and balloon vanished without a trace—reinforcing the dangers of such attempts.[10]

Although events such as these brought the balloon into the American spotlight, they further tarnished the image of both aviation and aviator. The circus was a perfectly respectable entertainment for the public to attend, but people felt there was something unsavory about those who worked there. Pilots often worked under pseudonyms to save their loved ones the embarrassment of having the family name associated with "show business."[11] It was interest in the European sport of long-distance balloon racing that helped rescue American aviation from this disreputable image.

Sport ballooning had developed somewhat differently on the continent. There the same predominantly west-to-east winds that hindered long American flights tended to carry balloons further inland. Although the sport was still hazardous, the terrain above which the pilots flew was substantially more settled than that in America. A pilot could feel reasonably assured that he or she would be able to land in an inhabited area, where return transportation for crew and balloon could be secured.

It was a pivotal point in time—one when technological history unfolded within a matrix of social developments. With the turn of the century came a new America. Census statistics indicated, as noted in a widely read treatise by Frederick Jackson Turner, that the entire country was finally settled.[12] Railroad lines brought regions together. New roads and the automobile promised to make even the smallest of towns accessible. The challenge of a geographical frontier was gone and only the sky was left to conquer.

In the vigorous sociopolitical environment of Progressivism, the country collectively flexed its muscles with a new nationalistic spirit. America had to compete with—and surpass—the industrial progress of other nations. Leaders of industry, such as those who comprised the membership of the Automobile Club, felt it was their responsibility to establish American technological superiority.

The wealthy in America, as elsewhere, espoused a new doctrine known as social Darwinism, a convolution of Charles Darwin's *The Origin of Species.* This pseudoscience taught—and the powerful eagerly believed—that the principles of biological evolution also worked within the social structure. It stated that those who were characteristically brave and strong were the fittest leaders, ones who must, by the "laws of nature," inevitably assume positions of power.[13]

The wealthy set about confirming to themselves that they were, indeed, the best suited to leadership. They participated in vigorous sports like big game hunting, long-distance automobile touring, and aviation. It was men like these, with their wealth, influence, ability, and need to prove themselves masters of their environment, who took the Aero Club of America on its maiden flight. And it was these men who would see American aviation through the tragedies and triumphs of the soon-to-dawn era of the airplane.

PROMOTING THE DEVELOPMENT OF THE PRACTICAL FLYING MACHINE | 2

The Debut of the Aero Club and Its First Aviation Exhibit

According to a news article of the time, one of the initial acts of the Aero Club's first president, Homer W. Hedge, was to send a telegram to Courtland Field Bishop in Paris, authorizing him to act as the organization's European representative. Bishop, an Automobile Club member, was in France learning to fly balloons. President Hedge hoped he could persuade some of the leading European aviation experts to come to America as guests of the Aero Club. Perhaps, he told the press, even the great Alberto Santos-Dumont might be induced to lecture on the science of aerial navigation.[1]

Bishop's appointment appears, from the early news accounts, to have come at an extremely opportune time—it allowed him to participate in an international conference of "air balloon" enthusiasts, held in Paris during October 1905, as the representative of a fast-growing American aviation club. The world's leading aeronautical associations attended, including the Deutscher Luftschiffer Verband of Germany, the Aero Club of Spain, the Aero Club of Belgium, the Aero Club of America, the Aero Club of the United Kingdom, the Italian Aeronautic Society, the Swiss Aero Club, and the host for the meeting, the Aero Club of France. These eight aero clubs, including the Aero Club of America, became the founding members of an organization of national aeronautic associations, the Fédération Aeronautique Internationale (FAI). To this day, the FAI remains the international sanctioning body for all aviation records and record attempts, and the NAA, successor to the Aero Club of America, still represents the United States in FAI matters.[2]

Yet the formation of the American aero club was hardly as spontaneous as the early reports make it appear, nor was Bishop's presence in Paris at the founding of the FAI entirely a matter of fortunate chance. Bishop, an avid automobiling enthusiast in the days when being a motorcar "tourist" was synonymous with the pursuit of romance and adventure, had spent most of 1905 in Europe and Africa.[3] During June of that year, in Brussels, Belgium, a meeting of the Olympic Congress resolved that a world federation of aeronautics be formed, and plans were made to hold a meeting for that purpose on October 12, 1905, in the Paris rooms of the Automobile Club of France.[4] Whether or not Bishop actually attended the Brussels meeting is uncertain, but it appears probable that he did, because on June 7, 1905, the articles of incorporation for the Aero Club of America were filed with the secretary of state in Albany, New York. Named as the board members, and the sole owners of stock in the corporation, were Augustus Post, Homer W. Hedge, Dave H. Morris, John F. O'Rourke, and Charles J. Glidden.[5] When, in October, the leaders of the various national aviation organizations met to form the FAI, the organizational structure of the Aero Club of America was apparently firmly in place. All the new Aero Club needed was members, and the announcement of the formation of an international aeronautic federation—one in which Americans already held a place—proved to be the ideal way to launch a successful membership drive.

President Hedge stated that the Aero Club's purpose would be largely educational. Its policy, he said, would be to encourage "a proper interest in the possibilities of aeronautics." He hoped the members would be able to secure a balloon for the club to use by spring, but was emphatic that they would not limit themselves to ballooning. They would perhaps attempt to build their own balloon or dirigible, or even an "aeroplane," during the following year.[6]

For its first official event, the Aero Club engaged Charles M. Manly to speak to the combined membership of the Automobile Club and the new Aero Club. During the evening of November 14, 1905, Manly, former assistant to Smithsonian secretary Samuel P. Langley, told them about the aeronautical experiments he had conducted with his former employer. Manly reviewed the history of man's attempts at flight and brought the club up to date on developments in aerial navigation, showing photographs of flying machines being built in the United States and elsewhere in the world. The lecture, it was reported, "was frequently interrupted by questions by the listeners showing that many at least were not only interested in the subject but well posted."[7] Manly's presentation had such a profound impact that the Automobile Club members in attendance resolved that their 1906 automobile show in New York would also exhibit the most advanced developments in aerial technology.[8]

The club appears to have entered its first full calendar year with at least one hundred founding members.[9] Although the exact organizational structure of the original club is unclear, there was later mention of "a few who had previously thought of a club and arranged the preliminaries" before the membership rolls were opened at the Manly lecture.[10] The founding members who can be identified are listed in Appendix F.

An editorial in the *New York Times* prophetically noted that the Aero Club

had developed an association of men interested in the navigation of the air from which some real help in solving the great problem can be expected with some confidence. Included in the membership of the new Aero Club are possessors of money who are also equipped with more or less knowledge of machinery and mechanical principles, obtained in the practical operation of automobiles, which are devices with several close relationships to the coming airship . . . to carry the work into more practical lines. It is time to abandon the "balloon with a paddle" [the dirigible] . . . and to concentrate attention on the moving plane.[11]

The Sixth Annual Official Show of the Automobile Club of America opened on January 14, 1906, in the newly built 69th Regiment armory. "Only the latest models, latest appliances and creations never before exhibited will be shown," the advertisement read,[12] and the club made good on that promise. There were two novel attractions: motion pictures, some of which depicted automobile races, and the Aero Club's aviation exhibit.

Compared to the showing of cars, trucks, and motorcycles representing 75 different manufacturers and 205 exhibitors, the size of the aeronautic display was small. Nevertheless one reporter claimed that it threatened to upstage the automobiles. Many of the visitors who had come to see automobiles seemed more amazed by the impressive sight of three fully inflated balloons and a seventy-five-foot dirigible suspended from the high ceiling inside the huge building.

The newest of the balloons bore the name *Aero Club No. 1* painted on its side, identifying the prospective owners. It had been completed by balloon manufacturer Leo Stevens just before the opening of the show and needed only to be test-flown before the Aero Club would take delivery. Stevens already had plans for a flight following the show's close. Another Stevens creation, the dirigible *No. 3,* appeared nearby, also inflated as if in flight. A French balloon, *L'Allouette,* brought to America by pilot Charles Levee, and a smaller one designed to carry scientific instruments on unmanned flights completed the "in-flight" portion of the exhibit, but there was much more to be seen on ground level.

The walls of the armory's gymnasium were lined with photographs of flying machines, both functional and fanciful, from all over the world.[13] Models of proposed heavier-than-air craft filled display cases, and kites of every conceivable design were exhibited by proud builders. The largest of the kites was Alexander Graham Bell's *Oinos,* a 408-cell tetrahedral design, constructed from bright red silk (so it would show up better in black-and-white photographs). The great inventor himself visited the auto show and favored the crowd with a lecture on his kite-flying experiments. They were awed to learn that the huge kite on display was but a smaller model of his 1300-cell *Frost King,* which had successfully carried a man aloft.[14]

The framework and propulsion systems of two dirigibles, Thomas Baldwin's *California Arrow* and Santos-Dumont's airship *No. 9,* were mounted at eye level for the crowds to examine closely. The gas bags of these machines were not inflated. Suspending one of the sausage-shaped dirigibles from the ceiling was, it seems, more difficult than hanging a spherical balloon. On the evening of the first day, Leo Stevens noticed that his machine was beginning to sag in the middle. He ordered a crew of workmen into the overhead girders, intending for them to lower the dirigible and attach more supporting lines. In the process one of the workmen lost his footing and, in order to save himself from falling, dropped a pulley he was carrying. The falling pulley ripped through the envelope of the dirigible. Stevens was able to patch the fabric sufficiently to last out the exhibition, but lamented that a new panel would have to be installed before the machine would again be airworthy.[15]

The show also provided a glimpse of the future—it displayed a series of winged machines. Perhaps the best known of these were the Lilienthal glider and the *Aerodrome* built by Samuel P. Langley. Otto Lilienthal was a German engineer who made several hundred gliding flights in primitive hang gliders during the latter part of the nineteenth century. His untimely death came just before he was to begin experiments with motorized machines. Langley successfully flew a motorized model plane for well over a mile, but his attempts with a larger, manned airplane were unfortunate—and very thoroughly publicized—failures. Both Lilienthal and Langley were considered to be among the most reliable of the experts from whom scientific solutions to the problems of heavier-than-air flight might be forthcoming.[16]

There were other gliders and flying machines on display, but one small exhibit, centered around the crankshaft and flywheel from a gasoline engine, drew some particularly curious looks. The parts, it was alleged, were from the first engine to power a successful heavier-than-air flying machine—one using plane-configured surfaces to move through the air. This "aero plane" flying apparatus would indeed have been a marvel—if it had in fact flown. The reason that only the crankshaft and flywheel were shown, it was explained, was that the cylinders from the original engine were still being used, along with a newer and lighter crankshaft, in the inventors' latest flying machine.[17] The engine parts had been built by two Ohio brothers, Wilbur and Orville Wright, who had been secretly working on the project for years. Careful readers of the *New York Times* would have noticed a story about the Wright brothers among the flurry of aviation articles preceding the auto show's opening. The remarkable account stated that the two sons of an Ohio bishop had been flying since 1903, and that, only the year before, they had flown for thirty-eight minutes without stopping, covering a distance of twenty-four miles.[18] Skeptical visitors, wanting to decide for themselves if men had actually flown a machine without a balloon attached, crowded around the exhibit.

The show was a commercial success for the Automobile Club and the new Aero Club was congratulated for having staged an aeronautical exhibit that *Scientific American* magazine called ". . . the most complete of its kind ever held in any part of the world," adding that the club's exhibit should "stimulate interest in the art of flying . . . [and] greatly promote the development and perfection of the practical flying machine."[19]

Leo Stevens's earlier disappointment with the damage to his dirigible was assuaged. Race car designer Carl Fisher bought Stevens's dirigible for $8000, and Cadwalader Kelsey ordered a balloon to be built identical to the one awaiting delivery to the Aero Club.

Stevens and the other members of the Aero Club looked forward to the end of the exhibition. They were anxious to fly. Although the Aero Club's new balloon had not yet been tested, arrangements were already being made to match it against Levee's *L'Allouette* to see how American construction compared with that of the French.

But, as club members readied themselves to test the latest in ballooning technology, they were compelled to take a stand on the possibility that a far more advanced form of aerial navigation—the flying machine—had already made its debut. Had the young men from Ohio actually built, as they claimed, a practical heavier-than-air flyer? What would the consequences be for the members of the new club if they endorsed the Wrights without seeing proof that they could actually fly?

ENDORSING THE WRIGHT BROTHERS

The Aero Club's Early Support for the Fathers of Powered Flight

3

A surprisingly large number of people were trying to invent flying machines at the beginning of the twentieth century. The press seemed to group them into two categories: experts with scientific credentials who admitted they had not yet solved the problems of flight, and borderline madmen who claimed they had. The Wright Brothers were a problem for the media because they did not fit neatly into either category.

It was difficult for news reporters, who often understood little of what the experts told them, to explain the new science of aviation to their readers, who understood even less. It was even more difficult to determine who the true experts were. Some qualified physicists stated without reservation that it was theoretically impossible to build a flying machine without a balloon to lift it. Other well-educated persons said it certainly could be done and presented a wide range of proposals for achieving flight. The theories for building flying machines were as varied as the people who fostered them. A doctor named Daniel Caulkins, from Toledo, Ohio, claimed, for example, that he could build a gargantuan flying cube powered by "electro-magnetic circular power"—a force he had discovered while dissecting the muscles of a frog.[1] Amid such varied and often peculiar claims, it is easy to understand why the press and the public remained cynical.[2]

But by the turn of the century the airplane was an invention whose time had come. Recent advances in automotive and other technologies had created a general optimism that more long-dreamed-of inventions would soon materialize. Some of the greatest scientists in the world—men like Alexander Graham Bell—were addressing the problems of manned flight. Still, when the airplane finally did arrive, it was difficult to convince people that it really existed.

The founders of the Aero Club were the first group in this country to support the Wright Brothers officially. Soon after its exhibit at the New York automobile show closed, and amid a pervasive public attitude of skepticism regarding the Wrights' claims, the Aero Club adopted a congratulatory resolution commending them. It read:

Whereas, The Messrs. Wright Brothers, Wilbur and Orville of Dayton, Ohio, have developed an aeroplane type of flying machine that many times has carried a man safely through the air at high speed and continuously over long distances, and therefore is of practical value to mankind: therefore be it

Resolved, That the Aero Club of America hereby expresses to them its hearty felicitations on their great achievement in devising, constructing, and operating a successful man-carrying dynamic flying machine.[3]

It was a bold move from the standpoint of public opinion, for no member of the Aero Club had actually seen the Wright machine fly. The resolution came after a letter prepared by the Wrights, at the request of the Aero Club, was circulated among the members. This letter detailed their experiments to date, giving distances and times flown, and provided some sketchy information about the plane itself.[4] It is obvious that the Aero Club hoped the Wrights would respond by demonstrating their airplane to members of the organization, but that was not to happen for over two more years.

At the time of the Aero Club resolution, the Wrights were on the verge of entering into a long battle with the very people who would eventually profit most from their invention: airplane pilots and future airplane designers and builders. Throughout this prolonged conflict, the Aero Club strove to remain fair and impartial. It continued, as an organization, to support the brothers, in spite of later opposition from many of aviation's most powerful figures—including individual members and officers of the club itself.

The Aero Club had been following news of the Wrights for some time and had attempted to learn more about their flying machine, but that was not always easy to do. At the time of the automobile show, the Wrights had been experimenting with powered airplanes for more than two years, and with gliders since 1900. As their machine improved they began carefully guarding information about the methods they used to achieve flight, thereby becoming known as "the mysterious Wrights."[5]

Some of the Aero Club's first substantial evidence that the Wrights were actually flying came to it, oddly enough, through sources in France. Frank S. Lahm, Sr., an American who lived in Paris and was a prominent member of the Aero Club of France, read reports about their flying machine that the two Ohio brothers had sent to French aviation magazines. Lahm wired his brother-in-law in Mansfield, Ohio, and asked if he would investigate the stories about the Wrights. Honoring Lahm's request, Henry M. Weaver traveled to Dayton early in December 1905. After speaking with the Wrights and interviewing several witnesses to their flying experiments he wired Lahm in France: "Claims completely verified." Weaver followed the telegram with a letter giving details of his findings in Dayton. Lahm in turn notified the French Aero Club and his son in the U.S. Army that he had confirmed the stories from America.[6]

The press reports from France, based on information supplied by Lahm and the Wrights, actually did more to convince Americans of the Wrights' veracity than anything theretofore published on this side of the Atlantic. Perhaps the most persuasive argument that the Wrights might have accomplished something substantial was a subsequent report that the French government was negotiating a $100,000 contract for rights to the brothers' flying technology.[7]

If the French were that interested, the U.S. press reasoned, it should find out more about the mysterious fellows in Dayton. After years of indifference and abuse, the news media finally wanted to see what the Wrights could do. But their interest came too late. The Wrights, believing that they were on the verge of marketing their invention, and smarting after years of anything but benign neglect by the fourth estate, refused to display the airplane itself to reporters.

There is a common belief that the Wrights were always secretive and carefully hid their achievements from other aviation experimenters, as well as the press, from the outset. One often-advanced argument against the Wrights is that they availed themselves of the successful developments of others, but failed to share their own findings.[8] This view is not entirely accurate. In the early days of their experimenting they seemed quite willing to have their accomplishments publicized. Wilbur freely discussed the brothers' progress with gliding machines before the Western Society of Engineers in Chicago on September 18, 1901, and again on June 1,

1903, just over six months before their first powered flight at Kitty Hawk, North Carolina.[9]

After the Kitty Hawk flights of December 17, the brothers sent a telegram to their Dayton home, briefly reporting the facts and telling the family to "notify press." Attempts by the Wright family to arouse interest among local newsmen proved fruitless, but the story was made public—in a most unfortunate manner—by another source. The telegraph operator charged with forwarding the message passed the story without permission to a reporter from the Norfolk *Virginian-Pilot*. Unable to obtain further details of the flights, the reporter nevertheless forged ahead, publishing a story that was so obviously contrived that even the most gullible reader would dismiss any thought that it could be true. This ridiculous account—Orville later stated that the only accurate thing about it was that there *had* been a flight—was eventually picked up by the Associated Press and published in major U.S. papers, including the *Washington Post*. Every subsequent publication based on the Associated Press release seemed to get worse, with outlandish illustrations and absurd quotations attributed to the fliers. A clarification of the story the brothers sent to the Associated Press received some press attention, but the papers tended to print their own belittling remarks in conjunction with the Wrights' explanation. The Associated Press report was to damage the brothers' credibility severely for years to come.[10]

However, as yet undaunted, in May 1904, the Wrights attempted a practical demonstration for the press. More than thirty invited reporters came to their flying field outside Dayton. But first the wind, then engine trouble, kept the plane on the ground. As the first day concluded with no flying attempt, the reporters began leaving, convinced they had been led to witness another fraud. Toward the end of the second day, the Wrights' engine, firing on only three of its four cylinders, managed to drag the plane a few feet into the air for a flight of less than twenty yards. The plane suffered a hard landing, during which the propellers and other parts were damaged to the extent that the brothers could not try to repeat the demonstration. The few remaining reporters were unconvinced that they had witnessed a true flying machine in action.[11] The event received scant mention, even in publications conspicuously promoting aviation. *Scientific American,* for example, devoted two short paragraphs to the flight, concluding only that the machine "had another trial near Dayton, O., on May 26, which the brothers say was successful."[12]

An incredible paradox thus developed. Stories about the brothers' flights that found their way out of Dayton were discredited because the Dayton papers were not covering the events, and the Dayton papers made no attempt to confirm the persistent reports of a flying machine because they assumed that flying was impossible. Asked later to explain why the flights were ignored for so long, the former city editor of Dayton's *Daily News* admitted "the truth is we were just plain dumb."[3]

From that point on, Wilbur and Orville concentrated on developing the airplane and their piloting skills instead of on generating publicity. They became convinced that the essentials of their invention would be too easily stolen and resolved not to display their airplane until they had secured a reasonable contract for its sale. Their flights grew longer in distance and duration and were seen by a number of people working near, or passing by, the field they used for their experiments. These were the witnesses Weaver later interviewed for his report to Lahm.

The brothers first attempted to sell their invention to the U.S. government, but they were met with bureaucratic ineptitude. The government officials charged with receiving such inquiries were predisposed to believe that only balloons could fly. Their unenthusiastic replies to Wilbur and Orville insisted that the brothers furnish detailed construction drawings before the proposal would even be considered.[14] But to the Wrights compliance with this demand was out of the question. They had no intention of risking the theft of their invention in such a careless manner. They knew that they had a functional airplane, and the government's stance appeared to question their personal integrity. Having fulfilled their moral obligation to the government by giving it the first opportunity, and having been rejected, they now felt entitled to offer their airplane to foreign governments. As the overseas negotiations got underway, their domestic flight experiments became even more secretive.

By the time the 1906 exhibition opened, the members of the Aero Club of America had few doubts that the Wrights had achieved powered flight, but were unable to convince them to demonstrate the airplane. As the brothers' reputation spread across the Atlantic, news of their flights met mixed reactions. "Perhaps so far the most successful are the brothers Wright," wrote London balloonist Gertrude Bacon in 1905, "up to the date of writing this the full details of their work are not yet made public, but it is known that on the 17th of December 1903, their machine . . . started along a short track on level ground, rose into the air and flew for about half a mile."[15]

Other would-be airplane manufacturers, like British inventor and aviation experimenter Sir Hiram Maxim, became less charitable toward the Wrights as time passed. Three years after Bacon had given them a vote of confidence, the brothers still had not made public flights. The exasperation of one who had been continuously teased with wild tales showed in Maxim's writing: "As there seems to be much doubt regarding these alleged flights," he fumed in a 1908 book surveying flying machine progress, "we cannot refer to them as facts until the Wright Brothers condescend to show their machine and make a flight in the presence of others." Just before Maxim's book was published, Wilbur Wright traveled to France and finally "condescended" to show his machine. Maxim graciously ate his words in concluding remarks added just as the book went to press:

A few months ago the remarkable feats of the Wright Brothers in the States were discredited in Europe. It was claimed that "the accounts were not authentic," "too good to be true," etc., but recent events have shown that the Wright Brothers are able to outdo anything that was reported in the American Press . . . in fact, the remarkable success of the Wright Brothers has placed the true flying machine in a new category.[16]

More than three years after the Aero Club had first officially stated its belief in the Wright Brothers' claims, a Wright airplane finally flew before the public in France. The members of the Aero Club regretted that these first public flights were not made in the United States, but saw the demonstration as validating the faith they had all along placed in the brothers when skeptics called their flights impossible. The Aero Club's continued belief in the Wrights was expressed in sustained, and finally successful, efforts to have the U.S. military test their machine. Years later the NAA prodded the government to further recognition of the Wrights by promoting legislation to create the Wright Memorial in Kitty Hawk.

With the club's first exhibition of flying apparatus behind them, and the marvels of heavier-than-air flight still in their future, the spherical balloon held the members' immediate attention. The possibilities for the balloon's sporting, commercial, and military applications seemed to have barely been investigated, and they were men who deemed themselves of a class destined to explore.

SOCIETY'S SCIONS AND
SPHERICAL BALLOONS

4

Early Flight Experiments Conducted by
Club Members

After the automobile show, and with news of the Wrights' progress very much on their minds, the Aero Club members were eager to get into the air. Dr. Julian P. Thomas purchased Augustus Herring's 1897 Chanute-type glider, and said he planned to install a French-made gasoline engine on the glider and attempt to fly it as an airplane.[1] Another member, electrical engineer S. D. Mott, announced his intent to build a flying machine somewhat along the lines of the modern helicopter. He produced mechanical drawings of his machine and illustrations showing how it would appear in flight. The theory behind his ideas received the support of the dean of the School of Applied Sciences at Columbia University, who encouraged him to build a practical model.[2] Most members, however, pursued ambitions of flight in spherical balloons. Thomas himself also placed an order with Leo Stevens for a balloon.[3]

Members of the Aero Club were pleased when, on the night of February 5, 1906, an express package was delivered to them during their meeting at Automobile Club headquarters. The package contained a pilot balloon that was one of three launched the previous weekend from the grounds of the U.S. Military Academy at West Point, New York. Each of the three balloons carried a note asking the finder to return it to the Aero Club and offering a five-dollar reward for a letter containing details about where and when the balloon had been found, but only one was reported as having been returned.[4] As the members opened the package, they found that the balloon was undamaged.

The shipping papers indicated that it had been sent from Glen Head, Long Island—suggesting that it had flown at least seventy miles, crossing the Hudson River and Long Island Sound before coming to earth.

The Aero Club's West Point test of the pilot balloons was a small achievement, but it marked the beginning of an important and long-lasting association. It was the first experiment in which the civilian organization worked directly with the U.S. military to promote American strength through airpower. The test had been designed to evaluate the quality of the gas produced by the Army at its West Point facility.[5] Such gas needed to produce between thirty-six and forty pounds of lift per one thousand cubic feet of volume in order to raise a balloon. The test established that West Point was capable of producing gas of the highest caliber, yielding nearly forty pounds of lift per thousand cubic feet. The results were sufficiently encouraging that the club planned a manned flight for the following weekend.[6]

Looking at the clear blue sky above the military academy on the morning of February 11, 1906, Courtland Bishop exulted, "You wouldn't get a day like this in a thousand years for ballooning." Volunteers from the academy spread open the envelope of Charles Levee's *L'Allouette*, allowing the sun to warm it for an hour before inflation was attempted. One of the assisting cadets was a young cavalry instructor, Lt. Frank P. Lahm. This young army officer was the son of the Paris-based ballooning enthusiast by the same name who had earlier instigated an investigation to verify the Wrights' flights. Lahm, like his father, was a balloon pilot and a member of the French Aero Club. The West Point launch marked the beginning of his incredible career as a founder of U.S. Army aviation.

Also at West Point that day was the *Aero Club No. 1* of balloon manufacturer Leo Stevens. The Aero Club hoped to have the American balloon ascend along with Levee's, but the cold weather made it too brittle to inflate. *L'Allouette* took most of the day to fill and was not launched until late in the afternoon, when,

Amid a salvo of cheers from the officers and cadets of the West Point Military Academy and with the stars and stripes proudly flying from the French balloon *L'Allouette,* Charles Levee, a young Parisian aeronaut, who arrived in America about three weeks ago, made the first balloon ascension to-day conducted under the auspices of the Aero Club of America.

Standing among the cadets and the members of the Aero Club was another interested witness: E. R. Bronson, who, thirty-two years earlier, had been a passenger on the record-setting flight of the *Barnum* from New York to Saratoga.

Once aloft, Levee drifted slowly across the New York countryside and landed about thirty miles away, on the farm of Matthew DeWitt of Hurley, New York.[7]

The Aero Club members, and Stevens especially, were eager to compare the performance of Levee's balloon to that of craft built in America. They were also interested in trying new sources for lifting gases. So Levee and the club agreed to ship their balloons to Pittsfield, Massachusetts, for a competition between *L'Allouette* and the *Aero Club No. 1*.

The crowd gathered at the Pittsfield Gas Works on March 10, 1906, was estimated to number more than ten thousand. They were there to witness what had been advertised as the first international balloon race in America—and the maiden voyage of the balloon built for the Aero Club. At midmorning the aeronauts began filling their balloons from the gas works generators. Progress was slow. It was a windy day and the weather, coupled with the difficulty of trying to inflate two balloons at once from the same source, retarded progress. After more than six hours of work the balloons were finally ready, but it was still too windy to launch them, and they had to be weighted with dozens of sandbags to hold them in place. While the pilots attempted to secure the two balloons in this manner, a sudden gust pushed the *Aero Club No. 1* toward the crowd. It knocked down the first line of spectators before more than fifty volunteers took hold of the gas bag and brought it under control.

As night approached, the pilots informed a disappointed crowd that the race would have to be postponed until the following day, when, they hoped, the wind would subside. Levee considered deflating the envelope of *L'Allouette* for the night, but was persuaded to leave it filled in anticipation of an early flight the next morning. He was told that the area was protected from the strongest winds and that both balloons would be securely tied and ballasted for the night. Stevens's balloon also remained fully inflated.

At about 9:30 that night the *Aero Club No. 1* made its first—and last—flight. A sudden gale slammed the two balloons, tearing them completely from their moorings. *L'Allouette* blew into an iron post, tearing and collapsing the envelope. The *Aero Club No. 1*, still the property of the manufacturer, was last seen proudly flying solo toward the Atlantic Ocean. Later that year club member A. N. Chandler purchased a balloon of his own, named the *Initial*. It was the "initial" balloon owned by an Aero Club member and the first club balloon to fly with a pilot on board.[8]

Although the proposed race between Levee's and Stevens's balloons may have ended disastrously, the Aero Club found the Pittsfield Gas Works to be an excellent location for its experiments. The company offered the Aero Club free use of land adjacent to the gas works for a permanent launch site. It agreed to provide favorable rates on coal gas and pointed out that it was capable of manufacturing hydrogen, if club members desired. One problem previously encountered by Levee and Stevens—the length of time required to fill the balloons—could be solved: the Pittsfield company would generate sufficient gas in advance, then store it until it was needed. The filling procedure would also be speeded by the installation of a large-diameter pipe leading to the launch site.[9] Acquisition of the Pittsfield facility was fortunate. It came as the club finalized arrangements for a visit from Parisian balloon expert Count Henri de la Vaulx.

Count de la Vaulx was, at the time, vice president of the Aero Club of France and the international record holder for long-distance balloon flights. His visit would help to give the American aero club some of its first concrete international credibility.[10] The count was the only person to have ever crossed the Mediterranean in the air and the only pilot to have crossed the English Channel, traveling from France to England. Now he planned to make some preliminary flights with an eye toward a later American visit, when he hoped to undertake several record-breaking North American voyages.

De la Vaulx arrived on March 24 on the steamship *La Savoie* and was greeted at the pier by members of the Aero Club. He brought with him three balloons: the *Centaure,* in which he had made a 1300-mile trip from Paris to Kiev, the *Orient,* and the *Ludion.* De la Vaulx's stay in America was to be short. He needed to return to Paris in time to supervise the construction of a new balloon for the James Gordon Bennett International Cup in France and the Kaiser's Cup in Germany.[11]

On March 31 the count made his first American ascent, from the U.S. Military Academy at West Point. Only a small crowd was present. The forecast was for inclement weather to last throughout the day, and the Aero Club members, most of whom had not yet left New York, were notified to stay home because the flight was sure to be postponed. Lahm took charge of filling the balloon with gas in preparation for the next day's flight. By midafternoon, however, the weather cleared and the count, anxious to fly over America, opted to launch. He and his fellow countryman, Charles Levee, got away in a haphazard start that carried them first through the branches of a tree, then narrowly close to the academy's clock tower. An hour later they descended near Peekskill, New York. The count's long-awaited American balloon trip concluded, ironically, on the farm of a French immigrant. "It was," de la Vaulx remarked, "just as natural as being in my own country!"[12]

The Aero Club members took every opportunity to learn from this master pilot. De la Vaulx, Levee, and Dr. Julian Thomas flew from a gas works in the Bronx on April 2,[13] and the doctor, this time accompanied by his wife, went aloft again on April 11.[14] Throughout the rest of April other club members accompanied the count on flights from their newly established base in Pittsfield.

It appears that the would-be fliers were also learning how a new pilot's enthusiasm sometimes comes into conflict with the wisdom of more experienced airmen. At midday on April 14, de la Vaulx's giant balloon *Centaure* was three-quarters inflated for a flight scheduled to carry several club members on their first trip aloft. The count arrived at the field, apparently angry, and demanded that the gas be turned off. De la Vaulx, well informed of Levee's and Stevens's earlier problems with the wind, felt the day was too breezy to make an ascent safely in such a large balloon, and did not wish to risk his safety and that of his passengers. Rumors also spread that the count was upset because club members were unwilling to assure him that they would assume the expense involved in loss or damage to the $14,000 balloon. The newspapers reported that the very disappointed Aero Club members boarded a train for New York after having had a long discussion with the count. After so much preparation and anticipation, some members were, apparently, quite vocal in their protests. They could not understand why the count had canceled the event when flights in smaller balloons had been made under similar conditions. However, more experienced members like Courtland Bishop agreed with de la Vaulx.[15]

A resolution to the problem came within a few days. The Aero Club assumed responsibility for the equipment by purchasing the *Centaure* (now Americanized as the *Centaur*). On April 18 the count made an ascent in the huge balloon carrying club members Augustus Herring, Augustus Post, and Alan R. Hawley for a thirty-five-mile trip to Winstead, Connecticut.[16] On his next flight, on April 28, club president Homer Hedge and treasurer Charles Jerome Edwards went aloft.[17]

Before de la Vaulx sailed for France, the club also bought his balloon *Orient,* perhaps suggesting that the count's petulant behavior a few days earlier was part of a clever sales strategy. He was, after all, preparing to construct a new balloon for the upcoming Gordon Bennett competition, and the *Orient* and *Centaur* were both aging and probably considered outdated.

Whatever the case, it was in these, the first club-owned balloons, that members made thirty-three ascensions before the end of the summer of 1906. With every successful flight the Aero Club members' hopes—that America, too, might soon be able to field an expert balloon crew in international competition—must also have risen.

NATIONAL AND INTERNATIONAL FLIGHT COMPETITION

The Beginning of International Competition for Superiority in the Air

5

The first international competition for the Gordon Bennett prize, a long-distance balloon race, began in Paris on October 1, 1906.[1] Bennett, publisher of the *New York Herald,* had established the contest to promote aeronautics under the FAI. The winning pilot received a prize of 12,500 francs (then equivalent to about $2900[2]—a substantial sum for the time) and the sponsoring aero club took possession of the James Gordon Bennett International Cup for the next year. Bennett had specified that the first competition would begin in France, but thereafter the winning aero club would host the following year's race in its own country.[3]

Sixteen balloons were entered, representing France, Germany, Great Britain, Spain, Italy, Belgium, and America. The crowd of almost a quarter of a million spectators at the Place de la Concorde heard the cry, "*Lâchez tout!*" ("Let go all!") and watched the balloons rise. In spite of the race committee's careful planning to select a date when winds should have favored distance racing inland, to the east, the balloons slowly drifted westward, toward the Atlantic Ocean. There the few crews brave enough to continue found that the air currents turned sharply northward.[4]

There were two American entries in the race. Frank Lahm senior felt that the newly formed Aero Club of America should be represented in this historic event, so he had purchased a used balloon named *Eros* and rechristened it *United States.* But the balloon was an outdated model and stood little chance of winning against a field of specially built long-distance racers. Shortly before the race Lahm relinquished his position as pilot to his son.[5] The junior Lahm, newly transferred to the French cavalry school as a U.S. Army observer, had chosen a French pilot to be his partner, but, at the last moment, the Frenchman backed out. Major Henry B. Hersey, a veteran of Teddy Roosevelt's Rough Riders, happened to be present. Learning that Lahm was without a partner, he volunteered to join the flight, with only enough time to get his overcoat before takeoff.[6]

The contest committee recognized the Aero Club of America as an international organization representing all the nations in the Americas by accepting Alberto Santos-Dumont, the famed Brazilian airman, as that club's second entry. Santos-Dumont's balloon, *Two Americas,* had a unique feature. Instead of using sand bags for ballast, he mounted a sixteen-horsepower engine and propeller to the basket in such a way that it would move the balloon vertically, but not horizontally. It was an ingenious idea, but one that ultimately turned out to be Dumont's undoing. As he oiled the engine while it was running during the flight, his clothing entangled in the machinery, injuring his arm. He was forced to land the balloon to receive medical attention, thus disqualifying himself.[7]

As the competitors approached the Atlantic coast, most landed for fear of being blown out to sea. Lahm and Hersey, however, carefully examined their position and the movement of the air currents. As an experienced meteorologist, Hersey believed they would be able to reach the coast of England. Lahm concurred. They crossed the English Channel between eleven o'clock that night and three o'clock the next morning, then were able to find northerly winds to carry them further into England.

By the middle of the second day of the race, all but one of the balloon crews had been accounted for and the distance they had traveled determined. After many tense hours of waiting, in which it was feared that England's C. S. Rolls[8] might have been blown out to sea, his *Britannia* finally reported in, having also crossed the channel, along with *Elfe* of Italy, piloted by Alfred Vanwiller, and Count de la Vaulx's new *Valhalla.* Lahm and Hersey, truly the underdogs of the race, were pronounced the victors with a flight of 415 miles.[9]

Lahm's surprise win so pleased the members of the Aero Club that they prepared a silver trophy to present to the young lieutenant when he returned home from France. The Army, equally impressed with Lahm's accomplishment, granted him a year's leave of absence in order to study ballooning further, with an eye toward its military applications. Back in the United States the Army renewed an interest in balloons that had lagged since the Civil War, and members of the Signal Corps accompanied Aero Club pilots on flights from the Pittsfield site.

Yet with the honor of Lahm's win came a great responsibility. Under the conditions of the Bennett competition the winning aero club was required to sponsor the following year's event. The Aero Club of America, youngest of all the FAI affiliates, now faced the challenge of organizing the largest aviation event in the world.

Within days of the conclusion of the 1906 competition the French Aero Club issued a challenge to its American counterpart. They intended to bring the trophy back to France in 1907. The Aero Club named Courtland Bishop chairman of the newly formed Contest Committee and charged him with selecting a site for the 1907 race. The French race had been widely publicized in American newspapers, and reports of the huge crowds attending the Paris launch had not escaped the notice of real estate boomers in the west. Cleveland, Chicago, and St. Louis all soon offered to host the competition.[10]

The Aero Club entered its second full year with a new slate of officers to face a growing onslaught of responsibilities. The members elected Bishop president, Augustus Post secretary, Frank S. Lahm foreign representative, Leo Stevens advisor, and Charles Jerome Edwards and J. C. McCoy directors.[11] Along with the Gordon Bennett International Balloon Race, the club had a more immediate project: it was once again to sponsor an aviation exhibit as part of the New York Automobile Show.

The 1907 show (actually held on December 1–8, 1906[12]) featured fully inflated balloons and dirigibles, as had the exhibition the year before, but also displayed the basket from the balloon that Lahm and Hersey had used to win the Gordon Bennett competition. Another eye-catching display was the work of an early aero modeler. It was a five-foot-long dirigible labeled "The United States Air Line," complete in detail down to three passengers, a megaphone, the American flag, and a whiskey flask.

But there was now a new focus. Americans wanted to see prospective heavier-than-air machines and the engines that would power them.[13]

On the walls of the aviation section of the auto show, amid photographs of notable balloon and dirigible flights, were some of the first publicly displayed photographs of an airplane in flight. The heavier-than-air flying machine was the work of the famed balloonist and dirigible pilot Alberto Santos-Dumont, and these were photos of the first fully documented airplane flights in Europe. Detailed pictures of the engine and control mechanisms for the aircraft were included in the display.

There were also photos of the Wrights and some of their flights, but none of these were of powered aircraft—there were only photos of gliding experiments.[14] Even though the Wrights refused to substantiate fully their claims of having conquered the problems of powered flight, those at the exhibition showed a willingness to believe the brothers. Probably the most attention paid to the myriad of aeronautical engines on display was centered on a Wright twenty-five horsepower engine that was designed to power a plane capable of carrying both the pilot and a passenger.[15]

Several other aeronautical engines were present. Glenn Curtiss displayed an entire line of lightweight engines—from single-cylinder models to an air-cooled V-8, but the five-cylinder powerplant from Samuel Langley's failed 1903 *Aerodrome* was touted as having the best weight-to-horsepower ratio of any machine on display.[16]

With the auto show completed, Bishop and other board members began investigating potential sites for the Gordon Bennett competition, and they eventually selected St. Louis. The citizens of St. Louis offered $2500 to the winner, and the Association of Railroads and businessmen John Nugent and J. M. Schroerer posted additional cash prizes.[17]

The business leaders of St. Louis, who lost no time in finding ways to promote their companies, realized that balloons could serve as very effective aerial billboards. Although the actual participants in the race were prohibited from displaying advertising, there were no laws preventing nonparticipants, bearing commercial messages, from launching balloons at the same time as those entered in the competition. One wealthy, but egotistical, local manufacturer sought to sponsor a race contestant, hoping that a huge portrait of himself could be painted on the side of the balloon. After learning of the restriction against advertising on balloons actually participating in the race, and not having enough time to contract for his own balloon, he badgered another aerial advertiser to allow him to buy into a noncompeting machine already near completion. After much negotiation the owner agreed to sell advertising rights to half the balloon's envelope for a sum equal to one-third of the cost of construction. The manufacturer was very pleased at the prospect of his portrait occupying half of a balloon to be seen by thousands across America—until he discovered that the shrewd balloon owner intended to give him the *inside* half of the balloon envelope as his share.[18]

St. Louis, like so many larger cities, formed a local aero club under the umbrella of the Aero Club of America. The St. Louis Aero Club was initially formed expressly to manage the 1907 Bennett competition.[19] It created a trophy, the Lahm Cup, to be awarded to a member of the Aero

Club or an affiliated club who flew further than Lahm and Hersey had in the 1906 competition.[20] By accepting the responsibility of determining the winner of the Lahm Cup, the Aero Club marked the official beginning of its long history of officiating at American record attempts.

By February, German, French, American, English, and Spanish aeronauts had registered for the competition. An Austrian pilot also applied but he was turned down, for Austria did not yet have an aero club and the regulations stated that he could not compete in an FAI event without having a national aero club for a sponsor.[21]

The Aero Club members spent much of the year developing their ballooning skills and trying to determine who, besides Lahm, would represent the United States in the 1907 competition. By the time the event arrived, at least eight of their number were licensed to fly.[22] Members of a new affiliated aero club in Philadelphia developed plans for a new flying ground, complete with an enclosed hangar, and Aero Club director J. C. McCoy and Capt. Charles de Forest Chandler participated in experiments flying "war balloons," intended for observation use by the U.S. Army Signal Corps.[23]

The Gordon Bennett International Balloon Race of 1907 was a watershed event for both American aeronautics in general and the Aero Club in particular. Three American balloon entries sought to win the Lahm and the Gordon Bennett prizes, but, ironically, Lahm himself was unable to compete because of an attack of typhoid fever. His partner of the year before, Hersey, flew in his place with a companion named Arthur T. Atherholt. The other American teams were McCoy with Chandler and Alan Hawley with Post. A seventh American, Edgar W. Mix, flew as a team member aboard one of the French entries.[24]

On October 21, 1907, the St. Louis crowds, estimated at 300,000 people, were so large that President Theodore Roosevelt authorized the use of U.S. Army troops as police.[25] Aero Club advisor Leo Stevens was contracted to oversee the filling of the one British, two French, three German, and three American entries. The efficient manner with which he carried out the sizable task won him great praise from all the participants.

It was a long race, with each balloon remaining aloft for more than twenty-four hours. The German, Oscar Ebersloh, flying the balloon *Pommern,* won the event with an 872.5-mile flight. McCoy and Chandler, in the *America,* traveled 726.42 miles for a fourth-place finish; Hawley and Post were fifth with a distance of 714.5 miles in the *St. Louis;* and the team of Hersey and Atherholt placed eighth in the *United States* with a flight that terminated in Caledonia, Ontario. Although they finished at the back of the pack, this last pair may have had the most unusual experience en route. Flying three hundred feet over the Illinois countryside, and unsure of their exact location, Hersey shouted down to the crew of a railroad locomotive to ask the name of the nearby town. "Macomb," the man shouted back, "but don't run your damned old balloon into this smokestack!"[26]

The performance of the Americans notwithstanding, the race was a success for the Aero Club. It demonstrated that the club was capable of organizing an international competition and carrying it out efficiently. It also showed that long-distance flights across the United States were relatively safe. But perhaps of greatest value, given the original purposes of the club, was the U.S. government's and the American public's stronger interest in aeronautics after the widely publicized air meet.

The events of late 1907 foretold the beginning of an exciting year for aeronautics. New aero clubs formed in Boston and Philadelphia. Secretary of War William Howard Taft announced that the U.S. was lagging in aeronautical development and proposed steps to remedy the problem. Lieutenant Lahm investigated military dirigibles in Europe, while his mentor, Gen. James Allen, commander of the U.S. Army Signal Corps, sought $200,000 in congressional appropriations for an army dirigible program. U.S. military interest in aviation grew even stronger with reports from France that an airplane built by Henry Farman had flown more than a kilometer in a straight line, then later had flown in a complete circle. Finally, Brig. Gen. William Crozier, president of the Army Ordnance Board, announced that the U.S. Army would enter into negotiations with the Wright Brothers for the purchase of an airplane.[27]

It was the first sign of encouragement for the Wrights after almost three years of frustrating efforts to let the U.S. military be the first to have the use of airplanes. From the time they had sent their first letter to their congressman (R. M. Nevin, of the Dayton district, on January 18, 1905), and throughout the course of sending subsequent letters to Army officials, the response had always been the same. Even though their letters were accompanied by affidavits from reliable persons and reports from the Aero Club, they were repeatedly sent replies stating that it appeared that their machine had not yet "been brought to the stage of practical application."

In May 1906, the Wrights finally thought their problem had been solved. Senator Henry Cabot Lodge heard of their plight and personally brought evidence of the Wrights' success to the attention of Crozier, but the general did not follow up on his response to Lodge that he might send a representative to meet with the Wrights. Again in November of the same year, the press asked Crozier to comment on the status of his negotiations with the Wrights. He replied that he had made them an offer (he had not), and that the matter was in their hands. Even when the Ordnance Board was presented, in the spring of 1907, with a letter endorsed by President Roosevelt and Secretary of War Taft (at the request of New York Congressman Herbert Parsons, a friend of the Aero Club), the board's response to the Wrights was merely that, if they desired to "take any action in the matter, [the Board] will be glad to hear from you on the subject." After still further correspondence, and no doubt prompted by reports that foreign governments were becoming quite interested in the Wrights' airplane, Crozier, Allen, and Wilbur Wright finally met to discuss the terms under which the Wrights would demonstrate their machine to the U.S. Army.[28]

The year 1908 started off rather quietly. In January the club filed an official challenge for the Gordon Bennett competition in Germany later that year and nominated McCoy as the U.S. delegate to the international balloon conference in London, scheduled for June. Then, in late June, some of the club members found themselves engaged in a legal action of an unusual sort.

During a flight on June 20 from Pittsfield someone fired a rifle at Charles Glidden and Leo Stevens as they passed near the Vermont–New Hampshire state line. One of the two bullets glanced off the envelope without piercing the fabric, but the other penetrated the balloon, doing sufficient damage to cause them to land. The flight concluded in an even less pleasant manner as Glidden and Stevens landed in a pasture already occupied by a bull. They fled the charging animal and escaped over a fence, only to discover that they were lost. The grounded aviators wandered for hours through the dark, finally finding a farmhouse around midnight. One can imagine that the long walk heightened their resolve to locate and prosecute the person or persons who had earlier used their balloon for target practice.[29]

Five days later a deputy sheriff arrested two Vermont men and charged them with assault against Glidden and Stevens. One was eventually sentenced to six months to two years at hard labor.[30] Shooting at balloons was by then becoming a rather common practice, and the Aero Club determined to put a stop to it. On June 30 it posted a reward of $250 for information leading to the conviction of anyone shooting at a balloon or any other flying machine.[31]

Unfortunately the reward had little effect. The next year, during an Aero Club–sponsored balloon race from the newly opened Indianapolis Motor Speedway, Clifford Harmon reported passing over northern Alabama when a man yelled up to his balloon, "Come down here you—or I will bring you down!" The command was followed by three rifle shots, one of which penetrated the balloon's basket. Another competitor in the same race said that he had to fly at an altitude of at least two miles over most of Kentucky because of the numerous shots fired at his craft.[32] These events prompted an editorial in the *New York Times,* which noted that the phenomenon of people shooting at balloonists was not confined to America. It was becoming more prevalent in Europe, where "[balloons] have been viewed with some suspicion and hostility when they drift across European frontiers, but that is only part of the general war scare in that nervous part of the world, and no trace of such a feeling exists in this country." The editorial concluded, "some day one of these gunners will kill an inoffensive sky-traveler if the practice be not stopped, and it is therefore well that the practice to punish and suppress it be vigorous."[33]

An even more frightening experience—albeit of a different nature— overtook two officers of the club later that year at the 1908 Gordon Bennett race in Germany. Club secretary Post was in Washington, D.C., attending the first U.S. demonstration of a Wright airplane when he received a telegram from A. Holland Forbes. Forbes, a vice president of the club, had qualified to represent the United States in the Gordon Bennett competition, and he wanted Post to be his partner. Post left immediately to meet Forbes in New York, and they soon sailed for Europe, taking with them a new 80,000-cubic-foot balloon, *Conqueror.*

The fifty-foot-diameter balloon had an unusual experimental feature on its appendix, the long tube of gas-proof fabric extending from the bottom of the envelope to the basket, through which the balloon is filled and from which excess gas escapes under the pressure of expansion during the balloon's ascent. On the *Conqueror,* Forbes closed the appendix with a rubber band, loosely wrapped around the tube so that it could act as a one-way valve, thus conserving the small amounts of gas that might escape during flight. With this small innovation, they hoped to gain a narrow edge and win the competition.[34]

On October 11, 1908, the contestants prepared to launch their balloons from a field in a suburb of Berlin. The other Americans in the race included McCoy and one Lt. Foggman in the *America II,*[35] and Nason H. Arnold and Harry J. Hewatt in the *St. Louis.* Twelve German soldiers carried the basket of the *Conqueror* to the designated launch site and, at precisely 3:40, released the American team. The balloon had been carefully ballasted, but now it seemed to be slightly heavier than was necessary for a quick ascent. Rather than rising, it floated near the ground until a gust of wind blew it into a fence, tearing away two bags of ballast sand and spilling another. The sudden loss of weight caused the balloon to shoot skyward.

The rapid ascent made the internal gases expand, opening the experimental valve mechanism. Forbes had just commented on how well the device was working when, at approximately three thousand feet, the overpressurized balloon envelope burst. The valve had not permitted the expanded gas to bleed out quickly enough. Post and Forbes heard the explosive report and looked up to see a large hole in the side of the collapsing sphere. Post quickly released the rope that held the appendix near the gondola, and the lower half of the balloon crumpled upward to form a crude parachute. On the ground, thousands of spectators watched in horror as the collapsed balloon began falling. "She's gone," Post said matter-of-factly to Forbes.

As they fell back toward the city of Berlin, Forbes used his knife to cut away as many sandbags as possible and Post emptied still others by hand. Their rate of descent was checked somewhat by discarding this weight. As a last instinctive reaction, to lessen the shock of impact both aeronauts held onto the wooden ring connecting the gondola to the balloon's suspension lines. The gondola crashed heavily onto a housetop, partially penetrating the tile roof, while the collapsed balloon draped over a gable. Amazingly, apart from sustaining a few bruises, neither aeronaut was hurt. As Forbes unloaded the equipment, Post stepped out of the basket and began taking photographs of the wreckage.

The German press seemed fascinated with the Americans' calm demeanor in the face of death. The two might have perpetuated that image had not Post later admitted, "Perspiration was starting from every pore . . . thoughts came rushing in sentences. I found myself speaking German with a fluency that I never had before or have had since, answering questions with the greatest of ease, replying to the greetings and congratulations that came from every side."[36]

Yet, exciting though ballooning competition was, the Aero Club still longed to see "aeroplane" flights. Even though they were convinced that the Wright machine was actually capable of flight, it was apparent that the brothers could not be persuaded to put on an open flying exhibition. Public airplane flights would soon take place in America, but the Wrights would not be the pilots. Because of a peculiar set of circumstances, the Wright plane would first go on display in France, an Englishman turned Frenchman would bring his plane to the United States to fly, and a motorcycle racer sponsored by the inventor of the telephone would make the first American flights open to the public.

MECHANICAL FLIGHT

Introducing the Public to the Airplane

6

With all the pleasure to be derived from the modern motorboats, there will remain those who will regret the passing of the yacht, and others who, with the perfecting of the airship or airplane, will regret the passing of the good old balloon.

> —Homer Hedge, first president of the Aero Club of America[1]

During November and December of 1907, the press reported that Henry Farman, an Englishman's son born and raised in France,[2] was making remarkable flights in an airplane of his own construction. By early 1908 the flights had been officially certified: on January 13, Farman flew a circular path of 1300 meters before a committee of the Aero Club of France.[3] The achievement won him a $10,000 prize for the first circular flight of more than a kilometer and convinced the experts that "dynamic," or heavier-than-air, flight was possible.

The news had a profound influence on the members of the Aero Club of America, and their thoughts turned even more toward airplanes. At the March 9 meeting club member Stanley Y. Beach, who was science editor of *Scientific American,* provoked a lively discussion on the amount of energy per pound needed to lift a plane versus different species of birds. The *New York Times* reporter who attended the meeting captured an interesting quotation from Beach, one that reveals his disposition to believe that Samuel Pierpont Langley, more than the Wrights, was the true father of flight:

I predict that although Europe is way ahead as far as aeroplane flight is concerned, America will soon lead the world. The two most successful of the French machines, those of Farman and Bleriot, are prototypes [*sic*] of Prof. Langley's machine, which, had it been properly launched at Washington, would have undoubtedly obtained great success.[4]

His comments reflected the views of a small but prominent group within the aviation field who were beginning to minimize the achievements of the Wrights. No matter what the brothers had learned through their own experimentation, these people were convinced that all of the Wrights' success had been built entirely on the findings of Langley and others. Their influence is still reflected in recurring assaults on the Wrights' primacy as the fathers of airplane flight.[5] A year later, in the fall of 1909, Beach became a key member of a group that challenged the legitimacy of the Aero Club's corporate structure (see Chapter 7).

By April, President Courtland Bishop announced that the Aero Club would henceforth "devote practically all of its energies to the development of airships or flying machines which are heavier than air."[6] Declaring that "the balloon [has] no further worlds to conquer [and that] henceforth the mission of the club would lie in the development of aerial flight," Bishop and members of a newly formed Aviation Committee began experimenting with flight in a "Herring model" glider,[7] a machine built by Augustus Herring, assistant to American flight experimenter Octave Chanute.

Later that spring the club circulated a letter soliciting one hundred subscriptions of $250 each. It explained the need for the $25,000 fundraiser in the following, at times inelegant, manner:

To prevent the United States of America from remaining so far behind other countries in the art which is fast becoming one of the most important ones, namely, dynamic flight, the Aero Club of America has appointed a committee to determine the best means of promoting the art of aviation and after due deliberation this committee has decided that the following is essential:

To provide an aviation park with proper sheds for housing . . . gliders of different forms, propellers, motors, etc. Also a small machine shop. . . . Then to create interest and form an incentive to cause the inventors for which this country is noted [*sic*], it is essential to put up prizes and with this end in view the following is proposed . . . [the amount of prize money desired is specified and it is proposed that the public be required to pay to see flight tests conducted, with profits divided among subscribers].

One of the first exhibitions proposed is the inviting of one of the most noted aviators of France, either Mr. Farman or Mr. DeLaGrange [Delagrange], at the expense of $2,500 and make flights in their practical machines [sic] which will create more interest than any other suggested plan. . . .[8]

But it would appear that the subscription was not as popular as the Aviation Committee hoped it would be, and the idea was abandoned. In spite of the enthusiasm for airplanes among many members, most seemed satisfied to remain an organization of sportsmen balloonists.

In July, citing public apathy regarding the remarkable advances in aeronautics being achieved overseas, and "believing this abnormal condition was the result of inactivity by the Governors of the Aero Club," club member Albert C. Triaca and some fellow members formed their own organization, the Aeronautic Society of New York. They set about establishing a flying field on the Morris Park racetrack.[9]

While it was debating whether or not to pursue airplane development more actively and, at the same time, negotiating to have Henry Farman come from France to demonstrate his airplane, the Aero Club was presented with a surprise proposal for a flight by an American.

On June 30, 1908, the club hastily informed its members that Glenn Curtiss had petitioned to make a record attempt, within the week, under the auspices of the Aero Club. The flight, to be conducted in Hammondsport, New York, on the Fourth of July, would bid for the Scientific American Trophy by trying to cover a distance of one kilometer or more. The club arranged for a special Lackawanna Railroad car to take members up to Hammondsport on the night of July 3.[10]

Scientific American had originally offered the trophy in 1907, hoping to encourage airplane development. The Aero Club was charged with officiating at all attempts to win the prize and establishing the progressively more difficult criteria by which it would subsequently be awarded. Curtiss, a motorcycle and engine builder who had attained the remarkable speed of 136.3 miles per hour on one of his machines the summer before,[11] had caught the club off guard with his sudden challenge. He was a member of Alexander Graham Bell's Aerial Experiment Association—a group of bright young individuals the inventor had assembled to investigate ways in which to achieve powered flight. With financing from Mrs. Bell, the group—comprised of Bell, Curtiss, J.A.D. McCurdy, F. W. (Casey) Baldwin, and U.S. Army Lt. Thomas E. Selfridge—first formed at Bell's home in Baddeck, Nova Scotia, and then carried out gliding and powered aircraft experiments at Hammondsport, Curtiss's home. Curtiss was first brought into the association because of his expertise with gasoline engines, but he soon showed that he had abilities as an aircraft builder and pilot as well. The *June Bug,* with which the association intended to compete for the Scientific American Trophy, was the third in a series of planes built and flown by the association. Its predecessors, the *Red Wing* and the *White Wing,* were destroyed in crashes after making two and five straight-line flights, respectively.[12]

Before Curtiss issued his challenge, the general feeling had been that the trophy would go to the Wrights. From the time it was first announced, the prize appeared to be theirs for the taking, but the brothers seemed uninterested in pursuing such awards. The Wrights were even notified of Curtiss's intentions and given the opportunity to compete against him, but they refused.[13]

On July 4, 1908, the *June Bug,* piloted by Curtiss, flew twice. The first flight was a relatively short hop, but the second lasted one minute, forty-two and a half seconds. The craft flew six hundred yards further than the one kilometer required to win the Scientific American Trophy. Selfridge, secretary of the association, recorded the success in his report to the members, adding the comment, "The Wrights though have undoubtedly far outflown it in private."[14] The Aero Club awarded the Scientific American Trophy to Curtiss and the Aerial Experiment Association.

The club's negotiations to have Henry Farman come to America for a demonstration of his flying machine took a different turn when the members learned that a syndicate of St. Louis businessmen was also trying to engage Farman. After meeting with representatives of the syndicate, acting president Alan Hawley[15] agreed that the visit and all financial arrangements should be handled by the St. Louis group and that the Aero Club's involvement would be limited to sanctioning the flights.[16] The St. Louis syndicate contracted with Farman to make a series of demonstration flights in New York, Philadelphia, Boston, Pittsburgh, Chicago, and St. Louis over a period of ninety days. Farman agreed to receive $24,000, plus bonuses based on the number of flights he made.[17]

On July 26, the famed aviator and his wife arrived in New York to a hero's welcome. They were met in the harbor by a tugboat flying the newly designed flag of the Aero Club of America,[18] and escorted to the Hotel Astor by a committee of Aero Club notables.

Before leaving France, Farman had packed two disassembled planes to be transported under the supervision of his mechanics. But at the last moment the shipping company refused to load the airplanes, claiming that some of the crates were too long to be carried below decks. He sailed without them. The mechanics left behind with responsibility for the machines were unable to persuade any other shipper to carry them. Finally the Aero Club exerted its influence and asked J. Pierpont Morgan, head of the International Mercantile Marine Corporation, to intervene.

Morgan sent a cable to his company's Liverpool office, and the planes were loaded (strapped down above decks) onto the next ship bound for the United States.[19]

Although the impression he created may have been unintentional, Farman's early remarks to the U.S. press seemed to be aimed at needling the Wrights. Even though he expressed a belief that the Wrights knew "a great deal about the subject on which they are so successfully working," he went to great lengths to emphasize that all of his own experiments had been conducted publicly and that his plane was based, in part, on information shared by Langley and other experimenters. He announced that he would try for the second goal of the Scientific American Trophy (determined by Contest Committee chairman Charles Manly to be a twenty-five-kilometer flight) and offered the Wrights a side bet of $10,000. The brothers did not respond.[20]

As the mechanics prepared one of his machines at the Brighton Beach race track, Farman and his wife were wined and dined by the Aero Club. The night before his first scheduled flight attempt in America, the couple was honored at a reception held in the Hotel Astor. The centerpiece of the affair was a huge cake decorated with the chef's impression of what Farman's airplane looked like. In a scene likely to be repeated by any future group of aviators in the same circumstances, Curtiss and others of the country's top aviation experimenters gathered about the cake to discuss the potential airworthiness of the confectionery marvel.[21]

On July 31, Farman made two short straight-line flights before the members of the Aero Club and the St. Louis syndicate. The attempts were limited to about four hundred yards each because workmen had not yet covered over ditches in the portion of the flying field where Farman intended to land. During the test flights, aeronaut Charles Hamilton paid a surprise visit to welcome Farman, arriving at the field by dirigible.[22] The prospects looked bright for the success of Farman's American trip.

August 2, the day of the first public exhibition, arrived. The field was muddy and the ditches were still left uncovered. Farman, unwilling to risk damage to his machine, announced to the five thousand people who came that Saturday that he would not fly until conditions improved. The following day less than one thousand people appeared because problems on the field were still not resolved. The small crowd that did attend waited for more than three hours before the aviator made a forty-second hop over a portion of the field that was free of obstacles.[23]

Rain prevented flights for the next two days; then, in midweek, another group of about one thousand witnessed two short flights. The first was a straight-line race between the airplane and an automobile, and the second was a short, semicircular flight.[24] Once again the weather deteriorated. For two more days Farman could not get airborne, and the gate receipts for the few flights he had already made did not cover expenses.

Meanwhile, unknown to the pilot, all but one of the representatives of the St. Louis syndicate, their money spent and owing thousands of dollars to Farman and other creditors, had left town. T. R. MacMechen, the one remaining syndicate member, tried desperately to achieve an honorable solution to the problem.[25] Even as he tried to find new backers for the Farman trip, he hastened to exonerate club members from responsibility for the embarrassing situation. "The Aero Club of America," he told reporters, "had nothing to do with finances. The flights were merely under their auspices."[26] MacMechen still hoped that someone would recognize that a tour by the Farman plane could be profitable. He had the machine crated for shipping in the event that a backer could be located. Many people came forward with ideas, but none with cash.

While MacMechen attempted to salvage the bankrupt airplane exhibition tour, Farman and his wife continued leading the society life. On a visit with Thomas Edison, "The Wizard," as Mrs. Farman respectfully called him, sat down and sketched plans for an airship, signing the drawing before giving it to the French couple.[27]

Farman continued to believe that all was well and that the syndicate members would return to pay him the money they owed. But as he waited at the Hotel Astor he was informed that a municipal court judge had issued a lien against his airplane. The flying machine had been attached as surety against payment of a bill for the tent serving as the plane's hangar.[28] He soon learned that other creditors planned to have the machine confiscated and, possibly, sold to pay additional debts incurred by the syndicate. So in the middle of the night of August 13–14, Farman, his wife, MacMechan, and a crew of hired laborers stole their own airplane and had it loaded aboard a ship bound for home.[29]

The same day the collapse of the Farman tour was announced, newspapers published reports from France that Wilbur Wright, under the auspices of the French government and the Aero Club of France, had finally made a public flight. The aviation editor of *l'Intransigeant* wrote, "It is not without a certain sadness that we applaud Mr. Wright's success. The aeroplanes of Farman and De la Grange would seem to be only copies. When we contested the sincerity of Mr. Wright we were trying to believe that France would lead in aviation as in aerostatics, but Mr. Wright proves that we are but debutantes."[30]

While Wright was being feted in France as the "Conqueror of the Air," France's own hero of flight was forced to sneak out of the country like a thief in the night. "I bear no ill-will to the American people," he said as he departed, "Later I may come to America again, but I will do business with another class of people." Mrs. Farman was a bit less diplomatic in her parting comments: "I didn't suppose that a country existed where there was so much trickery, selfishness, and cowardliness as we have found here."[31]

Yet, a scant three weeks later, thoughts of Farman almost vanished entirely from American minds. On September 3, 1908, Orville Wright gave the first U.S. demonstration of sustained flight in a Wright airplane as he began the military tests at Fort Myer, Virginia. The circling flight, lasting one minute and eleven seconds, abruptly ended as, having inadvertently turned the steering lever the wrong way, he forced the plane to earth rather than chance hitting a shed. In spite of the rough landing, his performance clearly outshone that of the French plane.[32]

On September 9, Orville made a stunning, record-breaking flight of sixty-two minutes and fifteen seconds. That same day he took Lahm up for another world record of six minutes and sixteen seconds, the longest flight up to that time with a passenger.[33] Two days later he broke his own record by flying for seventy consecutive minutes, and then flew the following day for an unbelievable seventy-four minutes, carrying Maj. George O. Squier as his passenger.[34] There could no longer be any doubt that the Wrights were the masters of flight and that their claims had all been true.

Then, tragedy struck at the height of the Wrights' glory. On September 17, Orville again flew with a passenger. This time he took up Army Lt. Thomas Selfridge, the secretary of Bell's Aerial Experiment Association. During the flight the tip of a propeller blade struck a brace wire, causing the propeller to shatter and sending the plane crashing to earth, killing Selfridge and seriously injuring Orville. The military tests of the Wright plane ended for the time being. Nevertheless, in spite of the catastrophe, the U.S. Army had been given a remarkable demonstration of the airplane. Convinced that the crash did not justify condemnation of the machine itself, and that the Wrights' plane was capable of meeting or even exceeding their performance criteria, the military extended the qualification period.[35]

That December the same James Gordon Bennett who had earlier promoted balloon competition now commissioned an elaborate trophy to be awarded, along with a sizable cash prize, to the winner of a competition among powered flying machines. The trophy was a large silver sculpture by artist Andre Aucoc, depicting a human figure, poised as if about to leap into flight, holding a sterling replica of the Wrights' airplane.[36] The new Gordon Bennett competition would be one of several contests featured at the First International Air Meet, to be held in Rheims, France, late in August of 1909. The meet was sponsored by the FAI and, as such, was open to participants from all countries with affiliated aero clubs. The United States was entitled to field as many as three entries from the Aero Club of America.

The Aero Club was naturally interested in having the Wrights represent the United States. Bishop even pressed the Contest Committee to revise their rules, allowing aircraft without wheels, such as the Wrights', to be started with the aid of a launching device. The Wrights, however, declined to participate. Orville curtly informed Bishop:

I presume you already know that the race is for automobiles rather than for aeroplanes. The rules carefully provide against any test of the qualities desirable in aeroplanes such as reliability, ease of control, efficiency, dirigibility, &c., and provide only for a test of speed in which the machine is allowed to come down and run on the ground.[37]

With the Wrights removing themselves from a "flying" contest in which the entries were not required to fly the entire course, the Aero Club seemed to have few alternatives. In mid-April Bishop told reporters that Augustus Herring might enter a plane built in collaboration with Glenn Curtiss of the Aerial Experiment Association. The plane, Bishop said, would combine some features of the association's *Silver Dart* with others of a machine that Herring was preparing for the U.S. military. With studied casualness, Bishop indicated that the Aero Club would have "no objection" if Herring wished to enter the competition.[38] Bishop also mentioned the fact that he and Aero Club members Augustus Post, Alan Hawley, and Cooper Hewitt had agreed to finance the new Herring-Curtiss Company's endeavor.[39]

The Herring-Curtiss combination was predicated on Curtiss's ability to construct engines and flying machines and his facilities for doing so. Herring's part of the deal was to provide access to technology that he claimed to have patented earlier than had the Wrights, thus shielding the company from possible patent infringement suits. Only later would Curtiss learn that Herring's patent applications, though filed, had been denied by the Patent Office.[40]

The Herring-Curtiss company nonetheless contracted to build an airplane for the Aeronautic Society of New York for the sum of $5000. On June 10, 1909, the society announced that Curtiss had written a letter confirming that the machine, the *Golden Flyer,* was finished and had flown successfully. It was shipped to the Morris Park flying grounds a day or two later.[41]

While Curtiss flew the *Golden Flyer* at Morris Park, the workmen at his plant in Hammondsport were hurriedly building a second airplane, identical in most respects to the *Golden Flyer* (except for a larger engine and shorter wingspan), to race in the Gordon Bennett competition. Curtiss taught Charles Foster Willard to fly the Aeronautic Society's plane, then left for France with an as yet untested plane to represent America against the world in the first international air meet.

When Curtiss arrived at Rheims the press informed him that the Wrights' attorneys were proceeding with a patent infringement suit against the Aeronautic Society of New York. Curtiss showed no concern over the action and stated confidently that the Wrights, not having flown publicly until after he had won the Scientific American trophy in the *June Bug,* had no chance of showing that he could have appropriated any of their ideas.[42]

On August 28, Curtiss won the Gordon Bennett Aviation Cup and in the process set a world's record for speed in a flying machine. The only thing that marred his success was the surprise announcement that the Wrights' attorneys had named him as a defendant a second lawsuit, this one against the Herring-Curtiss Company. More suits against European airplane manufacturers and pilots followed. The brothers, who once had been called "the mysterious Wrights," were now dubbed with less flattering nicknames.[43] The Aero Club's joy at the Curtiss win was now mixed with concern that the Wrights would legally block the Bennett competition that it was obligated to sponsor in 1910. It was to prove a troubled time for the Aero Club—with challenges to be met from both within and without the organization.

BRINGING ORDER TO THE AIR

7

Promoting Flight and Flight Safety

With the growth of aviation the Aero Club assumed more and more responsibility as the governing body of flying in America. The club sought to promote the sporting aspects of aviation by making it more affordable and accessible to more of the public, but also charged its members with safe operations through licensing programs and regulated aerial competition.

In an effort to assure the continued growth of aviation the club established the Junior Aero Club of America in June of 1908. Members of the Junior Aero Club could be no older than twenty-one years of age, but there was no minimum age requirement. These young boys designed and constructed models of "flying apparatus," then demonstrated them at exhibition contests. By 1909 there were fifty-one club members in thirteen states. That year, the youngest member, a nine-year-old boy, displayed an eight-foot-long model he had built of a dirigible.[1]

The guiding power behind the Junior Aero Club was its founder and advisor, Miss E. Lillian Todd of Staten Island. Although little is known about the woman herself, she appears to have been a significant influence on many of the young men who would distinguish themselves as the second generation of aviators. Her mechanical abilities were reportedly evident in her early childhood days when she made improvements to a flying toy that she had bought. In her adult years she worked as a stenographer in the U.S. Patent Office in Washington, D.C., and invented a dirigible airship.[2]

She was an avid designer of model flying machines and displayed one of her airplane designs at the Aero Club's 1907 exhibition. The next year, in June 1908, she organized the Junior Aero Club of America, enlisting several members of the senior organization as directors. The constitution of the Junior Aero Club stated that one of the club's purposes was "to hold exhibitions and contests of apparatus designed and made by the *boys*" (emphasis that of the author). How ironic that this was an objective of an organization founded by one of the first women in the country to design aircraft! There appeared to be little objection from the male-dominated Aero Club to women becoming involved in flying activities, but it seems obvious that the women were not welcome to become members of the Aero Club itself. On March 28, 1909, Courtland Bishop announced that certain prominent New York women, including his own wife, planned to start their own "aeroplane club," but there is no evidence that their plan was ever carried out.[3]

Although it is uncertain whether Miss Todd ever piloted full-scale aircraft, several accounts tell of her building such a machine for the use of the Juniors. A September 26, 1909, account of the Aeronautic Society show at Madison Square Garden mentioned that she had the airplane under construction in a tent at the Aeronautic Society flying grounds in Mineola, Long Island. While she did not bring her full-sized plane to the exhibit—preferring to keep it from the public until she had made a successful flight with it—she displayed "a number of interesting models." A follow-up article printed September 29 reported that Miss Todd had mechanics working on the plane in the secrecy of a tent, and that it was hoped the machine would be completed within a few days. Yet it would appear that the plane did not fly after all, for nothing more seems to have been published about it. Nevertheless, a photograph still exists of Miss Todd sitting at the controls of an early airplane that may be the one she designed. She appears quite out of place—a schoolmarm in a floor-length dark dress, her gloved hands clutching the control wheel, her veiled hat placed squarely atop her head—but in her face one sees the set jaw and determined look of a pilot.[4]

Even the most farsighted of the Aero Club members could not have anticipated the long-term effects that this model airplane club would have on the future of American aviation. At the Aero Club–sponsored model airplane competition of 1912, the first-place award went to Jean (John) Roche for his original design of a monoplane.[5] Roche was to remain in aviation for most of his life. In the late 1920s he designed the Aeronca C-2, the first in a long series of Aeronca airplanes that marked the true beginning of America's light plane industry.[6] Third-prize winner in the same contest was George A. Page. Page also made a career of aviation, earning his pilot's license in 1914 even before he learned to drive an automobile. He worked as a draftsman during World War I, then flew a surplus float plane on a scheduled route between the United States and the Bahamas, thus becoming the first American to fly a regular over-water passenger route to a foreign country. Most of his working years were spent as a design engineer. During World War II he was director of engineering for the airplane division of the Curtiss-Wright Corporation. In the course of his lifetime he participated in the design, construction, or testing of more than ninety different aircraft, including many of our most successful military airplanes.[7]

Meanwhile, of growing concern to the Junior Aero Club's parent organization was the fact that European nations were quickly out-distancing America in military airpower. On January 19, Brig. Gen. Allen of the U.S. Army Signal Corps requested $500,000 for aeronautics as an amendment to the War Department's appropriations bill. The request was strongly supported by Aero Club president Bishop, whose enthusiasm for the measure was almost certainly boosted by Lt. Frank P. Lahm. Yet, despite passionate testimony about the progress made by the Wrights from Allen, Maj. George Squier, his assistant, and Lt. Lahm, not all of the members of Congress were convinced. It was the first request for appro-priations since the government had financed Samuel P. Langley's failed flight attempts in 1903.[8]

Following two hours of debate on January 31, the House approved the requested $500,000 as part of the larger appropriations bill, and the *New York Times* reported, "Members of the Aero Club of America were in a jubilant frame of mind yesterday when President Courtland Field Bishop showed a telegram received from Congressman Parsons stating that the House had appropriated $500,000 for development of aeronautics by the War Department." Bishop had discussed the matter with Parsons a few days before, urging him, on behalf of the Aero Club, to press for the amendment.[9]

The club's excitement turned out to be short-lived. On February 2, the House reversed its action, voting 161 to 90 against the aeronautics amendment as a separate issue. Hoping that the Senate might be induced to reverse the action, Bishop urged members to write to Senator Francis E. Warren of Wyoming, chairman of the Committee on Military Affairs, asking him to attach a corresponding amendment to a bill then before the Senate, appropriating the necessary money.[10] In spite of the Aero Club's efforts, no action was taken to provide additional funds for military aviation.

The club also tried to encourage long-distance ballooning by making it more affordable. When they learned that railway companies were overcharging for shipping balloons (at double the standard freight rate), the members took steps to obtain equitable treatment.[11] Leo Stevens led a successful effort to convince express companies that reduced rates for balloon transportation would, in the long run, lead to more business for them. As a result of this campaign, the companies cut their rates on balloon transport in half, effective March 10, 1909.[12]

But dissent within the membership created difficulties in the latter half of 1909. Holland Forbes, acting as president in the absence of Bishop, still hospitalized in France, called a special meeting in late September for the stated purpose of revising the club's constitution. The meeting was ostensibly intended to address a request from "the necessary number of members" that the board be expanded from five directors to nine, with the president, first vice president, and treasurer to be chosen from members of the board.[13] In addition to addressing the stated issue, however, the board members used the meeting to pass two other, unannounced, amendments: the first raising the annual dues from $10.00 to $25.00 and the second giving the board the power to expel any member at its discretion.[14]

Thereupon a faction represented by club members Orrel A. Parker, Wilbur R. Kimball, and Stanley Y. Beach mounted a drive to replace Bishop as president, and to force the expansion of the board of directors. These men stated that Bishop was an absentee president who led a group of men dominating the club "more for their own glorification than for the good of the art." The dissenters further maintained that the two amendments raising the dues and concentrating expulsive power in the board were illegal (because only eighteen of the necessary twenty members had been present at the meeting) and were designed to force out members who could not pay high membership fees or who disagreed with the Aero Club's leadership. The leaders of the dissenting faction further complained that the club's power and its assets were locked in the control of the five directors—the club's only stockholders.[15] Members were, they complained, welcome to control the club's liabilities, but not its future.[16] The movement to expand the board by six member-elected directors was obviously intended to give the membership that control. The directors' amendment, giving themselves the power of expulsion, was just as obviously a mechanism by which they might rid themselves of dissenters such as Parker, Kimball, and Beach.

The schism soon caught the attention of the press and the New York newspapers took sides, with the *New York Press* favoring the opposition and the *New York Herald* supporting Bishop and the other directors.[17] Amidst the furor created by this controversy, club member Albert Triaca (a respected authority on aeronautics, and a pilot licensed by the Aero Clubs of America, France, and Italy), sent a personal letter to each of his fellow members. The letter read in part as follows:

Returning January, 1908, from abroad, and amazed at the enthusiasm raised there by the first performances of the French aviators, I found that in this country public interest in aeronautics was altogether lacking.

Believing this abnormal condition . . . [was the result of inactivity by the Governors of the Aero Club] . . . , I grouped around myself a few men who assured me of greater progress in aviation, and I founded the Aeronautic Society [of New York], the heads of which [a group that included Parker, Kimball, and Beach] now direct the movement against the Aero Club and its president.

After a few months I clearly realized that the work of these men was not what I expected in the interest of the art, and that they tried to turn a popular association into a commercial enterprise, in which the word "business" had a much more potent sway than the word "sport"; and realizing that my endeavors were wasted, I resigned as director [meanwhile noticing that aeronautic events were in fact poorly attended].

All this convinced me that it was not the fault of the officers of the Aero Club that aeronautics was not progressing, but the lack of public interest.[18]

We see, reflected in Triaca's letter, the depth and complexity of the problems associated with advancing aviation in America. Even among the leading experts there was no consensus on how best to promote aviation—as a sport or as a business. Triaca seemed primarily interested in assuring that U.S. efforts remained on a par with those in Europe. First thinking that the lack of American enthusiasm for flying was the fault of the Aero Club's leadership, he formed a new organization, the Aeronautic Society of New York. But when the other members of this new, rival society eventually showed their inclination to approach aviation as a commercial endeavor, and to support what appear to have been efforts to gain control of the Aero Club, Triaca reevaluated his position. He chose to rejoin Bishop and his allies in the Aero Club.

Triaca concluded his letter with a strong defense of Bishop and the other Aero Club directors, stating that his work within the United States and his recent election to the vice presidency of the FAI had done much to give American aviation international status. He supported raising the club's dues on the grounds that it would "improve the standard of its membership," and admonished Parker, Kimball, and Beach to concentrate on improving their own Aeronautic Society, rather than meddling with the affairs of the Aero Club.

In spite of vigorous last-minute efforts on the part of the dissenters, including a court order attempting to block the use of proxy ballots, Bishop survived the Aero Club election on November 1, 1909. But an underlying cause of the controversy—whether Aero Club membership should be open only to wealthy industry leaders, or if it should include interested persons from all stations in life—remained a source of tension throughout the life of the organization, one which would eventually, thirteen years later, figure in its demise. Within a month of the election that reinstated Bishop, the club admitted twenty-one new members—all wealthy and prominent individuals, and all nominated by Bishop, the other directors, or their strong supporters.[19]

Apparently Bishop and the club's directors realized that their organizational structure was in need of modification to protect it from future attacks, so the original Aero Club was merged into a new corporation called Aero Corporation, Limited. In a letter sent to a member three days after his reelection, Bishop invited drafts of changes to the club's organic laws. On February 17, 1910, a letter went out to certain Aero Club members, stating, probably merely for the record, "The above club [the reorganized Aero Club] has to-day been formed and organized. You have been elected a member without payment of initiation fees or dues for the period ending November 1, 1910." The letterhead read, "Aero Club of America (membership corporation)," and it listed a slate of officers that included six officers and twelve governors.[20] Even though the organization would continue to be called the Aero Club of America for the remainder of its twenty-one-year existence, that ceased to be its official name on February 16, 1910, the date on which it was formally absorbed into Aero Corporation, Limited.[21]

With the introduction of the airplane came transition, triumph, and turmoil. Unexpected growth, increased responsibility for issuing licenses and conducting air meets, and a divergence of personal interests within the organization strained—but did not break—the Aero Club. But its idyllic days as a genteel and relatively small organization of wealthy balloonists gradually ended as the new technology of powered flight gained prominence.

Balloon racing was a sport for gentlemen. It seldom promised rewards greater than a trophy or, at best, a cash prize that hardly offset flying expenses. Balloons had obvious limitations. Because they could not take passengers to a predetermined destination, they seemed to have little commercial future. Some enterprising aviators attempted to find practical applications for the balloon, such as locating and identifying illegal auto racers,[22] but the crafts' most conspicuous commercial value remained their ability to attract large crowds. This appeal sometimes translated into profits for the merchants of a town sponsoring a large balloon race, but few pilots ever learned how to make any substantial amounts of money from balloons. Because the profit motive was missing, long-distance balloon aviation remained a sport of the wealthy.

The airplane, on the other hand, presented seemingly endless possibilities for commercial exploitation. Above and beyond military and transportation applications and opportunities in manufacturing planes, there developed an immediate demand for exhibition flying. People wanted to see airplanes. At first the curious public was willing to pay to see a real airplane sitting on static display.[23] But, soon enough, their demand for ever more spectacular flights—and more catastrophic crashes—was met by a new type of aviator: the exhibition airplane pilot.

Before the advent of the airplane, three distinct groups of fliers had existed: wealthy sportsmen balloonists; "smoke balloon" operators, who performed on trapeze apparatus suspended beneath or parachuted from hot air balloons at county fairs; and exhibition dirigible pilots, who seemed to possess a combination of the scientific and sensational aspects of the first two groups.

In its balloon racing phase, the Aero Club had grown slowly and steadily, as members brought in friends and new affiliate organizations formed in major cities. Invariably the new members were wealthy and influential persons in their communities. Aero Club membership carried sufficient status that many nonaviators joined just to be in the right company. Any time that a member of the upper crust even rode aloft as a passenger, the event was considered newsworthy.[24]

The carnival aviators, on the other hand, made news all too often when catastrophe struck. A typical Aero Club member felt that he had nothing in common with the "professors" who entertained at the county fairs; they were mere circus performers whose activities did nothing to progress the practical development of the balloon.[25]

The newest group of the three was made up of the exhibition dirigible pilots. A cut above the carnival balloonists, they were still conspicuously performance-oriented. The Aero Club members generally admired them for their skill and tended to accept them as peers in the air, even though few came from upper-class backgrounds. Although most exhibition dirigible pilots were paid performers rather than sportsmen, their metier had distinct advantages over that of the smoke balloon pilots, which made them more acceptable to the rank and file Aero Club member. For one thing, the dirigible had potential applications as a functional piece of military equipment, and at the turn of the century the wealthy considered it their duty to support a strong national defense.

The dirigible manufacturers and pilots were also at the forefront of the development of light, powerful, internal combustion engines. Most of their earliest powerplants were motorcycle engines that they modified by removing unnecessary accessories and drilling "lightening holes" in various parts to reduce the weight of metal components. It was not long, though, before dirigible operators sought from engine builders improved powerplants designed specifically to power their airships. The best known of these relationships, of course, was that between Thomas Baldwin and motorcycle builder Glenn Curtiss, which eventually led Curtiss to build both aircraft engines and airplanes. But there were others. Lincoln Beachey, who began his professional flying career as a dirigible operator for an "airship impresario" named Charles Strobel, designed a dirigible engine, two copies of which were later modified to power early airplanes, and automobile race car designer Carl G. Fisher displayed his own lightweight dirigible engine at the Aero Club's December 1906 exhibit. These fliers, as well as those attempting to solve the problems of heavier-than-air flight, knew that such engines would be necessary if ever a functional airplane were to be developed.[26]

The leading U.S. expert on dirigible construction was Aero Club member Capt. Thomas S. Baldwin, a former smoke balloon performer. Baldwin and his fellow member and engine manufacturer, Curtiss, built the first U.S. military dirigible. By bridging the gap between aviation performers and sportsmen, they helped open the doors of the Aero Club to airplane pilots of nearly every social stratum.

After the Wright flights of 1908–1909 and the Curtiss victory at Rheims, Americans developed an intense interest in aviation. In Philadelphia, Aero Club member Alfred W. Lawson launched a new magazine called *Fly,* dedicated to the science of mechanical flight. Aviation appealed to such a large segment of the population that the president of the Virginia College for Young Ladies chose the magazine's first issue to advertise her school to prospective students and their parents.[27] The airplane was the talk of the country.

The next few years brought a surge of airplane construction and flight attempts. Publishers advertised books and magazines telling how to build various airplanes. With these new guides, would-be middle-class pilots joined the wealthy aerial sportsmen in homebuilt machines (see Chapter 8). Scores of these fliers followed Selfridge to the grave, but even greater aerial mayhem might have resulted had the members of the Aero Club not had the foresight to put various control mechanisms into place at the outset of the airplane era.

In little more than three years the sportsmen balloon pilots had created a network of aero clubs and a licensing system that easily adapted to the coming of the airplane. As ballooning grew in popularity, so did the number and size of local aero clubs affiliated with the Aero Club of America. By the end of 1908, affiliates were active in Pittsfield, North Adams, and Boston, Massachusetts; Canton, Ohio; Milwaukee, Wisconsin; St. Louis, Missouri; Springfield, Illinois; Denver, Colorado; Los Angeles, California; Hartford, Connecticut; and Seattle, Washington.[28] The number increased significantly throughout 1909, and by the end of that year there were affiliate clubs in nearly every region of the country.[29]

Vigorous competition developed between these clubs, spurred by prizes sponsored by members.[30] By insisting that balloons participating in these sanctioned contests carry at least one licensed pilot, the club encouraged proper training, but there were no laws requiring flight training.[31] An FAI license issued through the Aero Club merely attested to a degree of competency on the part of the holder. It carried no legal weight.

In the fall of 1908, acting Aero Club secretary Alan Hawley and Gen. James Allen, Commander of the Army Signal Corps, met with other aeronauts and enthusiasts who were attending Orville Wright's Fort Myer airplane trials to discuss the future of aviation. The group proposed the passage of federal laws to require licensing of pilots, primarily as a method of preventing flights by inexperienced persons. The primary requirements for obtaining Aero Club licenses were training by an already licensed pilot, having made at least ten balloon flights, and possessing an endorsement of ability from two existing license holders. Hawley and Allen's legislative proposal recommended mandatory certification by an affiliate of the FAI, but they conceded that they would be satisfied if some agency of the federal government chose to take responsibility for issuing licenses.[32] The issue of federal licensing would again come before the Aero Club in 1909, when member Leo Stevens appealed to the club to request government intervention following an inexperienced pilot's balloon crash in the Sierra Madre Mountains.[33] Although there is no clear indication whether or not the government officially responded to these public proposals for mandatory licensing, it is likely that they did not (probably because there existed no government agency that would logically regulate aeronautical activities). Supporting this contention is the fact that pilots' licenses continued to be issued by the Aero Club (and later the NAA) until the federal government formed an Aeronautics Branch of the Department of Commerce in 1926.[34]

In November 1909, the Aero Club announced that it would extend its licensing program to certify airplane pilots as well as balloonists and dirigible operators, in order to prevent "indiscriminate flying." The club's criteria (slightly modified early the following year) stated that a candidate must make application in writing; be at least twenty-one years of age; have made at least three solo flights under the general supervision of the Aero Club (at least one of which went further than one kilometer), in which the plane returned to the point from which it had started; and have demonstrated flight skills that were "reasonably safe and prudent." The board of directors also had the power to grant an American license to any applicant who was already certified by a foreign affiliate of the FAI. In announcing the new licensing requirements, the Aero Club stated that Glenn Curtiss and the Wrights were already qualified as "aviation pilots."[35]

Unfortunately, even though this early licensing program was an idea very much in step with its time, the manner in which it was administered later inspired one of the great myths of American aviation history, which was used to perpetuate anti-Wright sentiment. The first ten Aero Club airplane licenses were issued in early 1910[36] in the following order:

License number	
	1—Glenn H. Curtiss
	2—Lt. Frank P. Lahm
	3—Louis Paulhan
	4—Orville Wright
	5—Wilbur Wright
	6—Clifford B. Harmon
	7—Capt. Thomas S. Baldwin
	8—J. Armstrong Drexel
	9—Todd Schriver
	10—Charles F. Willard

In a series of magazine articles published in 1947, General H. H. (Hap) Arnold, who had completed service as commanding general of the U.S. Army Air Force the previous year, pointed out that Curtiss, rather than the Wrights, had been issued license number 1. The general explained this circumstance thus:

The real reason for this may have been that the Aero Club of America was "peeved" at the Wright brothers because of the scanty information anyone received from either Kitty Hawk, North Carolina, or Sims Station [outside Dayton], Ohio, during those early pioneering days. Glenn Curtiss, on the other hand, gave information of his flights "upstairs" very freely.[37]

General Arnold's speculative explanation caught the fancy of aviation enthusiasts and, over the years, gradually became accepted as fact. Certainly a number of people had reason to be unhappy with the Wrights early in 1910, but to say that the Aero Club deliberately issued Curtiss the first license in order to spite the Wrights is inconsistent with the honors that the club bestowed on the brothers during those years (see Chapter 8).

Perhaps a more accurate, albeit considerably less intriguing, explanation can be found by examining the evidence. There were three ways to qualify for an Aero Club airplane license: to have already demonstrated proof of one's flying ability to the club prior to the time it started issuing licenses; to demonstrate one's ability by flying the required test before the club; or to have demonstrated one's ability by holding an FAI license issued by an aero club in another country.

The Aero Club records do not show a date of assignment for the first five licenses. The first dated license, number 6, awarded to Clifford Harmon, was assigned May 24, 1910, after he passed his flight test before representatives of the club. The five pilots preceding Harmon had all demonstrated their ability to fly in the presence of Aero Club officials (Paulhan held an FAI license from the Aero Club of France[38]) before the club actually began issuing airplane licenses.

The historical record thus suggests that the original five previously qualified applicants were assigned their licenses in alphabetical order and that the Wrights were victimized only by their last name. Subsequent licenses seem to have been issued in order by date of flight test before club officials or by date of application for a license based on previously demonstrated ability. Indeed many very early pilots did not apply for a license until long after they started flying—and some were never licensed at all.

Although the Aero Club's licensing program no doubt helped to make flying safer, it carried with it no weight of law. Indeed, the only way that the club could enforce any of its safety measures was by excluding the offender from record attempts and sanctioned competitions—events in which only a relatively small number of pilots participated. As the number of airplane pilots increased, local airplane-related legislation began to appear in municipalities where the flying machines were little understood, and often feared.

A proposal was put forward in Grand Rapids, Michigan, for example, to levy a fine on any pilot who fell from his plane and landed on a pedestrian. The fine was to start at $10 and increase in amount, based on increases in the height from which the aviator fell.[39] (Although there were no reported cases of pilots falling from their planes onto pedestrians, one unfortunate low-flying student pilot in the Los Angeles area was knocked out of his machine when he struck a cow. The pilot was uninjured and the plane came safely to rest against a haystack some two miles from the collision site, but the cow tumbled end over end for several feet.[40]) Jefferson City, Missouri, legislators proposed that all aviators be required to post a bond of $10,000 as surety that they would not fly any higher than one thousand feet—and that they be imprisoned for five years in the event they exceeded that altitude, on the grounds that such flights constituted attempted suicide.[41] There were even laws in effect to protect the souls of the living. The members of some two hundred Louisiana churches warned:

We condemn the use of flying machines as against the teachings of our forefathers. The airship craze is involving these United States in a helpless financial and moral curse. If the average young American is mortgaging his home to buy an automobile, what may we expect when the skyship has been perfected? We shall be a nation of beggars, and our women, now the chief sufferers from the automobile curse, will be further humiliated. If for no other reason, the protection of womanhood demands that a halt be called in these hellish devices miscalled scientific achievements.[42]

Ministerial opposition was not limited to Louisiana, and pilots Lincoln Beachey and J. A. D. McCurdy were arrested in Tampa, Florida, for flying their airplanes on Sunday. The clergy of that state, some of whom reportedly used the evils of airplane flying as a topic for their sermons, managed to have a Sunday ban on flying enacted into law.[43] Other proposals dealt with prohibitions against flights over cities and aerobatics. The public opinion of aviators was, it seemed, that of "a man who goes up for the primary purpose of coming down upon the landscape in a crumpled mass."[44]

If the outside threat of legislation to curtail flying activities was not enough to hinder the club's desire to see the airplane developed, disputes within the budding industry were. During the same era the Wright Brothers were to square off against some of the top exhibition fliers in the country, leaving officials of the Aero Club caught between the combatants.

THE CURTISS V. WRIGHT DILEMMA

The Influence of the Wrights' Patent Suits on American Aviation Development

8

As 1908 came to a close, the Aero Club prepared to honor the Wrights for their contributions to American aviation. A committee including Alexander Graham Bell, Charles Manly, Octave Chanute, Maj. Henry Hersey, Charles Glidden, and several others among the more prominent members set about procuring medals to be presented at a banquet in the brothers' honor.[1] The Aero Club commissioned the medals at a cost of $1000 each, to be paid through contributions from the membership.

In an editorial discussing the proposed honor to the Wrights, one newspaperman humorously remarked that the job of designing such a medal would be exceptionally difficult. Fortunately for the artist, the article read, one side of the medal would pose little problem because the Wrights appeared to possess "precisely what the features of men who have achieved the conquest of the air should be—lean and eager and strongly marked . . . and with something added that speaks of courage and originality." The other side, however, would be more difficult, because it had to portray the plane itself. The writer lamented that, in this part of the job, the designer would not be so fortunate, for airplanes did not have the same grace and beauty as the birds whose flight they emulated. "As a matter of fact," he concluded, "they could resemble nothing less than birds and are of a really dreadful ugliness."[2]

Even more of a problem than choosing the design for the medals was arranging a time and place for the commemorative dinner. The club was determined to give the Wrights the kind of honor they deserved from their country and decided that the dinner, to be held on or before April 1, should be attended by none other than the President of the United States himself. However, getting the schedule of President Theodore Roosevelt to coincide with that of the Wrights proved difficult. When first contacted, Roosevelt informed the committee that he would be unable to attend a function in New York, and suggested that the banquet be held in Washington, D.C. Then the Wrights, who seemed genuinely uninterested in such ceremonies and awards, notified the Aero Club that they would be in Europe for an extended period of time and would thus be unable to attend such a banquet.[3]

Finally, on June 10, 1909, Roosevelt's successor, William Howard Taft, presented the Aero Club medals to the Wrights in a White House ceremony. In his speech before the crowd of more than one thousand gathered in the East Room, Taft joked about his and his predecessor's paunchy profiles. Former President Roosevelt, he assured his audience, would have gone up in an airplane had he possessed a more aerodynamic shape. The Wrights, he noted, "are constructed more on the plan of the birds than some of us." In the same speech the President touched on the key issue of a controversy that soon would explode, dividing the aviation community for years to come. As he paraphrased Justice Brown (who had recently commented to him about patent laws), President Taft said:

it is the last step that counts—that is the difference between failure and success, and that step you gentlemen have taken. I doubt not that whatever improvements are hereafter made for sailing in the air in machines heavier than the air, the principles that you have discovered and applied and the method of their application will be the basis of all successful ones.[4]

Whether or not the President's words influenced the Wrights, there can be little doubt that they found them encouraging. Slightly more than two months later the Wrights filed the first in a series of many patent infringement lawsuits.[5]

The Wrights claimed that their patents on airplanes, dealing with devices for simultaneously controlling flight along each of three separate axes (pitch, yaw, and roll), covered every functional airplane known to exist in the world. As we have seen in Chapter 6, soon after the Herring-Curtiss company produced the *Golden Flyer* for the Aeronautic Society of New York, the Wrights sued for patent infringement. The suit was to be the first of some dozen actions filed in the United States and about the same number lodged against European builders.

In the United States Glenn Curtiss became the focus of the Wrights' greatest efforts. He featured so prominently in the American patent infringement suits that the entire affair is often called the Curtiss v. Wright litigation, even though many other pilots and manufacturers were involved. In his own case, Curtiss succeeded, through legal maneuvering, in holding off the final judgment until the matter was concluded by the U.S. government for the good of the nation during World War I (see Chapter 11).

For their part, the Wrights sought only what they felt was reasonable compensation for patents on devices they had invented through hard work and no small expenditure of resources. The Wrights placed no restrictions on those who wished to build and operate planes purely in a spirit of scientific investigation, but demanded royalties—often as high as $1000 per flight—of those who built or used airplanes for commercial gain, and they considered any flights before a paying audience, such as those at aviation exhibitions, to fall into the commercial category. It was this last condition, more than any other single stipulation of the Wright requirements, that most directly involved the Aero Club.

When Curtiss had won the Gordon Bennett aviation speed competition at the first international air meet in Rheims in the summer of 1909, he was flying as an Aero Club entry. As with the Gordon Bennett ballooning trophy first won by Frank P. Lahm, this award mandated that the winning aero club sponsor the competition the following year. Thus, it became the responsibility of the Aero Club of America to hold the 1910 Gordon Bennett competition in the United States.

As noted in Chapter 6, while Curtiss was competing at Rheims the Wrights filed two lawsuits. The first was against the Aeronautic Society of New York for operating the *Golden Flyer,* the first Herring-Curtiss airplane. The second suit was filed jointly against the Herring-Curtiss Company and Curtiss as an individual. The aviation community—and Curtiss—had expected the Wrights to file lawsuits. Everyone involved knew that it was inevitable that the patent questions would eventually be settled in the courtroom. But they had also expected the action to be purely a business matter—a dispute settled between two corporations.[6]

By naming Curtiss himself in their complaint, the Wrights put the issue on a personal level. Pilots and airplane manufacturers who might otherwise have tried to be objective found themselves on the defensive. Many felt they had to oppose the Wrights, if only for their own protection. When, in September of 1909, the Wrights initiated legal action to prevent the importation of a Bleriot airplane and a Farman craft, European builders realized that they, as well as Americans, were potential targets for legal action.[7] A few weeks later the newspapers announced that the Wrights' invention would be marketed—and protected—by a million-dollar corporation backed by Cornelius Vanderbilt, Howard Gould, August Belmont, and seven other of the country's wealthiest financiers.[8] It had become apparent that the questions regarding legal rights to the airplane would have expensive answers.

The Aero Club spent the fall of 1909 preparing for a busy year to come. In September the members mourned the death of the club's first President, Homer W. Hedge, from typhoid fever.[9] In October, Courtland Bishop was elected to a vice presidency of the FAI. At the same FAI meeting the governing board decided that the 1910 Gordon Bennett aviation race, to be held in the United States, would be a timed competition over a closed course of not less than 3.1 miles and would cover a total distance of 62.1 miles. As had been the rule the previous year, the airplanes would be allowed to make stops during flights.[10]

The Aero Club determined to hold the 1910 race in the New York area and planned to include a competition for the Michelin Cup, the winner of which would have to better Wilbur Wright's 123.2-kilometer flight of 1908.[11] The owners of Belmont Park racetrack immediately offered their facilities as the site of the event. Eventually the club would choose this site, and the series of competitions became known as the Belmont Meet.[12]

As the club began preparations for the 1910 event, its attention was diverted by the first of several distractions. A telegram was received requesting sanction for another international competition being promoted in Los Angeles. The west coast event, scheduled for January 10–20, 1910, presented a new range of problems. Club officials responded to promoter Dick Ferris that they would sanction the meet only if it were conducted as a sporting event. In addition to requiring assurances that the cash prizes offered actually existed, the Aero Club mandated that no paid exhibition flights be performed during the meet and that licensed aviators not be permitted to fly in competitions with unlicensed pilots. As with the earlier balloon competitions, this was to be a gentlemanly competition for prize money and trophies only.[13]

Much to the members' surprise, promoter Ferris countered that all the licensed airplane pilots he had invited to fly at the meet, including Curtiss, had "demanded [guaranteed individual payments] ranging from $3,000 to $10,000 each." The aviators' response to his assurance of sporting prizes totaling $50,000 was, Ferris said, "Keep your prizes. We cannot fly unless [it is for] real money."[14] Ferris made it clear that he and the pilots were willing to defy the Aero Club, guaranteeing pay to the top pilots, if necessary, and continue with the meet whether it was sanctioned or not. It must have been obvious to Bishop that the potential profits to be realized in airplane flying were too great for aviation to remain the realm of the sportsman. Thus the Los Angeles meet received last-minute Aero Club sanction and the boom years of the airplane exhibition pilot began in earnest.

The first international air meet in America opened in January 1910, at the Dominguez Ranch near Los Angeles. During the course of the ten-day event an estimated 500,000 people watched airplanes, balloons, and airships sail through the California skies. The Americans, most notably Curtiss, Charles Willard, and Charles Hamilton, all in Curtiss planes, put on a good flying show for the crowd, but the unquestioned hero was Frenchman Louis Paulhan in his Farman. Unlike Curtiss, the top American competitor, who was described as being "cold and re-served, almost to moroseness," Paulhan appealed to the crowd as a warm and lighthearted young man. The young Frenchman far outdid the Americans with displays of his flying abilities: once by leaving the safety of the exhibition area to fly nonchalantly to a nearby city; another time by challenging Charles Hamilton to an impromptu race, in the course of which he demonstrated the ability to pull ahead of the American seem-ingly at will; and finally, by setting a new world's altitude record of 4165 feet—significantly higher than the previous record of 3600 feet.[15]

A week before the meet began the Wrights won a temporary injunc-tion against flights by Curtiss, but, not wishing to impede such a well-publicized event, agreed to suspend it the day before the meet opened so that Curtiss could compete. Paulhan remained in America after the Los Angeles meet, making exhibition flights at various places throughout the country, until he too was stopped by court order in mid-February. On March 17, a New York District Court justice set a reduced bond of $12,000 to allow Paulhan to continue flying until the Wright claims against him were settled. But by the end of the month the Frenchman had boarded a ship bound for home, leaving his airplanes in the custody of the New York Superior Court as surety against claims from his manager for contracts left unfulfilled.[16]

Whether justified or not, the Wright patent claims were a tremendous obstacle to American aviators. One alternative action, suggested by one W. M. Page at the March 25, 1910, Aero Club dinner, would have had the patents condemned for the good of the American public. Under this proposal the U.S. government would buy the Wrights' patents in much the same manner as property is purchased for a highway right-of-way. Although this idea had a great deal of merit and may have, in retrospect, been the ideal solution, there appears to have been no immediate action to get government support for the measure.[17] Still, it was a sound idea—one that would come up again. In October 1915, publisher Robert J. Collier, then a former president of the Aero Club, and Harry Payne Whitney offered to buy the Wright Company from Orville. Their intention was to then make the Wright patents freely available to U.S. airplane manufacturers. Unfortunately, Orville had by then already committed to sell the company to a syndicate of investors that included William Boyce Thompson and Frank Manville.[18]

Uppermost in Aero Club president Bishop's mind was whether or not the club would be able to hold the Gordon Bennett race. The world was watching the episode between the Wrights and Paulhan when Bishop stated that he had been assured by "all the foreign aviators of note . . . [that they] would not sign contracts to appear in this country until the suit against Paulhan [was] decided." Bishop continued, "If Paulhan wins, they will be glad to compete. If he loses, they do not care to place themselves within the jurisdiction of American courts."[19]

In April the Aero Club reached an agreement with the Wright Company. It essentially acknowledged that the club recognized the Wrights' ownership of certain patents for flying machines and agreed not to sanction any event at which flying machines would operate without first compensating the Wright Company. In return, the Wright Company agreed to "encourage the holding of open meets or contests, whenever approved . . . by the Aero Club of America, by granting licenses to promoters who make satisfactory arrangements with the company for its compensation. . . ." The agreement further held that "at such licensed meet any machine of any make may participate freely without securing any further license or permit."[20] In accordance with this arrangement, the Aero Club agreed to pay the Wright Company a percentage of the Belmont Meet proceeds in exchange for immunity from prosecution for all competitors.

This agreement served the club's immediate need of clearing the way for the upcoming Gordon Bennett competition, but prevented it from sanctioning any future meets unless given prior approval by the Wrights. The contract also implied that any airplane pilot licensed by the Aero Club who competed or performed for compensation without prior approval from the Wrights would be subject to license revocation for flying at an unsanctioned meet. In the eyes of its membership, Bishop's agreement had put the Aero Club directly under the Wrights' control.

The contract would probably have been satisfactory in the days when wealthy New York sportsmen had monopolized the Aero Club, but the makeup of its membership was changing. The new members could not afford the luxury of an expensive sport and aspired to make their flying pay for itself, if not turn a profit. Affiliate clubs now existed on both coasts and in smaller cities and universities throughout the country. These middle-class aviators openly asked if the Wrights and their new corporate board were not, in effect, trying to monopolize flight by creating an aviation trust. They cast the brothers in the role of men who had deserted the flying fraternity and sought personal wealth at the expense of all others.

In this environment the compact between Bishop and the Wrights immediately came under fire. Some of the same members who had opposed Bishop's reelection in 1909 led the attack by filing a protest with the FAI.[21] This time they succeeded in gathering substantial support from the membership and, on May 23, 1910, formed the American Aeronautic Association in opposition to the Wrights. The new organization proposed to circumvent the Wright agreement with the Aero Club by undermining the parent organization. The leaders called for all affiliates of the Aero Club to regroup under a new national association in order to avoid the conditions of Bishop's agreement with the Wrights, and twelve soon did so.[22]

Approximately one week after the American Aeronautic Association was formed, the Aeronautic Society of New York hosted a meeting to create the Aeronautic Federation of America. Including the twelve clubs comprising the American Aeronautic Association, this new federation boasted that it represented at least seventy-five American aero clubs, and a total of more than seven thousand members. Representatives of the American Aeronautic Association and the Aeronautic Federation of America planned to meet on June 22 to propose a convention, at which their members would consider joining forces under the name American Aeronautic Federation.[23]

The published objectives of this new national organization were nearly identical to those of the Aero Club of America. The only real differences were that the member organizations would not be bound to conform to the Wright patent agreements and would, they believed, have a stronger voice in future national decisions. In the federation's plan, the Aero Club would be reduced to having authority only to sponsor the upcoming Belmont Meet in accordance with their previously signed agreement with the Wright Company. From that point on the American Aeronautic Federation would take over (and, presumably, become the new American representative to the FAI).[24]

By the time of the proposed June 22 meeting, however, there was no longer a need to circumvent Aero Club agreements with the Wrights by forming new associations. On June 14, a U.S. Court of Appeals in New York dissolved the temporary injunctions against flights by Paulhan and Curtiss. The Court ruled that aviators accused of infringing on the Wright patents could operate their flying machines without bond until the case was decided in court. On June 17, the Aero Club instructed its Law Committee to investigate the impact of the court's ruling on the agreement between the Wrights and the Aero Club. They decided that the ruling left the Aero Club free to sanction aviation meets without prior approval of the Wrights until the courts judged whether the Wright claims were valid.[25] The matter of the Aero Club's agreement with the Wright Company for the Gordon Bennett competition, which guaranteed the Wrights "a large percentage of the proceeds," was later resolved when Wilbur Wright himself, in an apparent attempt to demonstrate his compliance with the spirit, as well as the letter, of the law, suggested that the agreement be abrogated.[26]

At the June 22 meeting convened by the four different aeronautic associations—the Aero Club, the Aeronautic Society of New York, the American Aeronautic Association, and the American Aeronautic Federation—it was concluded that disputes such as those concerning the agreement signed with the Wrights could be avoided in the future if policy decisions were handled by a separate National Council, rather than individual Aero Club officers. The council was formed, and club member Clifford Harmon was chosen acting chairman. Because this step seemed to resolve the complaints of various members and affiliated aero clubs, further plans to proceed with the American Aeronautic Association and the American Aeronautic Federation were dropped. At an Aero Club meeting held on April 4 of the following year, it was decided that the National Council would be the official governing body of U.S. aero clubs, but that the Aero Club of America would retain its distinct position as the American representative to the FAI.[27]

The court's ruling also seems to have forced a change in the Wrights' attitude toward exhibition flying. Once freed by the courts to do so, Curtiss and a newly created team of exhibition fliers resumed their highly lucrative business of flying at county fairs and grand expositions. Unable to rely on their patent claims to protect them from financial loss, the Wrights had to form their own troupe of fliers or lose their share of the profits from flight. They engaged Roy Knabenshue, the former dirigible exhibition pilot, to manage their new flying team.[28]

This temporary solution to the Wright patent problem, although welcome, hardly cured all the Aero Club's ills. A minor scandal soon developed when Hamilton, a pilot on the Curtiss exhibition team, broke away from Curtiss to fly on his own. Claiming that Hamilton was violating his contract, Jerome Fanciulli, business manager for the Curtiss Aeroplane Company, applied pressure to the management of the Harvard/Boston Aero Meet, in which Hamilton was to appear that September. If they allowed Hamilton to fly, Fanciulli threatened, none of the remaining Curtiss pilots would participate.[29]

The Harvard authorities banned Hamilton rather than lose several other prominent participants. Hamilton in turn protested to the Aero Club. Because the Harvard meet had been sanctioned, he contested, and since he was a licensed member in good standing, the management had no right to exclude him. Hamilton maintained that Fanciulli's action would have been inappropriate under any circumstances, but was particularly odious in light of the fact that Fanciulli was also secretary of the Aero Club!

The Aero Club executive committee, in a meeting from which Fanciulli exempted himself in order to assure that Hamilton received an impartial hearing, ruled that the Harvard meet promoters had acted improperly in banning Hamilton, and withdrew its sanction of the meet. At the same time, the executive committee gave Fanciulli a vote of confidence for his performance as club secretary, but he nevertheless resigned soon afterward to avoid further conflicts of interest.[30] He was replaced by Israel Ludlow, an early aviation experimenter and the attorney for Paulhan.[31]

There were many such instances of conflicting interests within the leadership of the Aero Club. In retrospect they might easily be misinterpreted as signs of corruption within the organization. In actuality they indicate that the officers and governors were personally involved in the leading edge of aviation technology. Certainly partisan politics was involved, but the overall makeup of the Aero Club leadership was fairly well balanced among all aviation interests. Compromise, rather than conquest, appears to have been the objective of the club's policy makers. Throughout the seemingly rocky early years, individuals and factions who vigorously opposed each other legally and philosophically outside the organization managed to work together to achieve the Aero Club's goals.[32]

Amid the confusion born out of the Wright patent controversy, and the uncertainty as to whether the event would even take place, the committee designated to organize the Gordon Bennett competition had in the meantime made no significant progress. After several weeks of planning they had not even decided on a location for the meet. Gage E. Tarbell, the manager, resigned in frustration over the committee's inability to act. With little more than two months remaining before the competition was scheduled to begin, the club selected Belmont Park racetrack and appointed August Belmont as the new manager.[33] Within days the management was again transferred, this time to A. A. Ryan.[34] Under Ryan the Belmont Meet got underway, but only after the FAI had granted permission for a postponement of several days. The international nature of the contest was underscored as the British pilot Claude Graham-White, flying a French-built Bleriot, won the competition.

The dissolution of the Wright Company injunction against Curtiss and Paulhan by the U.S. Court of Appeals was a signal to the American public that they could begin to build airplanes with little fear of reprisal. In late 1909, Victor Lougheed—the older half-brother to Allan and Malcolm Lougheed, who later founded the Lockheed Aircraft Company, and one of the more outspoken members of the anti-Wright contingent within the Aero Club—published a book entitled *Vehicles of the Air*.[35] The book contained sufficient drawings, photographs, and technical data to give a person who was mechanically inclined a good idea of how to build a flying machine. Lougheed followed this book by writing an extensive aviation segment for the textbook for an automobile engineering correspondence course, the *Cyclopedia of Automobile Engineering*. The four-volume set of reference books was first published in 1909 and was revised at least through 1912. Each new edition added more information about airplanes until, at last, an entire volume was devoted to building and flying them, with blueprint-like sketches and relatively complete instructions for building various craft, including the Bleriot and the Curtiss.[36]

Other popular how-to articles appeared in 1910. The June and July issues of *Popular Mechanics* magazine published drawings and construction methods for the Santos-Dumont *Demoiselle*, and *Aero* magazine, a new publication for the aviation enthusiast, printed a monthly series by Howard Gill that showed, step by step, how to build a copy of the Curtiss airplane.

These articles inspired a new American industry that catered to the homebuilder. New businesses like the E. B. Heath Aerial Vehicle Company of Chicago published catalogs offering everything for the airplane, from small hardware items, through subassemblies, to complete flying machines. A copy of the Curtiss machine that cost $5000 from the factory could be had knocked down in a Heath kit for $125—less fabric, propeller, and engine.[37] A Roberts 4X aero engine, derived from that manufacturer's two-cycle marine engine, could be bought new for less than $1000, or factory reconditioned for as little as $400.38 All told, a thrifty would-be aviator could break into the flying business for about $1000. Although this still represented a substantial investment in pre–World War I terms, there was the enticing prospect of recouping many times that amount in just a few exhibition flying engagements.

The new breed of aviator was neither wealthy sportsman nor aerial circus performer. This was the true beginning of America's grass roots aviation. Across America enterprising young men, and a few women, bought or built their own airplanes. They were inspired by the stars of aviation—the professional exhibition pilots.

SPORTSMEN PILOTS AND SIDESHOW FLIERS

9

How the Aero Club Dealt with Early Attempts to Exploit the Airplane

Throughout the second decade of the twentieth century the Aero Club actively supported competition that encouraged airplane development and advanced flying technology. Sanctioned meets and competitive distance flights drew together the top licensed pilots as they vied for substantial cash prizes. In 1910 alone, the *New York World* offered a $10,000 prize for a flight from Albany to New York; Glenn Curtiss won a prize of $15,000 for a flight from Cleveland, Ohio, to Cedar Point, near Toledo; the *New York Times* and the *Chicago Evening Post* promised a $25,000 award for the first flight between Chicago and New York; and a New York to St. Louis flight brought $30,000 from the *New York World* and the *St. Louis Post Dispatch*. In 1911 the Grant Park Meet in Chicago guaranteed $100,000 in total prize money and the Illinois Aero Club Meet offered $80,000.[1]

While some of the best-known fliers competed for the grand sums of money offered at these sanctioned events, many others among the famous and less than famous engaged in exhibition "stunt" flying. This was a predominantly American phenomenon, as aviation in the United States temporarily strayed from the scientific course along which it was developing in Europe and began pandering to perverse human curiosity in a way not unlike the Roman circus. The Aero Club officially denounced this kind of flying, but it was powerless to control it. Many of the same pilots who had contributed—and continued to contribute—to the genuine advancement of flight were unable to resist the lucrative exhibition business. Even the Wrights, perhaps the most conservative of all American aviators, fell under the spell of this unique trade, until the deaths of their two best pilots caused them to disband their own exhibition company.[2]

Long after the residents of large cities came to accept the existence of airplanes as fact, there were still millions of people in remote areas of the country who remained skeptical about newspaper reports of flying machines. These people wanted to see an airplane for themselves, and it did not take entertainment promoters and amusement companies long to capitalize on this curiosity.

The newer of the exhibition fliers realized that they could not compete with experienced pilots like those on the Curtiss and Wright flying teams. Rather than enter sanctioned events in which they stood little chance of placing in the money, these pilots preferred to engage in a business that was more certain to pay off with each flight. A 1914 British publication made note of these exhibition fliers in the preface to a list of American pilots:

Only a few American aviators have bothered to obtain the Ae. C. [Aero Club of America] Certificate. America produces a large number of aviators who fly for pleasure or exhibitions only and have not gone into competitions under the International Rules. These consequently do not bother about certificates; but most of those recorded could easily obtain them, if they cared to try.[3]

The airplane rode the rails into rural America. Exhibition aircraft often had to be transported hundreds of miles between flying engagements. In order to be moved they were partially disassembled and packed into railroad cars. Wright airplanes usually traveled relatively intact. Their outriggers (the long booms supporting the control surfaces) were removed and the rest of the plane was placed intact into a boxcar that opened at the ends, rather than along the sides. Although this method required relatively little labor, the special end-opening boxcars were sometimes difficult to locate, had to be scheduled in advance by the railway line, and had to be disconnected from the rest of the train before cargo could be put aboard or unloaded.[4]

The Curtiss design, on the other hand, could easily be broken down into much smaller components and packed into a series of shipping crates. The wings were usually reduced to panels measuring about five feet by five feet[5] and stored in one crate, the engine and tools in another, the long outrigger booms and struts in yet another, and so on. These shipping containers often had palanquin-like handles built onto them for easy carrying and proved especially valuable when a Curtiss exhibition plane had to be stored for any length of time. They took up relatively little space and spared the exhibitor the cost of building a shed or hangar large enough to hold an assembled plane.[6]

In spite of the amount of labor required to ship and assemble a Curtiss-type airplane, it appears to have been the machine of choice for American exhibition pilots. The cost of the labor was relatively modest and the convenience of being able to transport the plane in nearly any standard freight car more than offset the extra assembly time. A quantitative study of American airplane pilots who began flying prior to 1917 indicates that 47% learned to fly in Curtiss or Curtiss-type planes, compared to slightly less than 18% in Wright or Wright-type machines. Out of all these, nearly 68% of the pilots started out doing exhibition work. In most cases a pilot continued to use the same type of airplane for exhibition flying that he or she had first learned in.[7]

While superstar aviators thrilled crowds at huge regional celebrations, lesser-known pilots flew at festivals in the smaller towns, usually those built along the railway lines. A typical American exhibition flight was usually the feature event concluding several days' worth of activities sponsored by local business owners. Hoping to bring in large crowds from the surrounding countryside, the merchants' association would organize a celebration typically dubbed Harvest Days or the Founders' Festival. These were major events for area citizens. Often a midway would be set up, featuring carnival rides, lemonade, ice cream, cold beer, and other rare delights. Horse races, another popular entertainment of the time, drew thousands of spectators to the fairground. The merchants themselves held special sales, in anticipation that the money they had invested promoting the fair would yield a high return.

An exhibition pilot usually traveled with a skilled mechanic and a mechanic's assistant, who assembled the airplane. Additional local help was sometimes hired to move the machine from the train to the flying field and to perform other odd jobs. The airplane exhibition began the moment the train carrying the flying machine rolled into town. The public was interested in seeing every aspect of the flight and the preflight preparations. They would watch intently as the shipping crates were unloaded from the train and carted to the exhibition site. Once there, the mechanics, or "mechanicians" as they were called in the vernacular of the times, unpacked and carefully assembled the flying machine.

The airplane was frequently displayed inside a tent for a day or more before the flight actually took place, thus whetting the appetite of the fairgoers for a flight. Anticipation grew as the pilot or mechanic—often assuming a degree of dramatic license—explained how an "aeroplane" worked and extolled the death-defying feats of the "birdmen" who operated them. Naturally, there was a modest admission charge for this preflight performance. For another few coins the awed spectator could purchase picture postcards of the airplane or a small pamphlet telling all about the aviator who would soon go aloft. In some cases the admission fee and revenues from the sale of souvenirs were the mechanic's only pay, but they could nevertheless amount to a tidy sum.

And there were other fringe benefits as well. To most of the men in these small towns, the aviator was a daring but foolhardy figure. To the women, he was dashing and romantic, and his flight crew shared the limelight. Were they not, after all, cut from the same cloth? None of the traveling aviators or mechanics who desired it was ever at a loss for feminine attention.

On the appointed day the crowds would gather to watch the flight. It was not unusual for the plane to take off from the horse racing track, with the spectators in the grandstand. Fair officials generally knew little about flying machines. Often their only previous experience, if any, was with balloons that ascended vertically. More than one aviator was assured in advance that the local fairground would be ideal for aviation, only to arrive and find the track surrounded by trees, fences, and telegraph wires. In such cases the aviator might try to negotiate to have certain of the obstacles removed, but he usually ended up trying to fly around, over, or sometimes through the hazards.

At first exhibition flights were simple because the audience was content merely to see a plane get off the ground. In 1909, for example, when Charles Willard first exhibited the *Golden Flyer* at Richmond, Virginia, the spectators filed into a grandstand masked by tall canvas curtains. They watched as the plane started at one end of the infield, rose a few feet off the ground, and landed at the far end of the track, then had to either leave the stands or pay another quarter to see the feat repeated.[8]

But as time went on the public wanted to see more thrilling forms of flying. Fair promoters offered top dollar to pilots who flirted with death by flying steeplechase-like paths close to the ground (a maneuver called the "ocean wave") or by plummeting hundreds or even thousands of feet straight toward earth in the "dive of death," only to pull out just as the spectators gasped, fearing (or perhaps hoping) that they were witnessing the aviator's last moments.

The ultimate feat of the exhibition pilot was the loop. First performed in America by San Francisco's Lincoln Beachey,[9] the loop became the hallmark of a spectacular flier. Beachey himself resented the implication that he was performing dangerous stunts. To him it was a matter of precision flying, of knowing the limitations of the airplane and the pilot. Unfortunately, less experienced fliers felt obliged to equal or exceed this master aviator's aerial gyrations. When one of these pilots—and there were many—fell to his death in an overstressed machine, it was said that he died "doing a Beachey."

The Aero Club officially disdained spectacular exhibition flying. It was not sporting competition and seemed to do little or nothing to advance aviation. A hint that Beachey's style of flying concerned the club can be found in a cryptic notation written across the face of his Aero Club license registration record card: "Do not issue license—investigate."[10] It is not known who called for the investigation or for what reason, but the Aero Club did ultimately award Beachey license number 27. In 1911 the club passed a resolution that licensed aviators would be suspended or otherwise punished for flying low over crowds at air meets or other sporting events. Beachey was among the first charged under this rule. The club suspended his license and banned him from participating in sanctioned meets for flying too low in meets at Chicago and Milwaukee. Two members of another daring exhibition team, the Moisant International Aviators, also suffered the suspension of their licenses. Fred Hild and Marvin Wood were punished under the same regulation for flying too close to the spectators and participants at a 1913 polo match. The Moisant family was among the better-known of the early fliers. John managed the exhibition team, and brother Albert operated an aviation school. Their younger sister, Matilde, obtained Aero Club license number 44 (the second license issued to a woman in the United States) and she flew with the Moisant International Aviators until her plane burst into flames at the conclusion of an April 14, 1912, flight. She recovered, but retired from flying after the incident.[11]

It was truly an era of aerial mayhem. Beachey himself explained the reason for the huge crowds and the high fees paid to fliers:

there was just one thing which drew crowds to my exhibitions—a morbid desire to see something happen. They all predicted that I would be killed and none wanted to miss the sight. They paid to see me die. They bet, and the odds were always against my life.[12]

In the three years from 1911 through 1913, nearly sixty persons in the United States died in airplane accidents.[13] Beachey felt a responsibility for the death of these pilots. In a speech announcing his (short-lived) retirement, he declared, "I have been a bad influence, and the death of a number of young aviators in this country can be traced, I believe, to a desire to emulate me in my foolishly daring exploits in the air."[14] Later, after reading a list of twenty-four exhibition pilots killed emulating his stunts, he emphasized that "You could not make me enter an airplane at the point of a revolver."[15] Yet, despite his well-intentioned words, Beachey could not stay away from the excitement of aerobatic flying. His own death came in his native San Francisco in 1915 as he flew a new type of airplane and pushed it beyond its structural limits. A crowd of nearly a quarter of a million people saw the star fall to his death.[16]

Most Americans felt that the growing number of pilot deaths signified that flying was out of control. In search of a measure to reduce flying fatalities, the Secretary of State of New York introduced a bill to require all "aeronauts" to be licensed.[17] The Governor of Massachusetts soon followed the lead with an act requiring licenses for aviators in that state.[18]

Ironically, the Aero Club's licensing program, which was intended to assure a degree of safety by determining that a pilot was competent, instead became a valuable promotional tool in the hands of the exhibition pilots. There were many fraudulent operators intent on bilking local promoters. An early pilot told this story of one such flimflam artist:

I can recall a fellow who really pulled off a dandy down at Stark County [Ohio]. His plane was made out of pipe with cloth stretched over it. He said he couldn't take off from the track, he wanted to take off in the oval center in the track. Well, during the night this fellow goes to work and builds a mound of dirt up right in the center of the field. He had enough cloth for buoyancy, which lifted him up and he left the ground for a second [after driving over the mound]. It never flew, yet he lived up to the contract. The landing wheels did bounce a couple of inches. He shut the motor off quick, and lived up to the contract which stated all three wheels must leave the ground. So he got $300 a day for three days; he had hooked them for $900.[19]

For reasons like this, fair sponsors soon became suspicious of those who purported to be fliers. As more and more pilots began competing for fewer and fewer exhibition contracts, the term "Licensed Pilot" took on significant meaning when it appeared on the letterhead of an aviator soliciting exhibition business. An Aero Club license was considered to be positive proof that the aviator was a genuine flier.

In 1911, amid the flurry of exhibition flying, the club faced another situation that, although perplexing, was more easily solved. That January, Charlotte Granville, a young woman from England, applied to the Wright

Company for airplane flight instruction. She had already been aloft in English airplanes piloted by C. S. Rolls and Frank Hedges Butler. She was also an avid balloonist, with more than fifty lighter-than-air flights to her credit. Now she wanted to learn the art of flying airplanes and asked Wilbur Wright to accept her as a student. Wright agreed to teach her.[20] Next, Granville applied to the Aero Club for membership. At the time she was already a member of both the Aero Club of France and the Aero Club of the United Kingdom. Yet, despite those credentials, in his reply, club secretary C. F. Campbell Wood said, "I beg to convey my regrets that the club does not at this time admit lady members." Her reaction to the club's refusal? "How perfectly stupid!"[21]

Perhaps the Aero Club secretary's response was a bit hasty and what he had intended to say was that the question of admitting a woman member had never yet formally come before the club. Or perhaps many club members agreed that excluding women was, indeed, "perfectly stupid." (This latter possibility is supported by the fact that, early that same year, prominent members of the Aero Club had encouraged their wives and other female friends to fly with Wright aviator Frank Coffyn.[22]) In any event, the club did not maintain its men-only stance for long. That summer Harriet Quimby, a writer for *Leslie's Weekly* magazine, received Aero Club of America license number 37. Hers was the second airplane license awarded a woman anywhere in the world.[23] The next month another American woman, Matilde E. Moisant, earned license number 44. By the end of 1916, eleven American women had been certified as airplane pilots through the Aero Club of America.[24]

Two of these women, Katherine and Marjorie Stinson (license numbers 148 and 303, respectively) figured prominently in one of the most important roles played by the Aero Club. Their flying school helped numerous pilots from the United States and foreign countries earn the coveted Aero Club license for a most serious purpose. These individuals—most of them Americans and Canadians—needed flying credentials so that they might join the aerial forces fighting the war in Europe.[25] Although the world would be slow to learn the lesson, the machinery of war was indifferent to sex.

THE WINGS OF WAR
American Aviation in World War I

10

Even before the airplane became a practical reality, the military had recognized the potential value of such a device in wartime. The concept of gaining a strategic advantage by occupying the high ground was as old as combat itself, and a flying machine would afford such a position regardless of the terrain. Very early in the life of the airplane, military theorists developed strategies for using fleets of airplanes against an enemy force. One 1909 plan even suggested that "The nation which had the aerial fleet would detach part of this for a daring raid timed to be almost simultaneous with the declaration of war."[1] Indeed, the brutal effectiveness of this tactic was demonstrated in the Japanese attack on Pearl Harbor more than thirty years later.[2]

In nearly all the tactical scenarios an aggressor relied on having superior air strength. The key, then, was for all the major powers to maintain parity in air power. Most authorities believed that, if such a balance of power could be achieved, war would become unnecessary. As a virtually irresistible weapon, the airplane would pose a strategic deterrent. With a powerful air force, America would be, it was often said, like the porcupine—a creature so well armed he need not attack or fear being attacked. This way of thinking fit nicely with turn-of-the-century American Progressivism: one of the basic principles of the Progressive school of thought was that modern machines would bring about an orderly society.[3]

In a book published eight years before the Wrights first flew, another Ohio native and would-be airplane inventor set forth his belief that airplanes would be among the greatest tools for creating this social order:

The best constructed air-ships will cost hundreds of thousands of dollars and some of them millions. They will be immense palaces with wings, whose natural element is the atmosphere, and whose movement is like the flying eagle's. Their highway of transit will be over seas, hills and deserts, over every man's house and every king's fort, making all men neighbors, and causing the sympathetic heart of all nations to beat within every man's door. This will be by far the safest method of transportation, for these aerial palaces will not move by the way of rocks, breakers, storms or cyclones. This being the greatest war-power, and being in and of itself a humanitarian institution of universal peace, by bringing the interests of all men into a cöoperative union, it will finally put an end to all wars and poverty, and establish social harmony, universal justice, peace and plenty.[4]

Given the existence of a sincere and widespread belief that military applications for the airplane would bring about peace, it is not paradoxical that the Wrights, sons of a bishop in the Church of the United Brethren in Christ, first tried to market their invention to the military.

From the beginning, the Aero Club of America had sought to achieve American equality in the field of aviation. In its early days, this had been measured by successful competition with other nations in the sporting arena. As signs of an impending European war grew clearer, however, the club assumed an aggressive position to promote American military use and development of the airplane.

In September 1910, at the Harvard/Boston Aero Meet, a group of concerned men formed the United States Aeronautical Reserve. Nearly all of the charter members of this organization were also prominent in the Aero Club. Not wanting to be a socially exclusive organization (in spite of the fact that the earliest members included the Hon. John Fitzgerald, Clifford Harmon, and other captains of American industry) the USAR charged a nominal membership fee of $1.00 and opened its doors to all who had a patriotic interest in developing military aviation. The members' aim was to raise money to provide airplanes for the different branches of the military and to train and maintain a pool of pilots ready to serve their country.

Adopting the same methods used by the Aero Club to promote the development of civil aviation, Commodore John Barry Ryan, a member of the USAR and the Aero Club, posted a $500 prize for the first person to fly an airplane from the deck of a U.S. naval vessel. Curtiss exhibition team member Eugene Ely soon won that prize.[5] On November 14, 1910, Ely's plane rolled down a makeshift wooden runway built onto the deck of the cruiser *Birmingham*. As his plane left the ship, Ely dove toward the water in an attempt to gain flying speed. Barely brushing the ocean surface with his wheels and propeller, Ely slowly rose above the water and set a direct course for shore. A few minutes later he landed on the beach of Willoughby Spit, near Norfolk, Virginia.[6]

Early the next year, Ely improved on the feat in San Francisco—this time taking off from and landing on the deck of the cruiser *Pennsylvania*. There he used a wooden platform measuring about twenty-five feet wide by one hundred and twenty-five feet long as his "runway." In order to stop the plane in such a short distance, ropes were stretched across the landing deck at intervals of a few feet, with a heavy sandbag tied to the ends of each rope. When Ely touched down, grappling hooks mounted under his plane snagged one after another of the ropes, progressively increasing the amount of drag on the plane, and stopping it in a short distance without a sudden jolt.[7]

The identity of the actual inventor of this crude progenitor of the aircraft carrier arresting gear is a matter of some debate. It was rigged under the direction of Lt. Theodore (Spuds) Ellyson, but several others later took credit for the idea.[8] One compelling version of the story says that Hugh A. Robinson, a pilot and mechanic with the Curtiss company, gave Ellyson the idea. Robinson, a former trick bicycle and motorcycle performer, allegedly adopted the aircraft arresting system from a similar one he had developed years earlier for a circus act in which a young lady rode a small cart down a steep track at a high rate of speed.[9] Regardless of which claimant (and there were many) actually developed the system, it is one example of the many aviation problems that owe their solutions to the widely varied backgrounds of the early pioneers of flight.[10]

In March 1911, Gen. James Allen of the U.S. Army Signal Corps addressed the Aero Club on the progress of military aviation. He reviewed the history of the army's interest in airplanes, going back to 1907, when it had solicited bids for functional flying machines and announced a congressional appropriation of $125,000 to buy airplanes and develop a flying program. In his speech he recognized Robert J. Collier, Aero Club member and president of the National Council, for loaning an airplane to the U.S. government. The army posted Collier's plane in San Antonio, Texas, as part of an escalated military presence to safeguard against possible border problems resulting from political turmoil within Mexico.[11] The Mexican situation had increased awareness of the need for the United States to be able to protect all of its borders. To this end, the Aero Club announced that it would begin a program intended to equip each station of the United States Life Saving Corps (a forerunner to the U.S. Coast Guard) with a "hydro-aeroplane" and a trained pilot. These planes, the club stated, would serve the dual roles of aiding in sea rescues and patrolling the coastline.[12] The club's proposed program for buying planes to guard U.S. coasts did not gain much momentum in 1911, but it was revived in 1915 as the well-publicized National Aeroplane Fund (discussed later in this chapter).

Collier, only son of *Collier's Weekly* publisher P. F. Collier, was the epitome of the wealthy sportsman of that era. Following the example of his father, Collier participated in many of what were then considered the most dangerous sports, such as big game hunting, polo,[13] boat racing, and, eventually, flying "aeroplanes."

When his father died of apoplexy shortly after riding his horse through a series of jumps in a 1909 competition, his son inherited an estate estimated at $4 million. The younger Collier, who had been groomed for some time to head the family business, proved to be to an able, if contentious, publisher. He was often sued for libel as the result of his attacks on corrupt public officials and the scandal sheets of the time. One of the more famous of these cases arose shortly before his father's death: Collier's magazine criticized another publisher for comments he had made about the alleged social misconduct of Alice, the daughter of then-President Theodore Roosevelt. The case was eventually settled out of court at a cost to Collier's magazine of at least $75,000, but it won Collier the appreciation and friendship of Roosevelt (who later became the first U.S. President ever to ride in an airplane). It was largely through such political connections that aviation would later be accorded a favorable introduction at the highest levels of the U.S. government.

The Aero Club elected Collier president late in 1911.[14] As the former head of the club's National Council—a body originally formed to assuage fears of domination of the Aero Club by its New York members—Collier was perceived by the members as a leader who could give affiliated clubs throughout the United States an equal voice in the operations of the parent organization. They thus voted to do away with the National Council and more closely join the affiliated clubs into one unified body.

His new stance gave Collier a stronger position from which to promote military aviation. In his first speech to the club, he declared:

One of the most important duties of this organization should be to assist in building up a strong public opinion in favor of aeroplanes for the Army and Navy. The figures show that while we are second or third in naval strength, we are sixth or seventh in naval and military aviators. This is a pitiable showing in view of the fact that we have the mechanical genius, the men, the courage, and the money to equip the finest naval and military aviation corps in the world. Both branches of the service have given this club generous co-operation in making our pilot license their standard. The least we can do is help them by every means in our power to secure an adequate equipment.[15]

Collier also expressed his disdain for the sort of exhibition flying that had killed some of America's leading pilots the previous year. "Hoxsey, Johnstone, Moisant, Ely, St. Croix Johnstone and others are too heavy a toll to pay for the morbid curiosity of the public,"[16] he proclaimed.

Collier felt that he had an obligation to promote those aspects of aviation that would demonstrate to the public that the airplane was inherently safe and not particularly difficult to operate. He originally proposed to sponsor a trophy for the winner of the elimination race for the Bennett Cup, but later asked that the club instead allow him to give a trophy "for the greatest achievement in aviation in America, the value of which has been thoroughly demonstrated by use during the preceding year."[17] In the decades since, that award has come to represent the height of aeronautic achievement.

Since its inception, it has been presented every year, traditionally— even now a reflection of Collier's political clout—by the President of the United States, on the anniversary of the Wright Brothers' first flight. Known at first as the Aero Club of America Trophy, today it is recognized throughout the world simply as the Collier Trophy.

The large bronze Collier Trophy was commissioned of Baltimore sculptor Ernest Wise Keyser,[18] a student of Augustus Saint-Gaudens. It is said to represent "The genius of Man (chief figure), [which] having conquered Gravity (male figure) and Contrary Winds (female figure) and having touched the bird and found its secrets, soars from earth a conqueror."[19] When, in 1922, the Aero Club of America became the National Aeronautic Association, members began referring to the former Aero Club Trophy as the Collier Trophy. In 1944 the NAA officially renamed it the Robert J. Collier Trophy.

At first, the actual 525-pound trophy became the possession, for one year, of the recipient. But, fearing possible damage from frequent moving, in 1951 the NAA elected to put the trophy on permanent display in the Smithsonian Institution. (It is now in the National Air & Space Museum.) In 1949, Bill Lear, upon receiving the award for developing an automatic pilot and automatic approach control system, commissioned miniatures of the original trophy and had them presented to each living previous recipient of the award. In 1957 Look magazine agreed to underwrite the expense of annual maintenance to the trophy, and continued Lear's

Collier was among the few aviators of his time who were able to maintain a friendship with both the Curtiss and Wright camps during their long dispute. Although he was a founding investor in the Wright Company, he showed a particular fondness for the Curtiss "hydro-aeroplanes" and flying boats, seeing the tremendous potential of such aircraft for protecting the U.S. coast against enemy attack. In 1911 the Aero Club presented its first Collier Trophy to Glenn Curtiss for developing the hydro-aeroplane, and Curtiss again received the award in 1912 for designing and building a practical flying boat.

generous initiative of providing a miniature to each winner of the prize. In exchange, the magazine asked only that it be allowed the exclusive right to announce the yearly winner of America's highest aviation honor. Since 1986 the expense of presenting miniature replicas of the Collier trophy has been borne by the Collier Trust, a perpetual fund established by the NAA with contributions from members of the aerospace industry.

The story of the Collier Trophy—of the individuals and organizations who have been named recipients throughout its eight-decade history—is very much the story of American aviation. Collier winners constitute a pantheon of aviation's best and brightest, judged by their contemporaries as responsible for the greatest achievements of their time. This volume uses the Collier Trophy as the armature that gives shape and structure to its narrative. Throughout the book, the winners of the Collier in every year in which it was awarded are highlighted in sidebars that place them within the context of world aviation at the time. (The sidebars do not always present the winners in strict chronological order, and a more condensed listing in that form is included as Appendix A.)

During the New York Aero Show of 1912—by now the Aero Club's exhibit at the Automobile Show had grown into a self-contained annual event—Collier asked pilot Walter Brookins to take him on a flight. Without announcing their destination, the two boarded Brookins's hydro-aeroplane and flew out into New York harbor. There they paid a visit to Rear Adm. Hugo Osterhaus aboard the cruiser *Washington,* inviting him to be the guest of honor at a dinner held by the club. Aero Club members first learned of the flight when the operator of a wireless telegraph machine that had been installed in one of the airplanes on display, to demonstrate future air-to-ground communications capabilities, received a message from the *Washington* that Collier and Brookins had arrived.

Once aboard the cruiser, Brookins, Collier, and Osterhaus discussed the potential for using aircraft in naval warfare. The trip was a modest effort, but it further demonstrated the practicality of the airplane. When Collier returned to shore he commented to the press:

The thing that most pleases me is that it means the passing of the day when the aeroplane's chief use was to make yokels gape at a county fair. We are going to have something more than that now—aeroplanes to carry the mails, to perform speedy messenger work, to take a permanent place among the efficient means of transportation.[20]

Collier developed an instantaneous enthusiasm for hydro aircraft and, under Brookins's instruction, soloed in his own machine two weeks later. The wealthy publisher was so proud of his accomplishment that he chartered a train to take his office staff to his country home in Wickatuck, New Jersey, where he demonstrated his flying ability.[21] He established one of America's first private airfields at this country home, often inviting the better-known pilots of the day to compete in informal flying meets that demonstrated the practical capabilities of the airplane.[22] By having these pilots fly before his influential friends, and often take them for short rides, Collier was able to demonstrate the potential of the airplane to a class of individuals with the power to develop it. He was thus instrumental in reshaping the image of the airplane from that of a deadly carnival act into a technology with a safe and exciting future.

Indeed, aviation safety became almost an obsession with Collier. Early in 1912 he shipped his plane to Panama with plans to take the first aerial photos of the Panama Canal. Aerial photographs of the world's most modern engineering marvel would have undoubtedly boosted sales of his magazine, but once he and his crew, which included Wright exhibition pilot Al Welsh and famed photographer Jimmy Hare, arrived in Panama, they determined that a flight the length of the canal would be extremely hazardous because the terrain afforded no landing place in the event of an emergency. Not wanting to chance negative publicity for aviation, Collier decided that neither he nor Welsh would make the flight. The entire crew returned home with not a single aerial view of the canal.[23]

Ever the adventurer, Collier tried to purchase the huge Curtiss flying boat *America,* which, as discussed later in this chapter, was under construction for Rodman Wanamaker at the beginning of World War I. His attempts to buy the machine aroused speculation that Collier himself intended to fly the Atlantic, a report that Collier flatly denied, claiming he had not "the slightest desire in the world to be classed among the numerous fakers who are forever talking about a transatlantic flight. My only idea in purchasing this outfit was to use it as a pleasure cruiser . . . not to break records or seek publicity by talking about present-day impossibilities."[24]

Perhaps the real reason Collier had sought to acquire the flying boat was later revealed by a representative of the Curtiss company: the publisher, anticipating that the United States would inevitably enter the war then fermenting in Europe, foresaw a naval battle off Sandy Hook, New York. If his prediction became a reality, Collier hoped to have Curtiss fly the *America,* with him as a passenger, over the historic battle. He wanted to be the first aerial spectator for the first naval engagement in U.S. waters of the first world war.[25] Such a plan would have been an exciting adventure, but would also have demonstrated a practical military use for flying boats in the defense of the United States. It was certainly entirely in keeping with Collier's ideals and character.

In 1914 Collier contracted uremic poisoning and lay in a coma for days. He eventually recovered, but never seemed to regain his previous vitality. Following the experience he took pains to assure that *Collier's Weekly* would survive if he passed away. On November 8, 1918, Collier sat at the dinner table with his wife. Only hours before, he had gotten off a ship returning him to America after several months spent reporting on the war from battlefield positions. As he and his wife spent their first moments alone since he had left for the European war, Collier suddenly slumped forward. A doctor later said that he had died almost instantly from heart failure.[26]

In the fall of 1912, the Aero Club hosted an unofficial visit of the National Guard to the Mineola, Long Island, flying field. The club hoped to extend use of the aviation grounds to the military for training operations. They demonstrated the practicality of using aircraft in military service by allowing senior Guard officers, including Maj. Gen. John F. O'Ryan, to ride in a plane piloted by George Beatty. It was the first time that such a high-ranking National Guard officer had flown in an airplane, but that fact was eclipsed in the news by the first flight of a less-senior National Guard officer—the incredibly wealthy Col. Cornelius Vanderbilt.

Several other dignitaries had their first opportunity to fly that day. One of them, a little known but ambitious Collier employee named Henry Woodhouse, also got a taste of the public glory associated with aviation. He was pictured, smiling engagingly, along with the military and civilian dignitaries at the field.[27] In years to come Woodhouse would become well known among the flying community as an editor of popular flying magazines and a governor of the Aero Club—only to have a dark past revealed as he figured tragically in the demise of the Aero Club (see Chapter 11).

The Aero Club's commitment to military aviation grew over the next several years. The dynamic Collier's lead in promoting the use of naval aircraft was followed with equal enthusiasm by his successor, Alan Hawley. The Aero Club organized Navy Aviation Day, in July 1913. It was a gala event, with a battalion of sailors and another of Marines as honor guards. Some fifty aircraft were assembled for review, both on the ground and in flight, by the commandant of the Brooklyn Navy Yard. The list of invited dignitaries who might be able to influence the advancement of naval aviation was headed by the assistant secretary of the navy and chairman of the congressional Naval Committee—Franklin D. Roosevelt.[28]

When the nations of Europe went to war, the airplane soon showed itself to be a key weapon. Those in the United States who were attuned to aviation development saw quickly how important aerial forces were becoming to combat. Unfortunately, the U.S. military as a whole was not easily persuaded to accept new technology. It continued to distress Aero Club members that the United States was rapidly falling far behind the combatant European nations in air strength. They mounted even more determined efforts to keep America apace with the rest of the world. For much of 1914, the club remained preoccupied with a dream of helping the United States become the first country in the world to achieve a transatlantic flight. With Wanamaker's financial help, they organized an effort to build a flying boat capable of the task. The airplane, *America,* was completed and test flown, but the beginning of the war in Europe prevented the actual Atlantic crossing attempt.[29]

Although it never fulfilled its original purpose, Wanamaker's *America* played perhaps a greater role than that for which it had originally been intended. The large flying boat implemented a V hull with ventilated steps, a design for which Glenn Curtiss later received a patent. This feature made it possible for large machines to break away more easily from the surface of the water on takeoff, and it is a principle still used in the design of the flying boats and pontoon planes of today. Furthermore, Commander J. C. Porter, R.N., secured plans for the *America* and used them as a basis for England's Felixstowe boats of World War I. The Felixstowe design came back to America during the war in the form of the U.S. Navy's coastal patrol and antisubmarine boats, eventually evolv-

---

Orville Wright received the 1913 Collier Trophy for inventing an automatic stabilizing device, but the effectiveness of Wright's stabilizer was soon surpassed by a gyroscopic "automatic pilot" developed by the young Lawrence Sperry. Sperry's autopilot was adapted for aircraft use from gyroscopic ship navigation devices invented by his famous father, Elmer A. Sperry. Since Lawrence Sperry was still a teenager at the time of this invention, and because he had built and patented the stabilizer with the financial aid of his father's company, the Aero Club awarded the elder Sperry the 1914 Collier Trophy for the gyroscopic airplane controlling device. In 1916, the father was once again honored by the Aero Club for a drift indicator principally developed by his young son.

In the interim year 1915, the Collier Trophy went to W. Starling Burgess, a former yacht designer, who had built the innovative Burgess-Dunne hydro-aeroplane for the U.S. Navy (and who also built a custom flying boat for R. J. Collier). The Burgess-Dunne hydro-aeroplane was Burgess's modification of the Dunne, built under a license from the English designer. It was a "tailless" biplane with swept-back wings. Although several of the radically different hydro-aeroplanes were built for the navy just before the outbreak of World War I, the concept of a plane without a tail did not find widespread acceptance. Many years later the concept was rediscovered, and more modern tailless airplanes, including the Mitchell "Flying Wing" and today's stealth aircraft, can trace their design heritage directly back to these planes.

---

ing into the plan for the NC (Navy Curtiss) boats that made the first Atlantic crossing.[30]

In 1915, the U.S. Senate refused a request by Secretary of the Navy Josephus Daniels to fund a naval aeronautics program. At the time, the navy had a total of three airplanes, as compared to hundreds of planes each in the French and German militaries. As the American public read of incredible long-distance air attacks taking place in Europe (such as a raid carried out against Venice, Italy, from an Austrian air base one hundred miles away), they sensed their own growing vulnerability. Yet again the Aero Club demanded that the government take notice. In a letter to Secretary of War Lindley M. Garrison, Aero Club president Hawley protested, "The east is entirely without aeronautical protection. The military centers have no airplanes. . . . I submit that this is an unnatural and shocking condition. It is my duty to urge that steps be taken immediately to provide aeroplanes for the defense of this part of the country."[31] However, Garrison could do little to correct the situation because money for military aircraft was not available.

The Aero Club reacted to this shortsightedness by creating the National Aeroplane Fund (often called the National Aeroplane Subscription, because it was based on similar public subscriptions for funds to buy military aircraft that had been successful in France and Germany). The original purpose of the fund was to provide airplanes, trained pilots, and mechanics to National Guard and militia units in those states desiring them, and to establish a series of landing fields along the coastal areas from which patrols could be launched. The plan intended for these reserve pilots to be used in public service, carrying mail to areas that were difficult to access, until such time as they might be needed for military service.[32] No sooner had subscriptions to the National Aeroplane Fund been announced on May 21, 1915, than the need for such an effort was jarringly brought home to America. The *Lusitania*—a British passenger ship carrying hundreds of civilians, many of them American—was sunk in the Irish Sea on May 7 by a German submarine. With the sinking of the *Lusitania,* America moved a giant step closer to involvement in the war.

To kick off the National Aeroplane Fund, the Curtiss Aeroplane Company donated a flying boat and training for a pilot and mechanic. This first aircraft was assigned to a battalion of the New York Naval Militia and stationed to protect New York harbor. Members of the Aero Club hoped that enough private contributions might eventually be solicited to provide as many as one hundred planes for coastal defense and reserve military preparedness. The National Aeroplane Fund grew with donations of cash and airplanes. Large corporations (notably those with interests in airplane manufacturing) and business leaders gave their support to the effort, many donating thousands of dollars. A longtime Aero Club member from Guatemala even sent a personal contribution toward America's aerial defense—a donation made more impressive by the fact that the contributor, Emanuele Cabrera, was the president of that country.[33]

The U.S. government, finally realizing the benefits of the Aero Club's program, agreed in June to cooperate by providing instruction and training aircraft for reserve pilots. The government hoped the Aero Club could assemble fifteen aviation squadrons for the National Guard and twenty-two squadrons for the Naval Militia.[34] Many Aero Club members further assisted by contributing the use of their private airplanes for maneuvers or for training National Guard units.

In the first six months of its existence, the National Aeroplane Fund enjoyed great success: it organized an aviation unit of the New York National Guard and began training eleven pilots in that state. The New York Naval Militia received a flying boat, as did its counterpart in Wisconsin (presumably with the intention that Wisconsin soldiers be prepared in the event they had to serve as part of a coastal defense). Guard units and militia in Massachusetts, California, Arizona, Rhode Island, and Texas received funds for pilot training, and units in several other states were afforded the opportunity, for the first time in their history, to conduct military training against possible air attacks. The National Aeroplane Fund also made it possible for the Aero Club to launch a campaign designed to enlist the aid of the press, military officers, and political figures in the cause of developing strong U.S. aerial forces.[35]

The publicity campaign was exceptionally effective. In an article printed September 26, 1915, the *New York Times* asked several government officials to go on record with responses to Aero Club concerns about strong military aviation programs and aviation sections for guard and militia units. Senators from New York, Massachusetts, and California, and congressmen from Pennsylvania, Delaware, Wisconsin, New York, Kansas, New Jersey, Michigan, and Connecticut joined with Brig. Gen. L. L. Mills, chief of militia affairs, and Franklin D. Roosevelt, assistant secretary of the navy, to endorse heartily the efforts and objectives of the Aero Club.[36]

As America watched the war in Europe with growing concern, a threat closer to home once again mobilized the Aero Club. Trouble on the Mexican border prompted the U.S. Army to send Gen. J. J. (Black Jack) Pershing to Texas in pursuit of Pancho Villa. At the request of Gen. Frederick Funston, the Aero Club provided a list of aviators who were willing to volunteer their assistance to Pershing in the Mexican campaign.[37] The army was also in need of airplanes (the War Department had allocated funds for only eight planes to be used by Pershing's troops), but regulations prevented outright gifts. In order to circumvent the rule, the Aero Club offered to sell the army two airplanes for the price of one dollar each.[38]

Knowing that seasoned combat pilots would be an invaluable asset in the Mexican campaign, the club wired William (Bert) Thaw of the Franco-American Corps (later renamed the Lafayette Escadrille), offering to pay the travel expenses of American pilots willing to return to the United States. None of the fighters in France was able to return, but reserve troops, including some forty pilots trained by the National Aeroplane Fund and thirty additional pilot volunteers recruited by the Aero

Club, announced that they were ready to join the Army Air Corps to fight in Mexico.

The U.S. government—at last realizing the severity of this shortage of trained pilots and airplanes in a time of national emergency—in June 1916 authorized $3.5 million to train military pilots.[39] By October of that year, the allocation for military aeronautics had been increased to $18 million, and the secretary of war announced the goal of training one thousand aviators. Nevertheless, by the time our military was given the governmental resources to develop an aviation program, the Aero Club's National Aeroplane Fund had already generated close to $400,000 in donations, which were used to train and equip reserve aviators.[40]

Most conspicuous among these reserve pilots were the flying clubs from Yale, Harvard, Columbia, Princeton, and other universities. In 1916 the Aero Club joined with Robert Bacon, former U.S. ambassador to France, and other Harvard alumni to underwrite flying lessons for college men wishing to become reserve military aviators.[41] The Harvard Aero Corps led the way for other universities to form similar groups, also sponsored by the National Aeroplane Fund and alumni contributions. Yale could not, of course, permit itself to be beaten by Harvard, and immediately gathered together its own contingent of flying students, which became known as Aerial Coast Patrol Unit Number One. Such patriotic action from groups of college students prompted John D. Rockefeller, Jr., to donate $1000 to promote flight training on other campuses.[42]

On February 3, 1917, a *New York Times* news article was headed:

ARMY PAVES WAY FOR VOLUNTEERS
Country Divided Into Districts to Provide
for Quick Mobilization in Event of War
AERO CLUB IS READY

The following day the headlines blared:

RELATIONS WITH GERMANY ARE BROKEN OFF;
AMERICAN SHIP HOUSATONIC SUNK, CREW SAFE;
MILITIA CALLED OUT; GERMAN SHIPS SEIZED

The day after that, Yale's twelve-member Aerial Coast Patrol Unit Number 1 withdrew from school to begin advanced military training as naval aviation officers. These were young men with family names long familiar to the members of the Aero Club: F. Trubee Davison and Henry

P. Davison, whose father Henry Pomeroy Davison, Sr., was a senior executive with J. P. Morgan & Co.; Robert A. Lovett, son of Judge Robert Scott Lovett, chairman of the board of the Union-Pacific Railroad; John Farwell, III; Earl Gould; Albert Dallon Sturtevant; and Wellsley Land Brown, to name just a few.[43] Now the sons of the "men of wealth, influence, and ability" would take up their fathers' fragile wings and fly to war.

TIMES OF CHANGE

The Demise of the Aero Club of America

11

As the U.S. government set about building strong military air forces, the Aero Club of America's status as the nation's preeminent aviation authority eroded. The club enjoyed some last moments of glory as the administrator of the National Aeroplane Fund, but even that prestige was short-lived. After 1915, the U.S. Navy no longer designated active-duty officers and men as naval aviators based solely on possession of an Aero Club flying license. The navy elected to establish its own training schools, developing more rigorous flying requirements than those of the Aero Club and the FAI.

Most of the old guard among high-ranking naval officers objected to proposals to create a separate Naval Flying Corps in which officers and men might serve for the duration of their career. They felt that navy pilots should be recruited from the ranks of those already trained in traditional shipboard skills and customs—acquired over six years or more of sea duty—then returned to sea after their period of greatest usefulness as pilots was complete. This period of usefulness was estimated at five years. Policies formulated for military aviation in the National Defense Act of June 3, 1916, reflected this attitude, but did not anticipate the problems involved in producing qualified pilots in wartime. The navy was ill-equipped to train a large number of pilots quickly—especially if they could only be drawn from a pool of experienced fleet sailors.

Fortunately for the navy as it launched into war in 1917, a provision in the same 1916 act permitted the establishment of a Naval Reserve

Flying Corps. This allowed civilian-trained reserve pilots to be given some additional navy flight training, then put into active duty as fliers. Because they had had no time at sea, these pilots could not be designated as "official" naval aviators, but they could fly naval aircraft in times of national emergency.[1] The vast majority of the U.S. Navy pilots who flew in World War I were such reserve members, and nearly all of them had received their earliest training through collegiate and militia programs paid for, in part, by the Aero Club's National Aeroplane Fund.

Government intransigence on aviation matters sparked an incident at the 1917 annual dinner of the Aero Club, which in turn touched off a feud within the organization. The guest of honor was James W. Gerard, who, before the break in diplomatic relations with Germany, had been the U.S. ambassador to that country. Club governor Henry A. Wise Wood, a close associate of president Alan Hawley and Henry Woodhouse, took advantage of his position as toastmaster to launch into an hour-long tirade against the administration in which the ambassador served. Wood's comments were strongly critical, including such barbs as "the present government reminds me of a huge ostrich farm with nothing in sight but tailfeathers, the heads buried so far in the sand they are thinking in Chinese."[2] His lengthy remarks (Gerard followed the hour-long introduction with a ten-minute speech) obviously embarrassed the guest of honor and angered many others, including Howard E. Coffin, an Aero Club member since 1909 who was soon to be appointed chairman of the new federal Aircraft Production Board. The Aero Club soon divided into opposing camps.[3]

Only weeks later, Hawley and Woodhouse began offering their services as aviation experts to Coffin and other government members. They first proposed to have the club officially undertake the recruitment and preliminary training of all military pilots.[4] In spite of public claims by Hawley that the Aero Club had been "recognized" by the new Aircraft Production Board, and that it would soon "train thousands of aviators and manufacture thousands of airplanes,"[5] Coffin chose to develop his own training and manufacturing programs. It was the first of many proposals that Hawley and Woodhouse were to make regarding wartime aviation (others dealt with plans for increasing spruce wood production[6] and with pay for military aviators[7]), but the board seems to have adopted none of them. Indeed Coffin never accorded Hawley and Woodhouse the status as aviation authorities that they sought.

Once the government committed itself to a wartime aviation program, it took steps to expedite production of military aircraft on a large scale. Following the example of the automobile manufacturers who, years before, had formed an association in which member companies pooled their patents, the government sanctioned the creation of a similar aircraft builders patent pool. It was called the Manufacturers Aircraft Association (MAA).[8]

Howard Coffin's Aircraft Production Board was largely responsible for helping the MAA form. The problems associated with quickly building a U.S. military airplane industry from virtually nothing into a network of companies capable of manufacturing thousands of machines a year were formidable. At one point the board anticipated a need for 25,000 planes. In order to accomplish such a task, government officials made certain decisions that they never would have dared implement in peacetime— such as sanctioning the MAA patent pool. The MAA charged the U.S. government a royalty of approximately $200 for every military aircraft that a member firm built. These funds were then apportioned, according to a predetermined percentage based on the relative value of that member's patents, to each of the MAA members. In exchange, every member of the MAA was allowed free use of all patents on aircraft held by any other member.[9]

The association outraged many in the aviation community who recalled that an early trust created by the automobile manufacturers patent pool had virtually blocked any nonmember from building automobiles. Most of those who opposed the MAA had no objections to the formation of such an association for the good of the war effort, but they were concerned about the consequences of a patent trust remaining in effect after the hostilities ceased. They feared that postwar American aircraft manufacturing would also be monopolized by MAA members.[10]

The objections of the MAA's critics were strengthened by the fact that the Curtiss v. Wright patent dispute, still in litigation after so many years, had been resolved through government intervention by allowing the two entities to declare themselves the principal patent holders of the MAA. Both the Curtiss and the Wright interests received substantial sums of money for use of their (legally still not established) rights to airplane patents.[11] By sanctioning this patent pool, opponents of the plan felt, the government essentially ruled in favor of, and rewarded, the Curtiss and Wright companies in matters that the civil courts had never been able to resolve.[12]

For years the Aero Club's membership had included nearly all the scientists and aviators who were applying their efforts to solving the problems of aeronautics. At the outset of World War I, many of them became directly involved in the war effort, working for the aircraft manufacturers whose activities proceeded with significant assistance from the government. They tended to support government policies, feeling that the war effort justified certain legal liberties taken in the name of expediency. Other members, who did not become part of the manufacturing system, fashioned themselves as watchdogs of the government wartime aviation programs, publicly proclaiming that the programs were robbing American taxpayers.[13]

Hawley, Woodhouse, and certain other members of the Aero Club administration fell into the latter category. Whether or not the intentions of these Aero Club officials were honorable, each new cry of scandal retarded the pace of aircraft manufacturing in support of the war effort. Fear of being involved in an impropriety made members of Congress hesitant to fund aircraft construction. Time and again the aircraft industry was investigated for wrongdoing, and each time it was vindicated. Still, the leaders of the Aero Club continued to take potshots at the Aircraft Production Board and the MAA.[14]

In the fall of 1918, a group opposed to the Hawley administration mounted an effort to replace it with a slate of their own officers. The opposition party, which nominated Coffin for president and Courtland Bishop for first vice president, was refused access to club records, in particular to a list of names and addresses of club members. Because most voting was done by proxy ballot, such a list was essential for their campaign. It was only under court order that the Hawley administration finally compromised by releasing a set of envelopes purportedly addressed to all members of the club.[15]

In a letter to members, the opposition party charged that Wood had stated that certain cabinet members should be removed from office. These comments, made by Wood in 1917 at the beginning of the war, took on a somewhat treasonous tone in 1918. The letter further suggested that the Hawley administration wished to transform the Aero Club, "from a body of distinguished sportsmen, scientists, and public-spirited citizens into a sort of trade organization, which would enable certain interests to use the prestige of the club for commercial purposes."[16] Wood denied all charges, and the opposition party failed to elicit enough support to defeat Hawley.

The Aero Club continued to function, but lost much of the momentum of its earlier years. It became a club with limited purposes. The following account of attendance at the Aero Club–sponsored Pan American Aeronautical Conference was presented before a House committee hearing as evidence of the club's lack of effectiveness:

There are more or less glowing reports originating with the Aero Club of America, in which the names of men mighty in aviation are tossed about with

The war, and disagreements among Aero Club members, temporarily suspended the annual presentation of the Collier Trophy. No
award was given during 1917–1920, even though there were numerous worthwhile aviation achievements during those years. Among
the most prominent of those accomplishments were the 1919
attempts to cross the Atlantic. On May 6, four Curtis flying boats,
designated NC-1 through NC-4, left Newfoundland, en route to
England via the Azores and Portugal. One of these planes, the NC-4,
became the first aircraft to successfully cross the Atlantic.

much ado about flying. Then there are the more discriminating reports of careful observers on the spot. According to one of these observervers . . . at the
opening luncheon of the congress there were 32 persons present, 11 of whom
were women. This situation emphasizes the waning influence which the Aero
Club of America, a civilian flying body, is having on the sport of flying in this
country.[17]

The advent of wartime aviation had made sporting flight in America
seem a somewhat frivolous pastime and of course international competition was out of the question. The Aero Club continued to officiate at
record attempts[18] and competitions for trophies, but more often than not
the competitors were no longer sportsmen in private aircraft, but military
officers testing the limits of new war machines. Even the Aero Club's
licensing program lost some of its impact. Pilots trained by the military
and experienced in combat flying often saw no purpose in obtaining a
sportsman's certificate that carried no "legal" weight.

Military pilots returning from Europe after the war had little in
common with the prewar fliers. Military aviation had advanced so much
during the war years that prewar civilian flying now seemed tame and
almost comic. With the development of more powerful aircraft engines,
pilots could now far exceed what had been a "high-altitude" flight before
the war. Looping an airplane was no longer a death-defying stunt, but had
become a common maneuver, as had upside-down flying, barrel rolls,
figure eights, and most of the other aerobatic feats that had once thrilled
the county fair crowds.

During the war these pilots had developed close bonds with each
other. Now they wanted an organization of their own, and so formed the
American Flying Club, comprised of active-duty military pilots and
World War I veterans. The new club posed a potential threat to the status

of the Aero Club, for it was improbable that civilian fliers would be able to compete for altitude, speed, and distance records against military pilots with the latest in technology at their disposal. For a time, in the years following the war, nearly every new aviation record was held by a military flier.

Among the American Flying Club's many publicity-generating events was the first American Transcontinental Air Race of 1919. In this competition, sixty-three planes (forty-eight of them starting on the west coast, fifteen starting on the east) flew between Roosevelt Field, in Mineola, New York, and the Presidio in San Francisco, California, then back again. The winner, Lt. Belvin W. Maynard, completed a cross-country flight in twenty-four hours, fifty-nine minutes, and forty-eight and a half seconds of actual flying time. (His total elapsed time was three days, six hours, and four minutes.)[19]

NAA member George B. Weller of Rawlins, Wyoming, distinctly remembers this event. The contest committee chose Rawlins as a refueling and overnight rest stop for planes making the cross-country flight. Weller's Boy Scout troop was "drafted" to stand nighttime guard duty over the visiting planes and to protect them from the curious and from vandals. Weller recalls the winner: "[he was] 1st. Lt. Maynard—the 'Flying Preacher.' His mascot was a German Police dog who rode in the front cockpit, with a white silk scarf around his neck—just like his master. In fact, all the pilots wore them then."[20] It was images like these that turned the eyes of America away from the civilian fliers and toward the dashing young military pilots.

Eventually the American Flying Club formed its own contest committee and sought to be recognized by the FAI as the official U.S. representative in international aeronautic competition. This bid was endorsed by a group within the Aero Club led by none other than Courtland Bishop, the second president of the club. Bishop went before the FAI in Paris and recommended that the American Flying Club be recognized "if the Federation desires to retain the prestige it enjoyed in this country up to a few years ago." An opposing bloc of Aero Club members, led by Woodhouse and Hawley, enjoyed a position of power owing to their control of the club's positions of leadership. They charged that Bishop's comments were a reaction to his involvement in the failed attempt to regain control of the organization and install Coffin as president.[21]

The Aero Club's leaders demonstrated their ill will toward the American Flying Club with an action that today seems rather childish and petty. Six months after the end of the war, certain members of the American Flying Club undertook to organize a reunion, which they billed in their comically—and somewhat suggestively—worded invitations as "The greatest souse party of the century." The term "orgy" was used and the attendance of certain "wild persons" was anticipated. Although it was not an official function of the club, the organizers sent invitations to every member of the American Flying Club.

When certain unnamed officials of the Aero Club learned of the invitations, they attempted to use them to discredit their rival organization. They sent copies to the secretary of war and the secretary of the navy, along with a letter expressing outrage that such activities were taking place to the "disgrace of the air service" and recommending that they act to "prevent further reflections on the service." They also notified the press of both the impending bacchanal and the action they had taken to try to prevent it. Clearly, the Aero Club officers who sent the letter hoped to put the competition out of business. But the result was the reverse of that intended, as the Aero Club ended up looking rather foolish for concerning itself with a private celebration held by war heroes.[22]

Less than a year later, the Aero Club itself came under attack. On June 2, 1920, the New York *Evening Post* published an article raising questions about the Aero Club's handling of money contributed to the National Aeroplane Fund. The question of possible improprieties was brought forward by Emerson McMillan, a New York banker who had contributed $34,000 to the fund, because it was alleged that more than half of the contributions went toward the expenses of managing the fund, instead of purchasing airplanes for the military. Henry Woodhouse, one of the three men in charge of handling the money, responded by filing a $250,000 libel suit against the *Evening Post*. New York Assistant District Attorney Edwin P. Kilroe questioned Hawley, Wood, and Woodhouse in an informal hearing held on June 8.[23] The officers claimed that the National Aeroplane Fund had been audited, and all appeared to be in order, but the general membership nevertheless took steps to remove them from office, and installed a new slate of acting officers.

A month later Henry Woodhouse was again in the news as he tried to obtain an injunction against a merger between the Aero Club and the American Flying Club contemplated by the faction led by Bishop and Coffin. Woodhouse claimed that the American Flying Club was controlled by the members of the MAA and that the merger was an attempt by them to gain control of the Aero Club's assets and records. Those records, Woodhouse charged, could be used to support government investigations of unlawful acts by certain members of the MAA.[24] The Aero Club's board of governors, under acting president Charles Edwards, suspended Woodhouse for filing suit against the club.

Edwards denied having had any contact with manufacturers while making plans to merge with the American Flying Club. He counterattacked, charging that Woodhouse had "been very active since his admission to membership in 1911 in the Aero Club of America and among its membership in promoting his own commercial interests, and has utilized his connection with that club in exploiting his publications, especially, *Flying Age, Aerial Age,* and *Air Power,* and two of his text books." He went on to note that members had expressed dissatisfaction with Woodhouse's use of the club to his own personal gain (Woodhouse often referred to his publications as the "official" magazines of the Aero Club) and concluded, "The plaintiff fears that the advantages of personal exploitation of himself and his publications, which he has heretofore enjoyed through the commercialization of his relations with the said club may be prejudiced or impaired by the termination of the terms of the present Board of Governors. . . ."[25] That board was indeed terminated, and the new board moved to unite with the American Flying Club.

The amalgamation of the Aero Club of America and the American Flying Club passed by the unanimous vote of the latter and majority consent of the Aero Club on August 16, 1920. The new organization retained the name Aero Club of America. Of the union Col. (later Brig. Gen.) William (Billy) Mitchell said: "The combined clubs bring together all the best elements in aviation that this country possesses. There is nothing which has happened in the development of our whole national defense system which will have a greater effect than this consolidation."[26]

The emergence—and apparent early success—of a competing aviation organization certainly suggests that a substantial number of U.S. pilots felt that their needs were not being adequately served by the Aero Club. The fact that an apparently smooth and amiable merger of the two clubs took place, once the club's board of governors (including Woodhouse) was replaced, makes it evident that the need for a unified national organization was still widely recognized, provided that organization's leadership and goals had the support of the aviation community. Obviously, the Aero Club of Hawley and Woodhouse had lost that support, perhaps to the point that the once sterling name of the Aero Club was no longer considered an asset. This indeed appears to have been the case, for the Aero Club's new board of governors soon was at the center of a group working feverishly to create a different world representative of American aviation—one that would fight to take with it the assets of the Aero Club, but would have some distinctly new objectives and a new name.

In the fall of 1921, aviation leaders from across America convened in Omaha, Nebraska, for the First National Aero Congress. Those Aero

In 1921 the Collier Trophy was presented for the first time since 1916. Collier's death may have contributed to the long period of time during which the trophy was not presented, for the period corresponded to the interval spanning his death and the final, very complicated, settlement of his estate. The 1921 recipient was Grover Loening, a long-time Aero Club member who had pioneered the idea of collegiate divisions of the Aero Club before the war, while still a student. Loening received the trophy for his "aerial yacht," a large craft that rose to an altitude of 19,500 feet with four people on board—substantially bettering the previous seaplane record of 9,600 feet (also with four on board). The pilot for that record-breaking flight was David McCulloch, who had captained the NC-3 on its 1919 Atlantic crossing attempt. Among the passengers were Loening himself and L. R. Grumman—another name destined to become famous in American aircraft construction. It was to be the last time that the Aero Club ever presented the Collier Trophy.[27]

Club members who had grown increasingly dissatisfied with the policies of Hawley and Woodhouse were already working out details for "nationalizing" the organization.[28] In an effort to create a unified association representing all forms of aviation and all aviators in the country, the conference participants created the National Air Association. The members of the new association agreed to meet again the following year in conjunction with the 1922 Detroit Aviation Air Society's National Airplane Races,[29] and there they hoped to consolidate the Aero Club of America and the National Air Association into one powerful national organization to be called the National Aeronautic Association. Aero Club officials immediately began investigating the best method to achieve this goal without losing their status as American representative to the FAI.[30]

Even though the Aero Club owned property worth many thousands of dollars, much of it was in the form of illiquid items like the Collier Trophy, and by then the club had outstanding debts amounting to nearly $25,000. In an effort to balance the accounts of the Aero Club and transfer its assets, debt-free, to the proposed National Aeronautic Association, the club appointed trustees who bought the assets of the Aero Club at a price equivalent to the club's total amount of indebtedness, and who were later repaid with donations made specifically for that purpose.[31]

Once again Woodhouse filed suit against the governors of the Aero Club, seeking to halt the merger. In this, the newest of his lawsuits, Woodhouse charged that the governors sought to obtain the Aero Club's records in order to block a government investigation of contract fraud by wartime aircraft manufacturers.[32] Woodhouse claimed further that he had a list of 404 members who had signed over proxy ballots, authorizing him to act on their behalf. These members, he maintained, constituted a majority in opposition to the merger.

In a hearing before New York Supreme Court Justice Philip J. Mc-Cook, Aero Club trustee Charles T. Terry, a Professor of Law at Columbia University, explained the club's state of insolvency at the time that he and the other trustees had been asked to become involved. By receiving such valuable assets as the trophies, then returning them once the club's debts had been paid, the trustees were participating in a plan by which the club could resolve its financial obligations without having to dispose of historic materials. The records in question, he continued, were stored in a Brooklyn warehouse where Department of Justice officials had already examined them in order to determine if Woodhouse's fraud claims were valid. They, too, would be turned over to the new national organization.

The Judge then gave Woodhouse a deadline by which to produce proof of the alleged proxies. Woodhouse could not comply. His credibility was severely damaged when he admitted to Justice McCook that most of the ballots he had claimed to control had actually been signed over to three other club members. But this was a mild transgression compared to the bombshell that was dropped by Chester Cuthell, then one of the club's defense attorneys. Woodhouse was, in fact, an immigrant whose real name was Morris T. Casalegno. Furthermore, he had served over four years in prison for knifing an unarmed man to death in a dispute at a restaurant where he had worked as a cook. Emerging from prison in 1909, Casalegno, with no practical experience in aeronautics, declared himself an expert on the subject. He had changed his name to Woodhouse in order to hide his true identity and fraudulently obtained U.S. citizenship.[33] The court ruled against Woodhouse, clearing the path for the creation of the National Aeronautic Association.

After nearly seventeen years as the focal point of U.S. aviation, the Aero Club no longer had the power to serve as the national leader of the aviation community. It had become apparent that the views of the club's officers were no longer consistent with those of the majority of its members, who were interested in transforming flying from a sport into an industry. A change in the organizational structure of the club was inevitable, but the change would not be a minor one. The Aero Club was on the eve of being restructured into an entirely different organization—one that would remain a vital part of American aviation some seventy years later.

A NEW BEGINNING

Founding the National Aeronautic Association

12

The Second National Aero Congress met at Selfridge Field in Mt. Clemens, Michigan, near Detroit, in conjunction with the National Airplane Races of 1922. There, on October 12–14, contestants competed for prizes that included the Curtiss Marine Trophy, the Detroit News Aerial Mail Trophy, the Aviation Country Club of Detroit Trophy, the Liberty Engine Builder's Trophy, and the Pulitzer Trophy. It was the last event ever sanctioned by the Aero Club of America.[1]

In the skies over the field, aviators smashed one speed record after another. For example, Lt. E. H. Barksdale averaged more than 180 miles per hour in a Sperry high-speed pursuit plane.[2] Meanwhile, behind closed doors, a lawyer with a passionate interest in aviation development made final revisions to the charter under which the NAA would be incorporated. William P. MacCracken, Jr., who had distinguished himself with his work as head of the American Bar Association's Committee on the Law of Aeronautics, presided over meetings between representatives of the National Air Association and the Aero Club of America. By the time the historic conclaves concluded, the two organizations had established a framework for amalgamation into the National Aeronautic Association.[3]

This new association's bylaws proclaimed fourteen objectives and purposes. Prominent among them were:

To foster, encourage and advance the science of aeronautics and all kindred and allied sciences.[4]

To kindle and keep alive a general interest in the art of flying and to lend . . . aid and encouragement to any person, body or institution which is engaged wholly or partially in advancing this art.

To encourage, promote, arrange for and carry on aerial expositions, exhibits and contests, in order that the general interest in aviation may be kept up and sustained . . . to sanction contests and formulate rules, administer such rules, certify records, and to grant or contribute toward the granting of awards, prizes and distinctions for the improvement, encouragement, and advancement of any and all branches of aviation.

But the objective that seemed most important to the founders was:

To aid and encourage the establishment and maintenance of a uniform and stable system of laws relating to the science of aeronautics and the art of aerial navigation and all allied and kindred sciences and arts.[5]

A most distinguished company witnessed the birth of the NAA. Former rivals Orville Wright and Glenn Curtiss came together as the guests of honor at the Second National Aero Congress. They were joined by other powerful aviation personalities, including Secretary of the Navy Edwin Denby, Assistant Secretary of War J. Mayhew Wainwright, Chief of the Naval Bureau of Aeronautics Adm. W. A. Moffett, Chief of the U.S. Air Service Gen. M. M. Patrick, Assistant Chief of the U.S. Air Service Brig. Gen. William Mitchell, Superintendent of the U.S. Air Mail Service Carl Egge, and representatives of the air services from Great Britain, France, Italy, Japan, Canada, Poland, Brazil, and Mexico.[6]

True to the spirit of the new association, the founding officers placed a copy of the newly minted NAA charter aboard a high-speed military plane and raced it to Hartford, Connecticut, where an application for incorporation was filed. The same plane returned to Detroit the following day, carrying with it the incorporation papers of the NAA. Thus, before the conclusion of the National Airplane Races, the NAA had become an official organization and the new U.S. representative to the FAI.[7]

After the Aero Congress adjourned, the NAA transferred its offices from the longtime New York headquarters of the Aero Club to a new location at 26 Jackson Place, Washington, D.C. The United States was divided into nine districts, each having a governor and a second representative who served as a national vice president. The districts apparently were of approximately equal size based on the number of members. In addition to these district officers, the new association had five governors-at-large.[8]

This structure, the members believed, would solve many of the problems of equitable power sharing that had plagued the Aero Club. The new association was to be national in scope, as well as in name. It was, in appearance, composed of persons who were selflessly devoted to the advancement of aviation.

The founding officers represented a cross section of American industry in general, but none was, at the time, directly involved in aircraft manufacture or other forms of commercial aviation. Howard Coffin, the new president, had served as chairman of the Aircraft Production Board during World War I, but he was vice president of the Hudson Motor Car Company when elected to head the NAA. His national staff—which included national vice president B. H. Mulvihill, treasurer B. F. Castle, recording secretary John B. Coleman, and general manager H. E. Hartney—were prominent businessmen in nonaviation industries.

At least one noted aviation historian has stated that there was no visible reason for these men to use the power of the NAA to steer the industry in directions favorable to their own personal gain from aviation investments because none of them, at the time, had "sunk their money in air transport."[9] Although this may be true, it hardly puts them beyond all suspicion. All of these men were astute business leaders who would almost certainly have hesitated to invest in any endeavor in which the risks associated with their investment could not be controlled or at least predicted. In the case of the as yet undeveloped air transport industry, these investment risks could best be managed by the availability of insurance. Insurance companies in turn would only be willing to underwrite the fledgling aviation industry if mechanisms were available to them to predict accurately the extent of their own risks.

The surest way to achieve all of these objectives would be to have the federal government regulate the aviation industry. Once the government had established and begun to enforce air traffic regulations, set standards for pilot certification and aircraft airworthiness, and developed a national system of airways and airports, the amount of risk involved in the industry could be predicted. Not surprisingly, then, the NAA's first efforts were concentrated on achieving exactly that sort of government intervention. MacCracken's initial task, after seeing the new NAA through the chartering process, was to write proposals for federal regulation of the aviation industry.[10]

In spite of the conspicuous absence of financial ties between them and the aviation industry, the early officers were only an arm's length away from opportunities to profit from a healthy aviation industry. Coffin, the NAA's first president and former chairman of the Aircraft Production

Board, knew that virtually every automobile manufacturer in the United States had produced aircraft engines, or engine components, during the war. As vice president of the Hudson Motor Car company, it would be hard to imagine that he did not see opportunities that would profit his company, should a thriving civilian aircraft market create openings for automobile engine producers to expand by offering aircraft powerplants. Likewise, Frederick Patterson, the second NAA president and head of the National Cash Register Company, had been actively involved in the lucrative wartime manufacture of military aircraft components. He, too, would have had more than altruistic reasons for wanting the aviation industry to prosper.[11]

Many of the NAA's founding officers, in fact, did eventually profit from the aviation industry. Coffin became the first president of National Air Transport, the forerunner of United Airlines and an early airmail contractor; MacCracken was named the first chief of the Aeronautics Branch of the Department of Commerce, then later served as legal counsel to various airlines and airmail transport companies[12]; Harry Hartney eventually served as technical advisor to at least seventeen aviation concerns in his lifetime career in aviation.[13]

The NAA's founders projected a bright economic future for American aviation. Theirs was an honest mission to bring about government involvement because of the close relationship they foresaw between a vigorous civil aviation industry and national military preparedness. Aircraft had proven so effective in World War I that maintenance of an air force now seemed an essential prerequisite for every major country of the world. The best way for the United States to achieve a state of aerial readiness, they believed, would be to find immediate wide-scale civil uses for aircraft. The country would thus be able to maintain a pool of trained pilots and an aircraft manufacturing industry capable of quickly converting to wartime production.[14]

There were unmistakable military benefits to be derived from federal control and subsidization of aviation, but the benefits to industrial America were just as plain. A boom in the aircraft industry, like that in the automobile industry before it, would profit producers of steel, aluminum, wood, petroleum products, and providers of countless other goods and services. It was the kind of industry that would make America grow. It was also the kind of industry that could generate substantial profits for stock market investors. The founders of the NAA sincerely sought to promote American aviation, but perhaps not all of their aims were necessarily altruistic. In the pre-Depression days of American history, public policy was as likely to be born on Wall Street as on Capitol Hill.

The birth of the NAA may thus be viewed as a carefully orchestrated event intended to serve a specific role in strengthening the growing American military/industrial complex.

Indeed the NAA's real roots might be properly traced to events immediately following World War I. In 1919, after enjoying a brief but very profitable period of manufacturing military airplanes, the members of the Manufacturers Aircraft Association found themselves facing massive military contract cancellations and few prospective orders from the civilian market. Those members of the association who were not immediately forced out of business by the sudden manufacturing slump resolved to try to salvage their industry.[15]

At the request of these manufacturers, the U.S. government appointed a committee of aviation authorities to tour postwar Europe as the American Aviation Mission. The eight-man mission, including Coffin, then a member of the Council for National Defense, was charged with investigating aviation activities in the nations recovering from the war. The reports submitted by the mission at the tour's conclusion noted that the European governments were heavily subsidizing commercial aircraft manufacture and air transportation. The Europeans presumed that future hostilities would be so dominated by aerial warfare that any nation unable to field combat air forces readily would be condemned to defeat. The ability to produce warplanes and recruit pilots quickly would hinge on the preexistence of a civil aviation industry.

On their return to the United States, the mission members compiled an exhaustive set of recommendations that included the immediate and ongoing development of U.S. air mail service as a way of arousing interest in the commercial possibilities of airplanes; sufficient purchase of military aircraft to keep U.S. aircraft manufacturers going until a strong civil aviation market could develop; the establishment of commercial air routes with appropriate navigation facilities; and an all-encompassing set of federal regulations governing the licensing and inspection of pilots and airplanes.[16] The last recommendation was, it seemed, essential to ensure the kind of safe operations that would foster the public's acceptance of commercial flight.

But it would appear that Washington viewed the mission's recommendations only as a rationalization for putting a faltering industry on the federal dole. The government shelved the findings,[17] leading Coffin and others to conclude that only a powerful lobbying effort would force federal adoption of the proposed measures. So for more than two years Coffin and a committee of nationally known business leaders sought to build an organization capable of persuading the federal government to stimulate and legislate a viable commercial aviation industry into being. Such an organization would have to have the prestige of the Aero Club, and the combined support of military and civil aviators nationwide. The proposed National Aeronautic Association would try to unite these diverse groups under the common banner of aviation progress. But it was easier to raise the banner than gather an army to follow it. In spite of their noble ambitions, the founders encountered a paradox. Those most likely to benefit from federal control of aviation—wealthy potential investors— were often reluctant to believe in the future of aviation. And all too often those with a passionate commitment to the future of commercial flight were the "gypsy fliers" whose shoestring operations would not be able to survive the expense of the rigid government inspection programs proposed.[18]

The World War I years had brought about tremendous improvements in aircraft design and production and in pilot training. As the machines evolved from observation platforms to fighters and bombers, they required engines with far more power and efficient airframes. Nearly all of these high-powered war machines were designed and built by the European combatants. America's best-known contributions to mass-produced World War I aircraft were the Curtiss JN-4 series "Jennies," designed as training aircraft to meet an anticipated demand for thousands of military pilots. These planes had enclosed cockpits, dual controls, and comparatively reliable engines.

At the end of the war many young men, and a few women, chose to use their new flying skills to make a living in civilian life by teaching others to fly or offering passenger "hops" for a few dollars apiece. At first the prospects looked promising. Hundreds of surplus Jennies were available to the public at bargain prices. Some of these machines were in relatively good condition, but others were little more than flying crates.

Because the fabric-covered, wood-framed, military surplus planes were not designed for prolonged service, even the best of them soon began deteriorating structurally and mechanically. A young man who took some of his first flight instruction in such a war surplus plane, a Curtiss Canuck,[19] later recalled, "every time the pilot would bank the plane to make a turn, the whole fuselage would sort of 'flop' over in that direction. That plane was so worn out that there was slack in all the brace wires and joints. Of course, I was just learning how to fly then and didn't realize until later that there was anything wrong with his plane."[20]

Another safety problem was posed by the absence of uniform training requirements. Only a few states issued (or required) flying licenses. In most of the United States a prospective pilot could buy a plane and try to teach him- or herself to fly. One such young man bought a surplus Curtiss Jenny for $500; then, having never flown by himself (and with only a little informal flight instruction), he tried to take off. He rose slightly from the ground, realized that he did not have the plane under control, and chose not to continue the flight. He managed to get the plane back down without destroying it. Fortunately for him, another pilot gave him a half-hour free lesson before he took off again on his first solo flight. Although he did eventually become a skilled pilot, others who tried to learn flying by such haphazard methods were not so lucky as young Charles Lindbergh.[21]

It was not just the inexperienced who were unsafe, however. Independent pilots, commonly called barnstormers, or gypsy fliers, took ever-increasing chances with themselves, their equipment, and their passengers in order to generate enough cash to buy a meal and sufficient fuel to fly to the next town. Just as in the last days of the prewar exhibition era, these pilots found that there was a tremendous amount of competition for relatively few dollars and that they always had to outdo the last pilot who had visited a town in order to attract paying thrillseekers. Thus, as the 1920s progressed, mechanical problems inherent in the aging World War I aircraft, improper training of new civilian pilots, and reckless stunt flying combined to cause an alarming number of accidents, most of which, Coffin and his associates felt, could have been prevented by proper legislation.[22]

The founders of the NAA believed that American aviation had to overcome its reputation as a dangerous daredevil amusement in order to have a commercial future. Preliminary experiments with "official" mail transportation, begun in 1918,[23] showed promising results. Because the mail service had an exceptional safety record when compared to other forms of aviation at the time,[24] it served as a model of how safe carefully regulated flying could be. With time, mail carriers expanded their service and, in some cases, occasionally took passengers along on a space-available basis. There were people eager to travel by air—if air travel could be made safe. The mail service's experiences further assured the founders of the NAA that only federal-level legislation would make these budding industries safe enough to stabilize aviation insurance rates and attract money from private investors.[25]

In the summer of 1923, the NAA kicked off a national membership and public relations campaign, intended to make the average citizen "air minded." It offered one thousand tuition-free flying scholarships to individuals seventeen years of age or older who had aroused "a public sentiment in their respective communities in support of national aero-

The Air Mail branch of the U.S. Postal Service did, indeed, have an impressive record. In 1921, under the direction of the second assistant postmaster general, Col. Paul Henderson, the service was able to claim 90 percent efficiency, meaning that the mails were delayed by weather or other reasons on only 10 percent of their flights, including the route extending all the way across the United States. This was statistically better delivery service than that provided by the railroads, and often letters arrived at their destination as much as two days faster than those sent by rail alone. Because such efficient service showed the practicality of commercial aviation to business persons across the country, and because the Air Mail Service operated this coast-to-coast service for the first year without a fatality, the new National Aeronautic Association awarded Robert Collier's trophy to the U.S. Air Mail Service in 1922.

Using remodeled, open-cockpit, De Havilland 4 military aircraft left over from the war (eighty were available, but usually only forty were in service at a time), the daring airmail pilots flew their hazardous routes during the day, then transferred their cargo to railway carriers for nighttime travel. Following the lead of pilot Jack H. Knight, who years before had made the earliest trial nighttime airmail flights, a small group of pilots began flying experimental routes. These were laid out with emergency landing fields stationed approximately every twenty-five miles, with electric or acetylene beacons marking the way between them. In 1923 the NAA again awarded the Collier Trophy to the U.S. Air Mail Service for their night-flying accomplishments. Once more these efforts brought the practicality of commercial flight to the attention of the nonflying public. After mail delivery was proved to be safe and efficient, commercial air transportation would be the obvious next step in the advancement of aviation.

nautics [then got their community to demonstrate that sentiment] through membership in the National Aeronautic Association [and involvement] with the nationwide campaign now underway to put America first in the air." Out of the one thousand persons who earned free flight instruction by promoting NAA membership and community involvement in national aeronautics, the person judged most successful of all was to also receive a Curtiss JN-4D airplane and eleven dollars cash.[26]

The NAA's long-range plans for public involvement in aviation included a very aggressive campaign to interest youth in model aeronautics.

Following the lead established by its predecessor group's Junior Aero Club of America, the NAA created its own Junior Flying League and sought to interest Boy Scout troops in model airplane competitions.[27] Over the next few years the NAA further emphasized the importance of these modeling clubs by staffing their committees with aviation heroes such as Orville Wright, Charles Lindbergh, and Adm. Richard E. Byrd, and by promoting events like the National Playground Miniature Aircraft Tournaments.[28]

A young model airplane builder, in a book he wrote to help others learn to enjoy the sport of model aviation, lavishly praised NAA vice president B. H. Mulvihill for a competition trophy he had donated in 1923. The writer commended Mulvihill for the incentive the trophy provided boys and girls aspiring to become aviators. One can only speculate what Mulvihill's reaction would have been to the compliment, had he known that the writer, young Paul Garber, would someday be known as the father of the most-visited aviation museum in the world, the National Air & Space Museum of the Smithsonian Institution.[29]

NAA projects conducted during 1923 sought to promote all aspects of aviation. On June 10–16, the NAA sponsored the first sanctioned National Kite Flying Contest at Clarksburg, West Virginia. Orville Wright, chairman of the Contest Committee, traveled to Los Angeles in April of that year to inspect a site for the first international soaring competition to be held in the United States. The NAA announced its hopes to raise $10,000 in prize money to supplement the $5000 donated by the city of Los Angeles and a trophy donated by America's "Ace of Aces," Eddie Rickenbacker. The contest promised to draw contestants from Germany, France, and Great Britain.[30]

On December 1, 1923, the first issue of the *National Aeronautic Association Review,* a new membership magazine, appeared. Its feature story dealt with the so-called Winslow Bill, and clearly explained the new organization's main objective: enactment of "rigid" federal legislation over aeronautical activities.[31] The NAA's support of the Winslow legislation dated back to the birth of the organization itself. On January 8, 1923, Congressman Samuel Winslow of Worcester, Massachusetts, introduced a bill to create a Bureau of Civil Aeronautics in the Department of Commerce. The same attorney who had prepared the NAA's charter, William MacCracken, had also drafted Winslow's bill,[32] and the NAA backed it with an all-out lobbying campaign. In his official statement of endorsement, NAA President Coffin, drawing on convictions that dated back to the American Aviation Mission to Europe in 1919, declared:

In order that [aviation] may develop on sound financial and legal lines, the Civil Aeronautics Act of 1923 is absolutely necessary. It is plainly the duty of every thinking American who is interested in the general welfare of his country to demand the passage of this act, in order that air navigation may be established in this country on a scale commensurate with the importance of the nation in the affairs of the world, and in order that we may reap the full benefits of the inventive and productive genius of our native land.[33]

The notion that Wall Street had longstanding interest in Coffin's beliefs is supported by the fact that financial wizard Charles Schwab wrote a follow-up article for the *Aeronautical Digest* that was reprinted in the *New York Times.* The next generation, Schwab predicted, would make wide use of airplanes, and it was the responsibility of the current generation to lay the legal groundwork for their safe operation.[34] After four years of loading its guns, the NAA fired a full broadside at Congress in support of the Winslow Bill. The man chosen to chair the NAA's Legislative Committee and to urge its passage was, logically enough, William Mac-Cracken. MacCracken was a man who knew how to get things done.

The key selling point of the Winslow Bill was safety. Winslow proposed to promote aerial safety by means of a number of federal initiatives, including testing and certifying aircraft for airworthiness; issuing pilot licenses based on physical fitness, training, and practical experience; establishing civil penalties for violations of federally imposed flight regulations; investigating accidents in order to determine their cause and to take action to prevent similar mishaps; publishing regular bulletins of actions taken involving accidents and licenses issued and revoked; requiring appropriate aircraft identification markings; designating commercial air routes and providing navigational aids along them; and maintaining the sovereignty of U.S. airspace. Winslow maintained that there was ample precedent for the federal government to undertake such responsibilities. The new bureau of the Department of Commerce would merely extend to air transportation the same safety measures already enforced in the marine transportation and commercial fishing industries.

The NAA strongly encouraged its members to achieve passage of the Winslow Bill by instituting a campaign of letter writing and local publicity. The organization asked members to contact their local newspaper editors, congressmen, and senators, informing them of the need for such legislation. F. B. Patterson, elected NAA president in the fall of 1923, furthered the efforts started under the Coffin administration by commissioning a film entitled "Make America First in the Air." Members were allowed to borrow copies of the movie to show to local business and political leaders. Almost 100 percent of the membership, the *NAA Review* reported, complied with the organization's request by participating in some way in the lobbying effort for federal legislation.[35]

However, some reports in the *NAA Review* were rather misleading. In addition to his role as president of the NAA, Patterson, as noted earlier, was also president of the National Cash Register Company. When Patterson strongly encouraged his NCR salesmen to join the NAA, some five hundred of them complied.[36] It is not unreasonable to assume that these same five hundred NCR salesmen—few of whom must have had any genuine interest in aviation—made up a great many of those who reportedly lobbied for passage of the Winslow Bill. Although the total membership of the NAA in 1923 is uncertain, there were less than 5600 members in 1925 and under 5000 in 1926 and 1927.[37] One can safely assume that Patterson's 500 salesmen comprised a significant percentage of the total membership.

Indeed, in counterpoint to the *Review*'s claims of nearly unanimous support for the Winslow Bill, there is substantial evidence that many of the NAA members protested the bill rather heatedly because of its potential to cause hardship for the gypsy fliers and others.[38] Even some manufacturers complained that the bill would be detrimental to their business and would possibly allow more government intervention than would be good for the industry. Because the legislation seemed to favor big business over the small operator, NAA officials became targets for accusations that they were lobbying for industry. Pressured by representatives of both small-time operations and some big-time manufacturers, eventually most of the early supporters of the bill—including Coffin, for the remainder of his term as president—backed off from it, leaving MacCracken as the only staunch supporter.[39]

The NAA did initiate some programs that were favorably received by the majority of aviators. One program that had long-lasting effects involved navigational aids for pilots. The association asked members to encourage their communities to assist the aviation movement by creating these markers. All across America individuals and municipal governments declared themselves "air minded" by painting their towns' most prominent rooftops and water towers with an orange-and-white checkerboard pattern. This familiar checked design called a passing pilot's attention to other information painted on the structures, like the town's name and directional arrows indicating magnetic north and the mileage to nearby towns or airports.[40]

Even throughout its troublesome first years the NAA had a mission— the kind of unifying purpose that had been missing in the waning days of the Aero Club. Events in the early 1920s hinted at the spectacular aviation achievements to come, at flights that would soon mark the decade as the "Golden Age of Aviation." It was an era when Americans felt good about themselves. They had entered a world war and emerged as the deciding factor in victory. Unlike European nations, many of which had been ravaged by the war, the United States had not only survived physically unscathed but also, in many ways, benefited by the growth of its industrial machine. With Uncle Sam known as a world leader, the American public was not about to let him relinquish the title.

One way to prove America's superiority to the rest of the world would be by capturing as many military flying records as possible. The NAA and the aviation sections of the U.S. military worked together remarkably well in organizing record-breaking attempts, and at the end of the 1923 air racing season an NAA official could announce with confidence that "America's supremacy in the airplane field is complete," as military fliers set new world records in thirty-three of a possible forty-two categories for land and sea planes.[41] Military fliers continued, under slack reins, to prove American superiority in the air, until the policy was called into question in 1925, when the public learned that a total of some $433 million had been spent on military aviation during the preceding five years. But the NAA vigorously defended the military spending, calling the criticism unjust.[42]

The NAA's half-decade-long fight to have the federal government assume responsibility for legislating aeronautical activities was continued in 1925 by president Godfrey Cabot. New legislative proposals for aviation, jointly introduced by Senator Hiram Bingham and Representative James Parker, were circulating through the House and Senate. These would provide for federal control only over commercial flights between states or between the United States and foreign countries, and would therefore not affect the gypsy fliers. Cabot seemed content to allow such a measure to pass, counting on being able to encourage Congress to increase federal control at a later date.[43]

Indeed, it no longer appeared that the NAA really questioned whether or not the government *should* regulate flying; rather, its concern now seemed to focus on *how* it should go about doing so. Some favored a structure whereby all aviation activities, both civilian and military, would come under one governing body. Others felt that military and civilian fliers should each have their own regulatory division. The search for answers to such questions added to the delay in legislative action. After much complicated maneuvering, a modified form of the Bingham-Parker Bill was signed into law by Calvin Coolidge as the Air Commerce

---

The 1924 Collier Trophy was awarded to the U.S. Army Air Service
for an around-the-world flight by specially built Army airplanes. Out
of the four Douglas World Cruisers that left Seattle on April 6, 1924,
two completed the entire journey, returning on September 28, after
covering 27,553 miles. The third crashed into a snow-covered mountain in Alaska, and the fourth, after suffering damage in rough seas,
was further damaged as its rescuers attempted to hoist it aboard a
ship. The successful flights of the World Cruisers were only the highlight of a year in which well-supported U.S. Army pilots smashed
record after record.

The Army again figured in the events leading up to the awarding
of the 1925 Collier Trophy. U.S. Army fliers pushed their Curtiss racing planes to decisive wins in both the Pulitzer Trophy Race and the
Schneider Cup Race. Pulling the planes along that year was a new
type of metal propeller, designed by Curtiss engineer S. Albert Reed.
Using Duralumin, a new alloy of aluminum, magnesium, and copper
developed by the Aluminum Company of America, Reed was able to
fashion a light yet incredibly strong and efficient propeller. It revolu-
tionized an industry that had until then been the exclusive realm of
woodworkers. Unlike wooden props, which sometimes absorbed
water in rainstorms and were then thrown out of balance, the new
metal prop was not affected by moisture, and it was far less likely to
break in flight or deteriorate over time. For his development, Reed
received the 1925 Collier Trophy.

Act on May 20, 1926. This act allowed for state regulation of noncommercial intrastate flight, but put commercial interstate flying under the
control of the federal government. Coolidge kept military aviation separate by creating an Army Air Corps and the positions of secretary of
aeronautics for both the war and navy departments.[44]

Amid this controversy the NAA began to lobby for a resolution to still
another problem: unfair treatment of military pilots. The influence of
members incorporated from the old American Flying Club showed
clearly on this issue. Military members of the NAA, both retired and still
active, remembered the army's wartime attempts to cut aviators' pay and
enforce reductions in rank among flying officers. In peacetime, the
hazards faced by aviators were infinitely more numerous than those of the
average foot soldier, yet the army, traditionally dominated by infantry and
artillery officers, promoted aviators at a much slower pace than their
land-bound contemporaries. The NAA urged the government to estab-

lish a separate military air force in which aviators would compete only with other aviation personnel for advances in rank.[45]

As the NAA was finally on the verge of successfully ushering through legislation to create a Bureau of Civil Aeronautics under the Department of Commerce, one of aviation's most flamboyant characters stepped—briefly—into their spotlight. Colonel Billy Mitchell supposedly learned of a plan to install Rear Admiral Richard E. Byrd as new president of the NAA and rushed to put a halt to it. Byrd was, Mitchell explained, "a very good man, but he is just a representative of the vested interests in the Navy Department which is doing all in its power to keep aviation down." Mitchell insisted that the navy wished to hold back development of airplanes so that the government's funding would continue to focus on battleship construction. He concluded his anti-Byrd argument by saying that he, himself, would be willing to accept the position of NAA president.[46]

Mitchell's apparently self-initiated bid for leadership of the NAA was taken up by Frank Tichenor, an aviation magazine publisher and president of the NAA's New York chapter. Tichenor agreed to nominate Mitchell in order that the NAA could be totally overhauled into a civilian organization "ready to take up the fight of the men in the air service who are unable to help themselves."[47] Mitchell was a primary proponent of placing both civil and military aviation under one unified government agency.[48] He and Tichenor vowed to make the NAA stronger by raising the membership from 5000 to 100,000, believing that such a large organization of voters could force whatever legislation they desired from the government. But it seems that Mitchell soon saw signs that his run for the presidency was not going well. In a subsequent speech he began hedging, saying that he would devote his time to building some "great civilian body" and adding, "If we can rehabilitate the National Aeronautic Association, we will. If not, we will get another one."[49] Mitchell never did get his chance to rehabilitate the NAA. The association elected Porter Adams as president to succeed Godfrey Cabot.

Shortly before the 1926 elections, a dream held by most officers of the NAA since its inception at last came true. First, President Calvin Coolidge signed into law the Air Commerce Act of 1926, placing civil aviation regulation under the charge of Secretary of Commerce Herbert Hoover. After offering the position of asssistant secretary of commerce for aeronautics to two other men who declined, Hoover nominated Mac-Cracken.[50] The man who had for so long pressed for government legislation on behalf of the NAA now was in charge of implementing it. Less than a month after taking the oath of office, MacCracken addressed the NAA. His speech was exceptionally well received, as he advocated building municipal airports in every city of the United States and promoting an expanded airmail service with uniform rates.[51]

Once MacCracken had been sworn in, the long-sought-after federal regulation was less than half a year in coming. The Department of Commerce assumed responsibility for licensing civilian pilots and aircraft, with MacCracken himself receiving pilot's license number 1, after Orville Wright had, characteristically, refused the honor. MacCracken personally supervised the inspections of some of the first aircraft to go through the program, especially some new planes built for ocean crossing attempts as part of contests for the Orteig Prize sanctioned by the NAA (see Chapter 13). Early in MacCracken's new career it was his honor to look over one such machine, a Ryan monoplane piloted by a former airmail pilot named Lindbergh. As the plane was being readied to take off in the dark on its trip from New York to Paris, Lindbergh, in his typically honest manner, confessed to MacCracken that it did not have the lights technically required for night flying under the new laws. MacCracken reportedly gazed eastward toward the Atlantic Ocean and replied, "That's okay this time . . . I don't think you will be meeting anyone coming the other way."[52]

Indeed he did not. But Lindbergh's journey demonstrated that transoceanic flight was possible, and within months dozens of pilots would face the challenges of other over-the-ocean flights, sometimes lured to their deaths by the large sums of prize money that race sponsors would offer.

THE GOLDEN YEARS

The Triumphs and Tragedies of the Lindbergh Era and Over-the-Ocean Air Racing

13

It can be convincingly argued that Charles Lindbergh, in one flight across the Atlantic, did more to promote the image of American aviation than all the industry's publicists since the time of the Wright Brothers.

America's response to Lindbergh's flight had been foretold in a satirical cartoon published several years earlier in *Aero and Hydro* magazine. The drawing depicted scenarios of success and failure in an over-the-ocean flight. The side labeled Failure showed two wags looking at a pair of tombstones, each engraved "Fool: Tried to Cross Ocean in Aeroplane." Shrugging his shoulders, one says, "They had it coming to 'em." In the Success panel, the same two gents smile up at garland-crowned statues commemorating the Conquering Heros, affirming to each other their unfaltering confidence all along that the pilots would complete the flight.[1] Thus was Lindbergh later received as the conquering hero while those less fortunate lay in their graves.

The formula for creating heroic pilots had been developed in the earliest days of the Aero Club. First a goal would be identified, then an attractive incentive offered for the one who would be first to achieve it. Following this simple formula, the Orteig Prize, offered through the NAA, led Lindbergh across the Atlantic Ocean.

Remarkably, the prize had been posted some eight years before it was actually won, and with a rather less dramatic end in mind. Raymond Orteig, a prosperous restaurant owner, originally offered the $25,000 award in 1919. The prize would, the conditions stated, go to the first pilot to fly an airplane between New York and Paris. It did not matter whether the flight went from west to east, or vice versa, whether the plane was designed for land or sea, or how many crew members made the flight, as long as it was made without any stops. Orteig was not particularly interested in stimulating the development of aeronautical technology. Rather, he intended his prize as the incentive for a symbolic flight between two cities that had, not long before, been joined by strife during World War I. Instead, as the mid-1920s brought aviation technology to the point where such an ocean crossing appeared feasible, Orteig's prize became the goal of a frenzied race.

The competition began disastrously. In September 1926, four men, led by French war hero René Fonck, tried to fly from Curtiss Field. Their specially built Sikorsky aircraft, the *New York to Paris,* could not attain flying speed with its heavy load of fuel and went out of control on the runway. Two of the four crew members died in the fiery crash that followed.

Charles Lindbergh was a little-known airmail pilot when, on February 28, 1927, he filed an application with the NAA to compete for the Orteig Prize. The NAA had a mandatory waiting period of sixty days from the date of application until the actual flight attempt could begin, and Lindbergh had filed before his Ryan monoplane was finished, anticipating that it would be ready about the same time as he was eligible to start. Prior to announcing his intention to cross the Atlantic, Lindbergh's greatest claim to glory had been surviving four parachute jumps from mail planes caught in bad weather en route between Chicago and St. Louis.[2]

Lindbergh was the second person to file an official application with the NAA in 1927 for the transatlantic flight. The first to apply that year, Lt. Cdr. Noel Davis, also had an airplane built especially for the Orteig competition. He and Lt. Robert Wooster felt that they had the edge in both time and equipment as they tested their new Keystone airplane, *American Legion.* Because of the required sixty-day waiting period, they had the advantage of being the next crew eligible to make the attempt.

Others were less patient. On April 9, 1927, Leigh Wade of the Columbia Aircraft Corporation petitioned NAA president Porter Adams to waive the sixty-day waiting period for his plane. Adams refused to make an exception, but Wade's request gave a clear indication of how this test of technology was shaping up into a race to be first, no matter the risk.[3] By April at least six teams—five in the United States and one in France—were actively preparing for a transatlantic flight. As the competitors pushed harder to be the first across the ocean, the cost of the competition rose.

With the date for Davis and Wooster's departure approaching, they prepared to make a final test flight—one that would determine the plane's flight characteristics when fully loaded with 17,000 pounds of fuel, oil, and crew. On April 26, they took off from Langley Field in Virginia. The plane was unable to gain altitude and crashed into a marsh, killing both men.[4]

A few days later, on May 8, French World War I ace Charles Nungesser and his navigator, François Coli, left Paris in their plane, *Oiseau Blanc* (White Bird). They disappeared after last being seen by a fishing boat in the Atlantic. Some modern researchers speculate that Coli and Nungesser may in fact have made it to North America, only to crash in the wilderness; nevertheless, the plane and its pilots were never found.[5]

Other aspiring Atlantic fliers suffered serious, if ultimately less tragic, accidents. On April 16, Richard Byrd's trimotored *America,* undergoing final test flights before he accepted delivery of the plane from the Fokker Company, nosed over on landing. The crash broke Byrd's wrist and seriously injured two others aboard the plane. A Bellanca monoplane named *Columbia,* also making test flights before trying for the Orteig Prize, lost part of its landing gear on takeoff. The pilot and passengers were alerted to the problem by the crew of another plane that flew alongside them, waving and holding up a spare tire to indicate that they should check their own wheels. *Columbia'*s pilot was able to land the plane gingerly on its good wheel and none of its passengers was hurt as the plane slid to a stop.[6]

People on both sides of the Atlantic nervously followed the ongoing drama that had been inspired by the Orteig Prize. It was featured in newsreels in theaters and headlined the newspapers. The spectacular crashes, mysterious disappearances, and sudden deaths served only to heighten the suspense. When, on May 20–21, 1927, Charles Lindbergh finally flew solo from New York to Paris, the accumulated popular tension exploded into a riotous celebration held simultaneously on two continents. It was as if the airplane, long in its awkward teenage years, had finally been presented to the world as a breathtaking debutante— escorted by the Prince of Eagles.

So swept away were the French by the historic symbolism of Lindbergh's arrival that the NAA had to engage in several months of tactful negotiations with the Aero Club of France before they would return the plane's barograph, a sealed instrument installed in Lindbergh's *Spirit of St. Louis* to record his altitude during the flight. The NAA felt that the

Before he achieved fame as the "Lone Eagle" who crossed the Atlantic, Charles Lindbergh had already introduced himself to readers of the October 1926 *National Aeronautics* magazine. He was the airmail pilot who had saved his life three times by parachuting out of his fog-shrouded plane. His exciting story had hardly come out in print when Lindbergh again took to the silk, for the fourth time. This time the *National Aeronautics* account was entitled, "He Does It Again: Pilot Lindbergh's Parachute Jumps Have Become a Monthly Affair."[7]

Interestingly, the Collier Trophy for 1926, awarded shortly afterward, went to Maj. Edward L. Hoffman for developing a practical parachute.[8] After refusing to issue parachutes to World War I airplane pilots[9] for fear that they would abandon their machines under fire, the U.S. military eventually realized the value of parachutes and related rescue equipment. The army sponsored the development of canister-packed emergency parachutes for lowering supplies to persons stranded in remote places, and emergency parachutes designed especially for use in airplanes, most notably the Irving Airchute and Russell Lobe seatpack parachutes, which folded up into a container that the pilot could sit on like a cushion.[10] The navy conducted experiments with parachutes designed to lower entire airplanes to the ground.

The following year, even though Lindbergh's flight across the Atlantic was the front-page story, the NAA chose to honor someone who had played a less well publicized part in the transatlantic journey. The 1927 Collier Trophy went to Charles L. Lawrance, designer of the Wright Whirlwind air-cooled radial engine that had provided the motive power for Lindbergh's *Spirit of St. Louis*. The press may have been slow to acknowledge Lawrance's role in the famed flight, but other pilots and aircraft manufacturers recognized and appreciated the sensational breakthrough in combustion engine technology that the Whirlwind represented. Over the next few months, engines of the same type took fliers Lester Maitland and Albert F. Hegenberger from the U.S. mainland to Hawaii, flew Byrd and a crew of three on a flight duplicating Lindbergh's, and became standard equipment on the aircraft of many manufacturers, including all four of the airplanes used by a fledgling airmail and passenger service called Northwest Airways.[11]

Yet even that was not the full extent of the Whirlwind's contributions to aviation. As reliable and efficient as the new engine was, its large mass of radially organized cylinders created a great deal of aerodynamic drag. Over the next year, the National Advisory Committee for Aeronautics (NACA), the organization of volunteer aviation experts that later evolved into the National Aeronautics and

Space Administration (NASA), undertook a project to make the mar-
velous new engine design more aerodynamically efficient. The result
was a rounded aluminum cowling that covered the engine, causing it
to pose significantly less resistance to movement through the air,
while more effectively directing a flow of cool air over the cylinders.[12] The invention won the NACA the Collier Trophy for 1929.

Fortunately for Americans, another of Lawrance's endeavors met
with far less enthusiasm than his Whirlwind engine. Lawrance
teamed up with engineers at the Radio Corporation of America to
produce an aircraft equipped with huge external loudspeakers that
were powered by gigantic amplifiers. The plan was to fly over cities
while blaring advertising messages down upon the populace. The airplane was produced, but it met with little popularity.[13]

---

instrument's rightful place was in America's Smithsonian Institution,
where it indeed resides today.[14]

The incredible public response to Lindbergh's flight was a blessing for
the NAA and other aviation promoters. It unquestionably put flying in
the public eye. No individual could have been better designed for the role
of hero than young "Slim" Lindbergh. His shy charm and good looks
appealed to the hearts of women the world over. Men related to his
hard-working middle American background and reputation for forth-
right honesty. Children looked up to him as a true champion, possessing
more fortitude and pluck than any storybook character ever could. Two
decades of efforts by the Aero Club and the NAA to make America "air
minded" were surpassed in the thirty-three and a half hours of his
transatlantic flight. Americans took Lindbergh's style of aviation not only
into their minds, but into their hearts as well.

There was, however, a drawback to Lindbergh's success. It inspired a
kind of flight mania that threatened to return aviation to the bloody days
of the prewar exhibition fliers. Caught up in the enthusiasm of the
moment, James D. Dole, a wealthy pineapple grower, staunch NAA
member, and booster of the Hawaiian territory, posted a $25,000 prize
for the first pilot to fly from the U.S. mainland to Hawaii in an air race
beginning August 16, 1927.[15] Dole did the Orteig Prize one better by
offering an additional $10,000 to the second-place finisher. His ante was
followed by a bid from Sid Grauman, owner of the famed Grauman's
Chinese Theatre, to pay $30,000 for a nonstop Los Angeles-to-Tokyo
flight. Next, a San Francisco group proposed to raise a $50,000 purse to
extend the Dole flight from Hawaii to Australia. A few of the pilots who

had failed to make the New York to Paris flight, as well as many eager newcomers with publicity-seeking corporate sponsors, set their eyes on islands to the west.[16]

The Dole races, as the press called them, were a catastrophe. Most of the planes were ill equipped for such a flight (only four of the original fifteen even had radios). Three fliers died even before the contest began, and two more planes crashed on takeoff at the beginning of the race. Of the fifteen original entrants who left Oakland, California, only four planes actually got beyond the California coast, and only two of those made it to Hawaii. The others were never seen again. Still another pilot disappeared while searching for the missing contestants. The sense of tragedy at these losses was amplified by the fact that one of the lost planes, the *Miss Doran* flown by Augie Pedlar, had aboard it an attractive young schoolteacher who rode in the passenger seat as the flight's "mascot."[17]

As the navy's light cruiser *Omaha* and fifteen destroyers searched for the missing pilots, the press began publishing criticisms of the race. Aircraft manufacturer William B. Stout, designer of the Ford Trimotor, dismissed the race as a stunt and compared it to walking across Niagara Falls on a tightrope. The NAA announced that it would take steps to prevent future flights that appeared to be so ill prepared. Adams petitioned William MacCracken to use the power of his new position as Department of Commerce air chief to prohibit flights not having "a reasonable chance of success." Adams went on to say that the NAA would "do all in [its] power to continue the progress of flying no matter what steps have to be taken."[18] But Adams clearly intended for MacCracken only to determine if the planes and pilots involved in such attempts were properly equipped for the task. Others wanted more.

Within a few days the American Bar Association (ABA) announced that it was asking Congress to pass new legislation. Citing the loss of twenty-five lives between January and September of 1927, the ABA proposed putting *all* aspects of transoceanic flight under the direct control of MacCracken's branch of the Department of Commerce. This measure implied that the federal government could prohibit any flight attempts, regardless of the pilot's qualifications and the plane's equipment.

The ABA's proposal marked an important turning point for the NAA, setting the stage for what could be called the "modern" NAA. The organization's founding officers had been primarily in tune with the goals of industry (which, in their thinking, were synonymous with the best interests of the United States) and had sought increased federal control to stabilize the aviation industry. On the other hand, the Contest Committee of the NAA included many longtime pilots, among them Orville

Wright, Glenn Martin, and Frank P. Lahm, by then a general. These committee members saw a black side to government regulation. They believed too much federal control would stifle aviation development.

On the recommendation of the Contest Committee, Adams reconsidered the effect that strict legislation might have on future record attempts. He reemphasized his belief that all pilots considering such flights must be qualified, properly equipped, and well trained, but resisted placing control entirely in the hands of the Department of Commerce. He reasoned that having transoceanic flights controlled entirely by a government agency might "discourage individual initiative, even in the quest of new records." Future requirements of the Contest Committee, Adams maintained, would assure just the sort of qualifications sought by the ABA and MacCracken.[19] With that statement Adams demonstrated that the NAA, an organization originally formed with the primary goal of lobbying for governmental regulation of aviation, was also willing to protect American aviation from governmental overregulation. His stance received the wholehearted support of the Contest Committee.

The NAA was prepared to back up its position. Even though federal aircraft and pilot licenses were now issued by the Department of Commerce, the NAA still required FAI sporting licenses of all pilots entered in sanctioned competition or attempting to set records. The NAA could, at the Contest Committee's discretion, refuse to officiate at any event that was not deemed to be reasonably safe and in the best interests of aeronautical science. Indeed such was the case when, only months after the Dole races, the committee refused to sanction a New York-to-Bermuda seaplane race. Citing the lack of a radio navigation beacon on Bermuda, the NAA claimed that the race would be safe only if a beacon were installed on the tiny island or if the contestants flew from Bermuda to the U.S. coastline, which presented a far larger target. The Bermuda Trade Development Corporation, which had offered the $10,000 prize to the winner of the race, found the conditions unsatisfactory, and the contest never materialized.[20]

Just over a year after Lindbergh made his epic solo flight to Paris, a young woman pilot accompanied two male fliers on a historic transatlantic journey of their own. When chief pilot Wilmer Stultz, mechanic Lou Gordon, and Amelia Earhart landed their Fokker trimotor in Burry Port, Wales, on June 18, 1928, it marked the first time a woman had crossed the Atlantic by air. In spite of the fact that she was just a passenger on the trip (indeed the British press referred to her as "a sack of potatoes"[21]), she was feted in America as if she had crossed the ocean solo. In 1932, on the fifth anniversary of the Lindbergh flight, she did just that.

As if to reward government aviation officials for applying their efforts in the right direction, the 1928 Collier Trophy went to the Aeronautics Branch of the Department of Commerce for developing the U.S. airways and air navigation facilities. It was a well-deserved award. By the end of that year the department had activated forty-eight official U.S. airways (nineteen of them equipped with navigation beacons for night flying), extending over 9135 miles. In addition, another 4000 miles of airways were under contract or construction. Altogether they joined 386 U.S. cities, including a lighted airway from New York to San Francisco, with weather service, radio, telephone, telegraph, and radio beacon direction installations supporting the network. MacCracken and his staff had accomplished an incredible task in a very short time.

Earhart was no stranger to the NAA. In 1923 she had become the first woman, and the seventeenth pilot, to receive an NAA pilot's license. She actually flew her license trials under the Aero Club of America in Los Angeles on December 15, 1921, but administrative delays prevented her from being issued license number 6017 until after the NAA had been formed (NAA licenses started with the number 6000). For a year before her flight she was an active member in the Boston chapter of the NAA, the members of which, not knowing of her secret plans to cross the ocean, voted her vice president of the chapter only a few days before she departed. Her election to a leadership position at the chapter level was a portent of things to come. Three years later Amelia Earhart became the first female officer of the NAA when she was overwhelmingly elected to the office of national vice president.

The late 1920s was a "golden age" for the NAA itself. Membership nearly doubled between 1926 and 1929, with a record 4667 new members joining in 1929 alone.[22] Under the direction of Adams the association sincerely reached out to the average citizen, greatly modifying its strong early posture as a lobbying force favoring big business and strict government control. The NAA renewed efforts to support sport aviators of all kinds.

When Adams was succeeded by Connecticut Senator Hiram Bingham, a solid representative of industry was once again guiding the NAA. Yet Bingham's favoritism for big business was partially tempered by his awareness that markets, as well as industries, had to be nurtured. He recognized that the aviation industry and the NAA could not survive without support from the average individual who dreamed of flight. Bingham fervently promoted commercial air transport to the public, but also encouraged men and women of modest means to fly—in a manner that would boost the aircraft industry. Under him the NAA prepared a comprehensive set of guidelines for persons interested in buying a factory-built plane and forming a flying club. The guidelines outlined such parameters as the requisite number of members, annual and monthly costs for each member, and budget schedules for maintenance and fuel. The NAA even offered a national group plan to make insurance affordable to potential grass roots fliers.[23]

At the NAA-sanctioned air races in Los Angeles in September 1928, fliers Ernest (Ernie) Jones and Jack Vilas began reminiscing about the early days. A recently published *Blue Book of American Airmen*[24] listed the names and addresses of numerous flying personalities from their shared past. The two concluded that those names might someday be forgotten, and much of America's early aviation history lost, if they did not take action. So they began contacting old friends and renewing acquaintances from the early years of aviation, before airplanes had also become instruments of war.

On December 3, 1928, sixty-four aviation pioneers met in the Stevens Hotel in Chicago. They founded an organization incorporated as The Early Birds of Aviation, Inc., limiting membership to those persons who had flown as pilot in command of a balloon, dirigible, parachute, glider, or airplane prior to December 17, 1916. (This date was the thirteenth anniversary of the Wrights' first powered flight, but it also approximated a time just before Americans began learning to fly for military service as pilots in World War I.) Membership was automatic to those who were able to show that they had been awarded one of the early Aero Club licenses. Others were required to present documented proof that they had flown before the cutoff date.

For years thereafter, the Early Birds held their annual meeting in conjunction with the Cleveland Air Races. After the Cleveland races ceased to be held, they chose various locations, and lately their meetings have coincided with those of the OX5 Pioneers, another group of early aviators whose membership is limited to those persons who first flew aircraft (such as the Curtiss Jenny) powered by the Curtiss OX5-series engines that were popular from World War I through the 1920s. At any gathering, they are identifiable by their adopted trademark—a black-and-white checked hat styled after the herringbone golf caps made popular by Lincoln Beachey and others among the early aviators.[25]

In 1962, the Early Birds unveiled a plaque at the National Air Museum in Washington, D.C., which listed the names of 593 members of the organization. Since that time an updated version has been installed in the National Air & Space Museum in Washington, D.C. It lists every one of the 598 members ever admitted to the Early Birds.[26]

Originally, the Early Birds was intended to be a "last man" organization, meaning that it would be made up only of the founding members, dissolving when the last member died. But with surviving members reaching remarkably advanced years, and with a need for assistance in planning and carrying out the objectives of the organization, the membership eventually voted to admit certain associate members upon the recommendation of two Early Birds.[27] The present body of associate members is largely composed of persons related to Early Birds, but also includes members with a particular interest in preserving the early history of flight. At this writing, there are seven surviving members of the Early Birds of Aviation. Paul E. Garber, Ramsey Fellow and Historian Emeritus at the National Air & Space Museum, passed away on September 23, 1992. He was, at age ninety-three, the youngest member of the organization.[28]

In December 1928, the NAA commemorated the greatest event in the history of flight. A motorcade carrying hundreds of dignitaries from all over the world traveled along rough country roads and crossed inland waterways on ferries. These men and women made the long pilgrimage from Langley Field near Norfolk, Virginia, to Kitty Hawk, North Carolina, to join more than three thousand others in honoring Orville Wright and his late brother on the twenty-fifth anniversary of the first powered airplane flight. Because federal funds were limited, NAA President Bingham personally underwrote the cost of this pilgrimage.[29] There Bingham, flanked by Orville Wright, Amelia Earhart, and the surviving "Kitty Hawkers" who had helped the brothers in 1903, unveiled a granite marker at the site of the first flight and dedicated the cornerstone for a federal monument atop Big Kill Devil Hill.[30] MacCracken had earlier encouraged the original Kitty Hawk locals who had assisted the Wrights in their flying experiments to identify the exact spot from which the Wright Flyer had left the earth on its historic journey. That point was marked with a copper rod until the NAA's granite monument was installed some three years later. Although those in attendance could not know it at the time, the ceremony would also mark the symbolic end of the Golden Age of Aviation, for the Depression and World War II would soon permanently change the nature of America's flying practices.

THE TURBULENT THIRTIES

American Aviation Survives the Great Depression

14

The Depression years severely tried the organizational strength of the NAA. During this time the association saw its leadership split on key issues, was nearly forced into bankruptcy, and found itself subjected to widespread and severe public criticism over its elitism and, in particular, its handling of the National Air Races. Ironically, it was through the temporary loss of working-class support during the early years of the 1930s that the NAA eventually realized how much of its strength lay within that segment of the flying public, and during the latter half of the decade it entered a period of reevaluation and reconstruction. As a result, the egalitarian association that emerged from the Depression was much stronger than the elite association that had entered it. It was willing and eager to meet the needs of the new middle-class pilots.

For a time in the 1930s the public lost faith in the NAA. Many saw it as a heavy-handed organization that was insensitive to the problems of the average pilot trying to make a living. Because all of its presidents had been wealthy men—including the current leader, Senator Hiram Bingham—the association was automatically an object of suspicion in some quarters. In 1930, an editorial entitled "Air—Hot and Otherwise: The NAA—That's Enough" in *Aero Digest,* one of the nation's leading aeronautical magazines, blasted the NAA and its president: "They have been responsible for various disastrous deeds, including old Hire'em Bingham, apostle of an air force for which every nut and bolt must be carved from a wooden nutmeg by a highly protected Connecticut

That Bingham loved the limelight was an assertion few would dispute, and his yen for Washington publicity could not have been better illustrated than by his staging of the Collier Trophy presentation for 1930. The award that year went to Harold F. Pitcairn and his staff for their development of Juan de la Cierva's autogiro, a new type of flying machine that used a twirling rotor to create the lift normally produced by a "fixed wing."[1] The autogiro was truly a unique aircraft in both performance and appearance. It could land in exceptionally short distances—even without power—and Pitcairn's addition of a device to start the rotor spinning before the machine began its rollout allowed it to take off in a matter of yards. It was this short-field capability that Bingham exploited.

In a well-publicized ceremony, a Pitcairn Autogiro flew into Washington, landed before President Herbert Hoover and the press gathered on the south lawn of the White House, and served as a photogenic background while President Hoover, with Bingham always close at his side, presented the Collier Trophy to Pitcairn. To borrow words from Bingham's critic, there was indeed an abundance of brass buttons and epaulets at the White House affair.

Pitcairn had begun his aviation enterprises by giving flying lessons and transporting Prohibition-era gamblers by air to casino ships anchored beyond the three-mile limit. Later he landed some of the earliest east coast airmail routes, first flying the mail between New York and Atlanta, then adding on the Atlanta-to-Miami run. While on a 1928 trip to Europe, Pitcairn saw de la Cierva's autogiro and predicted that it would be the future of aviation. He sold his airmail routes and planes in order to concentrate on producing the Pitcairn Autogiro under a license agreement with the Spanish inventor. Within a few years, autogiros were still little more than rare flying curiosities—whereas Pitcairn's former airmail company had grown into Eastern Airlines.

The following year the Collier again went to the developers of an aviation device that never found the success initially predicted for it. Packard Motor Company received the award for its nine-cylinder radial engine, designed to operate on diesel fuel. This engine performed extremely well, both on the bench and in practical flight tests, but Packard was unable to find a market for it in the financially troubled aviation industry of the 1930s.

Another Depression-era Collier recipient was Glenn L. Martin of Baltimore, Maryland. He won the 1932 award for a high-performance, twin-engined bomber designated the XB-907. Although it was highly advanced for its time, the XB-907 was soon surpassed by new Martin designs.

Although some of the Collier winners of the 1930s enjoyed only fleeting fame, others were to have a long-lasting impact on the American aviation industry. Among the best-known inventions to bring its developer the Collier was that by Frank W. Caldwell, chief engineer of the Hamilton Standard Propeller Company. In 1933 he and his company were given the Collier for a propeller with a controllable pitch that could be changed in flight—a design concept still in common use after sixty years. The 1934 award went to Capt. Albert F. Hegenberger for developing an instrument landing system that has, in the intervening years, been refined to the point that airline flights are now seldom delayed by inclement weather.

---

manufacturer." The article continued by reminding its readers that the magazine had warned the NAA four years earlier that "with proper leadership and a worthwhile program, no occasion would exist for the independent clubs which now for perfectly good reasons ignore the NAA." It concluded that, "the NAA was far too asleep to read or heed, or perhaps too busy down in Washington playing brass-button, brass-button, who's got the brass-button—and epaulets—to have time to think, or care." The writer was none other than Frank Tichenor, whose backing of Billy Mitchell for the NAA presidency some three years earlier had come to naught. Tichenor concluded that the NAA had fallen into the hands of officers who used its prestige to further their own political careers, rather than the good of aviation as a whole. He proposed, as a solution, that Orville Wright be awarded an honorary lifetime presidency, with William MacCracken elected president.[2] But this recommendation too was not followed, and Bingham was reelected president each year until 1934.

Among the main problems plaguing the NAA in the 1930s was one common to almost all organizations of the era—a lack of money. From its inception in 1922, the NAA had experienced financial problems, but the early presidents were men of means who had made up deficiencies from their own pockets.[3] Bingham, on the other hand, tried to make the organization self-sustaining by instituting membership and licensing fees and insisting on a commission of $25,000 from the sponsors of the National Air Races.[4] Still, these measures did not generate enough revenue to meet its growing operational costs, and the NAA was forced to make cutbacks. Even as the association shone publicly with the election of Amelia Earhart as national vice president, it suffered internally. But the symptoms of financial ills became readily evident in the spring of

1931, when the secretary of the Contest Committee, Maj. L. C. Christopher, resigned because his annual salary had been cut from $5600 to $3600.[5]

The grass roots pilots barely surviving the Depression far from Washington politics found it difficult to have faith in an organization founded and run by the same wealthy class that many blamed for their economic hardships. Membership decreased drastically, dropping by one thousand between 1929 and 1930, then plummeting from 5892 in 1930 to only 1699 in 1931. There was a slight comeback in 1932 as total membership almost reached 3500, but statistics indicated that most of this increase was attributed to new members who joined for only one year and then did not renew their memberships.[6] The treasurer's report for 1932 indicates that on June 30 of that year the organization had only $1690.44 in total cash and total assets of $21,398.09.[7] As with the assets listed in the closing days of the Aero Club, the valuable (but illiquid) trophies awarded through the NAA undoubtedly counted for much of this total. Realistically speaking, the NAA was in dire straits.

Yet throughout these bad times one of the NAA's most significant assets was never carried on its books: its vice president's public appeal. Amelia Earhart's flying exploits were front page news across the nation. Amid their economic problems the American people gathered strength from the "Lady Lindy" who had soloed the Atlantic in 1932 in her Lockheed Vega monoplane. She became a popular symbol of courage, and the NAA's public image reaped the benefits.

In 1933, further declines in the economic condition of the association forced Bingham to take an action that quickly proved very unpopular among his fellow officers and the general membership. He turned the organization's magazine, now called the *NAA Review,* over to Stuart Gayness, a private publisher. In return for the right to publish the NAA magazine commercially, Gayness agreed to pay a percentage of the profits back to the NAA.[8]

Bingham saw this move as a way to maintain the magazine without continuing to lose money on its publication, for the *Review* had traditionally operated in the red. But other officers, including Glenn Martin and Earhart, vehemently opposed the move. The new publisher, whose previous business enterprises had included questionable real estate deals in Florida,[9] now had editorial control over the voice of the NAA. In a letter to MacCracken, Martin expressed his concern:

I believe our President, Senator Bingham, and the board members present at the meeting, are aware of the fact that they have disposed of their magazine for all time except at the option of the "first party." I believe that the governors generally feel that the execution of this contract is another important step down the ladder of strength, instead of up the ladder, and further they feel they have no better alternative.[10]

At the height of the magazine controversy, Earhart gave up her office: "Finding myself at variance with the views of those who dominate the organization, I feel that it is for the best interests of all concerned that I resign."[11]

However, although the magazine problem seems to have been the proverbial last straw for the famed pilot, it was far from the main reason for her resignation. She was reported to have already been at variance with Bingham on numerous other key issues, including whether or not the association should expend its already limited resources in trying to recruit new members. Earhart believed that the NAA should operate as a skeleton operation through the lean years, whereas Bingham thought it should put forth an all-out drive to increase membership.[12] But even this matter was not at the core of her dissatisfaction.

Earhart's resignation, not clearly understood by either the public or the NAA's general membership, evoked an outcry. Dudley M. Steele, an NAA regional officer from California, implored MacCracken:

Do you mind giving me the real reason behind Amelia Earhart's trouble with the National Aeronautic Association and her resignation therefrom? It is causing a lot of smoke out here, and people are talking about it. I am afraid that unless we are able to give an explanation it may result in considerable harm to activities here.[13]

The "real reason" seems to have been the negative publicity the NAA received from both the press and air race pilots over its handling—or mishandling—of a Chicago air meet. The NAA subsequently suspended all pilots who participated in that meet from air racing for a period of three years.[14]

Air racing had been one of the foremost spectator sports of the 1920s. The National Airplane Races, overseen by the Contest Committee of the NAA, became so popular that large U.S. cities competed fiercely for the honor—and resultant business revenues—associated with these events.

The 1932 National Airplane Races, held in Cleveland, Ohio, had still proved the event's drawing power, but the NAA determined that the event's ten-day running time had led to excessive overhead. The officers thus resolved that the 1933 races would take place over only four or five days. Of course, shortening the races would lower the cost of managing the event, but also decrease total revenues. As a result, the cash prizes offered winners would have to be lowered.

To offset this reduction in the cash incentive for race plane builders, NAA officials discussed the possibility of holding preliminary races in other cities. One of the ideas that was tentatively—but nonetheless publicly—considered was coupling a preliminary airplane race with an upcoming U.S. Gordon Bennett balloon race. (As in the early days of the Aero Club, the winning country sponsored the balloon race the following year, and Americans had won the international competition in 1932.)

Promoters in Los Angeles submitted a bid for the 1933 National Airplane Races and a group in Chicago, sponsored by the Chicago *Tribune,* proposed a combined Gordon Bennett competition and preliminary airplane race series, as had earlier been considered by NAA officials. After reevaluating the logistical problems that might be involved with two large-scale airplane events, the NAA made a counterproposal to the two groups, that Los Angeles apply for the National Airplane Races, to be held early in July, and that Chicago apply for sponsorship of the Gordon Bennett balloon competition (without airplane races) early the following September. However, because of unclear communications resulting from NAA officials negotiating with different groups in Chicago and Los Angeles over what the NAA intended to be separate balloon and airplane races, the Chicago group assumed that they had been given permission to hold the National Airplane Races. They announced their plans in a series of front-page *Tribune* articles.[15]

Hearing of the *Tribune* group's plans to hold its own American Air Races on the same July days as the Los Angeles National Airplane Races, the NAA informed the Chicagoans that their race was not sanctioned. NAA officials further stated that any pilots competing in the meet would receive the most severe penalty possible: a three-year suspension from competition.[16] But by the time the *Tribune* group was contacted by the NAA, their plans were too far developed to be canceled. They had made extensive commitments to competitors and the public and felt they must continue as scheduled.

So the American Air Races and the National Airplane Races both took place as planned, on the Fourth of July weekend of 1933. The NAA maintained that the airplane races in Chicago violated the limits of the agreement between the promoter and the NAA and drew nationally known competitors away from the sanctioned Los Angeles meet. Feeling that the pilots had been adequately warned in advance not to compete in Chicago, NAA officials followed through on their threat and imposed on each of them a three-year suspension from competition. In the 1930s, any such highly publicized action that deprived a man or woman of the means of making a living was bound to draw criticism. Beyond that, several of the Chicago competitors were quite famous and popular with the public, and all were longtime racing friends of Earhart's. As a leader in American air racing herself, Earhart felt strong ties to her fellow competitors. Caught between their needs and a questionable decision made by the NAA, Earhart sided with the fliers and public sentiment went with her. Thus the embarrassment caused her by the heavy-handed action of the association against her racing friends was apparently the major factor leading to Earhart's resignation from the NAA.

When the press, spurred on by the *Chicago Tribune,* evoked a public outcry against the NAA for suspending the popular air race pilots, NAA officials convened an appeals panel. The panel concluded that the suspensions had been warranted, but greatly reduced the length of time during which the pilots could not compete. They were all soon back on the racing circuit.[17] But the damage had been done. In spite of the fact that the NAA carried out the majority of its numerous duties with relatively few problems, its public image was severely damaged by the resignation of Earhart and the attendant condemnation by one of the country's leading newspapers. It would be several years before the association was able to regain the public's confidence.

In retrospect, Earhart's loyalty to her air racing associates is easy to understand. In those days, even if they fought among themselves, pilots, both male and female, traditionally united against outside opposition. In the 1920s women had gained a great deal of freedom through aviation, and several new stars were born in the world of airplane racing. Other talented women fliers like Bobbi Trout, Jacqueline Cochran, Marvel Crosson, Thea Rasche, Louise Thaden, Neva Paris, Phoebe Omlie, and the legendary Florence (Pancho) Barnes joined Earhart in the spotlight.[18] These women were tough competitors, but their underlying spirit of unity was reflected in an organization called the 99s, founded within the small circle of female air racers and licensed pilots.[19] To this day the 99s remain the most prestigious organization of women pilots in America.

At first, race officials balked at allowing women to compete against men in flying events, especially the closed-course pylon races. They considered the speeds at which men competed to be too dangerous for women. Instead, female pilots were encouraged to fly in their own timed, long-distance "Powder Puff Derbies,"[20] or in circuit races limited to women. By the mid-1930s, officials had dropped some of the restrictions, but still used every incident involving a woman pilot (even those proven to have resulted from flaws in airplane design) as a rationale for attempting to bar female competitors. Such was the case when Florence Klingensmith died in one of the Granville brothers' Gee Bee racers in 1933. The accident was used as an excuse to bar women from some races the next year, even though the same type of race plane—essentially a huge engine with only enough wing and control surfaces to keep it flying and control its direction—had killed male pilots as well.[21]

No matter what they were called, female competitive flying events were hardly "powder puff" affairs. Several women lost their lives in air races. Yet, partially because they were so dangerous, the contests were exceptionally popular with the public. The races, unlike many other women's activities, received press coverage that was approximately equal to that given the men's races.

In 1935, women were allowed to compete against men for the first time in the four-year history of the Bendix Transcontinental Race. Earhart and Cochran, the first female competitors in the race, broke no records that first year, aside from shattering the gender barrier. But the following year Thaden and Blanche Noyes, flying together, landed in Los Angeles as the first-place winners. They were followed by Laura Ingalls, who placed second. Two years later Cochran led all pilots, male and female, across the United States in a Seversky P-35 that averaged just under 250 miles per hour on the 2042-mile flight between Burbank, California, and the site of the Cleveland Air Races. After refilling her gas tanks in Cleveland, Cochran continued on to New York, where the NAA certified a new women's record for transcontinental flight. Her total flight time was slightly over ten hours.[22]

Women racers were generally accepted by their male peers, but they were also the subject of a few practical jokes. Cochran seemed to afford an especially appealing target. In addition to her flying abilities, she was a hard-nosed businessperson and was considered by more than one pilot to be a "tough cookie."[23] Hers was the kind of personality that provoked strong reactions—positive or negative. Her warm friendships with such flying greats as Chuck Yeager (with whom she shared the honor of being the first man and woman to break the sound barrier in an airplane) were reportedly matched only by her raging feuds with others, like fellow racer Pancho Barnes.

Soon after learning to fly, Cochran had founded a cosmetics firm, and she later capitalized on her fame as an air racer to promote her own line of beauty products.[24] One of her best-known marketing gimmicks made its debut at the 1949 Cleveland Air Races. Cochran loaded a large batch of Shining Hour, one of her best-selling fragrances, into the tank of an airplane equipped for agricultural pesticide application, then, flying low, sprayed it over the crowd of thousands during the opening day's events. Her stunt attracted so much attention that she had the plane reloaded with perfume for a repeat performance the next day.

But not all of the responses to Cochran's publicity stunt were positive. Some married men, attending the event on business as representatives of aviation companies, feared they might have trouble explaining the lingering aroma when they returned home to their wives. Others simply didn't like the way it smelled. "I'd rather be sprayed by a skunk!" exclaimed Casey S. Jones of the La Guardia College aviation school.[25] That night the subject of the spraying run came up among a group of socializing male pilots. They concluded that Cochran's stunt was missing just a little something. Fortified with strong drink, some of the top fliers in the country (a group that reportedly included Roscoe Turner, Jimmy Haizlip, A. L. Williams, and Frank Hawks) crept into the darkened hangar later that night and took turns contributing their own personal ingredients to the tank full of perfume that Cochran sprayed onto an unsuspecting crowd the next day.[26]

Although the prank may not have helped Cochran's perfume sales, it did not slow down her drive to be the best at everything she did. In addition to holding the most international speed, distance, and altitude records of any pilot of her time, she would later become the founder of the Women's Airforce Service Pilots (WASPs), president of the 99s, and the first (and, thus far, only) female president of both the NAA and the FAI.[27]

The public's desire to fly—much of it born during the "Golden Years of Aviation" of the 1920s—lasted long after the Depression had crippled the market for expensive private planes. The nation's oldest group of aviators, the balloonists, continued flying higher and further. Proponents of the least costly form of aviation, model flying machines, actually prospered. And a group made up largely of professional exhibition parachutists emerged under Joe Crane as the Parachute Jumpers of America and began making jumps strictly for fun; they would eventually evolve into the Parachute Club of America and emerge as today's United States Parachute Association. Some energetic souls even built their own airplanes and gliders.

As the Aero Club had evolved into the NAA, its members had continued to believe that an interest in aviation should be inculcated at an early age. The Junior Aero Club of America was thus reborn as the Junior NAA. Although this branch of the NAA prospered for a while, the cutbacks of the 1930s caused it to, in the words of one author, "struggle

The award for 1935 heralded the coming of a true aviation classic. The 1935 Collier Trophy was actually given to Donald Douglas and his staff for his DC-2 transport plane, but the DC-3 that evolved directly from it the following year soon proved itself to be the military and civilian workhorse of the free world and the cornerstone of the developing U.S. airline industry. Tough, durable, and able to haul twenty-one passengers in relative comfort, the DC-3 soon became the backbone of transport fleets owned by companies like American Airlines and Trans World Airlines.

While the DC-3 was making a name for itself on the U.S. overland air routes, another plane was becoming an air transportation legend in flights across the ocean. The romantically named *China Clipper,* one of the first of the giant Baltimore-built Martin flying boats of Pan American Airways, bridged the Pacific. The pilot on this historic trip was Capt. Edwin Musick and the navigator was Fred Noonan—who would later disappear over the Pacific with Amelia Earhart. Forging the eight-thousand-mile route from California to mainland China was a task tantamount to building the Pony Express outposts in the wild west. Under the direction of William Grooch, a crew outfitted way stations on the Hawaiian Islands, in Manila, and in Canton, China. On Guam, Midway, and Wake Island they had to build channels through the coral reefs so that they could unload the necessary supplies. Everything they used for the mammoth construction project had to be brought to these islands aboard a chartered ship, the steamer *North Haven*.[28] The Pony Express analogy holds true in another sense as well, for the route they established for the huge flying boat helped Pan American win the first U.S. airmail contract for service to China. For accomplishing this herculean task, Pan American Airways was awarded the 1936 Collier Trophy.

along as sort of an orphan."[29] Most of the models used in those days were free flight gliders and rubber band–powered aircraft, but gasoline engines and radio control were starting to appear in experimental forms—in spite of the fact that some state governments tried at first to ban them for safety reasons.[30] Aero modeling was a popular activity in the 1930s. In 1935 there were 215 chapters (with 4000 members) in the NAA-sponsored Philadelphia Model Airplane Association alone. A group in New Jersey claimed 2500 members, and the Junior NAA of Akron, Ohio, listed 3700 enthusiasts on its membership rolls.

In 1936 about one hundred model airplane devotees, most from NAA-affiliated organizations, organized into the American Academy for Model Aeronautics, a title that was soon shortened to the Academy for Model Aeronautics (AMA). They merged with the International Gas Model Airplane Association in 1937 and joined the NAA as a separate modeling division. By the mid-1980s there would be over 100,000 members in the AMA. The AMA's member-officers took over most of the duties involved in organizing and promoting model airplane competition, with the NAA primarily formulating competition rules and processing membership applications. This relationship would continue until 1966, when the AMA formally incorporated as a separate entity. It has operated since that time as the franchised U.S. aero modeling representative to the FAI through the NAA.[31]

Depression-era aviation of all forms seemed to scale down to match limited economic resources. In contrast to the larger, more expensive, airplanes of the pre-Depression years, a new line of aerial "flivvers" evolved in the late 1920s and early 1930s. Beginning with the Aeronca C-2 and C-3, a host of small manufacturers began producing light, low-horsepower, low-cost flying machines aimed at a relatively new customer—the private pilot. The Aeroncas (affectionately known as "air knockers" or "flying bathtubs") were joined by other entries in the light plane market, and soon airplane manufacturers, both well known and unknown, had created the beginnings of America's light plane industry. Planes like the Curtiss-Wright Junior and the Cessna EC-2 darted around the sky along with the Cycloplane Solo and the Buhl Bull Pup.[32]

For those who could not afford a factory-built plane, popular flying magazines advertised blueprints that do-it-yourselfers could buy to manufacture their own planes. The modern homebuilt airplane movement was founded on such designs as the Heath Parasol, powered by a Henderson motorcycle engine, and the Pietenpol Air Camper, utilizing model A and B Ford engines. One of the many men and women smitten with dreams of building an airplane of their own during this period was a Milwaukee teenager named Paul Poberezny. He would later found the Experimental Aircraft Association, which would eventually grow to be the world's largest organization devoted to homebuilt aircraft.

While Poberezny and most other grass roots aviators of the 1930s pursued powered flight, many others chose to remain in the aviation field in which Poberezny himself had first learned to fly. Gliding and soaring made up the form of popular flying that owed its development perhaps most directly to the Depression.

In the years following World War I Germany found itself with a large number of young men and women eager to fly. Many of them had, or were in the process of earning, degrees in aeronautical engineering when the war came to an end. When the conditions of the Treaty of Versailles placed severe limitations on German development and use of airplanes in order to prevent the nation from developing an air force as strong as it had had in the war, young would-be fliers found themselves without an avenue to pursue their interest or to practice the engineering specialty for which they were trained. The ingenious young Germans circumvented such restrictions by building and flying motorless aircraft.

At first these gliders were primitive affairs that afforded little more than short-distance downhill rides, skimming along at best a few feet above the ground. By 1921, however, their technology had advanced to the point that the motorless machines were able to take advantage of air currents forced up the steep slopes of the Wasserkuppe mountains to actually gain altitude during a flight. In that year Wolfgang Klemperer, flying a plane named the *Blaue Maus* (Blue Mouse), stayed aloft for thirteen minutes.[33] It was not long before American corporations like Goodyear and General Electric recognized the valuable resource available in young German engineers such as Klemperer and brought them over to work in the United States. With them came their newly developed love for soaring flight.[34]

In the summer of 1928, J. C. Penney (whose father founded the department store chain that bore his name) financed flights by the American Motorless Aviation Corporation (AMAC). Using the *Darmstadt I,* a soaring machine designed and built by students at Germany's Darmstadt University, AMAC pilot Peter Hesselbach launched off a sand dune in Cape Cod for a soaring flight of fifty-seven minutes' duration.[35] Later that year Penney joined forces with Detroit businessman Edward S. Evans, whose interest in motorless flight had prompted him to start an American manufacturing company producing primary gliders. These were primitive training aircraft that consisted of little more than an uncovered frame, wings, and an empennage. The pilot sat out in the open air while making what were usually short, straight, low flights down a hill or sand dune. Together they formed the National Glider Association in January 1929. By August of that year, gliders were being featured at the Cleveland Air Races, with Lindbergh, Earhart, and other nationally known pilots trying their hands at flying the unpowered machines. Within months of its founding the National Glider Association was recognized by the NAA.[36]

One of the events intended to be a highlight of that year's Cleveland Air Races literally fell short of its mark. Klemperer was to fly a new glider, the *Akron Condor,* designed by Frank Gross (one of the students involved in designing the *Darmstadt I*) and built in Akron, Ohio, by the Baker-McMillen Company. The plan was to present the glider in a unique manner. Klemperer left Akron for Cleveland in the *Condor,* towed behind a Goodyear blimp. However, a few miles before reaching its destination, Klemperer's glider encountered turbulence that first caused the tow rope to go slack, then jerked it tight again, in an increasingly violent game of aerial "crack the whip." Klemperer elected to disengage from the tow vehicle. In spite of efforts to soar to the site of the air races, his motorless plane landed short of the Cleveland airport.

The Baker-McMillen Company played a brief but important role in America's soaring history. Prior to building gliders the company had, for nearly one hundred years, specialized in manufacturing lathe-turned wood products, such as knobs for teapots and handles for garden tools. Willis (Doc) Sperry, the younger brother of company president Jack Sperry, later explained that Klemperer and his brother had met at a party in Akron shortly after Klemperer came to the United States to work for the Goodyear Corporation. In the course of their first conversation the two former World War I pilots established that they had met—briefly—once before. Klemperer had shot Sperry down during the war![37] The two soon became friends and Klemperer convinced Sperry to hire a young engineer named Frank Gross to design American-built soaring machines. The result was the *Akron Condor,* followed soon after by the *Cadet II.*[38]

In the summer of 1930, Baker-McMillen pilot Jack O'Meara launched the *Cadet II* from a pasture on South Mountain near the town of Elmira, New York. His subsequent flight lasted one hour and thirty-four minutes, immediately drawing the attention of glider pilots to the mountainous area around Elmira and gaining it the nickname the "American Wasser-kuppe." Based on O'Meara's flights the National Glider Association elected to hold its first national contest in Elmira.[39] The town has been closely associated with the soaring movement since that day and is now the site of the National Soaring Museum.

In 1932 the National Glider Association was replaced by the Soaring Society of America; among the new organization's founders was William R. Enyart of the NAA.[40] Enyart's influence would continue to be felt in the American soaring movement as he rose in status within the NAA, eventually becoming the association's president in early 1944. "My memories of Enyart are not as a pilot," recalled Paul Schweizer, "but he was there at nearly all of the early meets, helping out in various ways. He was one of the founding fathers of the Soaring Society, but I remember him best for his association with the NAA."[41]

Another of the early members of the Soaring Society was just out of high school when he competed in the first National Soaring Competition at Elmira's Harris Hill. Floyd J. Sweet, an Elmira local, began flying in a homebuilt primary glider, then advanced to a Franklin PS for the competition. It was the beginning of a long relationship with the Soaring Society and the NAA. Sweet holds NAA "C" soaring license number 45, signed by Orville Wright. Since his first flying experiences in the 1930s, he has served on several occasions as president of the society, and served on its board of directors for half a century. He is also a long-standing member of the NAA board. His valuable experience, spanning an aviation career of more than sixty years, has always been freely given to both organizations. In 1988, Sweet took his place alongside America's most revered aviation personalities as he was named one of the NAA's Elder Statesmen of Aviation (see Appendix E).

In the closing years of the Depression, with talk of another European war once more stirring concern among aviators that not enough trained pilots might be available in the event of American involvement, a group of some twenty Chicago pilots formed an "NAA" of their own in 1938. Although their organization bore the same initials, they were not part of the National Aeronautic Association. They were the National Airmen's Association—the first organization of black pilots in America.

Operating out of Harlem Airport in Chicago, this small group set about showing that black pilots were equal in ability to their white counterparts. In spite of having equipment that was inferior to that of many of the white exhibition fliers, the group organized a barnstorming tour sponsored by the *Chicago Defender,* a black-owned newspaper. This ten-city aerobatic tour, which featured pilots Dale White and Chauncey Spencer, ended in a flight from Chicago to Washington, D.C.

Upon arriving in Washington, the two pilots were introduced to then Senator Harry S Truman, who was surprised to learn that black aviators were unofficially—but very effectively—barred from pilot positions in the Army Air Corps. Truman took Spencer and White's pleas to heart. After visiting them at the airport and inspecting their airplane, he concluded that "if [they] had the guts to fly [the] thing to Washington, [he] had the guts to back them." Truman subsequently initiated legislation that gave black pilots assurance of receiving flight training under the Civilian Pilot Training Program.[42] It would still be years before blacks were able to enter the service as pilots, but, when they did, the NAA's magazine, *National Aeronautics,* voiced support for the efforts begun by this rival NAA. Once again, it would be the exigencies of war that would allow those who had long been disenfranchised to demonstrate their abilities.

A UNITED FRONT

The New NAA Organizes for War

15

In one sense, the NAA's efforts to promote commercial aviation during the 1920s were so successful that, by the early 1930s, it had worked itself out of a job. After spending years lobbying for the creation of governmental agencies to legislate aviation, in order to establish a stable business environment in which commercial aviation could develop, the NAA had watched from the sidelines as the air carriers and those same governmental regulatory agencies settled into a close working relationship that did not include the association. Indeed, some felt the relationship was too close. When the Roosevelt administration came into office in 1933, Senator Hugo Black, who would later serve on the Supreme Court, accused the former (Republican) postmaster general and the airmail carriers of collusion and contract rigging. One of those caught up in the scandal was NAA founding member and at that time general counsel William MacCracken.

MacCracken, who by then had left the Department of Commerce for a private Washington law practice representing some of the mail carriers, eventually served a brief jail term for contempt of Congress when he refused to produce files subpoenaed by Black.[1] At first believing that the subpoenaed records fell under the protection of attorney-client privilege, MacCracken hesitated to produce them until their status could be clarified. Later, after he had assured the court that he would comply with the order, some of the documents disappeared from his office. MacCracken endured the shame of a few days in jail, under Black's order, but he always maintained to his family that he had not been a party to the removal of the documents sought by Black. It might, in retrospect, appear that New Deal politics played a greater part in MacCracken's incarceration than any actual wrongdoing.[2] In his later years he focused his efforts on work with the American Optometric Association, but kept lifetime ties with aviation as NAA general counsel and a member of its editorial board.[3]

By presidential order the U.S. Army took over operation of U.S. airmail routes in 1933. Although Roosevelt could not have foreseen this outcome, the move dealt passenger service yet another setback. Public confidence in the safety of air transportation in general fell as military pilots, unaccustomed to the routes and hazards of civilian airmail flying, died in a much-publicized string of crashes. When aircraft accidents occurred, they were jointly investigated by the military or industry organization operating the airplane, as well as the Department of Commerce, whose Bureau of Air Commerce was responsible for maintaining radio and weather forecasting facilities along federal airways. There were frequent disputes among the interested parties concerning the causes of accidents, during which, not unexpectedly, each would try to shift the blame to the other. The result of this infighting was that identification of the true cause of an accident—and devising a solution to prevent further accidents of the same type—were often impossible.[4]

In 1938, five years after turning the airmail over to the military, Roosevelt, for political reasons, formed the Civil Aeronautics Authority (CAA) and once again the market for commercial aviation achieved some degree of stability through legislative control. All federal civil aviation was placed under the jurisdiction of the new CAA. Furthermore, within the CAA was an Air Safety Board that was beyond the reach of military or industry influences. This three-member investigative panel sought to discover the cause of accidents and recommend measures to prevent their recurrence.[5]

As we have seen, although the late 1930s were, in some ways, the weakest years in the NAA's history, they proved to be a time in which the grass roots strength of the American aviation movement made itself felt. Men and women who were truly devoted to flying found ways to express their love of the air in spite of restrictions on their financial resources. Recognizing that it was the dedication of these average American citizen-pilots that would nurture the spirit of future aviation, a wiser national association entered the 1940s proclaiming itself to be "the *new* NAA."[6] With their attention no longer focused primarily on the aircraft manufacturers and wealthy sportsmen pilots, the leaders of the new NAA addressed themselves to general aviation, the populist flight phenomenon that had arisen from the ashes of the 1930s.

Aviation progress hardly came to a halt during the Depression. The government, industry, and a few individuals of means still could afford to pursue excellence. The 1937 Collier Trophy went to the U.S. Army Air Corps for achieving substratospheric flight in a specially designed Lockheed XC-35 airplane. The project was able to send the crew safely to high altitudes by equipping the airframe with special sealing materials and pressurizing the plane's entire cabin.

Another custom-built Lockheed airplane, a Wright Cyclone–powered Lockheed 14, helped win the 1938 Collier Trophy and further established the flying reputation of a man who eventually became one of the wealthiest—and most eccentric—people in the world. On July 10, 1938, Howard Hughes and a crew of four left Floyd Bennett Field in Brooklyn, New York, for a record-breaking trip around the world. Ninety-one hours later the plane touched down at its starting point. Hughes had rounded the world at an average flying speed of 206 miles per hour.[7]

The last Collier Trophy of the 1930s was awarded, collectively, to all of the airlines of the United States for their unsurpassed record of safe air transportation. In presenting this award, the NAA recognized the efforts of three doctors—Walter M. Boothby and W. Randolph Lovelace of the Mayo Foundation and Capt. Harry G. Armstrong of the U.S. Army Medical Corps—for their contribution to flight safety through aviation medicine and, in particular, the instigation of measures to eliminate the danger of pilot fatigue. The NAA's dream of creating a viable transportation industry based on the once-frail airplane seemed finally to have become a reality.

Two strong forces were pushing for a change in the NAA's focus at the end of the 1930s. The first was internal: a need to address the concerns of a more middle class membership. The other was external: America's commercial aviation industry no longer suffered from many of the problems that had previously occupied the NAA's attention. Because it no longer needed the help of the NAA, the commercial aviation industry gradually lost interest in supporting the organization.

But, as the NAA entered the 1940s, the members soon perceived another venue for their efforts: the war in Europe now threatened to engulf the United States. True to the warnings of NAA officers over the years, it was clear that this second world war would be won or lost in the air. Even before America entered the conflict, association officers cautioned, "The imminence of a military threat must not overshadow in the public mind the fact that air mastery is not built simply on a preponderance of war planes. It is a challenge of war planes backed by a united nation believing in . . . and organized for air supremacy."[8]

The new NAA came to life early in 1940 under the guidance of a dynamic leader named Gill Robb Wilson. Wilson approached his job of promoting aviation with the enthusiasm of an evangelical preacher spreading the gospel—an analogy rendered even more fitting by the fact that he was also an ordained minister! Wilson came to the NAA with several years' experience as the director of aviation for the state of New Jersey and as a past president of the National Association of State Aviation Officials. He was the ideal man for reorganizing the association to address the needs of general aviation. He had previously served as the first spokesman and advisor to the Aircraft Owners and Pilots Association (AOPA), and it is his home address that appears on their incorporation papers as filed with the state of New Jersey. To show its gratitude for his service the AOPA gave Wilson membership number 1. The idea for the AOPA had arisen when two acquaintances of Wilson, the Sharples brothers, were told by the first chairman of the CAA, Edward J. Noble, that he had never been contacted by any formal organization representing the needs of noncommercial aviators.[9] When Wilson took over leadership of the NAA, he resolved that it, too, would accommodate all forms of aviation. Following the advice of a committee charged with formulating suggestions for reorganizing the association, Wilson concluded, "The result is today that the NAA offers, for the first time, to everyone who is interested in aviation, whether layman or experienced air technician, the opportunity to join within a United Front to advance through the strength of united effort the important needs that lie ahead."[10]

In addition to carrying out the programs already underway at NAA,[11] Wilson undertook a mobilization effort that would, he hoped, give participants in all fields of aviation a forum through which their ideas could be channeled and their needs could be communicated directly to aviation leaders. Wilson visualized the NAA as an arrowhead: the leaders of all aviation interests and activities would form councils at the point; specialist groups such as those for women pilots, college pilots, air transport crews, private pilot organizations, and aero modelers would back up the councils; and air-minded individuals from the NAA chapters and the general public would make up the broad base of the arrowhead.[12]

One of the first problems that Wilson set out to tackle with this new "United Front" involved preparation for the possibility of war. The tone of the association's magazine, *National Aeronautics,* turned more serious as the war progressed in Europe and the threat of American involvement increased. One issue of *National Aeronautics,* published just prior to Wilson taking office, featured a rather eye-catching advertisement for a British firm seeking American companies to manufacture aircraft subassemblies.[13]

Throughout these years, the NAA's official journal sought to deal with aviation issues in an impartial manner. In November 1940, *National Aeronautics* discussed concerns that the Civilian Pilot Training Program, enthusiastically backed by the association, might lead to overly congested airspace. In the same issue, the NAA was credited with reviving federal airport construction by pointing out the potential shortage of landing fields in the event of all-out involvement in war. By the end of the war the Civilian Pilot Training Program had trained some 330,000 pilots,[14] but fears of them all remaining active civilian fliers after the war proved to be unfounded.

The NAA's magazine addressed other issues well ahead of their time. A January 1941 article called attention to the government's need for aero technicians and strongly encouraged young men and women to take up aviation as a profession. One particularly insightful article was written by Bettie Gillies, National President of the 99s and a contributor to the magazine's regular "99s" column. She proposed that women pilots could perform a valuable national service by flying military aircraft in noncombatant roles, such as on ferrying missions. This approach, she believed, would free experienced male pilots for combat duty. Gillies's proposal would not be long in being enacted, as the government was soon to institute the WASP program (mentioned later in this chapter) under Jacqueline Cochran's leadership.

Overall, Wilson's changes in the NAA met with approval. A letter from Gen. Frank M. Andrews, published in January 1941, remarked: "The NAA has not always been what it should be to aviation but a lot of us stood by it in its off days because we knew it could be brought to serve a useful and patriotic purpose. I feel confident it is on the right road now."[15]

Encouraged by such reactions, Wilson continued down the same road. In early 1941 the NAA affiliated with the Air Reserve Association, an organization endeavoring to establish centers at which military reserve officers could go to maintain their proficiency in high-performance aircraft.[16] In April 1941, the magazine sadly reported that one of the earliest Air Reserve Association members, Lt. James H. Perry, had lost his life in a plane crash near Atlanta. At the time he was piloting an Eastern Airlines DC-3 in which airline president Eddie Rickenbacker was riding. Rickenbacker was severely injured in the incident.

As American sentiment in favor of supporting England in the war grew stronger, the NAA magazine featured advertisements and articles that solicited funds for the Royal Air Force Benevolent Fund. Some of the money raised by this fund purchased forty-eight Piper Cubs, one named after each state of the union. A group of pilots flew the training planes, affectionately referred to as "Flitfires," en masse from Loch Haven, Pennsylvania, to La Guardia Airport in New York, where they were turned over to the RAF.[17] Another story in the magazine concerned the making of the movie *A Yank in the RAF* and featured actor Tyrone Power. If articles in *National Aeronautics* were to be believed, American aviators were ready to go to war.

In spite of some early wartime shortages, NAA members tried to carry on business as usual. In the spring of 1941, over 1200 planes—most carrying ration books provided by Gulf Oil—participated in the 1941 Aero Cavalcade in Miami, Florida.[18] It was to be the last event with such an enthusiastic turnout for some time. Civilian aviators would soon find aviation fuel difficult to obtain and some would even have their airplanes impressed by the government into military service.

As the NAA's war effort continued, well-known personalities wrote to or visited the national office to wish the staff well and offer their services. Among them was Howard Hughes, who was listed as a "Cooperating Member" of the NAA. The organization also had the distinction of receiving correspondence from a self-acknowledged dummy. The world-famous Charlie McCarthy wrote to express regrets that he and his companion, ventriloquist and avid pilot Edgar Bergen, would be unable to attend an NAA banquet but, in a style all his own, wished "all the fellers" well and promised that the NAA could count on him to do his part.

When reports surfaced that Germany had used troop-carrying gliders in an effective attack on the island of Crete, the army's interest in such planes heightened. Officers were dispatched to Elmira, New York, to learn about flying motorless machines from members of the Soaring Society. At the time there were only about two hundred expert glider pilots in America.[19] Over the next few years the military would train thousands. Other longtime NAA—and Aero Club—members contributed what they could to the war effort. When the army began training parachutists, the diminutive former balloon exhibition jumper Georgia (Tiny) Broadwicke, then a grandmother, toured army training centers. If a burly would-be paratrooper had sudden doubts about the course he had chosen, a talk with the courageous lady would do much to put him at ease. Asked if she had used a reserve parachute for her more than one thousand jumps, Broadwicke replied, "Oh, yes, I always had a reserve chute in the hangar in case the one I was using got wet or torn."[20]

Perhaps the most long-lasting effort of the NAA's new president was similar to an idea the Aero Club had implemented before World War I. Wilson did not want to see the talent and equipment of the civilian aviation sector go to waste, nor did he wish to see private planes grounded for lack of available fuel. So, starting with his native state of New Jersey, Wilson pressed for formation of an organization intended to harness the resources of civil aviation for national defense. It was his belief that private planes might be of great service to the defense of the country, especially when used to patrol harbors and coastlines for submarines.[21] In the summer of 1941 the states of New York, New Jersey, and Alabama led the way by adopting plans for civil air patrols. By December of that year the government, urged on by a coalition of NAA and AOPA officers as well as other civil and military leaders, was meeting with them in Washington to discuss ways in which the civil organization could be structured to address the needs of the military. The January 1942 issue of *National Aeronautics* further defined the role to be played by the new Civil Air Patrol (CAP)—officially founded the day following the Japanese attack on Pearl Harbor.[22]

The NAA supported the CAP throughout the war. Members of the patrol provided courier service, towed targets, and performed search and rescue missions, in addition to providing basic aviation training to hundreds of cadets who later served as military pilots. In the course of this service, some fifty CAP members lost their lives. Periodically, *National Aeronautics* reported the CAP's activities to its readers. At the conclusion of hostilities, when the future of the CAP was in doubt, the NAA loudly protested the possible loss of such a vital organization and supported proposals that the life of the CAP be extended.[23] As the March 31, 1946, deadline marking the expiration of funding for the CAP approached, wings in Pennsylvania and Minnesota prepared to merge with their states' National Guard, while others in the organization investigated the possibility of continuing as a training element of the Reserve Officer Training Corps (ROTC).[24]

As U.S. involvement in World War II grew, participation in civilian aviation, predictably, diminished. Owing to shortages of materials, *National Aeronautics* shrank to a fraction of its prewar size, but it still kept the membership posted on aviation and association activities. In March 1942 the NAA moved its headquarters to 718 Jackson Place, Washington, D.C. The issue for that month included a cartoon illustrating all the activities associated with such a change. One panel showed an office worker dropping folders of records from past years into a wastebasket marked "permanent file." The label beneath it read: "NAA has no past!"[25]

But, contrary to what the cartoon claimed, not only did the NAA have a history, its publication foretold important future trends. In January 1943, for example, *National Aeronautics* published an article dealing with programs to accommodate women who had joined the work force for the wartime effort. In order to make it possible for housewives to take (supposedly temporary) jobs in the aviation industry, aircraft manufacturers were establishing in-house nurseries for the children of working mothers.[26]

In recent years historians have, rightfully, made much of the phenomenon of women working in the wartime aircraft factories, pointing out that "Rosie the Riveter" changed forever the role of the American woman.[27] Perhaps, though, even Rosie owes a debt to the women who had proven their equality in the sky for years before the war. Perhaps the more fitting symbols of mid-twentieth-century women's rights are the 99s and the other early women pilots who showed that aircraft were, and are, indifferent to gender and race. Rosie was indeed heroic, but her bravery was undoubtedly inspired by Amelia Earhart, Bobbi Trout, Phoebe Omlie, Jacqueline Cochran, Pancho Barnes, Marvel Crosson, and dozens of other courageous women who showed America that women's abilities extend far beyond—and high above—the boundaries of the household.

In 1943 the 99s and Jackie Cochran were still leading examples of women in the war effort. Cochran headed up the Women's Flight Training Division of the Army Air Force and fifteen of the members of her division came from the 99s. Other 99s served their country in different ways. By March 1943, 149 members of the 99s were active in the CAP; 154 held private pilot's licenses, 35 had commercial pilot ratings, and 3 had glider licenses. Women also found an important niche in aviation as wartime flight instructors. From the 99s alone, one served as a glider instructor, fifteen were commercial flight instructors, twenty-two were qualified to teach ground school, and seven held ratings that allowed them to work with pilots in the Link Trainer.[28]

By July 1943, Cochran's group had evolved into the Women's Airforce Service Pilots (WASPs). They were 1830 women who served their country in wartime by flying some sixty million miles while towing targets, ferrying combat aircraft, and flying aircraft to test experimental smoke and chemical dispersion techniques. In all, the WASPs suffered thirty-eight fatalities in their noncombat role. In later years the WASPs would have to fight another war—one to receive military benefits equal to those given men, some of whom had served under far less hazardous conditions.[29]

Another group heralded in *National Aeronautics* during 1943 were black American aviators. In February of that year the magazine announced an expanded program to be implemented by the U.S. Army to train black fliers. The program began just before the first black aviators who had received advanced training through the Civilian Pilot Training Program, conducted at Tuskegee, Alabama, saw combat as members of the 99th Pursuit Squadron. These military pilots—who first had to fight for their right to fly in combat by filing a lawsuit through the National Association for the Advancement of Colored People—distinguished themselves by flying P-40s (later P-51s) out of North Africa.[30] By the end of World War II the 992 pilots who made up the group known as the "Tuskegee Airmen" had destroyed 261 enemy aircraft, had damaged nearly 200 others, and were members of the only U.S. escort group that never lost a bomber while it was under their protection.[31] Charles A. (Chief) Anderson, one of the original instructors who taught the Tuskegee Airmen to fly, later received the NAA's Brewer Trophy in 1985 for his contributions to aviation education.

Throughout the war *National Aeronautics* reported the triumphs and tragedies of American pilots. In 1943 it sadly informed members that two longtime NAA members, Col. Sumpter Smith, formerly chief of the Airports Division of the Works Progress Administration, and Maj. Lewin B. Barringer, had disappeared over the Caribbean and were presumed dead.[32] Their C-47 airplane, a military version of the Douglas DC-3, disappeared near Puerto Rico on a return flight from Europe. Barringer, who at one time had held the post of general manager of the Soaring Society, had been one of the most enthusiastic of America's soaring pioneers.[33]

A year later the same magazine reported the death of another well-known American flier. In February 1944, *National Aeronautics* published an article about the passing of one of the Marine Corps's best fliers in the South Pacific, complete with a photograph of the "late" war ace. Fortunately for Maj. Gregory (Pappy) Boyington, the reports of his death were premature by nearly forty-five years. It would take far more than being shot down in the Pacific to pull the leader of the famed Black Sheep Squadron out of the war.[34]

The wartime support of U.S. servicemen by civilians was manifested in one particular honor that remains with us today. In the summer of 1943, Birmingham, Alabama, businessman Frank G. Brewer established a $10,000 foundation in honor of his two sons, who were serving in the military, one as a bombardier, the other as a paratrooper. Originally called the "Junior Collier Trophy," this award soon became known simply as the

The NAA's support for American military development was decidedly evident in the Collier Trophy presentations made throughout the war years. In 1940, Dr. Sanford A. Moss and the Army Air Corps received the Collier Trophy for development of the turbosupercharger, a device that increased both the power of an aircraft engine and its ability to climb higher into the air. It was soon put to practical use in American military aircraft.

The next year the U.S. air forces and airlines shared the Collier for their ability to supply the materials of war rapidly to troops overseas. Early in the conflict, the military relied heavily on the systems already established by civilian airline companies and their pilots to carry out the most extensive aerial supply operation ever known to mankind. The following year the emphasis shifted from aerial supply to aerial combat, and Gen. H. H. (Hap) Arnold received the 1942 Collier Trophy. The inscription on his citation was an elegantly simple statement of his awesome achievement: "For Organization and Leadership of the Mightiest Air Force in the World."

The 1943 Collier ceremony was one of the most impressive in history. At that ceremony half of the past Collier recipients, or their representatives, gathered together. Orville Wright (1913), Grover Loening (1921), Elmer Sperry, Jr. (1914), Charles L. Lawrance (1927), and Arnold (1942) were among those who helped the NAA present that year's Collier Trophy to Captain Luis DeFlorez, USNR, for developing wartime "synthetic training devices" for fliers. These were simulators that allowed student combat pilots to gain flying skills while still on the ground—and without risking men and aircraft. Two years later, Dr. Luis W. Alvarez received the Collier for developing a ground control approach radar landing system. The needs of wartime provided a forum in which the NAA could recognize two Americans of Hispanic ancestry with the country's top honor for aviation achievement.

General Carl A. Spaatz was the 1944 Collier recipient. Under his command, U.S. and allied forces had confirmed that air power, vigorously promoted by the NAA for many years, was the decisive factor in modern combat. Spaatz commanded the U.S. Strategic Air Forces, consisting of the Eighth Air Force bombing command under Gen. James H. Doolittle and the Fifteenth Air Force bombing command under Gen. Nathan F. Twining. These combined forces sent some three thousand B-17 Flying Fortresses and Liberators on devastating raids against military and industrial targets far inside Hitler's Germany. As part of the air power concept, fast fighter planes like the Mustang and Thunderbolt accompanied these long-range, heavy bombers to protect them far behind enemy lines.

Brewer Trophy. The conditions of the perpetual fund supporting the award were that the NAA annually present the trophy for "achievement in the field of Air Youth education."[35] As a longtime proponent of introducing young people to aeronautics, most often through the Academy of Model Aeronautics, the NAA began to emphasize a special Air Youth program in April 1942. Originally, its main goals were to form airplane model clubs under the AMA, and to create Junior Air Reserve flights and squadrons.[36] Throughout the war years, *National Aeronautics* magazine featured a regular column called "Air Youth Horizons" that was dedicated to the activities of these various chapters.

On December 17, 1943, during a ceremony commemorating the fortieth anniversary of the Wright Brothers' first powered flight, the first Brewer Trophy was awarded to the CAA for its program of preflight education. The presentation was purely ceremonial: there was, in fact, no trophy. Because the war effort had created shortages of metals, the actual trophy was not cast until 1949.[37]

It was at this same NAA celebration that Orville Wright announced that the original Wright Flyer would permanently return to the United States after the war.[38] This was news for which America had long waited. The first practical airplane ever built had been in England since early in 1928 because the leading museum in the Wright's own country, the Smithsonian Institution, had repeatedly refused to recognize the primacy of the brothers' plane. Smithsonian Secretary Charles D. Walcott had, instead, repeatedly maintained that the *Aerodrome* of his predecessor, Samuel Langley, was the first airplane "capable of sustained free flight under its own power, carrying a man," and the museum had, at one time, even refused to accept the plane when the Wrights offered it to them.[39] Orville Wright agreed to return the plane to the American museum only after being given firm assurance that it would forever be properly represented. Today it is the centerpiece of the National Air & Space Museum.

America united behind the war effort in a way that would not be seen again for half a century, and the NAA symbolized this unification. One of the NAA's most conspicuous Air Youth activities was known as the Junior Air Reserve, and nationally known celebrities volunteered to promote it. Among the first of the famous supporters were the tuxedo-wearing, monocle-sporting, Charlie McCarthy and his longtime companion, Edgar Bergen. After being sworn in as a Junior Air Reserve Cadet, McCarthy allowed ventriloquist Bergen to pilot him around the country, encouraging boys and girls aged ten to sixteen to join the organization and learn the fundamentals of flying.[40] Another avid private pilot who worked to promote the NAA's Air Youth program was the famed Robert

Ripley, known for his "Believe It Or Not" stories. In 1943 Ripley, like McCarthy and Bergen, embarked on a cross-country campaign to interest American youth in aviation.[41]

Throughout the war the NAA's magazine periodically reported on the development of a previously unbelievable flying machine. Inventors dating back to Leonardo da Vinci had dreamed of flying machines with whirling wings that could ascend vertically into the air. The Frenchmen Launoy and Bienvenu reportedly built models of such a feathered flying machine in 1784, and one of their countrymen, Paul Cornu, demonstrated in 1907 that a machine could be built on such a principle that had the capability of rising vertically from the ground, albeit without the added weight of a pilot. In 1910, a Russian named Igor Sikorsky duplicated Cornu's feat, but it would be many years and half a world away before he finally constructed a practical helicopter.[42]

In 1939 Sikorsky, then living in the United States and working for the Voight division of United Aircraft Corporation, proposed to his employers that he be permitted to build such a flying machine. United Aircraft granted him funds to build a prototype, which was officially known as the VS-300 (the VS was for Voight-Sikorsky), but was called the "Ugly Duckling" by its numerous detractors. On September 14, 1939, the machine managed to lift off the ground under the control of tethers, but it was not until May 15, 1940, that it hovered above the ground in free flight. For this accomplishment, the FAI, through the NAA, awarded Sikorsky helicopter pilot's certificate number 1.

Sikorsky's model VS-300 was replaced by the XR-4 and then the XR-5, each having more power and maneuvering capability than its predecessor. In 1943 *National Aeronautics* reported that the helicopter had undergone successful military tests, repeatedly landing on and taking off from the decks of a ship.[43] Later that year the XR-6, an even more advanced machine, flew from Washington, D.C., to Dayton, Ohio, under the control of an army colonel named Gregory. The 387-mile trip took four hours and thirty-five minutes.[44]

In May 1944 the helicopter made its entrance into battle as a rescue vehicle. That month Lt. Carter Harman of the Army Air Force used a helicopter to fly behind Japanese lines, making two trips over mountains as high as six thousand feet to rescue the downed pilot of a U.S. military plane and his three wounded passengers.[45] During the next few months helicopters performed dozens of other search, rescue, and emergency delivery missions, firmly establishing the vehicle's reputation as a dependable and versatile flying machine.

The helicopter's utility for search and rescue missions was eventually recognized by the NAA. In 1950, the Collier Trophy was jointly awarded to the helicopter industry, the military services, and the U.S. Coast Guard for "development and use of rotary-wing aircraft for air rescue operations." In awarding the Collier that year the NAA cited the use of rotary-wing aircraft by the U.S. Coast Guard in rescue missions at sea and during combat missions then taking place in the Korean campaign.

The rapid deployment of Army and Marine Corps helicopters to bring back troops stranded behind enemy lines was a lifesaver for many Americans and other United Nations soldiers. Still, the use of helicopters for the medical evacuation of seriously injured casualties proved to be the machine's most outstanding application in the Korean conflict. By greatly reducing the time that it took to get wounded soldiers from the battlefield to field hospitals, the helicopter saved thousands of lives. It was a role that helicopters would play thousands of times more in Vietnam two decades later.

In the years since World War II, helicopters have remained invaluable in both military and civilian activities. In 1942 Sikorsky predicted that, by 1955, the average American housewife would wheel her helicopter from the home's hangar to fly off for a visit to a friend.[46] Although their high purchase and operating costs have thus far prevented them from fulfilling their creator's optimistic expectations, the machines nevertheless have an enthusiastic following, supported by the Helicopter Club of America. The club, an air sport organization of the NAA, is the primary promoter of American helicopter teams in international flight competition.

Early in 1944, William Enyart, a founding member of the Soaring Society and a longtime NAA Contest Committee member, succeeded Wilson as president of the NAA. Enyart remained in this post throughout the remainder of the war and effectively anticipated many of the problems that would be faced by aviation and aviators as the NAA again became a peacetime organization.

The promise for postwar private aviation seemed bright. Manufacturers anticipated an explosive market for light aircraft as thousands of trained pilots returned from the war and other veterans learned to fly in GI Bill–approved flight schools. It appeared that the private airplane would soon become as common as the private automobile.

THE POSTWAR YEARS

Private Aviation's Boom and Bust and the Cold War's Chill

16

With the war ended and the NAA again turning its attention to civil aviation activities, the association's leaders faced the new problems encountered by returning GIs who had a desire to be involved in flying. Issues like these were ones that the association could identify and attack—but at the same time an invisible problem was developing within its own administrative structure. It would be an elusive enemy for NAA officers to identify, because it had been inherent in the association's very structure since the earliest days of the Aero Club. The problem stemmed from a gradual change in the collective identity of the association's membership that took place without a corresponding shift in the makeup of NAA officers and board members.

Traditionally, the heads of the association had been nationally prominent individuals, usually drawn from the upper ranks of wealthy capitalists, with a scattering of senior military officers. In the earliest days this situation was a given, for the Aero Club was, essentially, a rich man's sporting club. As the Aero Club evolved into the NAA, for a time it still made sense to keep such a structure. The NAA was created with direct and powerful links to aircraft manufacturers, military aviation, and the budding air transport industry, and NAA officers represented a pool of expertise in all of those fields. Besides, it was assumed, probably correctly, that rich and powerful people were necessary to generate the kind of large-scale financial support on which both the NAA and the Aero Club relied for survival. A peripheral result of having hard-nosed business leaders and military officers in charge of the NAA was that the upper echelon of officials tended to be politically conservative. They also tended to be men and women whose own economic good fortune distanced them from the concerns of the working class. Although few of these individuals seemed to be intentionally elitist by nature, occasionally the direction in which they steered the NAA was foreign territory to the average citizen wanting to hop on the postwar aviation bandwagon.

Other changes also took place during the 1930s and 1940s. Even during the Depression, small homebuilt airplanes and gliders had provided a low-cost method by which the working man and woman could participate in what had previously been a rich man's sport. World War II and the subsequent GI Bill of Rights benefits allowing for flight instruction further accelerated the development of grass roots aviation. During the same twenty years, the military, aircraft manufacturers, and the air transport industry developed networks of power and expertise separate from the old pool of experts once represented by the NAA.

The result of these parallel evolutionary processes was that the NAA's own base of power slowly shifted from expertise to constituency. Although a relationship with the NAA was still useful to military and commercial interests (largely because new FAI records validated their own expertise), it became less profitable for them to actually support the association. Thus the material and financial assistance they had once given the NAA gradually declined.

Some of the NAA administrators who served during this transitional period failed to adapt to the shift, clinging to the traditional alliances with government and industry while neglecting their membership. Still others, apparently unaware that the political views of a growing number of the members had become much different from their own, alienated the grass roots aviators by turning the organization's magazine into a personal political forum. The results were quite damaging to the national organization.

It was under William Enyart that the NAA began addressing the needs of postwar, military-trained pilots. In a reversal of the association's pro-regulatory stance during the 1920s, Enyart was concerned that the federal government might try to overregulate flying once the thousands of military pilots came home from the war. Concerned that wartime aviation regulations would remain in effect after the conflict, he lobbied for, and helped achieve, a timely lifting of many of the restrictions, such as those requiring pilots to carry fingerprint identification cards, closure of coastal areas to private flying, and bans against carrying cameras in aircraft.[1]

Enyart pushed to get American flying activities back to normal. The wartime hostilities had hardly ceased when the NAA announced that it would revive the National Airplane Races in Cleveland and the Miami Air Races as soon as its timing staff could be brought back to prewar strength. The demands of war had reduced the number of NAA officials trained to officiate at such events by two thirds since the National Airplane Races had been suspended following the 1939 competition. Timing staff director John P. V. Heinmuller, president of the Longines Watch Company, vowed that he would soon have personnel and equipment ready to handle the revived air races and the new speed record challenges sure to be presented by the jet-powered aircraft that had been developed during the war.[2]

The technological developments of war had indeed translated into new opportunities and challenges for peacetime record breakers—and record keepers. Flight speeds advanced from the 25-miles-per-hour record set in 1906 by Alberto Santos-Dumont to a 606-miles-per-hour flight by a British Gloster Meteor less than forty years later. Distance flights progressed from a few hundred yards in the days of the Wright Brothers to a 1945 flight from Guam to Washington, D.C., in which an American B-29 traveled 7933 miles nonstop. Such incredible advances in flight speeds had to be met with equal improvements in the way speed and distance records were verified. The old days of timers with stopwatches standing beside pylons along a marked course gave way to combinations of radar and movie cameras to determine the speeds of the powerful new machines.[3] Regulations governing the height at which speed records must be set were soon altered to accommodate the high-speed aircraft. The use of radar to time aircraft did away with the archaic, and unsafe, requirement that airplanes remain below 100 meters to permit visual verification that they had passed checkpoints. In 1949 the FAI changed regulations to allow such closed-course competitors to fly at whatever altitude they desired.[4]

Enyart encouraged the airplane manufacturers to anticipate a demand for inexpensive light planes and encouraged the government to give veterans priority in purchasing war surplus flying machines. He foresaw a bright future for light planes and his message fell upon a receptive aircraft industry.[5] For a while, at least, his predictions came true. Aviation and the light airplane seemed truly to be an integral part of postwar American life.

Air meets again became a popular form of relaxation and entertainment and everyone who attended dreamed that they would one day fly an airplane. It all seemed so easy—too easy for some. At the 1946 Miami

---

Wartime technological developments began finding applications in a peacetime aviation environment striving for flights that were higher, faster, and safer. Lewis A. Robert was honored by the NAA with the Collier Trophy for 1946 for his development of a thermal system that would prevent, or remove, ice buildup on aircraft wings and propellers. Radar and VHF radio improvements made during the war led to the receipt of the 1948 Collier Trophy by the Radio Technical Commission for Aeronautics, for its development of an air traffic control system that permitted safe flight operations under all weather conditions.

Maneuvers, sanctioned by the NAA Contest Board, one nonpilot member of the audience became caught up in the excitement and decided to go flying. He "borrowed" a parked plane and managed to get it started, but his wheels never left the ground. The would-be aviator's journey ended when he collided with the grandstand, the propeller of the plane taking its toll on some of the displayed trophies. Another dreamer at the same meet did see his dreams come true. On the first day a young Marine won a drawing for free flight instruction. At the end of the meet, only three days later, he soloed before the crowd.[6]

Following the armistice both veterans and civilians flocked to local airports for flight training. By the fall of 1945, the postwar flying boom was in full swing. Between July and October, the CAA added nine hundred flight examiners to its rolls. In August alone they licensed 5932 new pilots. During that same month 172,790 Americans possessed student pilot certificates.[7] Aircraft manufacturers responded by converting their wartime plants to produce civilian planes. Prewar civilian planes and light military aircraft designs were modified for private flying and turned out by the thousands.

Marketing methods were as creative as many of the designs. In New York the large department stores found it stylish to display and sell their "own" private aircraft. Macy's sold the Ercoupe, a two-place plane designed by Fred Weick to be "driven" through the air with automobile-like control inputs (the aileron and rudder controls were interconnected, so a coordinated turn could be made by "steering" the plane left or right with the wheel alone). Ercoupes listed at Macy's for $2994. Macy's traditional rival, Wanamaker's—the department store owned by the family of the Aero Club member who had financed construction of the transatlantic Curtiss airplane *America* before the beginning of World

War I—offered a complete line of small Piper aircraft, ranging in price from the $995.00 Sky Cycle to the $2995.00 Super Cruiser. By the end of November 1945, Wanamaker's reported advance orders for five hundred single-seat Sky Cycles and five thousand two-place Piper planes.[8]

Although they were not all represented by large department stores like Macy's and Wanamaker's, other manufacturers rushed to enter their nominees for America's favorite private plane. The variety of aircraft was seemingly limitless. A prospective buyer was dazzled by choices that included Cessna, Aeronca, Funk, Taylorcraft, Stinson, Luscombe, Interstate, and dozens of others.

Even the sailplane manufacturers capitalized on the postwar aviation boom. At its peak, Schweizer Aircraft of Elmira, New York, maintained a network of some thirty-five aircraft dealers. Schweizer required each of its representatives to offer a full line of sales, service, and training in two-place gliders. Like the pilots in Germany between the wars, the Schweizers subscribed to the notion that glider instruction was an inexpensive way to acquaint a student thoroughly with basic flying techniques. Once that student mastered glider flight, he or she would be well prepared to make the transition to powered aircraft. Many students did indeed participate in the Schweizer training programs before continuing on to obtain power plane ratings, but few escaped the magic of the sailplane. Eventually most of these same pilots returned to the genteel art of soaring flight.[9]

When sales of personal aircraft slumped later in the decade and many manufacturers went out of business, it was Schweizer's innovative sales techniques that kept the company alive. Their model SGS I-26 sailplane received a CAA Approved Type Certificate in 1955. Designed to be sold as an affordable kit, with major assemblies prewelded and components that needed specialized tools for construction already made, the I-26 possessed a combination of affordability and safety. These planes are now highly valued by vintage sailplane enthusiasts as one of the finer examples of American design.

Not all of the planes on the postwar market were new aircraft built for civilian use. Hundreds of the military trainers and liaison aircraft[10] manufactured during the war were no longer needed by the government. The NAA proposed that former military pilots be given the first option to purchase these surplus aircraft, but government officials (perhaps with some urging from airplane manufacturers who did not want the civilian market to be weakened by an influx of inexpensive surplus military machines) seemed eager to dispose of the planes quickly. W. Stuart Symington, the Surplus Property Administrator, proposed that the surplus planes be offered to the public for a period of only ninety days. Because of the large number of airplanes involved, all not sold in that time should be scrapped,[11] in order to provide, in Symington's words, a supply of "inexpensive light metals for commercial purposes."[12] Enyart opposed the plan.

Many of these planes, some quite airworthy, were sold to private fliers for as little as a few hundred dollars, but many more were eventually destroyed.[13] In retrospect, with so few of these warbirds surviving today, Symington might be perceived as an enemy of aviation for scrapping the planes, but in reality he should be praised for allowing as many as he did to be purchased in flyable condition. Symington's loyalty to aviation was recognized in 1957 with the presentation of the NAA's Wright Trophy. The certificate accompanying the award cited him for "significant public service of enduring value to aviation in the United States . . . based upon his distinguished career of public service in the field of aviation [since] 1941."

There seemed to be no end to the future of personal flying and the business opportunities that would spin off from the revived general aviation industry. At the war's end, Standard Oil of New Jersey announced production of a new aviation fuel offering a full 80-octane rating without the addition of tetraethyl lead.[14] This fuel would permit higher performance than existing aviation gasolines, which often had octane ratings of 73 and lower. The new gas, color-coded with a red dye, would remain a standard general aviation fuel for more than three decades. Refiners later added 100-octane low-lead fuel to the products available to general aviation, offering pilots a choice of fuel grades much like the specialized gasoline grades available to automobile owners.[15]

In the late 1940s, small airports that had previously lain unattended and offered few services became sources of community pride, developing into aviation filling and repair stations providing maintenance and line service on a par with that available from the best automotive garages. Within two years of the end of the war, the United States had 4490 public airports and landing fields, of which 1015 were lighted.[16] The NAA recognized the need for promoting such ground support. In 1945 it presented the Andrew J. Haire Airport Award to Beverly (Bevo) Howard of Orangeburg, South Carolina, for excellence of operation and service.[17] Howard's career in airport service had begun in 1932 when he took a job as a line boy at the newly founded Hawthorne Aviation. Four years later, at age twenty-one, Howard bought the company, supplementing his income as a commercial pilot flying for Eastern Airlines. At the time of his death, Howard had built Hawthorne Aviation into a multi-million-dollar aviation enterprise.[18]

With the war over there no longer seemed to be a need for youth programs like the Junior Air Reserve, which was military in nature, but the NAA maintained its long-term commitment to making young Americans "air minded." To this end the association joined with the Boy Scouts at the close of 1945 to form an aviation program for young men.[19] Although the Boy Scouts had had a long history of interest in aviation (a series of Boy Scout books published in 1915 included an episode centered around a Farman biplane[20]), their joint effort with the NAA actually followed the lead of the Girl Scouts. When the boys' group joined with the NAA, the Girl Scouts' Wing Scouts had been an active NAA affiliate for more than a year.[21]

Postwar America was a nation that accepted aviation as a part of everyday life. For a while it seemed that the longtime prophesies of airplanes becoming as popular as automobiles were finally on the verge of coming true. Heading the list of staunch aviation proponents was President Harry S Truman, whose own membership in the NAA dated back to 1938. On November 7, 1945, the NAA conferred the status of Life Member upon Truman for his support of aviation.[22] Although he was hardly the first American President to fly in an airplane, he was the first to travel regularly by air throughout the United States. Truman established the precedent of having a military aircraft designated exclusively for Presidential use. Unlike his successors, who would later dignify the Presidential plane with the title *Air Force One,* Truman referred to his lumbering C-54 as *The Sacred Cow.*

Yet, in spite of early evidence that America would see phenomenal growth in general aviation over the next decades, the boom did not materialize. Dreams of a plane in every garage gradually turned into nightmares for aircraft manufacturers.

At first, manufacturers were unable to keep up with their orders for new airplanes, especially two-seat trainers. The GI Bill for World War II veterans guaranteed them an opportunity to receive formal education or vocational training at government expense. In late 1945, President Truman signed an amendment to the bill that allowed veterans to spend as much as $500 in tuition for programs that did not take a full academic year to complete.[23] This amendment opened the way for veterans to enroll in condensed flight training programs. Many of the veterans had no desire to go to college and already knew the trade they wished to practice for a living. They saw the opportunity for flight training as a way to use their educational benefits to pursue a lifelong dream—that of becoming a pilot. The incredible initial spurt in sales of small airplanes was thus due, in large part, to the demand for training airplanes from hundreds of flight schools created primarily to teach veterans how to fly.

But once they completed their flight training (and many did not), few of these veterans bought planes of their own. Many others simply could not afford the luxury of a private plane. Learning to fly was just one of the dreams that these former soldiers had. Their other desires were to have a family, a home, and an automobile for reliable transportation.

For most of the young men and women trying to regain a peaceful life in postwar America an airplane simply was far too expensive to own as a hobby. All the economic indicators that had shown a nearly limitless growth potential for the aviation industry failed to take into account the simple fact that truly affordable private airplanes had few practical applications. Even if weather conditions allowed a pilot to make a trip on the schedule he or she desired, the amount of baggage and number of passengers these low-end planes could carry were limited. Furthermore, even after the airport closest to the final destination had been reached, transportation from the airport to the destination still had to be arranged. In most cases it was more practical, albeit slower and less exciting, for the average person to drive on a typical business or vacation trip.

One solution was proposed by a businessman named Joseph J. Stedem, whose Hertz Drive-Ur-Self car rental company made discount cards available to NAA members in the early 1950s.[24] Several aircraft designers tried to solve the problem by developing a private plane that would, once on the ground, convert into an automobile. Visionaries like Molt Taylor and Daniel Zuck spent years developing these machines. Although some were successful, and such ideas received enthusiastic support from magazines devoted to scientific and mechanical progress (as well as a boost from a then-popular television show starring flying enthusiast Bob Cummings), the roadable plane concept never really got off the ground.[25]

In spite of optimistic industry expectations for personal air transport, the new flock of pilots was disillusioned. They soon came to believe that affordable planes were an impractical means of travel, and that those airplanes capable of providing reliable long-distance transportation in nearly any kind of weather were beyond the means of the average person. The vast majority of these GI Bill–trained pilots soon added their pilot's licenses to collections of other wartime memorabilia and eschewed flying for the more mundane activities of raising a family and earning a living.

William Piper, president of Piper Aircraft, had his own explanation for their disappointment: "people were oversold on aviation at the end of the war. They expected everyone to own an airplane and the airplane to do everything an automobile [would]." The automobile, he concluded, was a "short-tripper" and the airplane was for long trips. His suggested solution was to make the private plane more practical by drastically increasing the number of small airports across the nation.[26]

But the response to Piper's call was too little and too late. The private plane market evaporated as quickly as it had formed. There were simply too many companies competing for a share of a market that was not, as many had believed, infinite. As early as the beginning of 1946, Piper had predicted that imprudent manufacturers of small airplanes "would go out of business when their stockholders' money ran out."[27] At the time, few seemed to believe him.

In the first week of 1946, aircraft manufacturers had cash orders for more than twenty-five thousand personal airplanes. In the final count, those same companies would manufacture more than thirty-two thousand planes during calendar year 1946. In spite of this appearance of prosperity, Piper's gloomy prediction proved accurate. In 1947, his own company's aircraft production nosedived from thirty prepaid airplanes per day in January and February to four or fewer per day in March.[28] Within a matter of months the private aircraft market collapsed, dragging with it some of the best-known names in American aircraft manufacturing. By the early 1950s, Waco, Stinson, Bellanca, Fairchild, Ryan, Ercoupe, Luscombe, Funk, Taylorcraft, Aeronca, Culver, Interstate, Porterfield, Rearwin, Monocoupe, Commonwealth, Navion, Republic Seabee, and Globe Swift were either out of business, in bankruptcy, or staying alive only by manufacturing nonaviation products.[29]

At the 1948 national convention in Minneapolis the NAA elected Louis E. Leverone, president of the Automatic Canteen Company of America, to head the NAA when Enyart accepted the presidency of the FAI (thus becoming the second American to hold the post after Godfrey L. Cabot, who had been president from 1941 to 1946).

Leverone sought to revive private aviation and once again have the NAA play a key role in U.S. air policy affairs. He and his board, largely comprised of nationally known commercial and industrial leaders, believed that the organization's strength lay in building a broad membership base. They tried to expand that base by strengthening the local chapters— providing monthly programs with suggested topics intended to focus the attention of all chapters on similar local issues, such as Air Youth activities, the formation of local airport committees to foster the development and improvement of landing facilities, legislative committees, and women's activities. Leverone and the board urged that each chapter sponsor an annual "clinic" to which all local persons would be invited (and at which they would, ideally, be recruited as new members of the NAA). These clinics consisted of a day-long series of meetings and exhibits designed to educate the public about aviation and to foster communication between the flying and non-flying sectors of the community. The model for these clinics proposed discussion of a series of topics of concern to the community, air show activities, model flying contests, soaring meets, and an airport party or banquet at which there would be roundtable reports summarizing the results of the day's activities for the press.[30]

Leverone's initial recognition of the need for a broad membership base and chapter activities proved to be correct, but his later attempts to make the NAA and its officers key players in national politics may have eventually cost the organization much of its grass roots appeal. The national posture he proposed for the organization was spelled out in the last of seventeen resolutions passed at the Minneapolis convention, requiring the officers elected at the convention to "implement as a part of the NAA program the integration of land, sea, and air power pointing toward the common objective of Air Power is Peace Power."[31] NAA members were concerned about national political issues, but proved to be more interested in local aviation matters over which they perhaps felt they had some control. The coming years would see grass roots aviators growing further away from the NAA and forming separate organizations that dealt specifically with the aviation form of their choice.

At the NAA's next national convention, held in Akron, Ohio, during the especially hot summer of 1949, members listened to a talk by Rear Adm. John P. Whitney, vice commander of the Military Air Transport Service. As the scorching heat melted an ice sculpture centerpiece of the American eagle into a shape more nearly resembling a penguin, the admiral told of the vital role aviation had played in the recently ended Berlin Airlift. It was an ironic setting in which NAA members were told of aviation's part in the beginning of what was to become a long "cold war"—one first fought not with fighter aircraft, but with planes configured for commercial transportation.

One man who sat in the audience that evening knew much about both flying and war. He was Gen. Frank P. Lahm, holder of Aero Club of America balloon pilot's license number 4, and airplane license number 2. One can only wonder what thoughts and memories went through his mind as he, a student of Wilbur Wright whose own first flights had lasted only minutes in a plane barely capable of carrying two people, heard of the thousands of flights that had brought millions of tons of supplies to the blockaded German city.

The NAA's renewed involvement with American aviation policy was reflected in the first of several resolutions passed at that convention. It said, in part, that "the Board of Directors . . . shall review annually the recommendations or resolutions of all agencies, public and private, bearing upon aviation policy and . . . the President of the NAA shall submit a statement of National Aviation Policy to the President of the United States in December of each year and to the Congress of the United States upon the convening of each regular session in January." The main criterion for the issues to be presented to the President was that they be only those on which there was "both a common meeting of minds and a common assent," rather than any controversial topics.[32]

The second resolution, one pledging the NAA's support in the advancement of American aviation technology, reflected the spirit and the fears that would mark an epoch in the country's history. It began, "That superior air power, coupled with the sole possession by the United States of the atomic bomb, gives reasonable hope that no nation will provoke the United States into war while such an advantage is ours. . . ."[33]

NAA President Leverone made good on the first resolution by polling the officers of seventy-six aviation associations and corporations in aviation or related industries. He was amazed to find that, of these, only forty-seven responded, and, of those, only twenty-six presented resolutions for consideration by the President and Congress. Even more amazing was the fact that, judging from the approximately 110 resolutions and policy statements presented, many of the aviation organizations were in direct opposition to each other over key policies. There was a clear consensus on only one issue, and even that was of concern to the commercial carriers alone.[34]

E. E. Wilson, Chairman of the NAA board, had explained the NAA's view of the problem when he argued that "regulation of [the airline] industry by political agencies under the doctrine of so-called 'reasonable regulation' has not only hamstrung the certificated airlines but nearly strangled an independent infant industry promoted by enterprising war veterans." Leverone presented this one common concern to President Truman and Congress, along with recommendations that the President appoint an advisory commission to investigate "the fundamentals of U.S. air policy."[35]

It is paradoxical that this particular problem was presented to President Truman by the head of an organization founded, in large part, to promote governmental flight regulation. Yet, in twenty-five years, the same federal regulation that the NAA originally thought would create a thriving aviation industry had turned into a monster threatening to devour it,

imposing increasing restrictions on private fliers without providing pro-
portionate benefits.

Had the NAA officials asked why there was such apathy and lack of
unanimity developing among those involved in aviation, instead of simply
expressing their shock that it existed, they might have realized that a
rapidly growing gap was developing between commercial and general
aviation. On the surface the two were cast from a common mold, but
underneath there were signs that the commercial and private sectors were
becoming less compatible.

As both segments of aviation experienced a growth rate exceeding the
pace at which new airports and other facilities were constructed, competition began between them for space on the ground and in the air. The
first signs of this rivalry were subtle. To be sure, they would have been
difficult for the NAA officials to see, even if they had been motivated to
look. Unfortunately, the NAA was staffed by men who were also national
leaders of finance and industry, and who were predisposed to promote
commercial enterprise under the traditionally unchallenged assumption
that what was good for American industry was good for America in
general. By focusing their attention disproportionately on commercial
aviation the NAA leaders created the impression that they were neglecting the needs of their own chapters. What the organization's officials were
late in realizing was that it was the individual members, rather than the
airlines, who were keeping the NAA alive.

The NAA's well-intentioned efforts to promote U.S. military aviation
were also futile. The military had developed their own experts and also
had those of their contractors to draw on for advice. Times had changed
and the NAA no longer played an important role in the new "Iron
Triangle" of Pentagon, Congress, and defense contractors developing in
Washington. Military and political leaders continued to listen politely to
the advice and admonishments of NAA officers, but the NAA's power
now lay more in the votes it represented and in its ability to certify
military flight performance records, rather than in its aviation expertise.
Very few of the NAA's suggestions to Congress were acted upon, and the
small number that were (like allowing liberal use of GI Bill money for
private flight training) proved of questionable long-term benefit to the
country. Their lobbying efforts afforded NAA officers a presence in the
Washington political scene, but they taxed the association's financial
resources without generating much tangible return.

In spite of their proclaimed efforts to reach the members of local
chapters throughout the country, Leverone and Kendall K. Hoyt,
editor of *National Aeronautics and Flight Plan,* were decidedly Washington-

One way in which the NAA maintained a strong influence among members of the U.S. government, the military, and the aircraft industry was the annual presentation of the prestigious Collier Trophy, and throughout the late 1940s and the 1950s, the Collier became a highly coveted symbol of excellence in supersonic flight.

The era began with a flight through the sound barrier by Charles E. Yeager in a bright orange aircraft that appeared to be more rocket than airplane. When his Bell X-1 was christened *Glamorous Glennis,* after Yeager's wife, little did the young Air Force officer realize that he was creating a memorial to her that would one day find a permanent place of honor in the world's most-visited aviation museum, represented in silent flight alongside the Wright Brothers' Kitty Hawk machine and Lindbergh's *Spirit of St. Louis.* Yeager and his team received many honors for flights in the rocket plane. In 1947 he shared the Collier Trophy with John Stack and Lawrence D. Bell for their joint effort, as pilot, engineer, and manufacturer, in achieving supersonic flight, and in 1954 he and Jackie Cochran both received Harmon International Trophies for being the first man and woman to fly faster than the speed of sound.

In 1951, John Stack again shared the Collier, but this time it was with his associates at the Langley Aeronautical Laboratory of the NACA. Their teamwork produced the transonic wind tunnel that allowed further experimentation and testing of supersonic aircraft without endangering the lives of test pilots. The contributions of Stack and other members of the NACA research teams to high-speed wind tunnel development were complemented by Richard Travis Whitcomb's discovery of the "area rule," an engineering principle that has facilitated the design of efficient fuselage shapes for supersonic aircraft. Working on the Collier-winning first project involving the transonic wind tunnel, this NACA scientist discovered a concept that enabled manufacturers to reduce greatly the drag induced by high-speed flight. He devised a series of calculations that enabled the designer to smooth the fuselage shape "seen" by the air flowing around it, thus producing stable aircraft capable of flying at far higher speeds than ever before under the same power. Whitcomb took home the 1954 Collier for his efforts.

William Lear's F-5 automatic pilot and control coupler system proved to the world that jet fighter aircraft could be designed with systems that would prevent the pilot from becoming fatigued by constant "hands-on" flying. For making the job of flying high-speed aircraft more accurate with a device that held the plane on a predetermined course, Lear earned the 1949 Collier Trophy.

oriented in their monthly messages to the NAA membership. It was the era of the Red Scare and the Korean War. In Washington, the communist witch hunts led by Senator Joseph McCarthy were the central focus of attention. The rest of air-minded America, while intrigued, might not have been so totally engrossed in the McCarthy frenzy that they wanted it to dominate each issue of their aviation magazine. Nevertheless, that is what Leverone and Hoyt gave them.

During the 1950s *National Aeronautics* shrank from a size and format similar to those of *Life* magazine to a newsletter of only a few pages. Leverone and Hoyt's front-page editorials regularly railed against the menace Russia presented to Americans. They criticized parents for letting their children play at being cowboys, arguing that they should be wearing leather flying helmets and aspiring to be future military aviators. The Reds, they maintained, had "burrowed into radio, movies, and television" and were responsible for turning the minds of children from the NAA's worthwhile air youth programs to frivolous wild west fantasies.[36]

Leverone and Hoyt became increasingly convinced that "Red chaos" was imminent and that the only thing that might be capable of moving on "A-Day," when the Russians would make their inevitable nuclear attack on America, would be American light planes. Issue after issue dwelt on the need to educate and mobilize American pilots to fend off the communist threat. Who knew, Leverone and Hoyt warned, how long it would be before "the Russian harvest is in."[37]

As time went on the McCarthy mentality took its toll on the organization. The editorials grew more contentious and alienated more and more members of the flying community who had previously been staunch supporters of the NAA. They criticized politicians for not following the NAA's suggestions and referred to CAP officers as "box-top colonels."[38] Grass roots aviation issues were relegated to back-page paragraphs or totally overlooked in favor of the political opinions of the president and editor. To judge by the tone of its national publication by the close of the decade, there was little evidence that the NAA was still in touch with its true constituency.

For many pilots of the 1950s, aviation provided an exciting escape from the fears of the new atomic age. Despite the sudden postwar crash in private aircraft manufacturing, interest in most of the forms of sport aviation that had been popular before the war gradually resumed. America's love for hot rods was carried aloft, as the revival of air racing inspired innovative designs for "hot" planes, many of which were quite affordable—if would-be aviators had the time and patience to build them

Airplanes and their engines merited the recognition associated with the Collier during the 1950s.

Leonard S. Hobbs received the award in 1952 for his Pratt & Whitney J-57 Turbojet engine. The thrust of this powerplant was rated at close to 10,000 pounds, making it the Air Force's engine of choice for the B-52 bomber, F-100 Super Sabre supersonic fighter, F4D Skyray, F-101 Voodoo, and F-102 Convair. Two aircraft designers shared the 1953 Collier Trophy for building supersonic military aircraft utilizing the J-57 engine: North American Aviation's James H. (Dutch) Kindelberger led the design team for the F-100, a land-based fighter that set an unofficial speed record of 757.5 miles per hour, and Edward H. Heinemann headed the Douglas team that produced the F4D, a carrier-based supersonic plane.

The 1955 trophy was jointly awarded to William M. Allen and his associates at Boeing Airplane Company and Gen. Nathan F. Twining, chief of staff of the U.S. Air Force, and the Air Force itself, for their development and operational use of the B-52. The long-range bomber design would be nearly as old as some of the men flying the planes when they went into service delivering cluster bombs in Vietnam. In 1956 the Collier was again shared by an aircraft manufacturer and representatives of a branch of the military. This time Charles J. McCarthy and his colleagues at Chance-Vought Aircraft and Vice Adm. James S. Russell and associates of the U.S. Navy Bureau of Aeronautics shared the honors for the conception, design, and development of the F8U Crusader.

The heavily armed F8U-2, designed specifically to meet the needs of the U.S. Navy, had the capability of exceeding one thousand miles per hour in maximum flight, but still could slow down sufficiently to land on the small deck of an aircraft carrier. The F8U was the first plane ever flown at supersonic speeds from coast to coast—by a young pilot named John Glenn. Another young naval officer who flew the Crusader the year it won the Collier was Richard M. Truly. Over the course of his career in naval aviation, Truly would rise to the rank of rear admiral and be the recipient of the Collier Trophy on two separate occasions, first as an astronaut, then as head of America's space shuttle program.

The 1958 Collier, collectively given to more people than in any previous year, was for achievements involving the F-104 Interceptor and its J-79 turbojet engines. In addition to the U.S. Air Force, the NAA recognized an industry team that included Clarence L. Johnson of Lockheed (for airframe design) and Gerhard Neumann of General Electric (for developing the engine), and U.S. Air Force pilots Maj. Howard C. Johnson and Capt. Walter W. Irvin, who shared the award for their record-breaking flights in the F-104, which set new records for world landplane altitude and world straightaway (straight line flight), respectively.

Amid so many awards for technological excellence in aircraft and engine design, the 1957 Collier recipient might seem almost out of place. Edward P. Curtis, a former World War I ace and long-time senior executive with the Eastman Kodak Company, received the prestigious award for a report he wrote while acting as a special assistant to the President. But Curtis's report was very much in keeping with the hardware developments that earned the other Collier awards. Titled *Aviation Facilities Planning,* it was a comprehensive national evaluation of the needs of American aviation in the jet age. It anticipated a need for, and recommended the construction of, expanded facilities to accommodate the high-speed commercial and military aircraft of the future.

---

themselves. At the opposite end of the spectrum of sound and speed from the powerful homebuilt racing planes, gliders were evolving into high-performance sailplanes, and a brilliantly simple design for a gliding device was about to give birth to a new sport flying industry.

Top: The Collier Trophy was first awarded to Glenn Curtiss (in 1911) for developing the hydro-aeroplane. Here Curtiss carries his hydro-aeroplane design a step further by adding wheels to the experimental U.S. Navy airplane *Triad*. Courtesy NASM.

Bottom: An unidentified artist captured the dramatic Paris demonstration of Lawrence Sperry's automatic stabilizer. In order to show its ability to hold a plane level under extreme conditions, Sperry removed his hands from the controls of a flying boat while his mechanic, Emil Cachin, off-set the normal balance of the plane by walking out onto one wing (Collier Trophy for 1914). Courtesy NASM.

Top: Awarded the first Collier Trophy after World War I (and the first presented by the NAA), Grover Loening's Aerial Yacht set a new world altitude record for flying boats and appealed to wealthy sportsmen seeking to buy a private airplane (Collier Trophy for 1921). Courtesy NASM.

Middle: An air mail plane lands at night with the help of lights on both the aircraft and the runway. For developing an airway system that allowed commercial aircraft to operate during hours of darkness, the U.S. Air Mail Service won the Collier Trophy for the second year in a row in 1923. Courtesy NASM.

Bottom: In 1923 U.S. Army pilots gained prominence among military aviators when Lts. Oakley Kelley and John Macready flew this Fokker airplane nonstop from New York to San Diego. The following year the Army built on the favorable publicity it had received for the long-distance flight when Lts. Lowell Smith and Erik Nelson, in two Douglas World Cruisers (out of four that started), completed a round-the-world flight in 175 days, winning the 1924 Collier Trophy for the U.S. Army Air Service. Courtesy U.S. Air Force.

Top: A crew of three manually starts the engine of a Curtiss Carrier Pigeon with a Reed Duralumin propeller using a technique similar to the children's game "crack the whip." The all-metal Reed propeller was nearly as light as, and far more durable than, its wooden predecessors (Collier Trophy for 1925). Courtesy NASM.

Middle: The problems of adapting the parachute for use with airplanes included finding a manner in which the bulky canopy could be stored, yet still be ready for immediate deployment with a minimum of danger that the device would become entangled with the airplane. The solution was to pack the parachute into a container and harness that allowed the wearer to use it as a seat cushion while flying. Here a parachutist demonstrates how he activates such a "seat pack" parachute after jumping clear of the airplane (Collier Trophy for 1926). Courtesy NASM.

Bottom: The Wright Whirlwind air-cooled radial engine that powered Lindbergh's *Spirit of St. Louis* across the Atlantic brought fame to its designer, Charles L. Lawrance (Collier Trophy for 1927), and quickly became the engine of choice for other long-distance fliers. Using the results of wind tunnel tests at Langley, Virginia, the National Advisory Committee for Aeronautics discovered a way to make such engines even more efficient by designing a cowling that would direct a flow of cooling air over the engine's cylinders, yet substantially reduce the amount of drag previously created by the exposed engine (Collier Trophy for 1929). Courtesy NASM.

Top: Harold F. Pitcairn's autogiro leaves a dust cloud in its wake as it dramatically departs the White House following the 1930 Collier Trophy presentation by President Herbert Hoover. Courtesy NASM.

Middle: Although propeller designers had long realized that there was no one optimum pitch (the angle at which the edge of a propeller blade cuts into the air) for all modes of flight, it remained for Frank Walker Caldwell and the Hamilton Standard Propeller Company to devise a propeller that could be adjusted, in flight, to give the best performance under every flight condition (Collier Trophy for 1933). Courtesy NASM.

Bottom: A crowd gathers around Howard Hughes's Lockheed 14 airplane, in which he and a crew of four others circled the globe in 91 hours (Collier Trophy for 1938). Courtesy NASM.

Top: Dr. Sanford A. Moss (right) explains the workings of a cutaway turbosupercharger. This device allowed combat aircraft with piston engines, such as the B-17, to operate at higher altitudes than previously thought possible (Collier Trophy for 1940). Courtesy NASM.

Bottom: A true genius of many talents, Captain Luis DeFlorez briefly worked in aviation during 1912, before going on to receive numerous patents for devices used in petroleum distillation. At the outset of World War II he returned to aviation as a U.S. Naval Reserve officer—developing a wide range of "synthetic" training devices used to simulate actual flying conditions encountered by aerial gunners and bombardiers (Collier Trophy for 1943). Courtesy NASM.

Top: On October 14, 1947, U.S. Air Force Capt. Charles Yeager became the first man to break the sound barrier while flying this Bell X-1 aircraft (named *Glamorous Glennis* after Yeager's wife). Lawrence D. Bell of Bell Aircraft Corporation and NACA research scientist John Stack shared the 1947 Collier Trophy with Yeager for making the flight possible. Courtesy U.S. Air Force.

Middle: At a ceremony in the White House Rose Garden, President John F. Kennedy awards the 1961 Collier Trophy to (left to right) pilots A. Scott Crossfield, North American Aviation; Maj. Robert M. White, USAF; and Joseph A. Walker, NASA. Their rocket-powered X-15 aircraft flew at speeds in excess of six times the speed of sound in flights that approached the lower reaches of space. Courtesy NASA.

Bottom: The B-52 Stratofortress became operational in the Cold War environment of 1955. This long-range bomber could operate at low level with a range of six thousand miles (even longer with air-to-air refueling) and a bomb payload of up to ten tons. Variations of the design remained in service throughout the Vietnam conflict (Collier Trophy for 1955). Courtesy Boeing Company archives.

Top: With its introduction in 1960, the Polaris missile became the heart of the U.S. nuclear strategic deterrence program. The missile could be launched from a submerged nuclear submarine, affording it a virtually limitless number of potential launch sites difficult to detect by an enemy (Collier Trophy for 1960). Courtesy NASM.

Bottom: The Collier Trophy is shown in the foreground of a photo of Project Mercury space capsule *Friendship 7,* which first took an American astronaut into space orbit (Collier Trophy for 1962). Courtesy Smithsonian Institution.

One of the many Americans who learned to fly as military pilots during World War I is shown standing beside a Curtiss R-2 after his first flight in 1917. The pilot is believed to be Lt. Adrian Williamson, a member of the Aero Club's Army/Navy division. Courtesy Diane Bleything.

Typical of the post–World War I pilots who made their living by barnstorming around the countryside, this unidentified "gypsy flier" and his surplus Curtiss Jenny were flying passengers for hire near Toledo, Ohio, in 1920. Grease stains on the aviator's hands and clothing testify to the fact that such pilots were often their own mechanics as well. Collection of the author.

World War I flight training programs were hard on both men and machines. Shown here are two Curtiss JN-series Jennies that probably did not survive the war to become surplus aircraft. Courtesy the family of J. Hayden Norwood.

Top: The first airplane to actually fly across the Atlantic was the Curtiss NC-4 (one of three NC boats to attempt the flight). It arrived in England, by way of Portugal, the Azores, and Newfoundland, on May 31, 1919—twenty-five days after it had left the U.S. Courtesy NASM.

Middle: The 1909 Herring-Curtiss *Golden Flyer,* whose sale to the Aeronautic Society of New York sparked the first of many lawsuits brought by the Wrights against pilots and airplane manufacturers. Glenn Curtiss is shown seated at the controls in Hammondsport, New York. Courtesy Glenn H. Curtiss Museum, Hammondsport, New York.

Bottom: Harriet Quimby, the first woman licensed by the Aero Club of America, is shown seated in a Bleriot airplane at the Moisant Aviation School, Garden City, Long Island, in 1911. Collection of the author.

Top: Flying apparatus on display at the first Aero Club of America exhibit, held in conjunction with the 1906 Automobile Club of America auto show. Courtesy William J. Hammer Collection, NASM.

Bottom: Aero Club members J. C. McCoy, C. J. Glidden, and Melvin Vaniman prepare to depart for a flight in *Aero Club No. 3* from St. Cloud, on May 13, 1908. Courtesy NASM.

A mass launching of hot air balloons at the 1991 Albuquerque International Balloon Fiesta in Albuquerque, New Mexico, illustrates how the sport has grown in popularity since Ed Yost flew the first modern hot air balloon in 1960. Copyright © 1992 Ron Behrmann.

Top: Georgia (Tiny) Broadwicke prepares to parachute from an airplane flown by Glenn Martin in 1913. The diminutive parachutist, who was the second American to parachute from an airplane, made her first parachute descent from a smoke balloon at age fourteen. Note that her single parachute is attached to the airplane above her. Courtesy NASM.

Bottom: Skydivers form the Olympic ring symbol in the air over Seoul, South Korea, as they fall at more than 100 miles per hour. The brilliantly executed maneuver was the highlight of the opening ceremonies at the 1988 Olympics. Sport parachutists from all countries hope that skydiving will eventually become an Olympic event. Courtesy Tom Sanders, Aerial Focus, Santa Barbara, California.

Top: Exhibition aviator Frank K. Miller, of Thayer County, Nebraska, pilots a Curtiss-type airplane above the grounds of the Republic County Fair at Belleville, Kansas, in September 1911. Even though this rare photo appears to be a composite of one of Miller's flights and a horse race held at a different time, it vividly conveys the atmosphere of the early airplane exhibition flights. Miller died a few weeks later when the same plane burst into flames while flying at another event in Ohio. He embarked on his final flight, in spite of the fact that his engine was not functioning properly, because the crowd had jeered at him and called him a coward. Courtesy of Virginia Priefert, Thayer County, Nebraska, Historical Society, Belvidere, Nebraska.

Bottom: An aerial view of the Experimental Aircraft Association fly-in at Oshkosh, Wisconsin, in August 1992. For the week of this annual event, the EAA's Whittman Field becomes the busiest airport in the world. Courtesy Experimental Aircraft Association, Oshkosh, Wisconsin.

William P. MacCracken, Jr., one of the principal figures who helped create the NAA in 1922. MacCracken's distinguished career included being named head of the Aeronautics Branch of the Department of Commerce—the first federal agency to regulate aviation activities. Courtesy NASM.

Officials clock then-Lt. Beverly Witherspoon and Cdr. Patrick L. Sullivan in their Navy Sikorski HSS-2 helicopter as they enter a three-kilometer course in hopes of breaking the two-hundred-mile-per-hour mark. Their speed of 192.9 miles per hour, albeit short of their goal, set a new world record. Courtesy Capt. Beverly W. Witherspoon, USN (Ret.).

Jackie Cochran emerges from her Lockheed Jetstar *Scarlet O'Hara* in 1962, after becoming the first woman to fly a jet airplane across the Atlantic Ocean. In addition to her many record-breaking flights and other aviation achievements, Cochran served as an officer of the NAA from 1955 to 1962 (including two terms as president), and was the first—and to date only—woman president of the Fédération Aeronautique Internationale (FAI). Courtesy Lockheed Aircraft Company.

Top: Jockey's Ridge, the sand dune formation from which the Wright brothers conducted many of their early gliding experiments, was the scene when pioneering Rogallo wing pilots gathered to participate in this 1976 East Coast event. Known as the Hang Gliding Spectacular, this annual event is the oldest continuously held hang gliding competition in the world. Courtesy Kitty Hawk Kites, Nag's Head, North Carolina.

Middle: The NAA's granite marker, with the Wright Memorial atop Kill Devil Hill in the background. Collection of the author. A bronze plaque on the marker (not shown from this angle) reads:

The First Successful Flight of an Airplane
was made from this spot by
ORVILLE WRIGHT
December 17, 1903, in a machine
designed and built by
WILBUR WRIGHT AND
ORVILLE WRIGHT

This tablet was erected by the
National Aeronautic Association
of the U.S.A. December 17, 1928
to commemorate the twenty-fifth
anniversary of this event

Bottom: The winner of the ill-fated Dole California-to-Hawaii race in 1927, Art Goebel is shown here with his Travel Air 5000, *Woolaroc.* Of the fifteen planes originally entered in the event, only two made it to Hawaii. Between January and September 1927, twenty-five U.S. pilots lost their lives in accidents related to such transoceanic flights. Courtesy NASM.

Jeana L. Yeager and Burt L. Rutan in a test flight of the airplane *Voyager,* which traveled more than twenty-five thousand miles in the first nonstop, non-refueled flight around the world. The flight by Yeager and Rutan captured the imagination and won the hearts of people around the world (Collier Trophy for 1986). Courtesy Pat Storch.

RENAISSANCE IN THE AIR

The National Races and International Competition

17

In spite of the Leverone/Hoyt perspective, not all aviation of the Cold War era was tied to domestic and international politics. Some future heroes were just beginning to show their abilities. Two of them were a young student from the California Institute of Technology named Paul B. MacCready, Jr., and Francis M. Rogallo of the National Advisory Committee for Aeronautics (NACA), which was later to become the National Aeronautics and Space Administration (NASA).

In both 1948 and 1949, while still in his early twenties, MacCready won top honors at the National Soaring Contest in Elmira, New York. Certainly none of those who witnessed his flights—especially the other competitors—doubted that he was an exceptionally skilled pilot. But none among them could have guessed that, thirty years later, he would achieve a goal as old as mankind's dreams of flight. For it was this young man who would later design and built a plane with the whimsical name *Gossamer Albatross*—the plane that pilot Bryan Allen, on August 23, 1977, would fly more than a mile in a figure-eight pattern to win the $200,000 Kremer Prize for the first craft to achieve controlled human-powered flight.

Rogallo was interested in low-speed flight, but he took an entirely different approach. In his search for a simple and inexpensive flying machine, he developed the flexible wing, known today as the Rogallo wing. Rogallo and his wife Gertrude began working on the flexible wing at home: his employer, NACA, was not interested in the concept, but gave him permission to pursue the project independently.

**On June 12, 1979, Bryan Allen again made history with the *Gossamer
Albatross* as he became the first person to cross the English Channel
by means of human-powered flight. Dr. Paul B. MacCready won the
1979 Collier Trophy for the conception, design, and construction of
the aircraft, with special recognition going to pilot Allen.**

In 1948 the Rogallos applied for a patent on their first flexible wing.
The prototype was a kite made from glazed chintz curtain cloth with a
floral pattern. They called it the Flexi-Kite. The Flexi-Kite flew so well
that a toy manufacturer licensed it for commercial production—thus
creating an unfortunate stigma that hindered future development of the
design. Rogallo soon adapted the flexible wing concept to gliders and
gliding parachutes, but the notion that the design was merely a toy held
it back from serious consideration by NACA.

It was not until the late 1950s that NASA, formed from NACA in
response to the Russians' successful *Sputnik* launch, "discovered" the
practical applications of Rogallo's design. NASA scientists began experimenting with flexible wing recovery systems for space capsules.[1] The
Rogallo wing would eventually be incorporated into a number of military applications, but its best-known uses in the sporting world have been
as the basis for the modern hang glider (and the ultralight airplanes it has
spawned) and the gliding parachute.

In contrast to MacCready and Rogallo's low-speed flight achievements,
another American aviator received worldwide recognition through the
NAA and FAI in 1949, but for taking flight into a new chapter of speed
and powered performance. At the annual FAI ceremonies for 1949, held
in Cleveland, Ohio, then–Capt. Charles Yeager was awarded the world's
highest aviation honor. He received an FAI gold medal for flying faster
than the speed of sound in the Bell X-1 rocket plane, an achievement for
which he shared the 1947 Collier Trophy. In accepting the gold medal,
Yeager became only the fourth American, following Charles Lindbergh,
Wiley Post, and Igor Sikorsky, to be given the FAI's most prestigious
award.

Amid other national displays of aeronautic power during the Cold War,
divisions of the NAA strove to establish U.S. superiority in all forms of
aviation. Not surprisingly, one of the most powerful, but least publicized,
of the NAA divisions led the way. In the fall of 1949 the Academy of
Model Aeronautics submitted five international model airplane speed

records to the FAI for acceptance. It was no secret that its main objective was to take away the Russians' lead. The model airplane record assault was sponsored by the Plymouth Motor Company, which made special timing facilities available to the NAA. By the end of the Plymouth meet, U.S. competitors had broken four international records for flights with various categories of model aircraft. A fifth international record—one that was also labeled a "world record" because it surpassed all previous records regardless of airplane category—was submitted to the FAI at the same time, but had actually been flown in Alameda, California, the previous month.[2]

It was hardly a smashing defeat for the Russians. Even with acceptance of the new U.S. speed records, the Russians still held the majority of international records and all but one of the world marks.[3] But the event served notice to Soviet airmen that the United States, headed by the NAA, was launching an all-out war on international records. In the next year the NAA would sanction more than two hundred model airplane competitions for the estimated three million Americans who were active participants in the sport. The NAA's renewed ambition to capture world records would last well into the 1960s and eventually involve all forms of air activities.

All of America's private aviation resources seemed to be behind the new effort to put the nation into the lead in every form of aviation— from model airplanes to rocket development and, eventually, space flight. Enthusiasm was so great that one magazine, *Southern Flight,* used the negative publicity from an air-racing tragedy as an effective forum to encourage even greater support for American flight competition. The unfortunate incident took place at the 1949 National Airplane Races in Cleveland. Race pilot Bill Odom, flying the highly modified P-51 Mustang *Beguine,* crashed into a home near the race course. Odom was killed instantly, as were a young woman and an eighteen-month-old child.

The tabloid press had a field day with the incident, decrying the NAA for sanctioning the race and condemning the use of military surplus "crates" in the competition. The newspapers demanded that such air races be immediately discontinued. But *Southern Flight* rallied to the cause, defending and even praising the activities of the NAA. The magazine pointed out that planes like Odom's were hardly rundown war surplus machines. Competitors had totally rebuilt and reengineered their planes, virtually converting them into new ones. The *Beguine,* for instance, had been modified for Texas oilman J. D. Reed at an expense of over one hundred thousand dollars. Reed sold it to Jackie Cochran, who, being

On the highest level of international competition, the United States and the Soviet Union feared each other's growing ability to deliver nuclear weapons by air. This led to a long period of escalating weapons deployment—first by airplane, then by missile—and a decades-long nuclear standoff during which each country was convinced that the other was the aggressor. To counter the Soviet threat, the United States formulated a policy of strategic deterrence, based on the assumption that the country could be best protected by possessing such devastating nuclear delivery capabilities that it would be futile for any other nation to launch an attack. The first of many missile systems designed to advance this policy was the Atlas intercontinental ballistic missile (ICBM). The U.S. Air Force, Convair (a Division of General Dynamics), and Space Technology Laboratories shared the 1959 Collier Trophy for developing the Atlas.

As a land-based missile, however, the Atlas had the shortcoming of being easily targeted, and possibly destroyed before it could be launched. The U.S. Navy's solution was to build a fleet of missile-carrying, nuclear-powered submarines capable of roaming undetected throughout the oceans of the world. Such submarines could launch their missiles from an infinite number of submerged launch sites, making it virtually impossible for them to be targeted by an enemy intent on eliminating U.S. defenses in preparation for a pre-emptive strike. The first of these Fleet Ballistic Missile submarines, the U.S.S. *George Washington,* went into service in 1960, carrying a complement of Lockheed Polaris missiles. For this achievement, Vice Adm. William F. Raborn received the Collier Trophy as the representative of the Navy-science-industry team that developed the Polaris.

---

ineligible to fly in the race herself because of restrictions against women competitors, chose Odom as the pilot. Odom was relatively inexperienced at pylon racing, but was a competent pilot. Earlier that year he had broken records flying in both directions between the U.S. mainland and Honolulu in one of Beechcraft's new Bonanzas.

Southern Flight also pointed out that such competitions were, through their association with the FAI, open to spectators and competitors from all over the world. It noted that FAI representatives from communist Poland had been shocked to see U.S. military jets perform high-speed passes at that same air meet, coming close to speeds of 630 miles per hour. The writer assured the public that such events were a showcase for American might, reminding them that it was from just such air meets that

Charles Lindbergh had brought home vital information, gathered from close-up looks at Hitler's aviation resources, before the beginning of World War II. The greater tragedy, the writer concluded, was not that the air races continued, but that the U.S. government failed to provide them with the same amount of support that its Cold War enemies afforded to similar efforts in their own countries.[4]

But the outcry was simply too loud to be stilled. In early 1950 the NAA finally gave in to public pressure and banned surplus military planes from competing in the National Airplane Races. Later that year it was decided that the competition could no longer be held over a congested metropolitan area and the era of the Cleveland Air Races came to an end.[5] For a time, at least, the thunderous roars of modified P-51s and other warbirds were silenced. They would be heard again more than a decade later over the desert sands near Reno, Nevada, but the old planes would then be flown by a new generation of pilots.

The Odom crash did not stop air racing, but it did cause the CAA to place restrictions on air show activities and the NAA to reexamine the safety of planes used in the National Airplane Races. During the ban on surplus airplanes the focus shifted toward a relatively new kind of competitor, the so-called "midget racer," which had first appeared on the official racing circuit in 1947. Throughout the 1950s these planes raced in competitions held throughout the country.

The opposite of the huge, highly modified, unlimited-horsepower military "muscle machines," the midgets had strict limitations on minimum wing area and the use of stock aircraft engines. Those restrictions and additional requirements, such as fixed landing gear, appeared to limit the top speed that such designs could ever achieve, but constant refinements moved the speed record for the class up from 165.86 to 207.27 miles per hour in the first fifteen years of competition.

The king of the midget aircraft movement was Tom Cassutt, an airline captain from Long Island. Cassutt designed a craft that, in its basic form, could be built for around six hundred dollars, plus the cost of the engine. He made blueprints of the plane available to the public, but purposely did not offer more than the basics of the design to potential builders, feeling that individual initiative and creativity were essential to the sport. Cassutt racers could be built in a year of part-time "hobby" work and had the potential of hitting speeds up to 230 miles per hour.[6]

The NAA's new emphasis on safety, brought on by the Odom incident, affected the midgets, too. The organization began requiring, rather than merely recommending, that all control surfaces of midget racers be dynamically balanced.[7] Eventually, all builders of midget racers were made to submit blueprints of their aircraft to the NAA in order to determine that they were safely constructed.[8]

An offshoot of the popularity of midget racing was that some enterprising designers turned to the compact airplane concept in efforts to make fast, affordable, factory-built light planes for the general aviation market. In 1963, *National Aeronautics* featured a sleek little prototype airplane predicted to fly 135 miles per hour and to cost as little as $2500 for a sixty-five-horsepower model. The concept was so promising—and so different—that the news release for Jim Bede's BD-1 was titled "Dare We Hope."[9]

Yet the ban on using fighter planes in closed-course racing did not exclude them from use in record attempts. And, as America entered the 1950s, it appeared that one woman had taken it upon herself to use such planes to single-handedly shatter the Russians' air records. In the first 1950 issue of *National Aeronautics,* a bold headline appeared that would be seen time and time again: "JACKIE COCHRAN SETS NEW RECORD." This time it was for setting an international speed record for propeller-driven planes by flying a P-51 an average of 444 miles per hour around a five-hundred-kilometer closed course.[10]

At the time, Cochran, a well-known racer in the early Powder Puff Derbies, already held three other open-class international speed records. Her previously set speed record for a propeller-driven plane around a two-thousand-kilometer course was even faster than times that had been turned in to date by jet airplanes, but the FAI had divided the aircraft types into separate categories shortly before her flight. Yet she was nevertheless destined to capture records in jet aircraft, flying with the advice and assistance of Chuck Yeager, and to become more involved in NAA matters by serving as the head of the 1951 American delegation to the FAI.

Other great racing pilots and airplanes set records early in 1950. Paul Mantz pushed his P-51 across the country at an average speed of 500 miles per hour, hitting speeds as high as 580 miles per hour at times. His coast-to-coast trip took less than five hours. Steve Wittman squeezed over 185 miles per hour from his homebuilt midget racer *Bonzo* on a twenty-mile course, with Phil Quigley placing fifth in the same race, flying another homebuilt plane called the *Pitts Special.*[11]

Designs like Wittman's *Bonzo* and the *Pitts Special* represented the kind of quality that could be expected from a revived grass roots aviation movement, and the NAA belatedly realized that its real strength, if it could regain it, would come from the support of local chapters all over America. "The only place I hear pessimism about NAA," wrote Mrs.

Mary Brown of the Akron chapter, "is in Washington. I have been in touch with all the NAA chapters this past month. Every one of them is working and getting more members."[12]

NAA officials proposed yet another program designed to reestablish their relationship with local chapters and special interest groups, but the effort may have represented too little, too late. Rumors began circulating that the NAA intended to discontinue its program of local chapters. In spite of fervent denials by president Leverone and his staff, the grass roots aviators lost faith in the NAA's desire to represent them.[13]

Devotees of different flying disciplines turned more to their own special interest organizations, or created new ones, to further their own forms of flying. As the Soaring Society of America and the Academy of Model Aeronautics had before them, the Experimental Aircraft Association and Parachute Club of America emerged as organizations devoted entirely to fostering one particular facet of sport aviation. The rapid growth of these new groups reflected a feeling that the NAA was not able to serve the needs of specialized flying interests.

In 1951, Leverone was replaced as president by Donald D. Webster (although Leverone remained on the NAA board as past president), and the next year Harry K. Coffey assumed the NAA's presidency.[14] Although Webster's tenure as NAA president was relatively short, he did much to make the NAA more appealing to the grass roots aviator. One of the first things Webster did was to bring former *National Aeronautics* editor Wayne W. Parrish back on board to run the magazine. Parrish had served as editor of the magazine in the mid-1930s, and had gone on to found his own publications, *American Aviation Magazine* and *American Aviation Daily.* The magazine and the NAA retained their long-stated goals of keeping America first in the air, and still printed news of national legislation, but fervent anti-Red rhetoric ceased to dominate the content of association communications. Instead, Parrish placed a greater emphasis on reporting chapter activities, featuring new developments in aircraft design, and spotlighting persons who had made significant contributions to aviation.

The first of the individuals honored in the "new" *National Aeronautics* was the man who held U.S. pilot's license number 1. William Mac-Cracken's long-time service to NAA had dated from his drafting of the association's original charter. In a ceremony held at the Aero Club of Washington, MacCracken was awarded a well-deserved honorary life membership in the NAA for twenty-nine years of service as general counsel, and for serving on or leading more than a dozen of the nation's most powerful aviation committees. President Webster characterized MacCracken as "the real daddy of American aviation, for my money."[15] The magazine again honored MacCracken in 1964, citing forty-three years of voluntary service as legal counsel to the NAA.[16]

Parrish's second term at *National Aeronautics* was short-lived, but his influence was long lasting. Other business responsibilities demanded his attention, and he was soon succeeded by Keith Saunders, a former newspaperman in North Carolina and Maryland, and an employee at Parrish's *American Aviation* magazine. Saunders, who was apparently hand-picked by Parrish as his replacement, had proven himself to be a friend of grass roots aviation in his days as aviation editor for the Baltimore *Evening Sun,* and had helped found that city's NAA chapter. For ten years, until January of 1962, he continued the tradition of good journalism rein-stated at the magazine by Parrish, presenting well-written news stories about flight activities on all levels and bringing back the often dramatic photographic illustrations long missing from the publication.

One of the first of these pictures was of NAA board member Arlene Davis and then-Maj. Chuck Yeager presenting a handsome trophy to ten-year-old Priscilla Henry, the winner of a Cleveland aeromodeling competition. Human interest articles such as this, reviews of the latest aviation books, and photos of unusual flying machines again made the NAA magazine interesting to a wide spectrum of flying enthusiasts. Throughout the 1950s and 1960s *National Aeronautics* reported aviation news from the nation and the world.

The magazine's editorial voice, although modulated, was far from stilled. Editorials continued to point out new dangers and policy prob-lems affecting pilots. One of these, peculiar to a new industry that had captured the public's eye during the 1950s, was a need for coordination between the Federal Communications Commission and aviation interests in order to control the navigation dangers created by the sudden prolifer-ation of television transmission towers. Saunders was among the first to recognize that the same centers of population that spawned air activity were the ones that attracted television station operators. He predicted, correctly, that the exploding popularity of television would result in more and higher towers being constructed, and called for the Air Coordinating Committee of the federal government to be responsive to the hazards these and other towers might present for fliers.[17]

Even though the NAA recognized the transmission tower problem early on, and tried to take steps to have federal agencies control their proliferation, the government maintained a laissez faire attitude. As a result, the problem of increasing numbers of ground-based hazards to air navigation still persists.

The magazine foresaw other issues that would grow in importance over time—among them, the restriction of airspace to use only by military aircraft[18]—but it would be the compatibility of aircraft operations with the desires of residential airport neighbors that would perhaps prove to be the most pervasive problem. Indeed, some of the events of the early 1960s might look familiar to those in general aviation today who are facing the possible closure of their local airport.

In 1955, *National Aeronautics* reported that a man whose house was nearly 1500 feet from Wichita Municipal Airport was suing that city for $25,000, charging that "tremendous wind, dust, roars, and vibrations" had devalued his property. Sadly, isolated situations involving disputes between airport operators and nearby property owners would evolve into ongoing problems throughout the country. A 1962 editorial confirmed that problems between homeowners and airports were on the rise—and that the homeowners were winning. "Almost everyone is an expert on converting an airport," noted Clyde P. Barnett, Director of Aeronautics for the State of Californa. "All the neighbors enthusiastically join any promotion that will get rid of it!" Between 1941 and 1962 the number of airports in the Los Angeles area diminished from sixty-four to eleven; nationally, the United States lost 1200 airports in twelve years. Barnett cited the vulnerability of small airports as the targets of land-hungry municipal developers:

It is always the last large "hunk" of real estate in one piece.... Chambers of Commerce see an airport only as an ideal factory site with a payroll. Real estate agents see airports as big fees for sub-divisions. Schools regard them as ideal sites for their large acreage needs. Local elected officials cannot solve this problem. They must win a popularity contest to get elected and stay elected. Airport supporters add up to less than one percent of the community.[19]

The problem is still with us, for many of the municipal airports constructed in what were then rural areas near cities and towns today face closure actions instigated by people who bought inexpensive land near the airport and built or bought their homes long after the airport was established. Even though the problem has been recognized by aviation officials for more than thirty years, it may prove to be the greatest long-term threat that general aviation faces in its first century of existence.

One of the smaller NAA affiliates began coming into its own in the 1950s, and would grow remarkably throughout the coming decades. This was the National Parachute Jumpers-Riggers, Inc. (NPJRI), a group that operated out of Mineola, New York, under the leadership of Joe Crane. Originally founded as an organization composed of a small number of exhibition jumpers, the NPJRI became the Parachute Club of America (PCA) in 1957, and, in 1968, the United States Parachute Association. It found a growing following among military parachutists and civilians who wanted to experience the thrill of falling through the air, often for thousands of feet, before deploying their canopies.

The NAA supported the efforts of this growing sport. In May 1956 it was helping to raise an estimated $25,000 to send a U.S. team to Moscow in order to compete in the Third World Championship of Parachuting. It would be the first time a U.S. team had ever competed in such a meet, and Marine Corps reservist Jacques Andre Istel was recruited to assemble the team and teach them the European technique of "skydiving." Among the recruits were George Bosworth and former overall U.S. national champions Bob Fair (1955), Lew Sanborn (1954), and Floyd Hobby (1953).[20] Sanborn later became the first person awarded a class D parachutist license, the highest rating of experience then given by the American FAI affiliate.

Sport parachuting appealed to the adventurous of all ages, civilian as well as military. As the sport began to attract more civilians, collegiate parachuting clubs emerged. In the summer of 1958 civilian and military jumpers competed against each other for the first time at the Eastern Sport Parachute Championship meet, held in New Castle, Delaware. There a nineteen-year-old sophomore from Amherst College named Stuart Rose (the youngest competitor in the meet) took top honors, winning the Mason Memorial Trophy for best individual score in accuracy jumping.[21]

In the 1940s and 1950s there were but a few parachuting enthusiasts—the PCA listed about two hundred members in 1958. By 1960 it boasted 2500 members, a number that had nearly doubled two years later. The popularity of the sport was growing, but it still suffered severely from a public perception that it was unsafe and foolhardy. In 1951 the CAA banned delayed, or freefall, parachute jumps, calling them reckless stunts. PCA President Crane sought, successfully, to have this rule rescinded, along with another requirement (imposed by twenty-two states and U.S. territories) that parachutists must possess a CAA waiver, issued before each specific jump.[22]

It was also during the 1950s that the Experimental Aircraft Association (EAA) began to show signs of how popular it would grow to be. The idea for such an association had germinated during the 1930s, when a Milwaukee teenager named Paul Poberezny had first become fascinated with aviation. Young Poberezny started, as did many of his friends, by building wooden model airplanes. When a high school history teacher gave him a Waco glider in poor repair, he not only rebuilt the plane but taught himself to fly it. Eventually he was befriended by a group of men who had, in the late 1920s, been members of a local homebuilt airplane club, the Milwaukee Lightplane Club. Their advice and guidance helped him develop the skills and knowledge needed to design and construct his own flying machine.

By the time he enlisted in the army Poberezny was already an accomplished pilot. His mechanical and flying skills were greatly increased during World War II as he earned every flight rating the army had to offer, piloting many of the military aircraft used by the United States. Once discharged, he rekindled his love of civilian flying, rebuilding and modifying a 1938 Taylorcraft.

In 1953, he and a small group of like-minded enthusiasts gathered at a Milwaukee airport for the inaugural meeting of the EAA. In less than forty years the organization grew from some thirty-five members into the largest experimental aircraft association in the world. The EAA's annual convention, today held at the association's permanent home in Oshkosh, Wisconsin, is the largest gathering of aviation enthusiasts and aircraft held anywhere.[23]

The NAA began the 1960s once again claiming to have a new look—and in at least one way it did indeed. For the first time in NAA history, the association's leader was addressed as "Madam President," as Jacqueline Cochran assumed that office. Cochran's "new look" program tried to breathe new life into the national organization by distancing it from the various special interest divisions. She attempted to convert regional membership divisions into separate aero clubs, encouraging members-at-large to ally themselves with, or form, such clubs. She saw the role of the NAA as an organization whose mission was to be primarily involved with issues at the national level: keeping the public aware of the importance of aviation to national security; pressing the federal government to foster programs that would keep the United States first in the space race; encouraging aviation and space education at all levels of learning; encouraging U.S. pilots to make, and sanctioning, record-breaking flights; and recognizing those who had made outstanding contributions to the advancement of aviation.[24]

Jackie, as she was known to friends, had served as first vice president under Thomas G. Lanphier, Jr.,[25] before her election to head the NAA. She was the kind of individual who would not take no for an answer when asking for assistance for the NAA from government or industry.

She even went so far as to invest in the association some of the personal assets she and her wealthy husband, Floyd Odlum, had amassed.

John Alison, a retired Air Force major general, former vice president of Northrop Aircraft Corporation, and later president of the NAA, recalled the first time he met Cochran:

I attended an NAA board meeting with my boss at Northrop, Whit Collins. There were representatives of ten large aviation concerns present at the meeting and Jackie told them that the NAA needed some money and she expected each of them to contribute $25,000. They knew that they were facing a pilot and business person as tough as any around, and the easiest way to deal with Jackie was to go along with her. When the meeting was adjourned, the NAA had $250,000 in contributions.[26]

Cochran was driven to shatter records and she aspired to have the NAA assist others in putting American names at the top of every FAI list. Month after month, *National Aeronautics* printed long lists of new marks set by American pilots in every form of aircraft. On June 3, 1964, the president herself set three world records in a Lockheed F-104G, including a women's speed record of 1429.297 miles per hour.[27] At the time she held more world flying records than any other pilot. In an era when breaking world records demonstrated U.S. technical and military superiority throughout the world, Jackie Cochran was the supreme symbol of strength.

Another of the many pilots who promoted the United States by pushing a flying machine to its limits was then-Lt. Beverly (Bev) Witherspoon. On May 17, 1961, he and Commander Patrick L. Sullivan tried to take a Navy Sikorsky HSS-2 helicopter beyond the two-hundred-mile-per-hour mark. They fell short of their goal, but their speed of 192.9 miles per hour was a new world record for helicopters flying over a three-kilometer course, breaking the Soviet-held helicopter speed record by more than twenty-five miles per hour.[28]

Looking back at that period of record attempts, Bev Witherspoon recalls the NAA's procedure for certifying the event:

At the time, Commander Sullivan and I were test pilots at Patuxent River, Maryland. We were evaluating the Sikorsky HSS-2 for acceptance by the navy during the year that just happened to be the fiftieth anniversary of U.S. naval aviation. The navy wanted to celebrate the event by setting as many records as they could, so they sent us to Windsor Locks, Connecticut, where the Sikorsky factory had a three-kilometer course already laid out.

The course was marked by four pylons, all set in a row. We would approach the outer pylon at as high a speed as we could attain, using it to help establish a straight track. The two inner pylons marked the actual three-kilometer course: while passing between them we had to hold a level, or climbing, flight path. After we had completed a pass in one direction, we had to turn around and fly the course the other way.

The NAA officials, who used cameras linked with timing devices to measure our rate of travel between the two inner pylons, then averaged the two speeds together to eliminate any advantage a tailwind might have given us. On some of our straight runs, we actually did break the two-hundred-mile-per-hour mark.[29]

International record-breaking helicopter flights like those of Witherspoon and Sullivan would eventually evolve into direct competition among helicopter pilots of all nations. In later years the Helicopter Club of America emerged to support the efforts of U.S. pilots in international meets, and an organization known as the "Whirly-Girls" encouraged women to become helicopter pilots.

And an entirely new category of flying machines took to the air in the early 1960s. When, on May 5, 1961, Cdr. Alan Shepard was thrust into space inside a Mercury capsule atop a Redstone missile, he established two records in new categories only recently developed by the FAI: "altitude without earth orbit" and "greatest mass lifted without earth orbit." When the rocket left its Cape Canaveral launch pad at the start of its historic journey, FAI president Jacques Allez and NAA president Cochran witnessed the departure, then tracked the progress of the flight from within the Mercury Control Center.

It was a spectacular flight, but one overshadowed by a trip made a month earlier in which a Russian cosmonaut, Maj. Yuri Gagarin, achieved space flight with earth orbit. Petitions by the Aero Club of Russia for the FAI to recognize the Gagarin space flight were, at first, met with a great deal of suspicion by noncommunist FAI members. The Russian government, unlike that of the United States, conducted its space flight in utmost secrecy. Many of those who lived outside the Iron Curtain doubted the Russian claims and insisted that records could only be certified if the flights had been witnessed by FAI representatives from nations not involved in the flight. Eventually the Russians did provide sufficient documentation of their space flight to the FAI and the Gagarin records were certified. At the FAI's fifty-fourth General Conference, held in Monaco during October 1961, Gagarin received the FAI gold medal for making the first manned orbital space flight.[30]

Such space age accomplishments spawned a new organization that became, for a time, an associate of the NAA. In 1957 a small group of model rocket builders formed the National Association of Rocketry (NAR). These were aero modelers of the space age. Their concerns for safety dictated that model rockets be built of light, safe materials like balsa wood and cardboard, and powered by factory-built engines. These rules distinguished them from so-called "amateur rocket builders," who made their own (often dangerous) engines and launched metal rockets. By the early 1960s the NAR had nearly one thousand members.[31]

In January 1962, Cochran became chairperson of the NAA's board of directors and Martin Decker assumed the presidency. A year later, a grateful board unanimously awarded Cochran the honorary title of "NAA President for Life." (Privately some now admit that they were grateful the strong-willed woman was gone!) Decker's NAA faced a large responsibility—helping to raise enough money to support an international aviation competition. For the first time, the United States was to host a championship event in the FAI's "Olympics of the Air." The 1962 World Parachuting Championships were slated for August at the Orange, Massachusetts, parachuting center, but there were early doubts as to whether the United States would support the event in a manner comparable to the efforts of the Europeans and Soviets in hosting their events.[32]

America had earned the honor of hosting the 1962 event after the U.S. Army's Golden Knights took top honors in the 1961 competition held in Paris. In the year leading up to the Orange championship, the Army team barnstormed America, changing the image of parachuting from county fair sideshow to precise aerial sport. In February and March 1962, the Army team filed no less than nineteen claims with the FAI for new international parachuting records—most of the previous recordholders had been from the USSR.[33]

When the time for the international competition finally arrived, both Orange and the U.S. competitors were ready. Out of a field of teams from eighteen nations, Americans took the world men's and women's titles, third place in men's team accuracy, and first in women's team accuracy. Americans also finished second and third in men's individual accuracy and second in men's individual style. For a country that had long condemned parachuting as an unsafe carnival act, it was a remarkable showing against competitors with nearly unlimited governmental support.[34]

Much of America's own support for the parachutists grew out of a fascinating perspective on the sport gained through the eyes of its participants. Even decidedly land-bound magazine readers were able to snatch astonished glimpses of what freefalling away from an airplane looked like when Bob Buquor and Army SFC Joe Gonzales strapped cameras to their helmets to record the sport as only another skydiver could. The color and breathtaking beauty of their fellow skydivers, engaged in an aerial ballet, portrayed the sport correctly for the first time. No longer could "wuffos"[35] imagine skydiving as a trial of terror endured only by those harboring a death wish. Here, before their eyes, was a celebration of life.[36]

The 1960s also marked a revival of the earliest form of flying, reborn through modern technology. Descendants of the hot air "smoke balloons" emerged, with huge, colorful bags bloated from the discharge of liquid propane burners. This new adaptation of the oldest flying machine had been developed under a contract from the Office of Naval Research. Enterprising homebuilders soon manufactured their own hot air balloons, and commercial models, called Vulcoons, were first manufactured for the civilian market in 1962 by Raven Industries.

No sooner were the new hot air balloons flying than a need to hold competition among them arose. At the 1961 St. Paul, Minnesota, Winter Carnival, University of Minnesota student Tracy Barnes won the first annual Jean Piccard Trophy for thermal balloon racing by navigating his homebuilt balloon to within two hundred feet of a predesignated target. Within two years the FAI voted to recognize hot air balloons as a special category for record attempts and international competition. Peter Pellegrino of the Balloon Federation of America and Frances L. Shields of the Balloon Club of America represented U.S. interests at the Paris meeting.[37]

At the same time a small group of aerobatics enthusiasts were, like the parachutists, also having their first experiences competing against well-trained European and Soviet aviation athletes. In 1962, a volunteer U.S. aerobatic team using clipped-wing Taylorcrafts and a borrowed Great Lakes biplane traveled to Budapest, Hungary, to face well-equipped Soviet fliers. It was only the third time the United States had entered international aerobatic competition. Three pilots represented the United States at the Hungarian meet: Rod Joclyn of Ottsville, Pennsylvania, Lindsey Parsons of Trenton, New Jersey, and Duane Cole of Fort Wayne, Indiana. Famed aerobatic pilot Bevo Howard headed the contingent, which also included a team coach, William Barber of Pinkney, Michigan, and technicians William Denight and Robert Nance.[38] Mike Murphy, of Findley, Ohio, served on the FAI international board of judges.

When the winners were announced on July 26, 1962, the United States finished fourth in team competition and Lindsey Parsons won fifth place (out of thirty-two pilots) in individual standings.[39] Perhaps though the real victory, in both the international aerobatic and skydiving competitions, was that Americans and Communist-bloc aviators found a common bond of friendship that transcended years of Cold War hostilities.

The aerobatic pilots had their own Aerobatic Club of America, sanctioned by the NAA. In 1970, internal dissent over contest operations, and feelings that the Aerobatic Club catered only to a rather small and elite group, led to the formation of the International Aerobatic Club (IAC), a Division of the EAA. In 1981 the NAA shifted its alliance from the Aerobatic Club of America to the IAC, feeling that the IAC might develop a program that would encourage a greater number of people to become involved in aerobatic flight. Since that time the IAC has remained America's NAA and FAI affiliate.

Even while American pilots were thawing some of the Cold War's tension behind the Iron Curtain, there were signs that a hot war might be slowly developing in Southeast Asia. In early 1962, *National Aeronautics* reported that more than four thousand American military personnel were stationed in the remote country of Vietnam. At the same time, five thousand more military men were undergoing training at Fort Bragg, North Carolina. These new "Special Troops," soon to be known as the Special Forces, were being groomed to act as "advisors" to the government of South Vietnam. But the advisors there were already suffering casualties.[40]

That summer the NAA held its annual Collier Trophy ceremony on the White House grounds. The activities began as President John F. Kennedy escorted the four award recipients, all test pilots in the X-15 program, from the Executive Office to the Rose Garden. Before one hundred guests and a score of newspeople, the President presented replicas of the trophy to Maj. Robert White, U.S. Air Force, Joseph A. Walker, NASA, Scott Crossfield, North American Aviation (the first man to fly faster than twice the speed of sound and also to fly faster than Mach 3 and survive the attempt), and Cmdr. Forrest S. Petersen, U.S. Navy. Following the White House ceremonies the recipients adjourned to a reception at a Washington hotel. There Congressman J. B. Williams of Mississippi addressed more than five hundred celebrants, pointing out that each of the X-15 pilots had begun his flying career by learning to fly in a Piper Cub or a similar general aviation aircraft. He cautioned America not to allow the "gap between the 70 mph Cub and the 17,000 mph space capsule" to grow so large that aspiring youth would not be able to pursue the same dreams as the Collier Trophy winners.[41]

Contributing writers to *National Aeronautics* also reflected the congressman's concern. In 1963 William MacCracken, who had provided legal counsel to the NAA since its conception, wrote an article in which he modified his support for the NAA's founding stance that "bigger and better airports" were the way to "make America first in the air." He called for small airports and heliports to be created in every community so that the trip up the ladder of pilot development could start in the small towns and reach to the stars. He reminded the American public that, on his return from Paris, Charles Lindbergh had toured the United States (under NAA sponsorship) to promote local airport construction, and urged that America follow Lindbergh's advice.[42]

Aviation writer Don Berliner also responded to the issue in the pages of *National Aeronautics*. He lamented that youth of the 1960s had few of the same opportunities to fly that had been afforded to young men and women of previous years. He pointed out that many children were fascinated with flying from an early age, but that children of the 1960s might not have the means to follow their childhood dreams. Gone were the days when an aspiring young pilot could swap a plane "wash job" for a ride in the freshly cleaned machine. No longer could a kid perform line service in exchange for flight instruction from a small fixed-base operator. Aviation was becoming too formal and bottom-line oriented. Even the starry-eyed boys and girls who had once hung onto the airport fence to watch pilots land and take off were being chased away by commercial operators who did not want them in the way. The only way such an operator would teach a young person was if he or she were able to pay the tuition—a cost few aspiring teenaged pilots, no matter how much they were willing to work, could afford. High school aeronautics programs, once an option in nearly every wartime curriculum, had all but disappeared. The CAP had reduced its youth programs to text study and uniformed drills, offering little or no opportunity for their cadets to learn how to actually operate a plane.[43]

In a companion article to Berliner's, William Strohmeier pleaded the case for those who were more advanced in their education. He urged college administrators to support campus flying clubs because of the maturity and confidence that their activities inspired in student members. He encouraged college men and women—even those not aspiring to careers as airline or military pilots—to learn to fly, pointing out that the ability to travel long distances quickly, on one's own schedule, was an invaluable asset for persons in sales, management, and engineering. Strohmeier was himself an excellent example of this kind of flight-oriented college graduate. His successful career as a national aviation advertising and sales executive had begun in 1935 when he was elected the first president of the National Intercollegiate Flying Club, formed under the NAA.[44]

Yet counterbalancing forces were at work. The immense popularity of America's space program served to stimulate interest in aviation and to aid in the preservation of America's aviation heritage. In February 1962, Lt. Col. John Glenn traveled eighty-one thousand miles in the nation's first orbital space flight. Over the next year his space capsule, *Friendship 7,* traveled an equal distance on land in a masterful effort to promote constituent support for the space program. This enthusiasm was further heightened when, on October 10, 1963, President Kennedy presented the Collier Trophy to the seven original Project Mercury astronauts, for whom the capsule had been named.

The space capsule drew crowds of the curious throughout its tour of America, but its attraction did not stop when the traveling exhibit did. Twelve months after the conclusion of its historic space flight, *Friendship 7* took a place of honor beneath Lindbergh's *Spirit of St. Louis* in a cramped facility of the Smithsonian Institution. Again, the crowds wanting to see the first U.S. space capsule to orbit the earth were overwhelming. In a move that reflected brilliant timing, the Smithsonian took advantage of the momentum generated by this enthusiasm to ask Congress for help in creating a permanent home for historic air and space craft. The ambitious project resulted in the world's most-visited collection of flying machines: the National Air & Space Museum in Washington, D.C.

Although a new era was born in space that year, 1963 also marked the death of the NAA's last living tie to its earliest glory as the Aero Club of America. That July, the aviation community mourned as the ashes of Gen. Frank P. Lahm fell to earth from an Army plane flying over Randolph Field, Texas, the Army's first Air Corps training base. The symbolic gap in a formation of T-33 jets flying the "missing man" formation should have been wide that day. Gone was the Wright Brothers' first Army flying student. Gone was the man who had brought honor to America by winning the first international flying meet, the James Gordon Bennett International Balloon Race. Gone was the only aviator to hold licenses issued by the Aero Club of America in all categories of early flying machines: Balloon Pilot number 4; Airplane Pilot number 2; Dirigible Pilot number 2; and Expert Aviator number 15. And gone was a dedicated American military officer of the highest rank and character.

Lahm's death came only months before the sixtieth anniversary of the Wrights' flight at Kitty Hawk. On that occasion pilots of all nations, and from all parts of the country, came together to pay homage to the Fathers of Flight. In Washington, D.C., the NAA, at a dinner hosted by the Aero Club of Washington presented the annual Wright Memorial Trophy to Donald Douglas, Sr., president of Douglas Aircraft and father of the DC-3. In Los Angeles, famed actor and U.S. Air Force Reserve Brig. Gen. Jimmy Stewart introduced Gen. Curtis LeMay, who spoke to sixteen hundred people attending the fourth annual Timers Aero Club[45] Wright Day Banquet. The Aero Club of Greater Kansas City marked the day with ceremonies and a talk by William P. Lear, Sr., who told the assembly about the test flights of his new prototype plane, the Learjet. And in Kitty Hawk, the nation and the state of North Carolina dedicated a new airport at the foot of Kill Devil Hill. Following the airport dedication, an exact, life-sized replica of the original Kitty Hawk plane, donated by the American Institute of Aeronautics and Astronautics, was installed in the two-year-old First Flight Museum and Visitors' Center.[46]

In the winter of 1963, a former NAA vice president undertook the dual role of NAA president and editor of the NAA magazine. Upon assuming office, William A. Ong broke with the long-standing tradition of announcing that the NAA would be revamped into a new and modern organization. Ong, in fact, entered the arena stating that he would scrap Jacqueline Cochran's "new look" program, instituted in 1961 and continued through 1963. To Ong, the "old look" was more appealing.[47] Cochran's programs had succeeded remarkably well in encouraging Americans who wanted to set new world aviation records, but they had lost touch with the regional and special interest divisions and almost entirely neglected the members-at-large. As in the founding days of the NAA, when all the presidents had been wealthy leaders of industry, Cochran sometimes kept things going by bearing expenses out of her own pocket or by soliciting sizable contributions from personal acquaintances. When she stepped aside, the organization found itself suffering financially. "Whatever Jackie decided she wanted, Jackie got," recalled fifty-year NAA board member and former Soaring Society of America president Floyd Sweet. "That was the way it was with her—if she said she was going to set a flying record, you could bet that she would do it. And she was the same way with the NAA. If she thought the NAA should do something, well, she would pay for it herself if she had to."[48]

Under Ong the NAA renewed an old commitment to lend maximum assistance to its divisions. Although he did not attack Cochran directly, Ong criticized many of the changes she had made to the NAA. He made a concerted effort to bring individuals back into the organization as members-at-large, assuring them that their participation was both wanted

Pilots and engineers associated with space and lunar exploration dominated the recipients of the Collier Trophy during the 1960s and early 1970s, but producers of Cold War hardware also shared some of the glory. Beginning with the 1961 Collier award, given to X-15 rocket plane pilots Maj. Robert M. White, U.S. Air Force, Joseph A. Walker, NASA, A. Scott Crossfield, North American Aviation, and Cdr. Forrest Petersen, U.S. Navy, the separate branches of the military were recognized for their members' contributions to the space program. Each branch was anxious to have one of its own become the first American into space.

Nearly all branches of the U.S. military were represented by the winners of the 1962 Collier as well. It is appropriate that the seven Project Mercury astronauts, after whom the space capsule *Friendship 7* was named, shared in the trophy for pioneering American manned space flight. They were: Lt. Cmdr. M. Scott Carpenter (U.S. Navy), Maj. L. Gordon Cooper (U.S. Air Force), Lt. Col. John H. Glenn, Jr. (U.S. Marine Corps), Maj. Virgil I. Grissom (U.S. Air Force), Cmdr. Walter M. Schirra, Jr. (U.S. Navy), Cmdr. Alan B. Shepard, Jr. (U.S. Navy), and Maj. Donald K. Slayton (U.S. Air Force). Of these seven, Alan Shepard was the first into space, but to John Glenn went the honor of being the first American to orbit the earth.

In the wake of the 1960 U-2 incident, in which Francis Gary Powers's secret spy plane was shot down over Russia, American military officials sought planes that would fly still higher and faster. One of the designs that came out of these efforts was that for the U.S. Air Force A-11. This aircraft, produced by Clarence L. (Kelly) Johnson and a group of engineers working in Lockheed's "Skunk Works," won the 1963 Collier Trophy. Another famous plane turned out by the Skunk Works only a few years later remained a secret for more than a decade—it was the SR-71 Blackbird, a high-altitude reconnaissance plane capable of flying more than two thousand miles per hour. Still another secret aircraft with a heritage rooted in Johnson's Skunk Works, the F-117A Stealth fighter, would earn the Collier for Benjamin R. Rich, and his Lockheed team, and the U.S. Air Force more than a quarter-century after the A-11 in 1989. Stealth technology would not have to wait long thereafter to show that its name was well deserved, as it served as the front line of aerial offense in Operation Desert Storm in 1991.

NAA officials presented the 1964 Collier Trophy to U.S. Air Force Gen. Curtis E. LeMay "For development of high performance aircraft, missiles and space systems which in 1964 significantly expanded the frontiers of American aeronautics and astronautics." LeMay had been affiliated with the U.S. Air Force Research and Development Division throughout the creation of the ICBM, and was a staunch believer that military control was just as critical in space in the 1960s as it had been in the air in the 1940s. An equally firm advocate of the use of air power in combat, LeMay later gained notoriety during the Johnson administration as the general who suggested that the North Vietnamese be "bombed back to the stone age."[49]

The latter half of the 1960s took America toward the moon in steps that were measured by almost annual Collier recognition. In 1965, James E. Webb and Hugh L. Dryden accepted the Collier trophy on behalf of the entire team of the Gemini program, which put U.S. astronauts into orbit for increasing lengths of time, conducting experiments to determine how humans could best adapt to living in the environs of space. James S. McDonnell, of McDonnell Aircraft (later to become McDonnell Douglas Corporation), won the 1966 Collier for "his leadership and perseverance in advancing aeronautics and astronautics exemplified by the F-4 Phantom aircraft and the Gemini space vehicles." Lawrence A. Hyland accepted the next Collier in 1967, as the representative of the Surveyor Program team at Hughes Aircraft Company, the NASA Jet Propulsion Laboratory, and other organizations that helped land remote photographic and data collection devices on the surface of the moon.

Exploration of the moon continued to be the priority of the U.S. space program, leading Apollo VIII Col. Frank Borman (U.S. Air Force), Capt. James A. Lovell, Jr. (U.S. Navy), and Lt. Col. William A. Anders (U.S. Air Force) to the 1968 Collier for the first manned lunar orbit. In 1969 the trophy was awarded to another Apollo team: Neil A. Armstrong, Col. Edwin E. Aldrin, Jr. (U.S. Air Force), and Col. Michael Collins (U.S. Air Force), received the award for the Apollo XI lunar mission, from which the world heard the electrifying words "The *Eagle* has landed." The giant steps for mankind continued as another Apollo crew won the Collier for lunar exploration again in 1971, when Col. David R. Scott, Col. James B. Irwin, and Lt. Col. Alfred M. Worden, all Air Force astronauts on the Apollo XV mission, shared the trophy with aerospace engineer Dr. Robert T. Gilruth. The explorers who were the first to use a motorized vehicle for exploration of the lunar surface were thus, fittingly, honored by an organization that had had its origins with a group of automobile enthusiasts in the days when the practicality of the horseless carriage had barely been proven.

and appreciated. A lack of financial resources forced him to reduce *National Aeronautics* to a quarterly magazine and to eliminate flying news that was not directly related to the NAA. His job, difficult under the best circumstances, was made even more unpleasant by two unfortunate occurrences. First Arlene Davis, a longtime board member and an active participant in operational affairs, passed away in July 1964. Then, while delivering his report at the NAA's annual meeting in Washington, Lucien DeTar, a regional vice-president, board member, and representative of the Aero Club of Kansas City, fell dead of a heart attack.[50]

William Ong remained president through 1965, keeping the organization functioning through difficult years. He tried to promote individual interest in the NAA by getting board approval for a plan that automatically made members of any NAA division also members of the NAA. But, with the assassination of Kennedy and the military action in Vietnam clearly escalating into an undeclared war, the nation seemed to lose much of the enthusiasm it had shown earlier in the decade. Save for a few notable exceptions (most conspicuously a flight by the Lockheed YF-12A that exceeded two thousand miles per hour), American record attempts slumped. In 1965 Ong gave up the presidency and attorney Edward C. Sweeney, the NAA's treasurer since 1932, succeeded him. Ong remained with the NAA as editor of *National Aeronautics* and chairman of the board of directors.

The decade of the 1960s closed on a particularly sad note. On September 19, 1969, William MacCracken died. With his passing the nation lost a devoted fighter for freedom in the American skies. He had drafted the NAA's first constitution and served the association for nearly forty-seven years, volunteering his assistance as general counsel for much of that time. He was a longtime friend of Orville Wright, Amelia Earhart, Charles Lindbergh, and countless others among those who built American aviation. He was the first leader of the governmental body that would eventually evolve into the FAA. He was the holder of the U.S. government's pilot license number 1, but was first in many ways beyond that. He was America's guardian of the Golden Age of Aviation.

POSTSCRIPT:
A RETURN TO ITS ROOTS

The NAA from the 1960s to Today

In the eighty-seven years since the Aero Club was first chartered, the role of first that organization, and then the NAA, has constantly evolved, adapting to the influence of a technological phenomenon that grew from a county fair curiosity into an integral part of modern society. As aviation grew more complex, and the needs of American aviators more diversified, it was inevitable that the scope of no one organization could remain all-encompassing. And so it was with the NAA, retaining its time-honored responsibilities as the American arm of the FAI and the presenter of this nation's highest honor for achievement in flight, even as new organizations formed to meet the specific needs of pilots in a multiplicity of new forms of aviation. The story of the evolution of these younger aviation groups—which signal a renaissance of sorts of many of the earliest forms of aviation in which the original Aero Club was involved—will enable the reader to understand the role of the modern NAA, and how it differs from the organization that was once at the center of all aviation in this country.

Throughout the 1950s and 1960s, the era gradually ended in which the NAA played an active role as a leader in national aviation policy and development. Both the commercial aviation industry and military aviation—two of the three primary causes long nurtured by the Aero Club and the NAA—matured into self-sustaining entities. The third of the NAA's three causes, sport aviation, became increasingly segmented as separate interest groups formed around each of the sporting activities.

The new environment of American aviation redefined the traditional role of the NAA. It became far more limited in scope, but hardly less important, than in previous decades. By the end of the 1960s, the NAA's chief role was that of serving as the American arm of the FAI. It remains today the official body in the United States that homologates (sanctions) attempts to break aviation records, maintains those records, and presents many of the nation's most prestigious awards for achievement in aviation and aerospace.

A summary of the NAA's activities in the last quarter century shows an interesting change in the relationship of the organization to the various forms of sporting aviation that it and its predecessor, the Aero Club of America, once helped to establish. No longer does the NAA serve as the parent organization, nurturing fledgling flying activities as they grow; it is more like a grandparent who records the remarkable achievements of fully grown, and independent, children and grandchildren. Symbolic of this change was the 1991 decision by the former "divisions" of the NAA to change their classification to the less subservient-sounding "air sport organizations."

Although the last twenty-five years or so of NAA history have been characterized by a constant struggle to remain economically viable, in the context of its eighty-five-year history, the organization today is emerging from another critical period during which the needs of American aviation have redefined its role. Occasionally during other such periods of readjustment, there have been those who have wondered if the NAA has become an archaic vestige of a past era, with no real place in the present aviation community. For the answer to this question one need look only to the achievements of American pilots. Their ability to continually expand the frontiers of flight through the application of new skills, knowledge, and technology has repeatedly confirmed that an organization that serves as the American arm of the FAI is essential. Above all else, the modern NAA is that organization.

Upon succeeding William Ong as president, Edward Sweeney chose one of the oldest endeavors of both the Aero Club and the NAA as his theme for a new administration. Inspired by a story told by Thompson Trophy recipient Col. Robert Stephens—in which Stephens related his childhood vow to someday emulate the 1934 Thompson Trophy winner, Roscoe Turner—Sweeney determined to use his office to promote activities that would engage youth in aviation. He declared that the theme for his first year as NAA president would be "Interest Our Youngsters in Aeronautics," and encouraged all members to "get away from special personal interests and endeavor to work with our youngsters so they will be better prepared to take over the duties of keeping aviation and aeronautics in the top position it so well deserves."[1] One can imagine that Sweeney, who was also a member of the U.S. Subversive Activities Control Board,[2] was influenced in his concern for American youth by a growing number of college campus protests. Images of students invading a hearing of the House Un-American Activities Committee in a well-televised San Francisco "sit-in" must have further convinced him that American youth badly needed the kind of help the NAA could offer. Both he and James Nields, who succeeded him as president of the NAA, pursued positive endeavors throughout a time of extreme civil unrest, but it was newly retired Air Force Maj. Gen. Brooke Allen who, as executive director of the NAA, truly met the new generation of aviators on their own turf.

Interestingly, some forms of aviation provided a common meeting ground for members of the hippie generation and their more conservative contemporaries. In the late 1960s and 1970s it was not uncommon to see crew-cut army parachutists competing at skydiving meets alongside long-haired, bearded skydiving teams with names like The Fabulous Furry Freak Brothers. Some of those who sought a sense of freedom in those years found it in the sky, particularly as parachutists and hang glider pilots.

In an interview with Allen and former NAA president John Alison, Allen recalled the first time that he attended a board of directors meeting of the Parachute Club of America (soon to become the United States Parachute Association) as a representative of the NAA:

Since the PCA was a division of the NAA, they were entitled to a position on our board, and we on theirs. When I told [then] NAA board chairman Bill Ong that I was going to one of their meetings, he advised me, "Don't go down there, General, those people will eat you alive!" Well, as it turned out, they did! They didn't care if I was a general or anything else—what they wanted to know was why they were paying money into the NAA, and the association seemed to be ignoring them—and they were right. After that I worked very hard to try to establish a close relationship between the NAA and the members of all its divisions.

Asked if he had problems dealing with the free-thinking young people whose appearance was often quite different from that of those he had

The late 1960s and early 1970s were times of paradoxical events in America's aviation development. Sport and recreational pilots experienced new highs of freedom, flying in the safety of U.S. air-space, while military pilots fought to preserve the purest form of that freedom as they streaked over the rugged terrain of Vietnam. Of all the wars in which Americans ever fought, it was perhaps the one that enjoyed the least popular support, yet the officers who led the NAA through those turbulent years had the skill and the courage to recognize impartially heroes on all fronts, based solely on their achievements.

In contrast to the tiny hang gliders and ultralight aircraft that be-came so popular in the late 1960s, the NAA presented the 1970 Col-lier Trophy to the Boeing Company for putting the first jumbo jet, the Boeing 747, into service. First proposed as a design in 1966 (Pan American placed an order for twenty-five planes while it was still on the drawing board), the 747 actually flew for the first time in Febru-ary 1969. Seating as many as 550 passengers (long-range versions seat fewer people as a tradeoff for increased fuel storage), the 747 has proven to be one of the mainstays of aviation by serving both the military and the air transport industry. In 1973 the U.S. Air Force contracted with Boeing for modified 747s designed to be used as advance airborne command posts, and in 1977 a Boeing model 747–123 made the first successful flight as a "piggyback" carrier for the space shuttle *Enterprise*. The Boeing Company again received the Collier in 1982, when the Company and T. A. Wilson were awarded the trophy for building on the success of the 747 with the 757- and 767-series aircraft. These new series of "jumbo jets" could be config-ured to carry as many as 255 passengers on medium-distance flights (the number of passengers carried varied from model to model, de-pending on the fuel requirements for the plane's intended purpose), or could travel for an estimated 2900 miles with a smaller passenger load.[3]

Most news stories of the early 1970s were, of course, about the war in Vietnam. On December 19, 1972, a series of intensive bomb-ing raids aimed at forcing the North Vietnamese back to the Paris peace talks began under the code name "Linebacker II." For twelve days U.S. forces relentlessly pounded North Vietnamese targets. They used B-52s that saturated areas with large numbers of conventional bombs, and fighter-bombers equipped with a new line of highly ac-curate "smart bombs" that were guided to their targets by laser beams or video cameras. By December 30, the North Vietnamese resumed earnest efforts to negotiate a peace, and President Richard Nixon ordered a halt to "Linebacker II." Less than a month later,

Henry Kissinger and Le Duc Tho signed a cease-fire agreement between the United States and North Vietnam. The personnel of operation "Linebacker II"—coordinated by Adm. Thomas H. Moorer and carried out by the officers and men of Navy Task Force 77 and the 7th and 8th Air Forces—were awarded the Collier Trophy for 1972.

The success of aircraft in Vietnam renewed government recognition that it was crucial for the United States not to fall behind in military air superiority. Two offshoots of this continued development won the Collier Trophy in successive years: David S. Lewis, the General Dynamics Corporation, and the U.S. Air Force shared the 1975 Collier for development of the F-16 fighter plane, a Mach 2 aircraft armed with a 20-mm cannon that was chosen as a key fighter plane by the air forces of several NATO organizations.[4] The Air Force again shared honors in 1976, this time with Rockwell International Corporation, for the design, development, management, and flight testing of the B-1 strategic aircraft system. But not all of the greatest achievements in American aviation during the 1970s related to air and space craft. Another development arising out of needs discovered during the Vietnam conflict won the Collier Trophy in 1977. Gen. Robert J. Dixon, Commander of the Air Force's Tactical Air Command, received the honor for creating "Red Flag," a simulated combat flight training program.

One of the last Collier recipients for the 1970s and one of the earliest recipients in the 1980s were to play a significant role in a war still a decade away. The 1978 Collier Trophy went to Sam B. Williams, of Williams Research Corporation, and the 1983 award went to the U.S. Army and Hughes Aircraft Helicopters. Williams developed a very efficient small turbofan engine that was capable of powering a new, surgically accurate, guided weapon. The U.S. Army and Hughes Helicopter collaborated on a replacement for the gunship model of the UH-1 Huey helicopter that had been the multipurpose workhorse in Vietnam. The Apache eclipsed the Huey Cobra as the premier helicopter gunship of the U.S. military. Designed to be able to withstand much heavier hostile fire than the Huey, the twin-engined Apache (the early UH-1s had been single-engine helicopters) also had much-improved fire control capability and could be equipped with an extensive array of weaponry.[5] In 1991 both the cruise missile and the AH-64 Apache helicopter contributed substantially to victory in Operation Desert Storm.

recently commanded, Allen replied, "I had to bite my lip a lot at first, but I soon learned that they had a great deal to say that needed to be heard." To which John Alison added, "The skydivers of the 1960s and '70s were a bunch of people who tended to be 'rugged individualists,' but you need to remember that it was exactly that kind of person who made this country in the first place."[6]

Over the past quarter century the NAA has witnessed a resurgence of many flying activities that have origins dating back to the earliest days of the Aero Club. Given new life through modern materials and technology, and re-pioneered by the same sort of "rugged individualists" that John Alison found in the skydiving movement, ballooning, aero modeling, hang gliding, ultralight aircraft flying, and homebuilt aircraft construction, as well as skydiving, have all experienced a renaissance.

A new version of one of the oldest forms of flying reemerged as a sport in the 1960s. It too was pioneered by youthful, free-thinking individualists. These latter-day disciples of Lilienthal, Chanute, Montgomery, and the Wrights began flying by building bamboo, wood, and polyethylene hang gliders, then launching them, with varying degrees of success, from available hills, slopes, dunes, or cliffs. Their designs were based on the flexible wing flying machines developed by Francis Rogallo and his wife in the late 1940s and 1950s.[7]

These new flying machines were both interesting and photogenic. A photo published in a North Carolina newspaper, showing a Utah hang glider pilot in flight, so excited one reader that he called the pilot and bought a hang glider kit from him sight unseen. Once the hang glider kit had been put together, and after watching a home movie of launches and landings that the dealer sent along with the glider, John Harris and his friend Otto Horton set out for Jockey's Ridge (near Kitty Hawk) to teach themselves to fly as the Wright Brothers had. There they were joined by Ralph Buxton, a Washington, D.C., enthusiast. Flights made by this informal "club" attracted a great deal of attention from tourists to the Outer Banks, and soon the men found themselves teaching others how to fly. Harris and Buxton eventually quit their jobs to begin instructing new pilots and sell hang gliders for a living. In the more than twenty years since they founded Kitty Hawk Kites, their company has taught nearly 150,000 people, between the ages of eight and eighty-eight, how to fly. These legions of new pilots learned on the same sand dunes where Wilbur and Orville Wright had experimented with their own gliders several decades before.

Another early east coast hang glider pilot, Victor Powell, organized a national gliding meet in 1973. He too chose Jockey's Ridge as a launch site. The annual Kitty Hawk Hang Gliding Spectacular still draws thousands of spectators to the dunes each year. It is the oldest continuously held hang gliding event in the country.

On the west coast, fliers were organizing more than just competitions. Experimenters, like Californians Barry Hill Palmer and Richard Miller, used the Rogallo concept to make foot-launched gliders. Their weight-shift-controlled craft were of interest to the small group of friends and the curious who saw them fly.

But it was a visit from two kite-piloting Australian water skiers that really called the sport to the attention of the general public. In 1969 and 1970, Bill Moyes and Bill Bennett toured America, demonstrating their ability to rise from the water, borne by curious flexible wings. At times they would release their tow ropes and glide back down to the water in controlled free flight. These two pilots took the concept of the Rogallo wing to its next level of refinement by developing a trapeze-like control bar, which gave the gliders much improved pitch and yaw control. Many of the future leading figures in the hang gliding movement, like West Coast pilots Bob Wills and Richard Eipper, were first exposed to the sport by the spectacular flights of Moyes and Bennett.[8]

A group of Southern California hang glider pilots, led by Eipper, formed the Peninsula Hang Glider Club in late 1971. By the next summer their name had been changed to the Southern California Hang Glider Association, and they began a publication called *Ground Skimmer*. The day after the seventieth anniversary of the Wright Brothers' first powered flight, the club members ratified a proposal to become a national organization, evolving into today's United States Hang Glider Association (USHGA).[9] In the twenty years since the USHGA was founded, it has registered approximately fifty-five thousand hang glider pilots. Of these, an estimated sixteen thousand are still active.[10]

During the same period the sport has advanced technologically. The early bamboo and polyethylene Rogallo gliders have evolved into rigid- and semirigid-winged high-performance fliers, some of them capable of performing aerobatic maneuvers. Flights have increased in distance and duration from short hops of a few yards to a recent "distance to goal" flight of 303.35 miles. During much of his eight-and-a-half-hour flight, pilot Larry Tudor cruised at altitudes between nine thousand and eleven thousand feet.[11] Clearly, the machines are no longer mere ground skimmers.

Still another air sport organization grew out of the hang gliding movement. The first experimenters with Rogallo's flexible wing had hardly become proficient at gliding flight before some of them tried attaching small engines to the hang gliders.[12]

The idea for ultralight airplanes was not a new one. Like the early machines that were revived as hang gliders by the discovery of new construction technology and materials, ultralight airplanes date back in American history at least as far as 1910. It was in that year that *Popular Mechanics* magazine had published, in two instalments, directions and diagrams for constructing Alberto Santos-Dumont's Demoiselle. This small plane was different from those previously constructed, in that it was a tiny "parasol" monoplane. The pilot sat below the wing, rather than in front or behind it, just inches behind the propeller, controlling the plane with one stick for the elevators, another to warp the wings (in the same method as the Wrights), and a wheel to turn the rudder. At the time it was billed as "the smallest flyer ever built."[13]

Santos-Dumont encouraged the public to learn to fly by making the design a gift to the world. It was in that spirit that the construction article appeared, with his permission, in *Popular Mechanics*. It is interesting to note that, in the days before experimental flying became fettered by threats of litigation, the authors of the article issued only this warning to prospective builders: "It is necessary to possess some mechanical skill and ability, and plenty of common sense . . . we trust that no one of our readers will start to build unless he possesses these qualities, especially the latter, without which he will never be able to accomplish anything."[14]

As modern hang gliders evolved from Rogallo's flexible wing into more rigid forms, so did ultralight airplanes. One of the most popular of the early commercially produced machines was the Eipper Quicksilver,[15] a derivative of Robert Lovejoy's hang glider by the same name. Lovejoy developed the prototype of the hang glider, then joined Eipper-Formance, Inc., where he and David Cronk further refined the design. The Quicksilver had a rigid wing with aluminum spars and curved ribs inserted into pockets sewn in the fabric covering. Lovejoy and Cronk called their early wing camber design the "six seventy fifteen," because they achieved it by bending half-inch aluminum tubing over a 670 × 15 automobile tire. In spite of the fact that they used a great deal of this type of intuition to design the hang glider (Lovejoy was trained in industrial design, not aeronautical engineering), it flew remarkably well. Later tests by a Northrop Institute of Technology professor showed it to be quite strong as well.[16]

The hang glider virtually begged to have an engine attached to it, and soon it did. Early Quicksilver ultralights were very much like the hang gliders by the same name, in that they utilized a swing seat and trapeze bar for weight-shift control. The first Quicksilver ultralight used a Chrysler West Bend water pump engine for motive power, but that was soon upgraded to a Yamaha KT100S go-cart engine of about fifteen horse-power. While the weight-shift control system was perfectly functional, it was familiar only to those trained as hang glider pilots.[17]

American tastes dictated that ultralight airplanes look and fly like traditional airplanes, so builders experimented with different forms of three-axis control systems.[18] Some manufactured aircraft with a variety of new and rediscovered features, such as the canard elevators used by the first Wright and Curtiss planes. There was an explosion of new designs, and advertisements for new makers appeared in nearly every issue of hang gliding and flying publications. Wanting to make their own product appear to be the reincarnation of America's quintessential light airplane, dealers for nearly every design boasted that their machine flew "just like a Piper Cub"—but few, in those early days, really did.

The FAA agreed to allow the ultralight flying community an opportunity to prove that they could maintain safe standards of operation while regulating their own activities—much as hang glider pilots and parachutists were already doing. Some restrictions were placed on the machines that prevented them from flying over congested areas and into controlled airspace, but, overall, ultralight pilots were allowed a great deal of freedom. The FAA defined powered ultralight aircraft as those

1. Having a single-seat and intended for one occupant.
2. Used for recreation or sport only.
3. Weighing 254 pounds or less.
4. Capable of reaching a speed of no more than fifty-five knots calibrated airspeed in level flight, with a stall speed of twenty-four knots, or less.
5. Able to carry no more than five U.S. gallons of fuel.

These criteria are more restrictive than those for the popular microlight category recognized by the FAI and popular in Europe. A microlight is allowed to weigh up to 330 pounds and carry one passenger.[19]

In the early days, both the USHGA and the Air Safety Foundation of the AOPA implemented training and registration programs for ultralight owners. Eventually, the FAA also granted these organizations the power to issue waivers to qualified instructors using two-place aircraft of ultra-light-type construction for training purposes.

The fanciful little flying machines captured the imagination of would-be pilots. In the early 1980s, ultralight manufacturers found a market much like that which had developed for light airplanes in the months after World War II. Ultralights seemed to herald the future of general aviation and sales figures for the first three years supported that dream. Eipper, for example, averaged sales of more than 2000 planes per year from 1981 to 1983.[20] Ultralights were relatively inexpensive, many of them could be disassembled for transport or stored in a garage, and the federal government did not require operators to possess a pilot's license.

At the height of their popularity in the summer of 1983, *National Geographic* magazine featured them in a beautifully illustrated cover story.[21] But a few months later the ultralight industry crashed as suddenly as the postwar light plane business had forty years earlier. This time the end was triggered by a single event—a segment on ABC's *20/20*. Prominent in the show were horrifying film footage of a Washington, D.C., newsman plunging to his death from an ultralight, and a heart-wrenching interview with the young widow of another ultralight pilot. Later, after talking with another man, a wheelchair-bound pilot who had been paralyzed in an ultralight crash, the commentators ominously con-cluded that, even though he was a licensed airplane pilot with several years of experience flying larger planes, he had not been able to control one of the "unsafe" little aircraft. The clear impression given by *20/20* was that ultralights were unavoidably hazardous.[22]

As typically happens with entertainment programs disguised as news reporting, members of the ultralight industry had no opportunity to present their side of the story. They could not point out that the Washing-ton newsman, for example, did not crash to his death *in* an ultralight, but instead fell *out* of one (a slow motion examination of the tape suggests that he might even have jumped[23]), or that he had told the operator of the flight center from which he had taken off that he was an experienced pilot—a statement that later proved false. At the very least, the newsman violated a cardinal safety rule by not wearing his seatbelt. Likewise, ultralight representatives could not explain to the public that the licensed pilot's years of flying experience were not necessarily the same as actual hours of flying time, or that flight time in heavier aircraft no more prepares a person for flying ultralights than driving an automobile pre-pares one to operate a motorcycle. In nearly every case in which *20/20* blamed ultralight airplanes for being "unsafe," the real problem lay with the persons operating them. They were either flying the planes in an unsafe manner or had failed to get proper ultralight flight instruction from programs like those offered through USHGA and AOPA (and now the U.S. Ultralight Association).

The ultralight industry felt immediate repercussions from the broadcast. Ironically, the 20/20 segment had the effect of frightening away many of the more cautious people who were learning to fly in approved training programs, while further encouraging some of the untrained and reckless, who now reveled in the "death-defying daredevil" image bestowed upon them by the report.

Ultralight airplane sales virtually ceased the day after the television program aired, and within two years nearly every major manufacturer (including Eipper-Formance) had gone out of business or was in bankruptcy. In 1985 the AOPA Air Safety Foundation discontinued its ultralight program owing to insufficient membership. Its responsibilities to pilots were assumed by a new organization, the U.S. Ultralight Foundation, organized by John Ballantyne, the same man who had headed the AOPA program in its later years. In 1986 the U.S. Ultralight Foundation became a division of the NAA, and has since evolved into the present U.S. Ultralight Association. Although Ballantyne recognizes that the 20/20 program did serious harm to the ultralight industry, he says that it also made the surviving manufacturers and dealers carefully reconsider their role in making self-regulation truly effective.[24]

Yet another air sport activity benefited from the advancements in technology of the 1960s and 1970s, as William Ivans, former president of the Soaring Society of America, relates:

Soaring made great progress during this period. The year 1970 was particularly important because it was at the World Soaring Championships in Marfa, Texas—hosted by the Soaring Society of America—that a number of "firsts" took place. Cameras were used for the first time to provide photographic evidence that the pilot had reached the required turn points. Before then, observers had to be positioned at each turn point, and the soaring pilot had to descend to 1,000 meters to be low enough to be positively identified—with a corresponding risk that the pilot would not find thermals to get back up to altitude.

Also, a simple but accurate starting "gate" was employed for the first time, using ground-based sighting apparatus. This assured that no pilot could have the advantage of starting a speed task at an altitude higher than that prescribed in the rules, typically 1,000 meters. Both of these innovations were adopted by the organizers of subsequent championships.

A new class of gliders was also introduced at Marfa, the Standard Class. This change came about in response to the need to provide a low-cost, uniform-construction glider that pilots around the world could use for competition, so that skills, not airplane design, would be the principal factor in determining winners. The recently introduced fiberglass sailplanes also dominated this championship. Their successors and carbon fiber derivatives have dominated every subsequent world championship.[25]

The years of Jackie Cochran's administration were both exciting and productive, but she was a hard act to follow, especially in a fiscal sense. Unfortunately, during the "Camelot years" when Cochran led the NAA, nobody foresaw the lean times that were to come in the 1970s and 1980s. Her ability to solicit financial assistance for the organization from corporations in times of economic prosperity, as well as her willingness (and that of her wealthy husband, Floyd Odlum) to use personal resources to finance NAA projects, left the association with aspirations that exceeded its resources once she had relinquished the presidency.

Two NAA officers who worked closely together in the post-Cochran era were president John Alison and Brooke Allen, who served as both executive vice president and executive director. From them we gain insights into the beginning of the NAA's most recent period of belt tightening.

A number of factors, most related to national economic conditions, affected the NAA at that time. The aircraft manufacturers, longtime supporters of NAA projects, remained faithful allies, but, because of budget constraints, were unable to be as generous as in the past. Another traditional supporter, the airline industry, over time cut back drastically, then discontinued entirely, financial contributions to the association. Alison offers an explanation for loss of support from the airlines:

For years the airlines were headed by people who were deeply immersed in aviation—many were pilots themselves. These were men and women who saw a need for the NAA and understood that, even though you could not, perhaps, directly account for the benefits of the NAA to the airline industry in terms of dollars and cents, that benefit was still there. It was very real.

Since then, the airline industry has grown and it is now operated by management structures much like those which run large hotel chains. It is extremely difficult for these accounting-oriented businesses to justify spending money when they can't quantify a return of some kind. It is just an unfortunate fact of modern life.[26]

Spacecraft—the newsmakers of the 1960s—were hardly forgotten in
the 1970s. On May 14, 1973, a Saturn 5 rocket thundered into space
carrying Skylab: an experimental living compartment built inside a
structure originally designed to be a fuel tank for prolonged flights.
All did not go well with the launch. The premature deployment of a
solar shield caused it to be swept away, damaging retractable solar
power panels as it went. On May 25, after a ten-day delay during
which NASA engineers frantically constructed a makeshift shield for
the "space station," a three-man crew left earth atop a Saturn 1-B
rocket for a rendezvous with the one-hundred-ton orbiting laboratory. The astronauts would have to function as space station repair-
men before they could live in their new orbital home. In a masterful
exhibition of space maneuvering, they docked with the space station
and entered it. The temperature inside the station had risen to 130°
after several days' exposure to sunlight, but deployment of their hastily constructed "parasol" gradually lowered the temperature by
some 50°. Then, nearly two weeks after they had moved into their
new home, astronauts Charles Conrad and Joseph Kerwin donned
their space suits and went outside the station to attempt a repair to
the damaged solar panel. After working outside the station for three
and a half hours, using rather primitive tools, the astronauts managed to extend the panel, eventually bringing it up to full power-
generating capacity.

Over its useful lifetime, the space station would be occupied by a
total of three different crews. Each gathered valuable information
from inside their orbital laboratory, but the greatest reward was perhaps the demonstration that a remote space station could be
launched and maintained for a prolonged period of time. For their
contributions to the exploration of space, the NAA presented the
1973 Collier to the Skylab program, with special recognition to William C. Schneider, its director, and the three astronaut crews who
proved the concept possible.

The NAA rewarded achievement in space with the Collier Trophy
again in 1974. In a world made ever more conscious of the limits of
its resources through pictures of earth taken from the distant perspective of space, efforts to examine environmental problems on a
global level met with appreciation. Dr. John F. Clark of NASA and
Daniel J. Fink of General Electric represented the NASA/industry
team responsible for the development and implementation of
LANDSAT, an earth resources technology satellite used to help manage the environment. Hughes Aircraft Company and RCA received
special recognition for the part they had played in making LANDSAT
a reality.

America entered the 1980s with an event that held the world breathless. The spacecraft *Voyager*—originally intended for exploration of the planet Mars but replaced by the smaller, less expensive, *Mariner* in 1966 budget cuts—flew past the planet Saturn, transmitting images of the planet's surface and mysterious rings. The NASA *Voyager* mission team, represented by chief scientist Dr. Edward C. Stone, won the 1980 Collier for the successful long-range mission.

The next year, the Collier went to NASA, Rockwell International Corporation, Martin Marietta Corporation, and Thiokol Corporation for the concept of a manned, reusable spacecraft—the space shuttle. Included among the recipients were astronauts John W. Young, Robert L. Crippen, Joe H. Engle, and Richard H. Truly. The space shuttle program remained the focus of America's pride until 1986, when the shuttle *Challenger* exploded shortly after takeoff, killing the entire crew. It was Truly, by then a rear admiral and no longer an astronaut, who was given the task of rebuilding the U.S. space program soon after the loss of the *Challenger*. As associate administrator for space flight of NASA, and chairman of the NASA task force that investigated the *Challenger* tragedy, Truly and the NASA team identified the cause of the accident and developed measures to assure that future space flights would be conducted with a significantly higher margin of safety. Truly was honored with his second Collier Trophy in 1988, for returning America to space only two years after the *Challenger* disaster.

The 1984 Collier was also presented for achievements in space. The Martin Marietta Corporation shared the trophy with NASA that year for the development of a "manned maneuvering unit" that allowed an astronaut to move through space and efficiently perform repair tasks such as the one that had proven so difficult for the 1973 space station astronauts. This device was used to rescue three disabled satellites that otherwise might have been lost. In presenting the award, the NAA recognized astronaut Bruce McCandless II, Charles E. Whitsett, Jr., of NASA, and Walter W. Bollendonk of Martin Marietta for their contributions to the design and construction of the unit.

In the same interview, Allen pointed out that corporate restructurings played yet another role in decreasing the association's income:

The aircraft manufacturers have always been good to us. We could, for instance, always count on a sizable contribution from Douglas Aircraft and another from the McDonnell Corporation. When the two merged into

McDonnell Douglas, the support continued, but it was half the amount we used to receive from them when they were separate companies. As an isolated case it was not too damaging, but when things like that happened over and over again—which they did—it really hurt us financially.[27]

The NAA had traditionally relied on persons willing to volunteer their time and resources to manage the association, employing a modest full-time staff to perform clerical duties. But, as air transportation gradually became an accepted way of life, the class of "wealthy sportsmen" with an interest in aviation, from which most of the early officers had been recruited, all but disappeared. It was obvious that the NAA needed to hire a professional staff, but it was equally obvious that its resources to do so were extremely limited.

Throughout the 1970s, Alison, Allen, and other former military men like Col. Everett Langworthy and Gen. John P. Henebry did much of the work of the NAA. They served as models for the type of person capable of leading the organization during times of little income. As retired officers they had extensive administrative experience and a keen interest and background in aviation. They were men with long-standing records of contributing to the public good who viewed the NAA as a public service organization in need of their talents. Because they had retirement income from the military, they were able to volunteer their time, or to work for substantially lower pay than the officers of comparable organizations.

In 1980 another former military officer joined the ranks of the NAA. Gen. Clifton F. von Kann began as senior vice president, and the next year succeeded John Alison as president. Von Kann's position was unique in that it was modified to include the duties formerly held by the executive director as well as those of the president. He was the first person to receive payment, albeit a nominal sum in the beginning, for serving as the NAA's president. Von Kann served the NAA in that post for ten years, before going on to serve two years as the president of the FAI.

The von Kann administration experienced difficult times. In the post-Vietnam years of the early 1980s, there was still lingering tension between the traditional military establishment and much of civilian society. Into this atmosphere the new president tried to introduce several laudable programs with the same methods he had used in the military. They seem to have met with only marginal success.

The first of von Kann's efforts was a series of in-depth proposals for national policies on such issues as space exploration, military aviation, the defense industrial base, commercial aviation, airports, and the airspace environment. National aerospace policies were matters in which he had particular expertise, and his lengthy proposals showed extraordinary insight into existing problems. At the top of the list of roles he felt the NAA should play were:

Spokesman and policy advocate for the U.S. air and space (aerospace) community—both civil and military.

 Watchdog over adequacy of programs that bear on U.S. leadership in air and space.[28]

 Also included among the numerous objectives distributed in his later proposal *Keeping the U.S. First in the Air and Space: A Review of Major Air and Space Issues*[29] were several affecting general and sport aviation, but to some they may have seemed lost on just two pages of the thirty-five-page document.

 Trying to pull all the nation's aviation elements together to gain input on aerospace issues, von Kann organized a series of symposia, entitled Aerospace I, Aerospace II, and Aerospace III. In much the same manner as the early Aero Club had drawn nationally recognized experts together to resolve national aviation problems, von Kann's meetings attempted to assemble the top authorities from all disciplines of aviation. The participants gathered in Williamsburg, Virginia, during 1981 and 1982, and in Washington, D.C., in 1983, where leading aviation notables addressed current issues and advancements. Later in the symposia members convened into panels charged with formulating proposals for a national aerospace policy.[30]

 Although such all-encompassing programs were well within the scope of traditional NAA objectives—indeed, they were very much in keeping with the approach to programs instituted during the Cochran era, which may have served as a model for von Kann—the various divisions were suffering from the same economic problems as was the NAA. Some of them were surviving only from month to month, and none seemed to have an excess of capital. Von Kann's efforts showed commendable foresight, but his timing was unfortunate. Division officers perceived that their organizations had more immediate needs on the local level and many of their members interpreted such national programs as signs that the NAA was yet again out of touch with the grass roots aviators. Because the problems that the von Kann administration encountered are fresh in the memory of those active in aviation today, and the buffer of time that permits an accurate historical perspective is so short, it is tempting to focus on individual issues over which some of those within the NAA disagreed. Yet assuming such a narrow focus would unfairly characterize the years of his tenure in terms of conflict.

History may well accord von Kann respect for trying to achieve a policy consensus with input from all levels of American aviation during a time when some of sport aviation's traditional freedoms were being challenged. It will be remembered, for instance, that during the years of his administration the NAA was among the leading aviation organizations in opposition to FAA regulations requiring expensive Mode C transponders[31] for operation in much of the country's airspace—regulations that would have excluded many gliders, balloons, and experimental and antique airplanes from enjoying flight as they had long known it. The NAA also supported legislation, introduced by Congressman Dan Glickman of Kansas, to control tort lawsuits involving aircraft manufacturers. Von Kann, and others within the NAA and its divisions, deemed it crucial to gain reasonable federal control over the exorbitant court awards that were destroying the light aircraft industry.[32]

In the overall picture of the NAA's long service as the American arm of the FAI, times of discord and reevaluation have almost always accompanied periods of national social or economic stress. Inevitably, the organization has emerged from these times having identified new trends and has made the adaptations necessary to carry it into a subsequent period of prosperity. From that perspective, the last decade appears to be no different from other eras when the NAA was—albeit painfully at times—slowly conforming to changes in the social fabric of America and new needs of American aviation.

Perhaps the best way of characterizing the past decade is by looking at the accomplishments and contributions of the NAA as a whole—including each of the air sports organizations involved with the NAA. In this light, the NAA shines very brightly throughout the 1980s.

On October 10, 1960, a pilot named Ed Yost left Bruning, Nebraska, on the first voyage in a modern hot air balloon; it was the birth of a modern form of the sport that had been responsible for the founding of the Aero Club of America. Kirk Thomas, director of the Soukup & Thomas International Balloon and Airship Museum, describes what he calls "the return of hot air" thus:

Ed Yost, regarded as the "Father of Modern Hot Air Ballooning," was working with balloons for the Office of Naval Research through the Aeronautical Research Division of General Mills. He was part of the effort that sent leaflets by polyethylene helium-filled balloons behind the Iron Curtain, some of which helped foment the Hungarian uprising of 1956. But his work with pilot training in balloons convinced him that a cheaper alternative to helium was necessary.

Yost and others founded Raven Industries in Sioux Falls, South Dakota, to develop what would become the modern hot air balloon.

On October 10, 1960, Yost made the first modern hot air balloon flight from Bruning, Nebraska (it was too windy in Sioux Falls). In 1961, Don Piccard, son of Jean and Jeanette Piccard and nephew of Auguste Piccard (all of whom had ascended into the stratosphere), was hired by Raven to promote hot air ballooning and try to sell sport balloons. In 1962, Piccard organized the first sporting event for hot air balloons, the St. Paul Winter Carnival Balloon Race and the first Hot Air Balloon Championship.

Later, other manufacturers entered the field to compete with Raven, including Piccard himself. From a slow beginning, the sport of Hot Air Ballooning has grown tremendously.[33]

In 1963, Piccard and retired Navy pilot Karl H. Stefan founded the first ballooning club dedicated to the modern hot air balloon, the Aerostat Society. Both men would also later be involved in the Balloon Federation of America, an air sport organization begun in 1967 under the leadership of Peter Pellegrino.[34] The first world championship of hot air ballooning was held in Albuquerque, New Mexico, in 1973, and the sport has grown remarkably ever since.[35] Over the next several years, balloonists continued showing the world that the oldest form of aviation had far from reached its limits. The 1980s began with the realization of a longtime dream held by balloon pilots—a nonstop crossing of the United States. Maxie L. Anderson and his son Kris came close to the goal with a 1980 gas balloon flight from Fort Baker, California. Their balloon traveled nearly the width of the North American continent, but they landed in Matane, Quebec, rather than the United States. Anderson was hardly a newcomer to long-distance balloon travel. He, accompanied by Ben Abruzzo and Larry Newman, had flown the Atlantic from Presque Isle, Maine, to Miserey, France, for a duration record in excess of 137 hours in 1978.[36]

But it was another balloon with the unlikely name of Super Chicken III, piloted by John Shoecraft and Fred Gorrell, that finally made the coast-to-coast American flight. Their trip from Costa Mesa, California, to Blackbeard's Island, Georgia, covered 2515 miles in less than fifty-six hours, averaging better than forty-five miles per hour.[37]

However, the undisputed kings of long-distance travel remain Abruzzo, Newman, Rocky Aoki, and Ron Clark. In 1981 they crossed 5208 miles of the Pacific, from Nagashima, Japan, to Covello, California. Their Pacific flight was more than 1650 miles longer than one made three years later from Caribou, Maine, to Montenotte, Italy, but that solo Atlantic crossing, made by Joseph W. Kittenger, nevertheless won the respect of the world.[38]

Another aviation rebirth of sorts took place in the late 1970s and early 1980s that again had its roots in the founding days of the NAA's predecessor, the Aero Club of America. The premier aviation competition of the Aero Club was the Gordon Bennett International Cup for gas balloons. Lt. Frank Lahm (later to attain the rank of general) won this honor for the United States at the Paris competition in 1906, only months after the Aero Club had been founded. Since then, Americans have won the contest ten times. The distance race was held annually for more than thirty years, with breaks only for wartime and one year in which worldwide economic depression kept the number of entries too low to hold the competition.

The 1939 Gordon Bennett International Cup, which was to have taken place in Warsaw, Poland, on September 3, was canceled as Hitler invaded that country two days before the scheduled launch date. During and after World War II, competition ceased, seemingly forever. It was not until 1983 that an international launch from Paris marked the official renaissance of the Gordon Bennett race. In the years since the competition's rebirth, Americans have always competed in the annual race, but victory seemed to remain just beyond their grasp. The remarkable Austrian team of Starkbaum and Scholz won first place in six of the ten competitions,[39] eventually being unseated by Volker Kuinke and Jörgen Schubert of Germany in 1991.[40] Finally, in 1992, the team of David N. Levin and James R. Herschend captured the trophy for the first U.S. victory in sixty years.[41]

During the 1980s the strength of interest in sport powerplanes could be characterized no better than by considering the EAA's annual gathering in Oshkosh, Wisconsin. The event has become so influential that aviators around the world instantly envision the ultimate flying extravaganza at the mere mention of the magic word "Oshkosh." For a few days each year, Wittman Field becomes the busiest airport in the world and the home of the largest aggregation of flying machines in the world. In 1992, for instance, more than twelve thousand aircraft (nearly 7 percent of America's privately owned machines), representing the United States and sixty-five other countries, accounted for more than fifty thousand air operations, controlled by a temporary FAA tower facility. Over eight hundred thousand spectators—including almost a thousand media representatives—watched the world's finest civilian and military pilots perform aerobatics, or wandered among the countless variety of airplanes parked on display.[42]

In spite of the fact that U.S. ultralights, by FAA definition, are restricted to performance far below that allowed under the FAI microlight category, some American ultralight pilots have managed to capture international records set in countries where the regulations are far more liberal. Sometimes they did this by modifying ultralight designs and licensing the planes under the experimental category.[43]

The Vietnam conflict, in the minds of many, was characterized by un-likely-looking machines with nicknames like "Huey" and "Jolly Green Giant." Thousands of soldiers owe their lives to the fact that helicopters could quickly extract them from areas under enemy fire or, if wounded, transport them to medical care facilities in a matter of minutes. American military forces—especially the U.S. Army—brought the art of rotorcraft flight to new heights during the Vietnam years.

In recent years, U.S. pilots have performed admirably in helicopter flight competition, but never more than during the 1980s. Under the auspices of the Helicopter Club of America, U.S. entrants placed first in both the individual and the team competitions at the international meets in Poland (1981), England (1986), and France (1989). At the Poland meet one civilian crew flew as part of the winning team, but otherwise the show has belonged entirely to the U.S. Army (including the National Guard).[44]

The Helicopter Club of America was originally formed as a group of sponsors, so that a U.S. team could compete under FAI rules. The club promotes international competition, sport helicopter aviation, and record attempts by American helicopter pilots. In addition to international competition, there have been two national meets, each sponsored by the military, held in the past decade. The U.S. National Helicoper Championship took place March 21–22, 1992, in Las Vegas with seventeen civilian helicopter crews competing in sanctioned categories for the first time in history. The military cited budgetary constraints as the reason for its failure to participate.[45]

Pilots of another form of helicopter also distinguished themselves during the past decade. In 1987 the Second World Radio Controlled Helicopter Championship convened in Bern, Switzerland. There, Curtis Youngblood took first-place honors in the individual category and an American trio composed of Curtis Youngblood, Bob Gorham, and Mike Mas placed a close second to the Japanese entry in the team competition. The U.S.

pilots were sponsored by the Academy of Model Aeronautics (AMA), one of the oldest air sport organizations associated with the NAA.[46]

Aero modeling may, at first, appear to outsiders to be a children's hobby. Indeed, as we have seen in Chapters 7 and 14, the NAA, and before it the Aero Club, has long sought to build interest in aviation in America's youth. Yet a close look at the division reveals an entirely different sport. In very few other aviation disciplines do the participants build, fly, and, sometimes, design their own aircraft. Once exposed to the level of skill required to construct and fly modern model aircraft, an observer cannot help but come away with respect for these practitioners of one of the oldest forms of the aviation arts. Still, as sophisticated as aero modeling has become, model aircraft fliers have held fast to their belief that aero modeling should be—and is—an open door for youth with a passion for flight. Perhaps this is why, with a membership approaching 200,000 in over 2500 chapters, today's AMA is the largest air sport organization associated with the NAA—a far cry from the fifty-one members on the rolls of the Junior Aero Club of America at the end of its first year of existence in 1909. The AMA lists among its members such aviation celebrities as Burt Rutan, Dr. Paul MacCready, and space shuttle pilot Robert "Hoot" Gibson.

One of the most spectacular events to ever bring the beauty of sport aviation to the world relied on a force of nature—gravity. It was September 17, 1988, and the Olympic Games were formally opening in Seoul, South Korea. Everywhere on the ground one could see visions of incomparable pomp and pageantry, but suddenly hundreds of thousands of spectators turned their eyes toward the sky. They and millions of others around the world, watching on television, saw seventy-nine parachutists streaking toward the ground.

At the focal point of these waves of skydivers, three came together. One after another, in rapid succession, a total of twenty-seven other national and international skydiving champions from twenty-four countries flew toward them. Falling at 120 miles per hour, the jumpers formed five circles, each one composed of six people wearing identically colored jumpsuits, helmets, and parachutes. They guided the falling formation through the air as a single flying machine—aligning it so that, from the ground inside the stadium, their interconnected bodies painted a perfect five-ringed Olympic symbol in brilliant colors against the clear blue sky.[47]

The 1980s marked an era of remarkable accomplishments, but none epitomized the vitality of modern aviation more than the nonstop, round-the-world flight of an airplane named *Voyager*. The story of this unprecedented flight is at once the epitome of the vitality of modern aviation and a fitting conclusion to this history.

The key players in the *Voyager* story could not have been more perfectly chosen to capture the spirit of aviation if they had been cast by Hollywood. The plane's designer, Burt Rutan, is an aircraft engineer whose impact on the advancement of aviation places him prominently within a small group of people whose influence is second only to that of the Wright Brothers. His composite construction designs have launched aircraft builders in a new direction: combining high-tech materials with new applications of such older concepts as the canard elevator to produce fast, fuel-efficient planes with a sleek, sculptured beauty. His newest creation, built with limited support from the industrial giants and partially funded by contributions from aviation enthusiasts, would hold the world breathless for nine days at the close of 1986.

The pilots, Jeana L. Yeager and Burt Rutan's brother Dick, possessed an extraordinary combination of flying skill and the look of aviation heros. Dick Rutan projected the smiling, self-assured image of the military pilot—an image he had earned, not merely affected. But it was Jeana Yeager who truly captured American hearts. News cameras revealed a shy self-confidence and a sparkling smile uncannily reminiscent of that of Mathilde Moisant, the petite pilot who had been the second woman ever awarded an Aero Club aviator's license. Yeager's impressive flying abilities are undoubtedly her own, but her courage, determination, and devotion to aviation reflected the inspiration of all women who preceded her into the air.

Following a six-year construction period, *Voyager,* the airplane that was to carry Yeager and Rutan around the world, set records even as it was being readied for the world flight attempt. On July 15, 1986, it completed a closed-course flight of 11,593.68 miles while investigating fuel consumption rates. The flight lasted a bit more than 110 hours and bettered a previously set unrefueled distance record by more than 250 miles. *Voyager*'s performance was spectacular. It averaged a speed of more than 105 miles per hour, consuming about 2695 pounds of fuel (approximately 450 gallons) at the rate of nearly twenty-six miles per gallon.

But the real test for the remarkable airplane came in December of that year. During the televised departure for the globe-circling flight, the plane's wings, sagging under the weight of fully loaded fuel tanks, scraped the runway, damaging the wingtip-mounted fins designed to reduce aerodynamic drag. These "winglets" soon broke off, but an in-flight examination determined that *Voyager* could continue without them. For the next nine days of December 1986—a period that, quite appropri-

Soon after the conclusion of their epic flight, President Ronald Reagan awarded the *Voyager* crew Presidential Citizens Medals. On May 15, 1987, Jeana Yeager, the Rutan Brothers, and Bruce Evans, representing the team of volunteers he had led, shared America's oldest flying honor as recipients of the 1986 Collier Trophy.

The other accomplishments rewarded with the Collier Trophy during the late 1980s may not have appealed to the public's sense of adventure so much as did the journey of the *Voyager,* but, taken as a whole, they represent an outstanding cross section of accomplishment in aviation.

The 1985 recipient was Russell W. Meyer of Cessna Aircraft Company, which has produced a line of business jets, the Citation series, that has maintained an unparalleled safety record. In the years since 1911, when Clyde Cessna built his first airplane and began Cessna Aircraft Company, Cessna had grown into a leading name in the light aircraft industry. In September 1969, the company entered the business jet market with the flight of their prototype Citation I (originally called the Fanjet 500).[48] Designed to operate from runways of the same length as those in use by most propeller-driven corporate aircraft, the Citation series has made Cessna a leader in the "bizjet" market.

Advances in the design and use of turboprop engines merited the Collier Trophy for 1987. The award went to the NASA Lewis Research Center and the NASA/industry Advanced Turboprop Team, consisting of NASA, Hamilton Standard, General Electric, Lockheed, the Allison Gas Turbine Division of General Motors, Pratt & Whitney, Douglas Aircraft, and the Boeing Commercial Aircraft Company. The turboprop engines and related systems developed by the team mark a new generation of fuel-efficient powerplants for subsonic aircraft.

Technological advances leading to the deployment of new and innovative types of aircraft have marked the most recent Collier awards. Ed Renouard of Boeing Helicopter and Jack Horner of Bell Helicopter Textron accepted the 1990 Collier on behalf of the Bell/Boeing team that produced the V-22 Osprey Tiltrotor aircraft. In spite of setbacks resulting from the 1992 crash of a prototype, the V-22, the first large-scale tiltrotor craft ever built and flown, promises to turn the page to an entirely new chapter in aviation industry. Tiltrotor technology is expected to allow aircraft capable of carrying substantial loads to operate from runways far shorter than those needed by conventional airplanes. It thus holds promise for the future development of commuter airports in areas where sufficient land might otherwise not be available. Likewise, the new technology

might bring air transport to parts of underdeveloped nations previously unable to construct and maintain conventional runways.

Finally, the most recent Collier award was presented for 1991 to the Northrop Corporation, the B-2 industry team, and the U.S. Air Force for bringing the B-2 aircraft through the design, development, production, and flight testing stages. This aircraft combined features designed to give it low observability with a highly aerodynamically efficient airframe, making extensive use of lightweight composite materials.

---

ately, spanned the eighty-third anniversary of the Wrights' first powered flight—*Voyager* slowly circumnavigated planet earth. In order to hold fuel expenditure to a minimum, Rutan and Yeager had to fly at altitudes that often subjected them to the most awesome forces of nature. This plan tested both their ability to control the plane precisely under adverse conditions and their power to withstand often-violent atmospheric conditions in an aircraft that sacrificed even the simplest of creature comforts for lightweight mechanical efficiency. Although sometimes bruised and often fatigued, they triumphed.

America followed the flight's progress on television, with national interest growing as the possibility of success grew brighter. Nightly news programs began featuring *Voyager*, with meteorologists and aviation authorities explaining to the nonflying public how the tiny plane was picking its way through the gigantic weather systems depicted in broadcast satellite images. When, on December 23, *Voyager* touched down in Mojave, California, the plane and crew had set a total of eight distance and speed records in completing the first nonstop, nonrefueled, flight around the world.

For a nation that had long viewed low-altitude airplane flights through eyes jaded by supersonic transports and moon-walking astronauts, the *Voyager* crew were Earhart and Lindbergh reborn. They reminded us that not all individual initiative has been smothered by corporate conformity and showed us that there would always be new frontiers for the courageous to conquer. And as these new pioneers of the air set ever more ambitious records, the NAA will continue to confirm and record them— watching over America's skyward reach as it and the Aero Club have done since the era of Kitty Hawk.

AFTERWORD:
THE FUTURE OF THE NAA

A Forecast from the President

*In October 1989, Malvern J. Gross, Jr., succeeded Clifton von Kann as president
of the NAA. Gross, newly retired from his position as a partner in the international accounting firm of Price Waterhouse, brought with him a unique background
that made him ideal for the position, including nine years' experience as the
NAA's vice president of finance; thirty-five years as a private pilot and sport
aviation enthusiast with more than four thousand hours of logged pilot-in-com-
mand time; and a widespread reputation as a leading authority on nonprofit
organizations, whose 1972 book on the subject is regarded as a definitive work.*

*Upon Gross has fallen the task of steering the NAA toward the conclusion of the
first century of American flight and the centennials of the Aero Club of America and
the NAA. What follows is his vision of the present role and the future of the NAA.*

The history of the NAA and the Aero Club of America is a history of
aviation in America. But, like the history of aviation itself, the NAA's road
has not been a smooth path from that day in June 1905 when the Aero Club
was incorporated in New York. As Bill Robie has clearly outlined in this
book, the Aero Club, and later the NAA, have frequently had to reexamine
and redefine their roles. We started out as a "gentlemen's club" for the
wealthy balloonist, later became an advocate of air power as the country
faced the prospects of World War I, and until the mid-1920s issued all pilot
licenses in the United States. At one time we issued an annual report to the
President outlining the nation's aviation priorities as we saw them.

But some of these early roles have long since been eclipsed by a mature industry now employing millions of people, and by a government that not only issues all pilot licenses but itself has a staff of thousands regulating the industry. Our lone voice advocating the nation's priorities has been largely replaced by those of a dozen aviation organizations whose function is to lobby for the specialized interests of individual sectors of this vast industry.

The NAA is a nonprofit organization. It has no right to continued existence just because it ably served the needs of the industry in the past. Like most nonprofit groups, it is a living organism, composed of individuals and supporters working toward a particular goal or set of objectives. It has no endowment or independent resources. Its survival is dependent on its ability to attract the volunteers and money that it needs.

As it has done so many times in the past, the NAA must still make continual course corrections to meet the needs of its constituencies in an ever-changing world. This is often most easily, and conspicuously, done at times of transition in leadership, since a new leadership is frequently not encumbered by the decisions of its predecessors. Such policy adjustments are often painful to those who have gone before, for the changes are sometimes perceived as a repudiation of past policies. In fact the policies of the past were usually appropriate *at that time;* they may simply no longer be appropriate today.

MISSION FOR THE 1990s

What then is evolving as the NAA's role for the 1990s?

In 1989 the board of directors adopted a broad mission statement (see Appendix K), the first sentence of which best summarizes the mission for the 1990s:

The National Aeronautic Association is the National Aero Club of the United States. Its primary mission is the advancement of the art, sport, and science of aviation and space flight by fostering opportunities to participate fully in aviation activities, and by promoting public understanding of the importance of aviation and space flight to the United States.

These words—except for the reference to space flight—could have been the words of the founders of the Aero Club in 1905.

At least for the next few years, the key words are in the first sentence— the NAA is the national aero club of the United States. This is our principal—but not our only—mission. It is a mission that, correctly or not, has been neglected in the last few years. The "aero club" function essentially relates to sport aviation.

The terms *sport aviation* and *general aviation* are often used interchangeably, but they do not refer to the same thing. General aviation is usually thought of as all aviation other than military flying and commercial air transport, that is, the public carriers. Sport aviation deals with that part of general aviation involving flying for which the principal motivation is pleasure and the exercise of skill and not commercial activities or air transportation. As the nation's national aero club, the NAA's principal job is the promotion and development of sport aviation in the United States.

In furtherance of this role, the NAA has as organizational members all of the major air sport organizations:

The Academy of Model Aeronautics

The Balloon Federation of America

The Experimental Aircraft Association

The Helicopter Club of America

The International Aerobatic Club

The Soaring Society of America

The U.S. Hang Gliding Association

The U.S. Parachute Association

The U.S. Ultralight Association

It is important to note that twenty-five years ago half of these organizations—and the disciplines they represent—did not exist. Air sports are an evolving area and it is the NAA's job to encourage and foster new sports as they do emerge.

New air disciplines—or offshoots of old ones—are evolving even as this is being written. A current example is the sport of paragliding, with probably less than a thousand participants in 1991[1] in the United States. Yet in Europe paragliding is an evolving sport that has already attracted more devotees than hang gliding—exactly the opposite of what has happened in the United States.

In years past several of the air sport organizations evolved into elitist organizations whose primary interest was only in top-level competition, without any real interest in stimulating broad participation in their sports. Today's NAA has a responsibility to encourage each of these disciplines to develop policies and procedures that will encourage the maximum possible number of participants.

FÉDÉRATION AERONAUTIQUE INTERNATIONALE

In its national aero club role, the NAA represents United States aviation—principally sport aviation—in the eighty-nation Fédération Aeronautique Internationale (FAI), of which it was a founding member in 1905. The FAI has several functions, but its most important is to establish competition rules for each of the air sport disciplines and conduct world championships, generally every other year.

The work of the FAI is far more complex than this mission might at first suggest. Whenever a multinational group comes together to establish sets of rules for individual disciplines, there is sure to be considerable debate and a need for negotiation and compromise. Furthermore, establishing rules and procedures for world aviation championships is a never-ending process because, as the equipment being used improves, new rules and procedures, or at least modifications of old rules, become necessary. Then too, within certain disciplines rules and procedures, as well as competitions for world championships, must be established for a number of subbranches of the discipline. Aeromodeling, for example, has aerobatic championships, free flight championships, and helicopter championships, to name a few.

Most of the work of the FAI is carried out by individual commissions that are established for each discipline, on which serve representatives from each of the countries of the FAI involved in that sport. In the case of the United States, the individual air sport organizations send representatives to the FAI commissions to represent U.S. interests. In all there are probably thirty to fifty Americans involved in FAI matters each year.

KEEPER OF AVIATION AND SPACE RECORDS

The FAI, like the NAA, has other roles, the most visible of which is to establish the rules under which "world" aviation and space records are established. The FAI is recognized as the world's recordkeeper of all aviation and space records. In the United States, the NAA serves as the FAI's agent in connection with overseeing and certifying world records. In addition to FAI-recognized world records, however, the NAA also recognizes U.S. national records that do not fit into record categories established by the FAI.

Clearly this record certification function will continue to be emphasized for the foreseeable future. Aviation records, and the publicity surrounding them, have always served to promote aviation by increasing public awareness of achievements. Robie's description in his Postscript of the *Voyager* round-the-world, nonstop, nonrefueled flight is ample evidence that record setting is not dead, and that the world's imagination can still be fired by such feats.

But the NAA also places emphasis on record setting of a different, less dramatic, type. We encourage pilots of all levels of experience to set speed records, established by weight categories, between any two recognized cities within the United States, or from the United States to any major city abroad. These records are set by weight category to permit the owner of a small single-engine trainer to set records in the same way as could the pilot of a larger, more advanced craft. And this is important. The more people we can get involved in setting records, and getting recognition for such flights, the more interest can be generated for aviation. In the years ahead we must all work toward getting more young people interested in aviation as a career, and we believe this is a major way of helping to do so.

HERITAGE

Another major function of the NAA is what is often referred to as our "heritage" role. The NAA is the custodian of many of the nation's most prestigious aviation awards. In recent years the NAA has been involved in presentations of awards and honors to more than fifty individuals and organizations annually. The early pioneers of aviation strongly believed that public recognition of aviation achievement was a major force in encouraging others to excel and make advances, and this function continues to be an important one for the NAA.

The most famous of these awards, of course, is the Robert J. Collier Trophy, which was established in 1911 and first presented to Glenn Curtiss. It is awarded annually for the greatest achievement in aeronautics or astronautics in America as demonstrated by actual use during the previous year. The recipients of this, the most prestigious of all aviation awards, have been highlighted throughout this book because they represent the history of aviation as perceived by the leaders at the time.

But the NAA's heritage function embraces more than the Collier Trophy, important as it is. No other aviation organization has this unique mandate to search out and give recognition to the "unsung heroes" of aviation, and our heritage role must receive greater prominence in the coming years.

AN ANALOGY TO THE OLYMPIC MOVEMENT

Another way of describing the national aero club function of the NAA is through an analogy to the Olympic movement. The NAA is—in many ways—performing functions for sport aviation similar to those that the United States Olympic Committee performs for general sports. (This olympic analogy can also be applied to the FAI and the International Olympic Committee.)

Both the NAA and the U.S. Olympic Committee are involved in sports, both in promoting competition and in recognizing achievement. One of the clear goals for the 1990s is to help foster this analogy in the minds of the public, and particularly the aviation public.

FINANCIAL VIABILITY

Finally, in discussing the 1990s and the direction in which the NAA must work, it is necessary to mention the need for the NAA to maintain its financial viability. Although the NAA will most likely never be a rich or well-endowed organization, it must develop the resources to keep its own financial house in order. The NAA is not exempt from bankruptcy, and it is important that whoever heads the organization in the years to come recognize this need. Otherwise one day the NAA could very well find itself with a mission, but without the financial means to fulfill that mission.

FINAL OBSERVATION

The 1990s promise to present an exciting opportunity for the NAA to resume its rightful place as a major aviation organization in the United States. It can best do this by recognizing that its mission is different but no less important than what it was more than eighty-five years ago when it was founded, different than what it was fifty years ago, and different than what it was twenty-five years ago.

NAA must build on its strengths—as the United States representative to and the leading member of the FAI, as the umbrella organization that promotes and coordinates sport aviation in the United States, and as the only nonparochial national organization that gives public recognition to men and women who have made contributions to the advancement of the art, sport, and science of aviation and space flight.

Our almost a century of service to aviation, and the heritage of the tens of thousands of aviation pioneers and leaders who have been members, place NAA in a unique and enviable position. We approach the final ten years of our first hundred years full of confidence in our role and its importance to aviation, and with the expectation that we will continue to serve well into the twenty-first century.

APPENDIXES

RECIPIENTS OF THE ROBERT J. COLLIER TROPHY

The entries in this list are taken directly and without editing from the base of the Collier Trophy—both the original base, now at the National Air & Space Museum's Paul E. Garber facility in Suitland, Maryland, and the newer base, still affixed to the trophy itself, on display at the National Air & Space Museum. It should be noted that published accounts of the award's presentation through the years have occasionally differed from the phrasing given here. The reader is referred to the sidebars placed throughout the text for further information on the Collier awards for particular years; sidebar coverage of individual recipients may be located using the index at the close of the volume.

1911   GLENN H. CURTISS
        For hydro-aeroplane development

1912   GLENN H. CURTISS
        For flying boat

1913   ORVILLE WRIGHT
        For automatic stabilizer

1914   ELMER A. SPERRY
        For gyroscopic control

1915   W. STERLING [sic] BURGESS
        For Burgess-Dunne hydro-aeroplane

1916   ELMER A. SPERRY
        For Sperry drift set

1917–1920   No award presented on account of World War I

1921   GROVER C. LOENING
For his aerial yacht

1922   U.S. AIR MAIL SERVICE
For a year's operation without a single fatal accident

1923   U.S. AIR MAIL SERVICE
For night flying in commercial transportation

1924   THE U.S. ARMY AIR SERVICE
For first aerial flight around the world

1925   SYLVANUS ALBERT REED
For metal airplane propeller

1926   MAJOR EDWARD L. HOFFMAN
For development of a practical parachute

1927   CHARLES L. LAWRANCE
For development of radial air-cooled aircraft engines

1928   AERONAUTICS BRANCH, DEP'T OF COMMERCE
For development of airways and air navigation facilities

1929   NATIONAL ADVISORY COMMITTEE FOR AERONAUTICS
For development of cowling for radial air-cooled engines

1930   HAROLD F. PITCAIRN AND HIS ASSOCIATES
For development and application of the autogiro

1931   PACKARD MOTOR CAR COMPANY
For development of the diesel aircraft engine

1932   GLENN L. MARTIN
For development of a high-speed weight-carrying airplane

1933   HAMILTON STANDARD PROPELLER COMPANY AND FRANK
WALKER CALDWELL, CHIEF ENGINEER
For controllable pitch propeller

1934   CAPTAIN A. F. HEGENBERGER, U.S. ARMY AIR CORPS
For development of a successful blind landing system

1935   DONALD W. DOUGLAS AND HIS TECHNICAL AND PRODUCTION
PERSONNEL
For outstanding twin-engined transport airplane

1936   PAN AMERICAN AIRWAYS
For the establishment of the trans-Pacific airplane and the successful
execution of extended overwater navigation in the regular operation
thereof

1937   U.S. ARMY AIR CORPS
             For developing, equipping and flying the first successful pressure cabin
             airplane, the XC-35

1938   HOWARD HUGHES AND HIS ASSOCIATES
             For their epoch making round the world flight in 91 hours and 14
             minutes

1939   AIRLINES OF THE U.S.
             For their high record of safety in air travel, with special recognition to
             Drs. Walter M. Boothby and W. Randolph Lovelace, II of the Mayo
             Foundation for Medical Education and Research and Captain Harry
             G. Armstrong of the U.S. Army Medical Corps at Wright Field, for
             their contribution to this safety record through their work in aviation
             medicine in general and pilot fatigue in particular

1940   DR. SANFORD A. MOSS AND THE ARMY AIR CORPS
             For development of the turbo-supercharger

1941   THE ARMY AIR FORCES AND THE AIRLINES OF THE UNITED
             STATES
             For pioneering world wide air transportation vital to immediate de-
             fense and ultimate victory

1942   GENERAL H. H. ARNOLD, UNITED STATES ARMY
             For his organization and leadership of the Army Air Forces through-
             out the world

1943   CAPTAIN LUIS DeFLOREZ, UNITED STATES NAVY RESERVE
             For his contribution to the safe and rapid training of combat pilots
             and crews

1944   GENERAL CARL A. SPAATZ, AAF
             For demonstrating the air power concept through employment of
             American aviation in the war against Germany

1945   DR. LUIS W. ALVAREZ
             For his conspicuous and outstanding initiative in the concept of, and
             his contribution to the construction, adaptation and effective use of
             the ground control approach system for safe landing of aircraft under
             all weather and traffic conditions

1946   LEWIS A. ROBERT
             Chief of the Flight Research Branch at the Cleveland Laboratory of
             the National Advisory Committee for Aeronautics, for his pioneering
             research and guidance in the development and practical application of
             a thermal ice prevention system for aircraft

1947   JOHN STACK
             Research scientist, NACA, for pioneering research to determine the
             physical laws affecting supersonic flight, and for his conception of
             transonic research airplanes

LAWRENCE D. BELL
President, Bell Aircraft Corporation, for the design and construction of
the special research airplane X-1
CAPTAIN CHARLES E. YEAGER
U.S. Air Force, who, with that airplane, on October 14, 1947, first
achieved human flight faster than sound

1948   TO THE RADIO TECHNICAL COMMISSION FOR AERONAUTICS
For the establishment of a guide plan for the development and implementation of a system of air navigation and traffic control to facilitate
safe and unlimited aircraft operations under all weather conditions

1949   WILLIAM P. LEAR
For development of the F-5 automatic pilot and automatic approach
control coupler system

1950   TO THE HELICOPTER INDUSTRY, THE MILITARY SERVICES, AND
THE COAST GUARD
For development and use of rotary-wing aircraft for air rescue
operations

1951   TO JOHN STACK AND ASSOCIATES AT LANGLEY AERONAUTICAL
LABORATORY, NACA
For the conception, development, and practical application of the
transonic wind tunnel throat

1952   LEONARD S. HOBBS OF UNITED AIRCRAFT CORP.
For design, development, and production of the J-57 jet engine

1953   JAMES H. KINDELBERGER
For the North American land-based F-100
EDWARD H. HEINEMANN
For the Douglas carrier-based F4D

1954   RICHARD TRAVIS WHITCOMB, NACA RESEARCH SCIENTIST
For discovery and experimental verification of the area rule, a contribution to base knowledge yielding significantly higher airplane speed
and greater range with same power

1955   WILLIAM M. ALLEN AND HIS ASSOCIATES AT BOEING AIRPLANE
COMPANY
For conception, development and quantity production of America's
first all-jet, long-range bomber, the Boeing B-52 stratofortress, and to
GENERAL NATHAN F. TWINING AND THE U.S. AIR FORCE
For sponsoring and making it operational in 1955 as a powerful
weapon of peace

1956   CHARLES J. McCARTHY AND ASSOCIATES OF CHANCE-VOUGHT
AIRCRAFT, INCORPORATED AND TO VICE ADMIRAL JAMES S.
RUSSELL & ASSOCIATES OF THE U.S. NAVY BUREAU OF
AERONAUTICS

For conception, design, and development of the F-8U Crusader, a carrier-based fighter which is the first operational aircraft capable of speeds exceeding one thousand miles an hour

1957
EDWARD P. CURTIS
For his report entitled "Aviation Facilities Planning," which represented a signal and dramatic advance in the field of long-range planning to meet the complex problems involved in the use by aircraft of our air space

1958
THE UNITED STATES AIR FORCE AND INDUSTRY TEAM RESPONSIBLE FOR THE F-104 INTERCEPTOR; CLARENCE L. JOHNSON OF LOCKHEED AIRCRAFT CORPORATION for the design of the airframe; NEIL BURGESS AND GERHARD NEUMANN OF THE FLIGHT PROPULSION DIVISION; GENERAL ELECTRIC COMPANY, for development of its J-79 turbo jet engines; MAJOR HOWARD C. JOHNSON, USAF, for establishing a world land plane altitude record of 91,243 feet; and CAPTAIN WALTER W. IRVIN, USAF, for establishing a world straightaway speed record of 1,404.09 miles per hour

1959
THE UNITED STATES AIR FORCE, THE CONVAIR DIVISION OF GENERAL DYNAMICS CORPORATION AND SPACE TECHNOLOGY LABORATORIES, INC.
For developing, testing, producing and putting into operation the Atlas, America's first intercontinental ballistic missile so vital to the security and space exploration needs of the United States and the free world

1960
VICE ADMIRAL WILLIAM F. RABORN, USN
Under whose direction the United States Navy, Science and Industry created the operational fleet ballistic missile weapon system—Polaris

1961
MAJOR ROBERT M. WHITE, USAF; JOSEPH A. WALKER, NASA; A. SCOTT CROSSFIELD, NO. AMER. AVN.; AND COMMANDER FORREST PETERSEN, USN
For invaluable technological contributions to the advancement of flight and for great skill and courage as test pilots of the X-15

1962
LT. CMDR. MALCOLM SCOTT CARPENTER, USN; MAJ. L. GORDON COOPER, USAF; LT. COL. JOHN H. GLENN, JR. USMC; MAJOR VIRGIL I. GRISSOM, USAF; CMDR. WALTER M. SCHIRRA, JR., USN; CMDR. ALAN B. SHEPARD, JR., USN; MAJOR DONALD K. SLAYTON, USAF
For pioneering manned space flight in the United States

1963
CLARENCE L. "KELLY" JOHNSON
For designing and directing the development of the USAF A-11 Mach 3 aircraft

1964
GENERAL CURTIS E. LeMAY
For development of high performance aircraft, missiles and space sys-

tems which in 1964 significantly expanded the frontiers of American aeronautics and astronautics

1965   JAMES E. WEBB AND HUGH L. DRYDEN
Representing all of the Gemini program teams which significantly advanced human experience in space flight

1966   JAMES S. McDONNELL
For his leadership and perseverance in advancing aeronautics and astronautics exemplified by the F-4 Phantom aircraft and the Gemini space vehicles

1967   LAWRENCE A. HYLAND
Representing the Surveyor Program Team at Hughes Aircraft Company, the Jet Propulsion Laboratory, and associated organizations that put the eyes and hands of the United States on the Moon

1968   COL. FRANK BORMAN, USAF; CAPT. JAMES A. LOVELL, JR., USN; AND LT. COL. WILLIAM A. ANDERS, USAF
As the crew of Apollo 8 and representing the entire United States space flight team for the successful and flawless execution of the first manned lunar orbit mission in history

1969   NEIL A. ARMSTRONG; COL. EDWIN E. ALDRIN, JR., USAF; COL. MICHAEL COLLINS, USAF
For the epic flight of Apollo 11 and the first landing of man on the surface of the Moon, July 20, 1969

1970   THE BOEING COMPANY
As leader of the industry-airline-government team which successfully introduced the 747 into commercial service with particular recognition to Pratt and Whitney Division of United Aircraft Corporation and to Pan American World Airways

1971   TO COLONEL DAVID R. SCOTT, USAF; COLONEL JAMES B. IRWIN, USAF; AND LIEUTENANT COLONEL ALFRED M. WORDEN, USAF
For demonstrating superb skill and courage and to DR. ROBERT T. GILRUTH as representative of the engineering genius of the manned space flight team, culminating in Apollo 15—man's most prolonged and scientifically productive lunar mission

1972   THE OFFICERS AND MEN OF THE 7TH AIR FORCE AND 8TH AIR FORCE OF THE UNITED STATES AIR FORCE AND TASK FORCE 77 OF THE UNITED STATES NAVY
For successfully carrying out operation Linebacker II, the air campaign against North Vietnam in December, 1972 which through precise, accurate, and determined attacks on key military targets in the face of unprecedented defenses, brought about a cease fire under terms which attained United States objectives in Southeast Asia

1973   THE SKYLAB PROGRAM, WITH SPECIAL RECOGNITION TO WILLIAM C. SCHNEIDER, PROGRAM DIRECTOR, AND THE THREE SKYLAB ASTRONAUT CREWS

For proving beyond question the value of man in future explorations of space and the production of data of benefit to all the people on Earth

1974   TO DR. JOHN F. CLARK, NASA, AND DANIEL J. FINK, GENERAL ELECTRIC COMPANY, representing the NASA/Industry Team responsible for the Earth Resources Technology Satellite Program, LANDSAT, for proving in 1974 the value of U.S. space technology in the management of the Earth's resources and environment for the benefit of all mankind, WITH SPECIAL RECOGNITION TO HUGHES AIRCRAFT COMPANY AND RCA

1975   DAVID S. LEWIS OF GENERAL DYNAMICS CORPORATION AND THE F-16 AIR FORCE-INDUSTRY TEAM
For significant advancements in aviation technology leading to innovative fighter aircraft effectiveness

1976   THE U.S. AIR FORCE/ROCKWELL INTERNATIONAL CORPORATION AND THE B-1 INDUSTRY TEAM
For the highly successful design, development, management, and flight test of the B-1 strategic aircraft system

1977   GENERAL ROBERT J. DIXON, COMMANDER, AND THE TACTICAL AIR COMMAND, USAF
For developing and implementing Red Flag, an unprecedented combat simulated flight training program for aircrews of the U.S. Armed Forces, a significant contribution to national defense

1978   SAM B. WILLIAMS, CHAIRMAN AND PRESIDENT, WILLIAMS RESEARCH CORPORATION
For conceiving and developing the world's smallest, high efficiency turbofan engine which was selected to power U.S. cruise missiles

1979   DR. PAUL B. MacCREADY
For the concept, design, and construction of the Gossamer Albatross, which made the first man-powered flight across the English Channel—with special recognition to Bryan Allen, the pilot

1980   TO THE VOYAGER MISSION TEAM, REPRESENTED BY ITS CHIEF SCIENTIST, DR. EDWARD C. STONE
For the spectacular fly-by of Saturn and the return of basic new knowledge of the solar system

1981   NASA, ROCKWELL INTERNATIONAL, MARTIN MARIETTA, THIOKOL AND THE ENTIRE GOVERNMENT/INDUSTRIAL TEAM that improved the concept of manned reusable spacecraft, with special recognition to astronauts John Young, Robert Crippen, Joe Engle and Richard Truly

1982   T. A. WILSON AND THE BOEING COMPANY
For the private development of two advanced technology transports—

757 and the 767—with the support of the Federal Aviation Administration, industry and the airlines

1983   THE UNITED STATES ARMY, HUGHES AIRCRAFT HELICOPTERS AND THE INDUSTRY TEAM
For development of the AH-64A Apache advanced technology helicopter weapon system

1984   NASA AND MARTIN MARIETTA CORP.
For the development of the MMUI and the NASA industry satellite rescue team and to ASTRONAUT BRUCE McCANDLESS II, NASA'S CHARLES E. WHITSETT, JR., AND MARTIN MARIETTA'S WALTER W. BOLLENDONK

1985   RUSSELL W. MEYER, CESSNA AIRCRAFT CO. AND CESSNA'S LINE OF CITATION BUSINESS JET AIRCRAFT
For an unparalleled passenger safety record during the past 14 years since the Citation's introduction.

1986   JEANA L. YEAGER, RICHARD G. RUTAN, ELBERT L. RUTAN, AND THE VOYAGER AIRCRAFT TEAM OF VOLUNTEERS
For the ingenious design and development of the Voyager aircraft and their skillful execution of the first non-stop, non-refueled flight around the world

1987   NASA LEWIS RESEARCH CENTER AND THE NASA/INDUSTRY ADVANCED TURBOPROP TEAM
For the development of advanced turboprop propulsion concepts for single rotation, gearless counter rotation, and geared counter rotation inducted fan systems

1988   REAR ADMIRAL RICHARD H. TRULY, USN
For his assistance for the successful return of America to space

1989   MR. BENJAMIN R. RICH, LOCKHEED AIRCRAFT CORP. AND THE UNITED STATES AIR FORCE TEAM
For the F-117A stealth aircraft development

1990   TO THE BELL BOEING TEAM
For the development of the V-22 Osprey Tiltrotor, the world's first large-scale tiltrotor aircraft.

1991   TO THE NORTHROP CORPORATION, THE INDUSTRY TEAM AND THE UNITED STATES AIR FORCE
For the design, development, production, and flight testing of the B-2 aircraft, which has contributed significantly to America's enduring leadership in aerospace and the country's future national security.

THE GORDON BENNETT CUP FOR GAS BALLOONS

B

Year	Starting point	Winner	Distance (miles)
1906	Paris, France	Frank Lahm (USA)	402
1907	St. Louis, USA	Osker Ebersloh (Germany)	872
1908	Berlin, Germany	Oberst Soheeok (Switzerland)	753
1909	Zurich, Switzerland	Edgar W. Hix (USA)	696
1910	St. Louis, USA	Alan R. Hawley (USA)	1173
1911	Kansas City, USA	Hans Gericke (Germany)	471
1912	Stuttgart, Germany	Maurice Bienhaime (France)	1334
1913	Paris, France	Ralph Upson (USA)	384
1914–1919	No events held during World War I		
1920	Birmingham, USA	Ernest DeMuyter (Belgium)	1098
1921	Brussels, Belgium	Paul Armbruster (Switzerland)	476
1922	Geneva, Switzerland	Ernest DeMuyter (Belgium)	852
1923	Brussels, Belgium	Ernest DeMuyter (Belgium)	717
1924	Brussels, Belgium	Ernest DeMuyter (Belgium)	444
1925	Brussels, Belgium	A. Veenstra (Belgium)	836
1926	Antwerp, Belgium	Ward T. Van Orman (USA)	535
1927	Detroit, USA	Edward J. Hill (USA)	745
1928	Detroit, USA	W. B. Kepner (USA)	460
1929	St. Louis, USA	Ward T. Van Orman (USA)	341
1930	Cleveland, USA	Ward T. Van Orman (USA)	542
1931	No event held		
1932	Basle, Switzerland	T. O. W. Settle (USA)	921
1933	Chicago, USA	Franoyzek Hynok (Poland)	848

Year	Starting point	Winner	Distance (miles)
1934	Warsaw, Poland	Franoyzek Hynok (Poland)	808
1935	Warsaw, Poland	Zbigniew Burzynski (Poland)	1025
1936	Warsaw, Poland	Ernest DeMuyter (Belgium)	1066
1937	Brussels, Belgium	Ernest DeMuyter (Belgium)	867
1938	Liège, Belgium	Antoni Januaz (Poland)	1051
1939–1982	No events held: Competition discontinued at beginning of World War II		
1983	Paris, France	Cieslak / Makne (Poland)	428
1984	Zurich, Switzerland	Spenger / Messner (Switzerland)	492
1985	Geneva, Switzerland	Starkbaum / Scholz (Austria)	212
1986	Salzburg, Austria	Starkbaum / Scholz (Austria)	169
1987	Seefeld, Austria	Starkbaum / Scholz (Austria)	528
1988	Bregenz, Austria	Starkbaum / Scholz (Austria)	689
1989	Bregenz, Austria	Starkbaum / Scholz (Austria)	565
1990	Lech, Austria	Starkbaum / Scholz (Austria)	429
1991	Lech, Austria	Kuinke / Schubert (Germany)	646
1992	Stuttgart, Germany	Levin / Herschend (USA)	598

THE WRIGHT TROPHY $\boxed{C}$

AWARDED FOR

The Wright Brothers Memorial Trophy is awarded annually to a living American for "significant public service of enduring value to aviation in the United States."

The words "public service" are interpreted to include either (1) public service whether as a full-time employee of the government or as an unpaid volunteer serving on a government commission or agency, or (2) service which made a major contribution of enduring value to the public. The word "aviation" is interpreted broadly to include aerospace activities.

ORIGIN

Following the death of Orville Wright in January 1948 the National Aeronautic Association established the Wright Brothers Memorial Trophy, which has been awarded every year since then by the president of the NAA on the anniversary of the historic flight.

COMMITTEE

The Wright Brothers Memorial Trophy Committee is appointed annually by the President of the NAA and consists of seven members, including the president, chairman, administrator, or a representative of each of the following:

National Aeronautic Association
National Aeronautics and Space Administration
Air Transport Association

Aerospace Industries Association

American Institute of Aeronautics and Astronautics

Aero Club of Washington

The aviation press

CHRONOLOGY

1948   Dr. William F. Durand
Dean of American aeronautical engineers, who developed the basic theories of aircraft propeller design and was a primary force in the establishment of the National Advisory Committee for Aeronautics.

1949   Charles A. Lindbergh
For his long and selfless career in aviation.

1950   Grover Loening
Who, over a period of more than forty years, has served aviation as a student, a pilot, an engineer, a manufacturer, an author, a consultant, and an advisor.

1951   Dr. Jerome C. Hunsaker
For his long career in public service in the field of aviation, dating back to 1913. He established the first course of instruction for aeronautical engineers at the Massachusetts Institute of Technology and also designed and built a pioneer wind tunnel for educational and research purposes. He was a founder and the first president of the Institute of the Aeronautical Sciences. He has been chairman of the (NACA) continuously from 1941 to the present.

1952   Lt. Gen. James H. Doolittle, USAF
For his service in a civilian capacity, which contributed to the progress of American aviation, dating back to his 1924 graduation from MIT with an aeronautical engineering degree. For development of fog-flying equipment and making the first successful flight, including takeoff and landing, while in a completely covered airplane cockpit. He organized the Air Force Association and was the first president of that organization.

1953   Honorable Carl Hinshaw
For his service as a member of the House of Representatives in fostering the sound and consistent growth of aviation in all its forms, so that it might become a deterrent to war and that it might increasingly become an important carrier of the people and the commerce of the world.

1954   Dr. Theodore Von Karman
For providing many of the foundation stones leading to the development of supersonic aircraft and guided missiles. No other man has had a greater influence on the development of high-speed aircraft in the United States.

1955   Dr. Hugh L. Dryden
For his pioneering work in the field of supersonic research. His studies of turbulence in wind tunnels and of the mechanics of air flow within the boundary layer made contribu-

tions of enduring value to aviation in the United States. He has had a distinguished career devoted entirely to the public service.

1956   Dr. Edward P. Warner
For continuous achievements over a broad range of aviation disciplines since 1917.

1957   Senator Stuart Symington
For significant public service of enduring value to aviation in the United States. Based upon his distinguished career of public service in the field of aviation, a career that began early in 1941. Senator Symington's belief in aviation, the energy and perseverance with which he has consistently fought for air power objectives, his high statesmanship, and his outstanding public service all combine to make him a most deserving recipient of the trophy.

1958   Dr. John Frederick Victory
In the building of the organization (NACA) that was selected to be the nucleus of the new National Aeronautics and Space Administration, Victory has exerted a driving influence to advance the progress of aeronautics in America and to promote the public interest. This he has done quietly and effectively with, at times, extraordinary courage, vision, and ability. His long record of unselfish service as a civilian to aeronautics is indeed significant and is of enduring value to aviation.

1959   William P. MacCracken, Jr.
Pioneer in aviation legislation. He has been a driving influence in the evolution of air travel and has, throughout his life, worked with great vision and ability in providing a sound legal foundation for the development of civil and commercial aviation in America. His long period of unselfish service is truly significant and of enduring value to aviation. His notable contributions fully qualify him for the award of the Wright Brothers Memorial Trophy.

1960   Frederick C. Crawford
Nationally known engineer and industrial leader, who has served the United States government on many occasions and over a number of years. He was a member of NACA (now known as NASA) and served as Chairman of NACA's Committee on Power Plants for Aircraft. Currently, he is chairman of the TRW Corporation, which offers talented scientific services to the nation.

1961   A. S. Mike Monroney
For more than three decades of public service dedicated to the advancement, safety, and equitable regulation of aviation in this country, first as a member of the House of Representatives, then as a member of the United States Senate. Some examples of his aviation leadership are: His continuous emphasis on air safety, his pressure for further advancement in the art of air navigation and traffic control, his leadership in the field of air cargo development, and the foresight that has put him in the vanguard of airport development throughout the country for over a decade.

1962   John Stack
For his outstanding career and reputation for spearheading advancement in supersonic flight.

1963   Donald W. Douglas, Sr.
For his many services to the nation and contributions to the advancement of aviation as a public servant. Probably best known for his role as the "father" of the famous DC-3

transport, the plane that ushered in a new era of air travel comfort and convenience during the mid-1930s, carried the logistics of global war during World War II, and, today, still serves as a feeder airline and business aircraft.

1964   Harry F. Guggenheim

For almost half a century, Harry F. Guggenheim has devoted a very considerable part of his time to advancing the science and practice of flight. The Daniel Guggenheim Fund for the Promotion of Aeronautics, which he administered, sponsored schools of aeronautics at New York University, the Massachusetts Institute of Technology, the California Institute of Technology, the Georgia School of Technology, and other institutions of higher learning. The Daniel and Florence Guggenheim Foundation, through his personal leadership, sponsored and supported jet propulsion centers at the California Institute of Technology and Princeton University, and for more than a decade was the sole financial supporter of Professor Robert H. Goddard, father of modern rocketry.

1965   Jerome Lederer

Aviation's extraordinary safety record to a significant degree is a result of the tireless and devoted effort of Mr. Lederer. For thirty-five years, he has worked unceasingly to improve all elements of the flight safety spectrum and concentrated on making compatible the primary elements of flight—the pilot, the machine, and the ground environment—to ensure maximum safety. In accomplishing this objective, he has taken the leadership in correlating, coordinating, and improving the flight safety activities of the many varied organizations and agencies comprising world aviation. For these selfless and inspired contributions, Mr. Lederer has received virtually every national and international safety award.

1966   Juan Terry Trippe

For significant public service of enduring value to aviation in the United States. Through his vision and practicality, Juan T. Trippe has played a unique role in helping to revolutionize air travel and promote international commerce and goodwill. More than any other man, he pushed the United States into international air transportation, where it is now the model for progress, efficiency, and safety. Through his forty years of leadership he has pioneered flight technology and accelerated the development of new aircraft, from the famous China Clippers of the Pacific routes to the supersonic jets of tomorrow.

1967   Dr. Igor I. Sikorsky

For public service of significant and enduring value to aviation through the design and production of the world's first practical helicopter, the conception and construction of the first successful multiengine aircraft, and the design and production of a series of amphibious aircraft that pioneered transoceanic air transportation.

1968   Senator Warren G. Magnuson

For more than two decades of dynamic leadership in developing national and international policy that has assured U.S. preeminence in aeronautics throughout the world and has contributed immeasurably to the health and vitality of America's economic structure.

1969   William M. Allen

For significant public service in the development of commercial airlines and civil and military aircraft, and for outstanding leadership and foresight in the establishment of policies and programs that have made possible U.S. preeminence in today's dynamic aviation environment.

1970   C. R. Smith
For significant public service of enduring value in the development of military and civil air transportation and for his contributions as a dynamic leader and articulate spokesman for U.S. aviation progress.

1971   Senator Howard W. Cannon
For his continuing energetic advocacy of and lasting contributions to the development and use of aviation, both as a viable national transportation system and as an essential element in maintaining a strong military posture.

1972   John H. Shaffer
In recognition of his outstanding leadership of the worldwide operations of the Federal Aviation Administration, which has greatly enhanced all aspects of U.S. aviation to the benefit and safety of the general public and of all who fly.

1973   Senator Barry M. Goldwater
For his leadership and inspiration to all elements of aviation in the United States, both military and civilian, and for serving as an articulate spokesman for American aviation and space in Congress and throughout the world.

1974   Dr. Richard T. Whitcomb
For his innovative research through the years, which has led to major advancements in high-speed flight and the continued technological leadership of U.S. aviation.

1975   Clarence L. (Kelly) Johnson
For his vital and enduring contributions over a period of forty years to the design and development of military and commercial aircraft.

1976   William Allan Patterson
For his contributions to the development of safe and efficient air transportation over the past half-century.

1977   Ira C. Eaker
For sixty years of significant public service: as pioneer flier, military leader, industry executive, and persuasive interpreter of aviation to the American people through the written and spoken word.

1978   Senator Jennings Randolph
For his distinguished support of aviation in the United States by successful initiation and advocacy of major aviation legislation over more than three decades of service in Congress, and as an airline executive.

1979   T. A. Wilson
Chairman of the board and chief executive officer of the Boeing Company. For distinguished and enduring contributions to the growth of American aviation as an essential element of national security and economic growth.

1980   Olive Ann Beech
Chairman of the board of Beech Aircraft Corporation. For five decades of outstanding leadership in the development of general aviation.

1981   Dwane L. Wallace
Former chairman and chief executive officer of Cessna Aircraft. For significant public service of enduring value to aviation in the United States.

1982   Willis M. Hawkins

For his vision, imagination, and dedication in more than forty years of public service to aviation through technical innovations and management leadership in the design, development, and production of military and commercial aircraft, space vehicles, and advanced missilery.

1983   John Leland Atwood

In recognition of his leadership in the development of air and space vehicles, spanning more than five decades, and his significant contributions in the public interest to the art of management in American industry.

1984   David S. Lewis

For his lifetime contributions to military aviation and national defense and his untiring efforts in the design, development, and production of superior combat aircraft.

1985   Harry Combs

For over half a century of significant and enduring contributions to aviation as a pilot, an industrial leader, an author, and an advisor to government.

1986   Joseph F. Sutter

In recognition of a career in aviation, spanning more than four decades, during which his technical leadership and management skills were instrumental in the development of three generations of advanced transports, which contributed significantly to U.S. preeminence in civil aeronautics.

1987   Allen E. Paulson

For his outstanding and enduring contributions to aviation as a pilot, designer, entrepreneur, industry leader, and employer throughout a career spanning over forty years.

1988   Sam B. Williams

For significant and enduring contributions to aviation and national defense over a period of thirty-five years. His invention and production of small, lightweight gas turbine engines and his leadership in the introduction and processing of new technology and new materials have provided major impetus to U.S. aviation progress.

1989   Thomas V. Jones

For his achievements, over a period of forty-seven years, in guiding the development of advanced aircraft, electronic systems, and manufacturing technologies. Visionary, bold designer, planner, engineer, and manager, he has significantly enhanced the defense and air transportation capacity of the United States.

1990   Edwin I. Colodny

For a lifetime of meritorious service to air transportation as an airline executive and public servant.

1991   Benjamin A. Cosgrove

For a lifetime contribution to commercial aviation safety and to the technology development of four generations of Boeing commercial jet transport aircraft.

1992   Senator Jake Garn

In recognition of a lifetime of public service in government and active participation in all segments of U.S. aviation—as a military and civilian pilot, astronaut, and one of the U.S. Senate's most effective aerospace spokesmen and legislators.

THE BREWER TROPHY

AWARDED FOR

The Frank G. Brewer Trophy is awarded annually for significant contributions of enduring value in the fields of aviation and aerospace education activities in the United States.

ORIGIN

The Frank G. Brewer Trophy was established in 1943 and was first awarded to the Civil Aeronautics Administration for its outstanding contribution to the education of youth in aviation and in recognition of its preflight training program in 14,000 high schools nationwide. Frank G. Brewer established the Brewer Trophy in honor of his two sons and the million and a half other American youths put into the air by World War II. The NAA has administered the trophy since it was founded.

COMMITTEE

The Frank G. Brewer Trophy Selection Committee is appointed annually by the president of the NAA. The size of the committee is also determined by the president.

PRESENTATION

The Frank G. Brewer Trophy is presented at an appropriate ceremony as determined by the president of the NAA.

CHRONOLOGY

1943   Civil Aeronautics Administration
For the Civilian Pilot Training Program, making it possible for 250,000 youths, fifteen to eighteen years of age, to exploit their interest in aviation by availing themselves of aviation education on a nationwide basis in high schools.

1944   Dr. Edgar Fuller, Assistant Director, Aviation Education Program of the Civil Aeronautics Administration
For the outstanding contribution of Air Youth, in his work as assistant director of aviation education, CAA. Fuller worked in each of the forty-eight states for organization of various phases of aviation education in elementary and secondary schools, as well as colleges.

1945   Dr. Huber W. Hurt, Director of Development and Research, Boy Scouts of America
For his outstanding contribution to the education of American youth, through his work in the Air Scouting movement. He organized a system of incentive awards for the study of aviation by members of the Boy Scouts. He authored the Scout handbook, *The Yearbook of Aviation for Young Men*.

1946   Dr. Frank E. Sorenson, Associate Professor of Education, University of Nebraska
Dr. Sorenson's work was recognized in determining just what knowledge teachers must have to instruct pupils effectively in becoming air-minded youth. He prepared such books as *Elements of Pre-Flight Aeronautics* and *Now We Fly*. He was frequently a consultant to NAA on aviation matters.

1947   Dr. Nicholaus L. Englehardt, Jr., Air Age Education Research
For his active participation in the field of Air Age Education in building up valuable aviation teaching aids, plus his 1947 teaching development, "Flying Classrooms."

1948   Philip S. Hopkins, President, Board of Education, Binghamton, New York
For almost a dozen air age education activities. Outstanding was his origin and promotion of the idea of an Air Age Center in each school, to contain visual aids, wall charts, pictures, maps, magazines, and other materials, which could be used by teachers. Hopkins traveled to over 13,000 teachers on aviation subjects. His trainer, similar to a small plane, led to the development of the "School Link" now used in many schools throughout the nation.

1949   Mrs. Elsie W. Adams, Supervisory Teacher, Denver Public Schools
For her practical and effective application of aviation to the processes of education. Her efforts made the Denver school system one of the most advanced in the nation in aviation education work. She wrote numerous articles and outlines for instruction on aviation education for leading education journals.

1950   Sr. Lt. John H. Burton, USN
For inspiring and effective leadership in planning and carrying out the 1950 air youth education and model airplane programs of the U.S. Navy.

1951   Dr. Harold E. Mehrens, Supervisor of the Aviation Education Program, Civil Aeronautics Administration
Mehrens conducted ground school courses as part of the CAA's Civilian Pilot Training Program and prepared instructional material in navigation and meteorology, and qualified

for all seven of the ground school ratings. He served with CAA's foreign national program and authored numerous magazine articles and books, including *Adventures in Aviation Education.*

1952   Civil Air Patrol
In recognition of the thousands of volunteer Civil Air Patrol members who have unselfishly devoted their time and effort in the development of the CAP Cadet and Teaching Training Program.

1953   Dr. Leslie A. Bryan, Director, Institute of Aviation, University of Illinois
Dr. Bryan, author of numerous books and articles on many aviation subjects, specifically developed a program for students and faculty at the University of Illinois that has supervised the training of over 7,000 without a single injury.

1954   Dr. John H. Furbay, Director, Air World Education, Trans World Airlines
For his outstanding contribution to the development of air youth in the field of education and training through his effective and inspirational series of talks to teachers about the responsibilities of citizenship in the air age.

1955   Willis C. Brown
For services rendered in seeking, through group action, to interest more youths in some phase of aviation through classroom and experience programs.

1956   Ray O. Mertes
For distinguished and unselfish service to the youth of America through his leadership in the field of aviation as a school administrator, lecturer, author, and Director of the School and College Services of United Airlines.

1957   Edwin A. Link
Whose inventive genius has resulted in the development of simulators and other devices that directly contributed to the education of hundreds of thousands of aviators and whose unselfish dedication to aviation education resulted in his establishing and liberally endowing the Link Foundation, which will provide, for years to come, financial support for students and research in the field of aviation education and training.

1958   Dr. Evan Evans
For outstanding service to aviation education as the executive director of the National Aerospace Education Council, and as a teacher and school administrator with a national reputation in aviation education.

1959   Dr. Paul E. Garber, Head Curator and Historian, National Air Museum
For thirty-eight years of outstanding service to youth and their education in aviation by planning, providing, and displaying education exhibits in the National Air Museum.

1960   George N. Gardner, Pan American World Airways
As Education Director of Pan American Airways, for his singular contribution to aviation education through the publication of materials tailored specifically to classroom use, through educational travel, and through the development and administration of an original and highly educational model aviation event.

1961   James V. Bernardo
For developing a plan of national spacemobile demonstration units to supplement high school science programs; personally organizing and teaching thirty-two aviation educa-

tion workshops in twenty-one United States colleges prior to joining the National Aeronautics and Space Administration; and authorship of the book *Aviation in the Modern World,* which covered both aviation and space exploration.

1962   Dr. Merlyn McLaughlin

For distinguished and unselfish service to aviation education over a period of years as a writer and lecturer, a pioneer aviation teacher and administrator, a Civil Air Patrol leader, and an officer of the U.S. Air Force.

1963   Marilyn Link

For her distinguished and outstanding meritorious service to the Air Youth of America in aerospace education, and for her work toward the stimulation, guidance, encouragement, and inspiration of young minds to make some truly great accomplishments in aviation and aviation safety. Her personal participation in programs for the Link Foundation and aerospace education have encompassed eighteen colleges and universities from Massachu-setts to the state of Washington, and from Michigan to Texas. The programs have embraced fellowships, scholarships, workshops, seminars, and conferences.

1964   Gill Robb Wilson

For his writing, his speaking, and his devoted public service, which have brought the message of aerospace to the minds and hearts of American young people. He has translated the knowledge and skills of the flier into language that is both meaningful and inspirational to the millions of young people who have heard him speak and read his prose and poetry. His entire career has been one of education, in the fullest and finest sense.

1965   Mrs. Jane N. Marshall

For her contributions to enlarged aerospace horizons for those who teach our nation's youth. Through her creative writing in educator-oriented aerospace publications, her development of timely bibliographies and teaching aids, and her leadership in the organization and administration of aerospace education workshops for teachers, she has contributed significantly to fuller understanding of the impact of flight upon all Americans.

1966   Dr. Mervin K. Strickler, Jr.

For his continuous and enthusiastic contributions to the education of youth as to the place of aviation in their lives today and its promises and challenges for tomorrow; for his energetic, imaginative, and innovative programs as special assistant for aviation education, Office of General Aviation Affairs of the Federal Aviation Agency, which have brought the educational community into closer contact with aviation; for the inspiration and encour-agement he has given to thousands of teachers and students; for his past leadership of the national program of aviation education of the Civil Air Patrol; and for his long years of service as a charter member and officer of the National Aerospace Education Council.

1967   Dr. Roland H. Spaulding

For forty years of continuous, outstanding, and pioneering contributions in aerospace education to the youth of the nation, as a classroom teacher and as an educational administrator; for his dynamic and inspiring teaching of thousands of students and teachers; for his efforts in organizing and directing aerospace educationworkshops for teachers; for his active participation and unstinting service as a member and as an officer of numerous aerospace organizations and committees, of many of which he is a charter member; and for his leadership and perseverance—resulting in significant achievements—in fostering the inclusion of aviation and space concepts in educational systems throughout the nation.

1968   Joseph T. Geuting, Jr.
For more than twenty years of dedicated involvement in numerous national aerospace education programs, and particularly for his influential and innovative leadership in general aviation through encouraging industry's active participation in aerospace education to enrich the school curricula and give to the youth of our nation a deeper understanding of the meaning of flight and its impact upon their lives.

1969   James H. Strauble
For outstanding contributions to the growth and development of aerospace education in the United States and abroad—as a stimulant, catalyst, and innovator—during more than two decades, as executive director of both the Air Force Association and the Aerospace Education Foundation.

1970   Dr. Walter Zaharevitz
For his unflagging endeavors in developing and introducing aviation and space concepts to the youth of the nation. His demonstrated ability in managing the National Aerospace Education Council, his writing and creative abilities, and his continuing contributions to education throughout his distinguished career as an aerospace education leader.

1971   Professor Harold S. Wood
For his unselfish dedication to the cause of youth aviation and education as a teacher at Parks College for nearly a quarter of a century and, specifically, for his leadership and exemplary efforts in founding and nurturing the National Intercollegiate Flying Association and Alpha Eta Rho.

1972   Dr. Wayne O. Reed
As one of the nation's foremost exponents of aerospace education on both the state and national levels, he has been instrumental in introducing millions of young people to an understanding of the air age.

1973   Dr. Frederick B. Tuttle
For three decades of outstanding contributions to air age education and training in the CAA, the field of higher education, the National Aeronautics and Space Administration, and through the National Aerospace Education Association. Hundreds of thousands of elementary and secondary school pupils and teachers have benefited from his innovative leadership in aviation and space education.

1974   Dr. Wayne R. Matson
For his outstanding contributions to the field of aerospace education over the years, serving as educator, author, lecturer, pilot, and consultant; for working for the educational community as well as government and industry in the furtherance of aerospace education; and most recently for creating, launching, and serving as editor-in-chief of the *Directory* and the *Journal of Aerospace Education*.

1975   Dr. Leslie L. Thomason
For his dedication in the development of creative and imaginative aviation education programs in government, industry, and the academic community, which have impacted and enlightened millions of people throughout the world about air transportation.

1976   Dr. J. Wesley Crum
For his dedication, enthusiasm, and contributions to aviation and space education over the past 20 years, and specifically for his sensitive responses and creative leadership, which have become a standard for all to respect and emulate.

1977   The Honorable Don H. Clausen
For outstanding leadership and performance in a number of activities in furthering aviation and space education, including chairmanship of the California Task Force on Aerospace Aviation Education. He also authored federal legislation establishing a civil aviation information distribution program designed to provide state and local school administrators and college and university officials with information, materials, and expertise on various aspects of civil aviation.

1978   Michael Collins, Undersecretary of the Smithsonian Institution and the Team
        of People He Assembled While Serving as Director of the National Air and
        Space Museum
He was elected for having put into place a vibrant and exciting education apparatus available to every citizen, reminding Americans of their proud heritage of aviation and space accomplishments, and inspiring young people to help contribute new advancements in aeronautics and astronautics.

1979   Paul H. Poberezny, Executive Director and President, Experimental Aircraft
        Association
For outstanding promotion of aviation education for the young for over a quarter of a century; for the motivational impact his aviation programs have had on thousands of young Americans; for his initiating Project Schoolflight, the program of building aircraft in the schools; for inspiring air-minded youth to work with hand and mind toward a common goal, the completion of an airplane.

1980   The Florida Institute of Technology and Dr. Jerome P. Keuper, President and
        Founder of the Florida Institute of Technology
For outstanding contributions of enduring value to aerospace education in the United States. The Florida Institute of Technology is unique, as it is the only university in the United States offering both aviation and space science programs and is the only independent technological university in the United States.

1981   Edward W. Stimpson
For over a decade of outstanding leadership in aviation education. He has personally been involved in instigating and promoting programs for teachers, students, pilots, and the general public. His efforts have been felt in high schools, colleges, flight schools, and aviation safety seminars, and have involved motion pictures, slide presentations, radio, television, and national magazine features.

1982   John V. Sorenson
His ability to combine superior qualities as organizer, administrator, educator, and orator, together with his practical wartime experience as a fighter pilot, has enabled him to accomplish outstanding improvements in many aeronautical organizations, including the Civil Air Patrol, the National Congress on Aerospace Education, and the World Aerospace Education Organization. His devotion to constantly learning more about aeronautics and sharing his knowledge with others, nationally and internationally, has provided outstand-

ing improvements in aerospace education. The whole science and art of flight have been advanced through his capabilities and dedication.

1983   Senator Barry M. Goldwater
For a lifetime of devotion to, participation in, and extraordinary support of all elements involved in aerospace activities and education. He has had a profound individual as well as professional impact on aerospace education during his many years as a pilot and a United States senator.

1984   Mary Jo Knouff
For outstanding contributions to the growth and development of aerospace education, across the entire spectrum, from the grass roots to high government and industry levels.

1985   Charles Alfred (Chief) Anderson
For nearly six decades of aerospace education leadership; attracting, motivating, and educating the youth of the nation; and exemplifying the very spirit and purpose of the Frank G. Brewer Trophy.

1986   Dr. Paul A. Whelan
For his outstanding contributions and enduring commitment to aviation and space education in both the military and civilian sectors.

1987   Dr. John D. Odegard
For his distinguished and inspiring leadership in creating new educational opportunities for future aerospace professionals. Moreover he has contributed immensely to the aviation training and motivation of young people and strengthening of the nation's air transportation system.

1988   Dr. Curtis M. Graves
For his many years of outstanding aviation/space educational leadership in the National Aeronautics and Space Administration education and governmental affairs programs. His efforts resulted in inspiring millions of young people and thousands of educators and public officials.

1989   (No Award Was Given)

1990   Lockhart J. Smith, Jr.
For his lifetime contribution of motivating, inspiring, and teaching aerospace sciences, aircraft design, construction, and maintenance to two generations of students at Wentworth Institute of Technology in Boston, MA. He epitomizes the very best of the many thousands of dedicated aerospace educators and leaders who motivate our young men and women to take up careers in aviation. Without the dedication of educators like Lockhart Smith, the Untied States could not have achieved its position of worldwide leadership in aviation and space.

1991   Kenneth L. Tallman
For over 40 years of creative leadership, personal accomplishments, and professional contributions to aviation and space education. As Superintendent of the U.S. Air Force Academy, as President of the Spartan School of Aeronautics and as President of Embry-Riddle Aeronautical University, he has been instrumental in developing and delivering aviation and space education to thousands of today's aviation professionals.

THE ELDER STATESMEN OF AVIATION AWARD

AWARDED FOR

The purpose of the Elder Statesman of Aviation Award is to honor outstanding Americans who, by their efforts over a period of years, have made contributions of significant value to aeronautics and have reflected credit upon America and themselves.

ORIGIN

The Elder Statesman of Aviation Award was established on October 16, 1954, by the board of directors of the NAA. The award is in the form of a handsome parchment certificate, suitably mounted, certifying the recipient's election as an Elder Statesman of Aviation.

NOMINATIONS

A nominee for consideration as an Elder Statesman of Aviation shall:

a. Be a citizen of the United States, who, for at least fifteen years, has been actively identified with aeronautics and has made contributions of significant value to aeronautics.

b. Have exhibited qualities of patriotism, integrity, and moral courage worthy of emulation.
c. Be at least 60 years of age.
d. Be well and favorably known as a person of ability and character.

COMMITTEE

The Elder Statesmen of Aviation shall be selected by a committee appointed by the president of the NAA. The committee presents to the association's board of directors those persons they select for consideration as Elder Statesmen of Aviation. The board then elects the Elder Statesmen of Aviation for the year being considered from among those nominations.

PRESENTATION

The Elder Statesman of Aviation certificates are presented annually at a time and place selected by the president of the NAA.

CHRONOLOGY

1955	Hiram Bingham		Clarence M. Young
	Godfrey L. Cabot	1957	Reginald M. Cleveland
	William F. Durand		Donald W. Douglas, Sr.
	Lester D. Gardner		Luis DeFlorez
	Jerome C. Hunsaker		John Jay Ide
	Frank P. Lahm		C. Townsend Ludington
	Emory S. Land		Charles E. Rosendahl
	Paul W. Litchfield		John F. Victory
	Grover Loening		
	William P. MacCracken, Jr.	1958	Preston R. Bassett
	Glenn L. Martin		Walter S. Diehl
	Frederick B. Renschler		Reuben H. Fleet
	Edward V. Rickenbacker		Gill Robb Wilson
	Igor I. Sikorsky		
	Carl Vinson	1959	Arthur B. Chalk
			Alexander P. De Seversky
1956	Richard E. Byrd		James H. Doolittle
	Frederick C. Crawford		Arthur W. Radford
	Harry F. Guggenheim		
	William T. Piper	1960	Ralph S. Barnaby
	Dewitt C. Ramsey		Edward R. Sharp
	Carl Spaatz		Theodore P. Wright
	Alfred V. Verville	1961	Arlene Davis

AWARDED FOR

The purpose of the Elder Statesman of Aviation Award is to honor outstanding Americans who, by their efforts over a period of years, have made contributions of significant value to aeronautics and have reflected credit upon America and themselves.

1961 [cont.]	Ira C. Eaker J. H. Kindelberger	1973	Bennett Hill Griffin James Joseph Mattern Maj. Gen. Leigh Wade
1962	Harry A. Bruno Maj. Gen. B. D. Foulois John K. Northrop Floyd B. Odlum	1974	Olive Ann Beech Cass S. Hough Jerome Lederer
1963	Henry J. E. Reid Howard F. Rough Gen. Nathan F. Twining	1975	Earl Dodge Osborn Dr. Oliver L. Parks Dwane L. Wallace
1964	F. Trubee Davison Dr. Paul Garber Charles Joseph McCarthy William A. Ong	1976	J. Leland Atwood Clifford W. Henderson Blanche Wilcox Noyes
1965	Joe Crane Leroy R. Grumman C. R. Smith	1977	Dr. Charles Stark Draper Congressman Melvin Price Congressman Olin E. Teague
1966	Leslie Aulls Bryan Smith J. De France Maj. George E. W. Hallett	1978	Senator Barry M. Goldwater Edward H. Heinemann Edward C. Wells
1967	William Littlewood George P. Miller Floyd L. Thompson	1979	Senator Howard W. Cannon Willis M. Hawkins Robert F. Six
1968	Tubal Claude Ryan Marjorie C. Stinson Charles Willard	1980	George E. Haddaway James T. Pyle Juan T. Trippe
1969	Adm. Joseph J. Clark Katherine Stinson Otero William A. Patterson	1981	Raymond L. Bisplinghoff Betty H. Gillies Frederick B. Lee
1970	H. Mansfield Horner James S. McDonnell, Jr. Capt. Henry T. (Dick) Merrill	1982	Glen A. Gilbert Robert B. Hotz Clarence L. (Kelly) Johnson Gen. Curtis E. LeMay Elwood R. (Pete) Quesada
1971	William M. Allen Col. John A. Macready Senator Jennings Randolph	1983	Gen. Joe Adams Harry B. Combs A. Scott Crossfield Elrey B. Jeppesen
1972	Michael C. Murphy Robert C. Reeve Col. Willard F. Rockwell	1984	John R. Clark

AWARDED FOR

The purpose of the Elder Statesman of Aviation Award is to honor outstanding Americans who, by their efforts over a period of years, have made contributions of significant value to aeronautics and have reflected credit upon America and themselves.

1984 Gerhard Neumann
[*cont.*] Paul Schweizer
Abe Silverstein
Fay Gillis Wells

1985 Robert T. Jones
Gen. B. A. Schriver
David D. Thomas
Richard T. Whitcomb
S. J. (Steve) Wittman

1986 J. B. (Doc) Hartranft, Jr.
Anthony (Tony) Levier
John Paul Riddle
John Worth

1987 Harold D. Hoekstra
Douglas T. Kelley
Frank N. Piasecki
Paul H. Poberezny
Crocker Snow
John H. Winant

1988 William S. Aiken, Jr.
Robert D. Beilman
William H. Conrad
Francis T. Fox
Michael J. Novosel
Floyd J. Sweet

1989 Walter J. Addems
Frank V. Ehling
Donald D. Engen
Najeeb Halaby
Don P. Hettermann
Egbert P. Lott
Jack G. Real

1990 John T. Griffin, Sr.
Everett W. Langworthy
Milton O. Thompson
Spann Watson

1991 Harold W. Buker, Jr.
Cornelius R. Coffey
Benjamin O. Davis
Robert A. Hoover
Ralph S. Johnson
Marie McMillian
Evelyn Trout

1992 C. Alfred Anderson
Alexander H. Flax
Jack S. Parker
Courtland D. Perkins
Richard W. Taylor
Clifton F. von Kann
W. Dillard Walker

FOUNDING MEMBERS OF THE AERO CLUB OF AMERICA | F

Homer W. Hedge, President, 10/18/05[2,5,6,7]
John J. O'Rourke, Vice President, 10/18/05[5,6,7]
Augustus Post, Secretary[2,4,5,6,7]
Charles Jerome Edwards, Treasurer, 12/20/05[1,2]
Charles J. Glidden, 10/18/05[4,6,7]
Dave H. Morris[7]
Courtland F. Bishop, Aero Club representative to FAI[4]

FOUNDING MEMBERS

John Austin Rooney, 10/18/05[6]
Dr. Calvin T. Adams, 10/19/05[6]

J. Seligman, 10/18/05[6]
Peter C. Hewitt, 10/20/05[6]

A. Lawrence Rotch[3]

J. C. McCoy[3]

O. H. P. Belmont[4]
Harry Payne Whitney[4]
Col. John Jacob Astor[4]
William K. Vanderbilt, Jr.[4]
J. Dunbar Wright[4]
Dave H. Morris[4]
Dr. Calvin T. Adams[4]
Robert Scott[4]
S. M. Butler[4]
A. A. Anderson[4]

Samuel Walter Taylor[4]
Rollin H. White[4]
Jefferson DeM. Thompson[4]
Jefferson Seligman[4]
Louis F. Bishop[4]
M. D. Chapman[4]
Robert Frothingham[4]
Albert R. Shattuck[4]
W. McMaster Mills[4]
Winslow Mallory[4]

Gen. George Moore Smith[4]
William Hawley[4]
A. L. Riker[4]
Robert Lee Morrell[4]
Peter Cooper Hewitt[4]
E. H. Fitch[4]
Winslow E. Buzby[4]
George O. Shields[4]
E. T. Birdsall[4]
Charles E. Miller[4]
Colgate Hoyt[4]
Charles W. Place[4]
Thomas L. Watson[4]
Louis R. Adams[4]
G. Mason Jenney[4]
Philip T. Dodge[4]

Curtis P. Brady[4]
A. N. Chandler[4]
A. H. Whiting[4]
Orrel A. Parker[4]
Horatio N. Adams[4]
William H. Butler[4]
John F. Carroll[4]
T. M. Hilliard[4]
A. G. Batchelder[4]
Herman F. Cuntz[4]
William H. Hall[4]
S. T. Davis, Jr.[4]
Emerson Brooks[4]
George E. Farrington[4]
A. E. Gallien[4]

A. M. Herring[5]
Mark M. Reeves[5]
Winthrop E. Scarritt[5]
George F. Chamberlin[5]
S. M. Butler[5]
Frank Eveland[5]
S. D. Mott[5]
E. M. Davison[5]

Leo Stevens[5]
William J. Hammer[5]
A. R. Shattuck[5]
A. H. Whitney[5]
Robert L. Niles[5]
E. P. Price[5]
G. C. Gillespie[5]

Charles M. Manly, 12/01/05[6]
Thomas L. Watson, 12/18/05[4,6]
Milton J. Budlong, 12/20/05[6]
A. L. Riker, 12/24/05[6]

Albert F. Zahm, 12/11/05[6]
Israel Ludlow, 12/20/05[6]
Mark W. Reeves, 12/20/05[6]

PIONEERS OF AMERICAN AVIATION

Aero Club of America License Holders
(1905–1919)

The names and license numbers of the pioneer aviators were taken from Aero Club file cards (believed to have been transcribed from license applications) and from lists compiled by the Aero Club in 1914 and 1919. The names herein reflect the spellings and typographical errors appearing in those sources.

SPHERICAL BALLOON

146	David J. Aaron	161	Emmann Bach	673	Harold W. Bell
481	Charles A. Abels	513	Charles F. Baer	29	James Bemis
502	George W. Adams	169	Harry D. Baird	515	Joseph W. Benson
448	Paul E. Adams	578	Murray A. Baldwin	592	Ward H. Bentley
192	John A. Allen	505	Harold P. Baldwin	33	Jay B. Benton
418	Harold D. Allen	191	Marion A. Baldwin	527	Thomas J. Berry
134	P. J. Allen	282	Samuel Y. Baldwin	24	John Berry
340	Richard H. Anderson	9	Thomas S. Baldwin	628	George U. Bertoniere
532	Andrew C. Anderson	710	Raymond S. Bamberger	440	Leon LeR. Biche
206	Martin M. Andrews	459	Winthrop Bancroft	414	John H. Bishop
301	Howard B. Andrews	130	Graves C. Barclay	521	Angelo P. Bizzozero
233	Guy Eugene Armantrout	160	Allen E. Bardwell	406	Horatio Blakeley
633	William L. Armstrong	575	Goerge S. Barker	344a	Robert K. Blakey
14	Nason Henry Arnold	279	Wm. S. Barker	202	Howard B. Blanchard
711	Ross O. Ashbill	419	Francis Barrington	478	Charles L. Blodgett
352	Thomas H. Ashton	257	Arthur H. Barry	700	George H. Bockius
35	Wm. T. Assmann	621	Orlo A. Bartholomew	65	Arthur Boettcher
36	Arthur T. Atherholt	625	Fred B. Barton	237	J. A. Boettner
491	Jasper C. Augustine	156	Joseph S. Batt	293	Ulysses H. Bonney
564	Harold B. Austin	730	Charles E. Bauch	145	Cliff Booth
76	Carl S. Axtater	529	Edward L. Baugh	433	Russell D. von Boren
734	John C. Ayling	524	Clare B. Bazart	712	Robert N. Borland
382	Fred D. Babcock	676	Ralph S. Beek	62	D. H. Bower

178	Aiden J. Gormann	724	Vernon B. Hill	330	Walter J. Krpof
441	George Grady	313	Arthur B. Hillabold	221	Clyde A. Kuntz
95	Frederic J. Grant	506	Harold K. Hine	4	(Col. USA) Frank P. Lahm
639	Alfred S. Gray	482	Harold M. Hine	3	Frank S. Lahm
689	Charles A. Greef	531	Harry E. Hoadley	18	(Maj. USA) A. B. Lambert
398	Paul A. Greene	671	Garrett F. Hoagland	645	Nathaniel R. Landon
705	Alfred S. Greene	296	Henry E. Hochettem	331	Ray Lane
623	Philip Van R. Griffin	604	George Hockemsmith	381	Frederick R. Lang
190	Leo J. Griffin	182	H. H. Holland	432	Leonard W. Larrabee
311	Walter B. Griffin	299	John S. Holloran, Jr.	464	Glenn R. Lassiter
674	Dorsey J. Griffith	302	Wm. H. Holmes	266	Earl H. Latimer
574	Harry B. Groony	239	Beverly W. Holmes	218	J. W. Lavers, Jr.
431	V. Vincent Guerin	626	Carl W. Holmguist	326	Lawrence A. Lawson
561	John W. Guinee	42	Albert Holz	325	Mortimer P. Lawton
173	C. C. Guthrey	20	H. E. Honeywell	580	Joseph G. Laycock
179	Leslie B. Haddock	654	Henry S. Honodle	396	Hunter J. von Leer
300	Harry C. Hahlbeck	472	Edwin M. Hooper	615	W. A. Leet
498	Stanley W. Hahn	736	Emery C. Hulett	497	Robert P. Lehr
155	James P. Haight	622	John M. Van Hulsteyn	87	James E. Lentz
718	Andrew Hale	298	Don L. Hutchins	582	Ottho Leutz, Jr.
319	John P. Hall	649	Norman H. Van Hyming	19	Charles Levee
446	Harold R. Hall	209	Robert V. Ignico	373	Harley B. Lewis
90	Joseph G. Halsey	85	Roland T. Ingels	573	Richard J. Lewis
421	Allen M. Ham	79	Joseph S. Jablouski	217	C. H. Lobitz
386	David H. Ham	41	Frank M. Jacobs	251	Barlett G. Long
148	David Q. Hammond	543	Hilding L. Jacobson	407	Charles W. Lorraine
679	Carl N. Hand	371	Gordon F. Jaques	583	August L. Loseth
66	Tolbert F. Hardin	276	Hollace N. Jennings	569	McDonald Lovell
463	Paul C. Harding	728	Harold L. Jeobes	420	Donald A. Loyhed
28	(Capt. USA) Clifford B. Harmon	287	Walter Jewell	470	Robert E. Lum
327	Richard S. Harper	530	Andrew N. Johnson	752	R. A. Lumphey
598	John J. Harrigan	620	Bert N. Johnson	334	Geo G. Lundberg
347	Harold C. Harris	129	George Call Johnson	659	Harold I. Lush
102	Richmond J. Harris	468	Lee B. Jones	250	Harry C. Lydiard
32	George B. Harrison	722	Victor H. Jones	483	Maynard F. Lydiord
668	Van Breed Hart	113	Thomas D. Jordan	650	Norman M. Lyon
631	Hysom R. Hartwell	61	John H. Jouett	495	Emmet K. MacArthur
634	Merrill Haskell	86	Robert J. Keefe	139	Angus W. MacDougall
303	Ruby F. Hatcher	640	George K. Keith	476	Thomas G. MacLaughten
383	Kenneth C. Hawkins	400	Cornelius J. Kellcher	354	George C. MacLeod
7	Alan R. Hawley	310	Wm. D. Kelley	292	Daniel D. Madden
147	Vincent J. Hays	150	Frank J. Kelly	523	Gustave H. Madsen
105	Charles L. Hayward	744	William H. Kelly	81	F. H. Maenner
158	William R. Healey	743	W. A. Kelly	636	Frank T. Magennis
568	Lawrence R. Heath	278	Herbert H. Kennedy	162	James P. Mahoney
240	Wm. H. Heftye	380	Rosewell W. Kennigner	684	A. G. Marnaville
264	Willard Heller	485	E. S. Kessler, Jr.	128	Emer G. Marschurty
687	Frank H. Helsley	426	Milton E. Keyser	335	Robert J. Marshall
455	Frank M. Henry	103	Elmer D. Kidder	364	Leslie Martin
75	E. A. Henshe	587	George S. King	488	Thomas C. Matthews
493	James W. Hensley	52	Jerome Kingsbury	55	(Lt. USN) L. H. Maxfield
321	Wm. N. Hensley, Jr.	494	George D. Kingsland	713	Kenneth S. McCall
171	Edward F. Hermanns	258	Edmund E. Kipling	610	Emmett K. McClintock
167	George F. Hersey	118	Joseph E. Kirkham	627	Thomas H. McClure
6	(Col. USA) Henry B. Hersey	603	S. R. Kirkpatrick	641	J. F. S. McCormick
		399	Louis Kent Klay	71	John H. McCoweley
727	Philip Heusel	31	Roy A. Knabenshue	1	(Maj. USA) J. C. McCoy
229	Kenneth P. Hill	611	Sheppard Knapp	265	O. McCrackin
153	Walter W. Hill	737	William D. Knox	54	(Lt. Cmdr. USN) F. R. McCray
186	Henry C. Hill	80	Ira R. Koenig		
		480	Frank H. Kramer	177	Roger S. McCullough

492	Carl E. Shumway	538	George L. Thompson	434	Arvin J. Welch
554	Joseph L. Silva	544	Arthur G. Thomsen	245	Herbert C. Welch
361	Robt. G. Simmons	415	George B. Thummel	548	Horace O. Welsh
332	Wm. D. Simpson	542	Harry J. Tillou	370	M. E. Welsh
246	Lawrence G. Simpson	608	Joseph R. Torrey	723	George P. Welzant
168	Gilbert M. Sipp	195	Wm. R. Toston	422	Clarence R. Westaby
365	Clawson Skinner	360	Gerald Towle	125	E. B. Weston
37	William Van Sleet	667	R. L. Train	234	John Whelan
605	Julian R. Sloan	619	M. D. Tremelin	220	Samuel E. White
290	Charles H. Smith	10	Albert C. Triaca	547	George C. White
262	Lawrence K. Smith	228	Julius C. Turcott	349	Dale White
465	Joseph N. Smith	466	William P. Turnbull	25	Wm. F. Whitehouse
436	Clarence F. Smith	417	R. Turner	617	Paul A. Whitney
98	Maurice R. Smith	411	Melvin M. Turner	362	King Whitney
747	Donald J. Smith	201	Edmond C. Turner	653	John R. Whitney
688	Clarence W. Smith	629	Clarence W. Tyndell	405	Henry R. Whitty
487	Frederick T. Smith, Jr.	706	William C. Uhri	73	F. Rozier Wickard
500	Victor A. Space	686	Dudley C. unt	252	Frederick C. Wiggins
504	Donald C. Spalsbury	48	Ralph H. Upson	40	Horace B. Wild
750	Joseph P. Spang	159	Edward Valentic	534	William H. Wilkenson
68	R. L. Sparks	44	J.J. Van Valkenburg	226	Robt. T. Williams
249	DeWitt T. Spence	59	H. R. Vaughan	223	Sanford E. Williams
473	John W. Spencer, Jr.	215	Howard C. Verbeck	152	Edward C. Williams, Jr.
261	George A. Spooner	317	E. J. Verheyden, Jr.	581	Charles D. Williams, Jr.
741	George A. Spragelberg	444	Joseph H. Vernon	467	Joseph R. Williamson
140	Donald R. Stevens	751	John W. Vernor	519	Ralph T. Wilson
2	A. Leo Stevens	646	Lloyd Volckening	503	Leon A. Winter
510	Don W. Stewart	333	Raymond T. Vredenburgh	99	M. L. Witherup
525	Alonzo E. Stone	403	Frank A. Wachob	142	Claude F. Wolfe
187	T. Aldin Straw	15	J. H. Wade, Jr.	388	Earl Wollam
198	Joseph I. Sullivan	556	Ray T. Wakefield	200	William E. Woodman
731	J. Monroe Sweeney	404	Glenn E. Wallace	490	R. S. Wright
630	Frederick G. Sweetland	600	Ezrom S. Walling	394	Merton L. Wright
555	Stanley T. Switze	17	Charles Walsh	664	Jacob W. S. Wuest
70	R. S. Tait	733	Richard S. Walton	82	E. A. Yeager
69	Roderick H. Tait, Jr.	648	Robert B. Wann	721	Thomas E. Yerxa
606	Andrew B. Talbot	435	Lot R. Ward, Jr.	157	Harold O. Young
439	F. L. Taylor	535	Chester T. Wardwell	180	William C. Young
402	Ora L. Taylor	541	Harry W. Warner	725	Richard Ziesing, Jr.
638	Alfons G. Taylor	368	Sanford M. Warren	112	James H. Zipp
704	William S. Taylor	591	Robert G. Washburn	222	(not assigned)
682	W. Griffin Temple	516	James A. Watt, Jr.	101	(not assigned)
517	William L. Thibadean	46	John Watts	13	(not assigned)
84	Arthur Thomas	551	Oran L. Weber	716	(not assigned)
338	Richard E. Thompson	363	Arthur R. Weigel		
121	Ray W. Thompson	661	Harold T. Weiss		

DIRIGIBLE BALLOON

21	Murray Baldwin	46	Lyscom A. Bruce	24	George Crompton
1	Thomas S. Baldwin	67	William R. Catton	62	Cyrus G. Davisson
52	B. S. Bamberger	10	Noel Chadwick	64	Gardner P. Eastman
61	Harold W. Bell	11	Warren G. Child	26	J. D. Ellis
69	George U. Bertoniere	50	Thomas J. Connelly	40	Raffe Emerson
42	George H. Bockius	70	La Vergne Cook	57	A. William Erdman, Jr.
13	J. A. Boettner	66	Richard L. Cooley	19	Albert W. Evans
32	William Brady	20	Rolland E. Corbin	47	Waymouth Finn

53	T. K. Gampper	43	George S. King	8	R. A. D. Preston
6	Frank W. Goodale	4	A. R. Knabenshue	41	John J. Quinn
65	Raymond F. Green	37	Herman T. Kraft	30	A. T. Sewell
15	Paul A. Greene	2	Frank P. Lahm	12	James F. Shade
29	Walter B. Griffin	17	Karl S. Lange	5	A. Leo Stevens
45	Carl N. Hand	71	R. A. Lumpkin	33	Donald R. Stevens
63	Van Breed Hart	55	Frank T. Magennis	68	A. G. Taylor
74	Richard Haworth	54	Edgar T. Manning	18	Joseph R. Torrey
44	F. H. Helsley	73	Albert A. Manson	7	R. H. Upson
27	George Hockensmith	39	A. G. Maranville	51	Lloyd I. Volckening
38	Henry W. Hoyt	22	Michael McDermott	3	Horace B. Wild
28	Norman H. Van Hyning	56	William J. Medusky	23	Clifford A. Wise
31	Bert N. Johnson	25	Thomas I. Morrow	36	C. K. Wollam
72	Decatur Jones	16	James P. Norfleet	59	Thomas E. Yerxa
60	Victor H. Jones	48	Scott E. Peck	35	W. C. Young
14	William D. Kelley	49	William L. Pemberton	58	Richard Ziesing, Jr.
34	Herbert D. Kennedy	9	Walter J. Pouchot		

AVIATOR (AEROPLANE)

The first one hundred license holders in this category are presented in a separate list in numerical order, followed by the complete list (including the first one hundred) in alphabetical order, as for the other categories.

1	Glenn H. Curtiss	32	Edson F. Gallaudet	61	A. B. Lambert
2	(Lt.) Frank P. Lahm	33	Harry N. Atwood	62	(Lt.) J. H. Toers
3	Louis Paulhan	34	Lee Hammond	63	L. E. Holt
4	Orville Wright	35	W. Redmond Cross	64	Jesse Seligman
5	Wilbur Wright	36	William Badger	65	Harold Kantner
6	Clifford B. Harmon	37	Harriet Quimby	66	Mortimer F. Bates
7	(Capt.) Thomas S. Baldwin	38	Ferdinand de F. Murias	67	George W. McKay
8	J. Armstrong Drexel	39	(Capt.) Paul W. Beck	68	Phillips Ward Page
9	Todd Schriver	40	William C. Beers	69	Clifford L. Webster
10	Charles F. Willard	41	George W. Beatty	70	Claude Couturier
11	J. C. Mars	42	Hugh Robinson	71	Beryl J. Williams
12	Charles K. Hamilton	43	Cromwell Dixon	72	Fred Dekor
13	John B. Moissant	44	Matilde E. Moisant	73	Max T. Lillie
14	Charles T. Weymann	45	(Lt.) R. Carrington Kirtland	74	Henry W. Walden
15	Arthur Stone			75	Albert Elton
16	Harry S. Harkness	46	Oscar Allen Brindley	76	John H. Worden
17	Eugene Ely	47	Leonard Warden Bonney	77	Clarence A. de Giers
18	J. A. D. McCurdy	48	(Lt.) John Rodgers	78	Francisco Alvarez
19	Walter R. Brookins	49	C. P. Rodgers	79	Alfred Bolognesi
20	Ralph Johnstone	50	Andrew Drew	80	Anthony Jannus
21	Arch Hoxsey	51	Louie Mitchell	81	Josef Richter
22	J. C. Turpin	52	James J. Ward	82	Henry D. W. Reichert
23	A. L. Welsh	53	Charles C. Witmer	83	H. F. Kearney
24	J. J. Frisbie	54	Shakir S. Jerwan	84	Arch Freeman
25	P. O. Parmelee	55	Norman Prince	85	F. T. Fish
26	Frank T. Coffyn	56	Glenn L. Martin	86	Frank S. Champion
27	Lincoln Beachey	57	Paul Peck	87	Earl S. Dougherty
28	(Lt.) T. G. Ellyson	58	Harold H. Brown	88	Frank M. Sties
29	(Lt.) H. H. Arnold	59	(Capt.) Chas de F. Chandler	89	Hillery Beachey
30	(Lt.) T. de Witt Milling			90	(Lt.) J. W. McClaskey
31	Howard W. Gill	60	John D. Cooper	91	William Hoff

92	S. C. Lewis	861	Hoxie Anderson	1409	(Lt.) Carl Wm. Badenhausen
93	Charles W. Shoemaker	666	Harry B. Anderson		
94	J. B. McCalley	1254	Warren Anderson	36	William Badger
95	Weldon B. Cooke	1207	Emil S. Anderson	1914	Milton D. Baer
96	Rutherford Page	1720	Harold Anderson	1664	Raphael Baez, Jr.
97	Frank M. Kennedy	1642	Richard M. Anderson	483	Harold S. Bagg
98	W. B. Atater	2857	Werner Anderson	1056	Marshall S. Baggs
99	Albert Mayo	3481	Walter Anderson	515	Edgar W. Bagnall
100	Frederick A. Hoover	2614	Louis A. Andregg	434	George Bagrie
		124	Wilbur David Andres	420	Charles L. Bailey
988	Henry Abbey, Jr.	929	Henry G. Andrews	502	Chas. W. Bailey
2177	Louis H. Abbott	3057	Elmer F. Andrews	1510	Elmer S. Bailey
2888	Wilbur K. Abernethy	1188	Malvin Carl Aney	1300	George B. Bailey
2656	Claude S. Abernethy	1839	Charles H. Anglin	2521	Henry F. Bailey
3434	Gene W. Acton	412	L. Carlton Angstrom	1912	Raymond L. Bailey
294	Baxter Harrison Adams	1943	Addison A. Apple	2147	Louis C. Bailey
215	Allen S. Adams	2561	Earl Appleman	3388	Augustus O. Bailey
937	John R. Adams	1960	Francis L. Appleton	1445	John Wm. Bailey, Jr.
1874	William T. Adams	418	Samuel A. Appold	433	John W. Baillie
395	Austin A. Adamson	886	Alfred Aram	1163	Eugene B. Baily
2698	Guy W. Ade	465	Fulsom Arbuckle	2363	Chester A. Baird
3404	Mariano L. Agramonte	1375	Allen T. Archer	1565	Herbert K. Baisley
426	Arthur J. Ahring	1556	C. E. Archer	1059	William F. Baker
2941	St. Claude Akers	1193	Rodney M. Armstrong	1321	Alfred B. Baker
3269	Thomas B. Akin			2652	Solomon F. Baker
2502	Truman H. Albe	2245	Max Vere Armstrong	3155	Foster K. Baker
3172	Freeman Albery	1955	Ralph S. Armstrong	2765	Harry S. Baker
3189	Joseph A. Albi	198	George H. Arnold	3540	Solomon F. Baker
3392	Kent A. Alcorn	29	(Lt.) H. H. Arnold	2626	Jason A. Balderston
217	Juan P. Aldasoro	1513	George M. Arnold	7	Thomas S. Baldwin
218	Eduardo Aldasoro	1786	Ivan T. Arnold	3136	Charles B. Baldwin
1302	(Lt.) Paul V. Alden	2397	Leslie P. Arnold	3007	Henry M. Baldwin
1278	Harry S. Aldrich	1518	(Lt.) Theodore Arter	3509	Errold G. Ball
1969	Robert P. Alecander	1123	Harry P. Ashe	507	Fred E. Banbury
447	William M. Alexander	3315	Goerge S. Aspinwall	3447	Amos R. Bancroft
335	J. Morrow Alexander	98	W. B. Atater	2673	Charles Y. Banfill
790	Junius B. Alexander	430	(Lt. USA) Bert M. Atkinson	3445	John J. Banigan
701	James R. Alfonte			1357	Frank Banke
582	Frederic S. Allen	1430	Harold K. Atkinson	3484	George H. Banning
2395	Albert A. Allen	2417	William T. Atkinson	3475	Martin Bruce Barb
2038	George B. Allen	2413	Frank G. Atwater, Jr.	2427	Frank H. Barber
2958	Albert G. Allen	2944	William B. Atwell	1989	John C. Barcklow
3163	Charles W. Allen	33	Harry N. Atwood	482	Louis T. Barin
3270	A. A. Allen	3195	Willie A. Aubert	2589	Donald V. Barker
2705	Oliver W. Alles	1562	Marion J. Aubimeau	139	Floyd E. Barlow
2998	Ernest McConnell Allison	497	Wellington C. Ault	674	Walter V. Barnebey
		2298	Eugene H. Austin	824	Philip J. Barnes
1826	Myron Aloe	2262	Joseph W. Austin	1112	Ray A. Barnes
78	Francisco Alvarez	2871	William J. Austin	1715	Percy Frederick Barnes
3168	James D. Alway	3386	Charles A. Austin	1365	Baron S. Barnes
3460	Theodore C. Ames	751	Theo. S. Avery	1738	Harold R. Barnes
2897	William N. Amis	3492	Edward Axberg	1639	Kenneth G. Barnes
2438	Roy W. Ammel	1341	Seth Axley	1932	Robert H. Barnes
1777	Karl J. Ammerman	2738	George R. Ayers	3141	Herbert T. Barnes
1116	Roger Amory	1428	(Lt.) Philip R. Babcock	560	(Lt.) Richard B. Barnitz
584	Francis I. Amory, Jr.	2165	Charles F. Bachus	3541	Tony Barone
617	Henry Andersen	579	William B. Bacon	1569	E. Osmun Barr
453	George B. Anderson	2978	Asaph P. Bacon	1555	William J. Barrett
1268	Richard Anderson	2912	Christian O. Bacon	3070	James R. Barrett

47 Leonard Warden Bonney	476 (Lt. USA) Geo. H. Brett	208 G. M. Bryant
651 R. Bonomi	1322 George J. Brew	879 Henry C. Bryant
1685 J. William Bonsteel	307 Griffith Brewer	1373 Douglas E. Buchanan
767 Arthur L. Boorse	1868 Percy O. Brewer	2883 Thomas S. Buchanan
970 Alfred B. Booth	1884 Henry Brewster	1682 James P. Buchannan
3082 John C. Booth	3202 Walter W. Bricka	1466 Francis J. Buckley
3499 William W. Booth	340 A. W. Briggs	2223 Cecil W. Buckley
516 John R. Booth, 2nd	511 (Lt. USA) Boyd F. Briggs	1371 Saml. A. Buckmaster
2301 William H. Boother	491 Chas. T. Brimer	2286 Denison M. Budd
742 Normna J. Boots	46 Oscar Allen Brindley	3464 Joseph Buffington, Jr.
2365 Eugene S. Borner	2006 Walter E. Brinkman	2874 Frederick C.
2634 Peter C. Borre	2659 Ralph R. Britten	Buffrum, Jr.
514 Henry G. Boswell	2854 Wm. A. Brock	1131 Louis M. Buggs
157 William Bouldin, 3rd	1586 Wm. J. Broderick	630 Walter R. Bullock
696 M. H. Boulware	135 Otto W. Brodie	601 G. L. Bumbaugh
1636 George L. Boulware	1593 (Lt.) Rudolph E. Brofft	3212 John H. Bumstead
322 Overton M. Bounds	2108 John A. Brokaw	2942 Walter M. Bunting
857 Leo R. Bourdon	1299 Tyler C. Bronson	154 (Sgt. USA) Vernon L.
858 Allen F. Bourdon	1947 Leon C. Brookes	Burge
2722 Joseph D. Boushall	19 Walter R. Brookins	2646 Fairfax C. Burger
1066 James M. Bovard	429 (Lt. USA) John B. Brooks	136 W. Starling Burgess
2490 Robert H. Bowen	1179 John P. Brooks	676 Clive Burke
2533 Claire A. Bower	2740 Thomas Brooks	3306 Harry L. Burkhardt
2655 Paul E. Bower	1436 Hugh M. Brosnan	2329 Gilbert W. Burnet
3211 Eugene Bowers	1314 (Lt.) Wm. E. Brotherton	967 Ernest R. Burnight
257 Winfield E. Bowersox	2112 William H. Brougher	370 A. C. Burns
3471 Lawrence J. Bowman	1085 LeRoy L. Broun	948 D. B. J. Burns
1222 Frank Lee Boyd	1318 Wilbur T. Broun	1566 LeRoy W. Burns
3409 James F. Boyd	413 William N. Brown	1621 (Lt.) John L. Burns
2479 Joseph B. Boylston	361 Arthur Roy Brown	1640 Ruel F. Burns
2707 Gail V. Braak	185 Ralph Myron Brown	3121 Kenneth Burns
834 Lloyd M. Bracken	267 Lindop E. Brown	2702 John V. Burns
3407 Frank M. Bradbury	394 (Lt.) Roy Stuart Brown	212 Frank H. Burnside
1084 Cecil H. Braddick	58 Harold H. Brown	3149 Hallett J. Burrall
444 Doyle Bradford	310 Lawrence W. Brown	964 John F. Burton
2514 Timothy W. Bradley	697 Michael Brown	3329 Charles H. Burton
2235 William T. Brady	707 H. M. Brown	744 H. B. S. Burwell
1895 V. A. Braincunas	650 Geo. S. Brown	2604 Harry N. Busch
1771 (Lt.) Geo. A. Brammer	1461 Willis C. Brown	2692 Albert E. Buser
2274 Walter O.	2593 Harold L. Brown	2323 Bradford S. Bush
Brandenburger	3068 Albert S. Brown	2786 Lyle K. Bush
2804 Howard C. Brandt	2774 Ronald W. Brown	3186 William R. Busher
2542 Harry E. Brants	2685 Thomas B. Brown	1815 Ralph J. Bushman
1127 W. Norman Bratton	3427 Raymond R. Brown	944 Louis T. Bussler
2404 Clarence A. Braukman	3293 Ernest L. Brown	3107 Melvin W. Buster
1888 William P. Braun	3351 William C. F. Brown	573 George Butler
1865 Bruce E. Braun	675 Belden B. Brown, Jr.	1366 Stuart M. Butler
2647 Arnold Wm. Braun	3074 Robert J. Brown, Jr.	1750 Clyde H. Butler
384 Lloyd S. Breadner	3115 William T. Brown, Jr.	3078 Lawrence O. Butler
417 George Breadner	885 Charles W. Browne	3416 Edgar M. Butler
2553 Leslie S. Brechon	1465 (Lt.) Chas. A. Browne	1076 Edward Butte, Jr.
850 Harold B. Breene	2573 Maxwell Brownstein	488 (Lt. USA) John W. Butts
1920 Winfield S. Breese	283 Augustus Jones	1527 D. E. Butts
2460 Augustus M. Brenneke	Brubaker	2537a George D. Buzano
2904 Charles G. Brenneman	2087 Louis M. Bruch	1355 Thomas V. Byne
423 Hibbert B. Brenton	2304 Russell L. Bruch	663 James F. Byrom
211 (Lt.) Lewis Hyde	400 Cecil G. Brunson	446 Gordon T. Bysshe
Brereton	580 Mahlon P. Bryan	923 C. R. W. Cabanies
248 A. A. Bressman	634 Frank Bryant	1396 James J. Cabot

95	Weldon B. Cooke	2094	Frank D. Croxford	3316	Harold C. Davis
572	Hamilton Coolidge	3159	Bruce D. Cruickshank	3198	Harris E. Davis
870	Clarence B. Coombs	3527	Gay Crum	3277	George L. Davis
1551	Cyril L. Coombs	2706	George R. Cullman	999	William R. Davis, Jr.
60	John D. Cooper	689	C. C. Culver	321	Dan Davison
2180	John H. Cooper	673	Howard P. Culver	1310	Ralph E. Davison
2483	Forrest G. Cooper	525	Barnard Cummings	2880	Kenneth S. M. Davison
2618	Edwin J. Cooper	2191	Frank J. Cummings	724	Frederick B. Davy
3242	Edwin H. Copehnaver, Jr.	2498	Charles M. Cummings	1103	Joseph M. Dawson
		1775	Wm. H. Cunliff, Jr.	1220	Athol A. Dawson
3279	Jay M. Copeland, Jr.	3275	R. M. Cunningham	2527	John C. Dawson, Jr.
2063	Charles R. Copp	1808	Robert O. Cupp	302	Curtis LaQ. Day
2086	Marsh M. Corbitt	1540	(Lt.) Andrew Currie	3322	Olin L. Day
3132	Frank D. Core	2161	Kent D. Currie	3179	William W. Deadman
1139	Duane D. Corning	392	(Lt.) John F. Curry	325	Thomas James Dean
2155	Laurence C. Couberly	839	Tobin S. Curtis	1546	Alex. R. Dean
1429	William Couch	2282	Thomas C. Curtis	1759	LeRoy P. DeArce
680	Ralph P. Cousins	1	Glenn H. Curtiss	1617	(Lt.) M. A. deBettencourt
70	Claude Couturier	1223	Patrick S. Curtiss	1117	Kenneth Decker
1176	William B. Cowart	3181	Dwight W. Curtiss	2247	Kenneth N. Decker
1697	Russell T. Cowgill	1658	Fredk. W. Curtiss, Jr.	1412	Wm. E. DeCourcy
1327	John D. Cox, Jr.	3139	Robert G. Cushman	1337	Leon deFremery
431	Stanley V. Coyle	2221	Clarence M. Cutler	72	Fred Dekor
837	Hubert M. Crader	1615	(Lt.) Chas. E. Cutter, Jr.	2423	John W. Delaplane
3221	Miller W. Cragin	2478	Newton A. Dahl	2852	Edwin S. Delaplane
3256	Brigg Craig	1689	Wallace W. Dahman	2748	George R. deLearie
2996	Philip B. Craighead	1287	Gardner A. Dailey	570	Raphael S. deMitkiewicz
3538	Norris I. Crandall	1472	(Lt.) Russell R. Dale		
1651	(Lt.) Oliver P. H. Crane	1679	Walter F. Daley	2011	Warren J. Dempster
1088	Edgar A. Craver	1862	Wilfred Dalton	2037	George R. Denie
1785	William J. Crawford	190	George B. Dalwigk	961	J. Murdock Dennis
1598	(Lt.) R. F. Crawford	678	Henry J. Damm	2713	Carl F. Denny
2151	Frank F. Crawford	2107	Deane Dana	3452	E. Harold DeNoyelles
2419	Will Clark Crawford	468	John B. Daneils	3473	Anthony dePodesta
363	Cutherbert J. Creery	3487	Lloyd A. Daniel	781	William H. Derbyshire
2222	John D. Crehore	2210	Julian S. Daniels	725	George M. Dery
563	Fred C. Cressman	242	(Lt.) Herbert A. Dargue	1539	(2nd. Lt.) Chas. B. DeShields
2322	Harry B. Crewdson	3264	Alfredo C. Daudt		
1984	John H. Crippen	2972	Laidey E. Dauthiett	1166	Lloyd M. DeShong
2471	Marshall C. Crisp	528	Howard C. Davidson	1706	Lawrence N. Despain
2538	Robert Critz, Jr.	1106	Frank G. Davidson	2240	Martin P. Detels
3126	Paul C. Croarkin	2522	Wilbur F. Davidson	741	Thorne Deuel, Jr.
379	Albert J. Croft	2101	Robert M. Davidson	531	Brian Devlin
829	Alfred J. Cromwell	2819	Rugus B. Davidson	2992	George M. Devlin
2466	Harvey H. Cronk	1836	John P. Davies	2887	Kenneth Lee deVose
1941	Marvin E. Croom	1549	Stuart J. Davies	2960	Orian L. Dhein
35	W. Redmond Cross	2811	Ward J. Davies	1456	(Lt. Cmdr. USN) G. C. Dichman
3398	John M. Cross	700	Michael F. Davis		
2311	Carroll B. Crossan	1156	Walter C. Davis	1447	Ernest W. Dichman
187	Samuel J. Crossley	960	John H. Davis	537	Fairman Rogers Dick
1079	George L. Crosson	1345	John E. Davis	2715	Guy H. Dick
1680	Robert O. Crosthwaite	1364	Albert J. Davis	1378	Paul Dickey
2942a	Homer L. Crow	2140	Edwin K. Davis	2781	Leslie J. Dickey
1829	Walter C. Crowdus	2027	William R. Davis	1824	Frank A. Dickman
513	Harry L. Crowe	2015	Franklin B. Davis	1529	S. H. Dicran
239	Henry K. Crowell	2238	Clarence A. Davis	877	William Diehl, Jr.
1735	Elmer A. Crowell	3088	Arthur O. Davis	2145	Richard H. Dietrich
3231	Harold O. Crowell	2701	Homer H. Davis	1719	Ralph C. Diggins
2104	Leon W. Crowl	3349	George E. Davis	2894	Roy W. Dikinson

3241	Manson M. Dillaway
1656	Edwin P. Dillion
2455	Elliott Dillman
1607	(Lt.) Harold E. Dimmick
3534	Beecher J. Dining
1489	Hugh A. Divins
43	Cromwell Dixon
2018	Jerome J. Dixon
3072	Edwin M. Dixon
3009	Oliver K. Dobbins
3157	Silas A. Dobbs
2530a	Matt H. Dobson
280	(Lt.) Townsend Foster Dodd
778	Wilburn C. Dodd
749	Percival Dodge
1526	Wm. K. Dolphin
1641	James A. Donaghty
3029	John W. Donahey
3335	John E. Donalds
2492	Harold R. Donaldson
716	Thorne Donnelley
1376	(Lt.) J. J. Donohue
1250	Bernard M. Doolin
603	B. McK. Doolittle
1702	James H. Doolittle
3147	Walker C. Dorsett
549	Lyman W. Doty
3498	Bernard M. Dougals, Jr.
87	Earl S. Dougherty
1227	Charles Douglas
1432	(Capt. USA) Walter C. Douglas
3237	Norman J. Douglass
2312	John R. Dow
2308	Joseph Dowdall
1674	John C. Doyle
3419	Arthur Doyle, Jr.
916	Alonzo M. Drake
1710	Chas. J. Drake
3225	Ernest E. Dreby
2154	Raymond C. Dreher
1781	Herbert C. Drescher
50	Andrew Drew
8	J. Armstrong Drexel
457	Harold Drummond
3377	Ralph LaF. Duba
377	Marcel C. Dubuc
1133	Charles S. Duddleston
810	Lloyd M. Dudley
1157	Frank B. Dudley
949	George L. Dudley
1629	(Lt.) LeRoy B. Duffield
3054	James R. Dugan
2056	Graham C. Dugas
3535	Malcolm Dugliss
3295	Harold E. Dujardin

2613	Wm. Britton Duke
3433	Paul H. Dunavan
2294	Thomas Duncan
735	Lawrence Duncheskie
2963	Samuel W. Dunferd
1516	Lionel H. Dunlap
1633	Thomas F. Dunn
2408	Walter V. Dunn
2848	Chas. A. Dunn
612	(Lt.) James L. Dunsworth
2196	Gardner Dunton
2959	Delmar H. Dunton
585	Francis V. DuPont
1592	George H. Durar
2778	Charles P. Durfee
2877	Ralph M. Durnell
1990	Leslie N. Duryea
2163	Florimond J. Dusossoit
1515	Rudolph W. Dussean
3408	Thomas A. Dussel
2509	Louis Dussere
3205	Robert D. Duthie
3061	Alfred G. Eager
2343	Kenneth L. Earl
903	Murray Earle
2259	Lawrence Early
705	Whitten J. East
2182	Andrew J. Eastman
128	Warren S. Eaton
1851	Alfred V. Eaton
2674	Charles F. Eaton
1335	(Lt.) Saml. G. Eaton, Jr.
2376	Solomon B. Ebert
688	Melchoir McE. Eberts
1235	Gerald L. Ebner
2851	McKendres A. Ecker
2545	Lawrence J. Eckstrom
191	David Edelman
331	F. C. G. Eden
1058	Harold H. Edgar
1793	Harvey W. Edmund
2993	Albert L. Edson
350	Stearne T. Edwards
888	Brooke Edwards
928	Fred E. Edwards
825	Nielson Edwards
1067	James L. Edwards
866	John W. Edwards
1740	Carl W. Edwards
2099	Lewis T. Edwards
333	Ferdinand Eggena
798	Frederick I. Eglin
2772	Geo. W. Ehlers
904	Henry S. Ehret, Jr.
1554	Ben B. Ehrlichman
1764	Frederick W. Eidermeyer, Jr.
1459	Herman A. Van Eiff
646	Gustav J. Ekstrom

3145	Warren B. Eldred
1748	John Rice Eldridge
2648	Loyal A. Eldridge
2657	Earl W. Elhart
3118	Carl G. Eliason
178	Robert Elliott
1002	John J. Elliott
2459	Clinton Elliott, Jr.
952	P. E. Ellis
1107	Lyman R. Ellis
1382	(Lt.) Robt. E. Ellis
1450	James A. Ellison
28	(Lt.) T. G. Ellyson
75	Albert Elton
1614	(Lt.) Chas. Elwell
17	Eugene Ely
2598	Newell D. Ely
3533	William H. Emery, Jr.
1427	Edmund M. Emmerich
770	Delos C. Emmons
1531	George N. Emory
1840	Oscar H. Engblom
2587	Connell A. English
2349	Charles R. Enlow
1293	Frank S. Ennis
1922	Grant W. Enrst
938	Carl R. Erdman
1477	Calvin P. Erdman
2141	Robert Erickson
1997	Eric Algot Erikson
339	H. B. Evans
1071	Thomas Roy Evans
878	Edward N. Evans
980	Elisha E. Evans
1405	Russell E. Evans
2547	Arthur H. Evans
2885	Stephen G. Evans
3364	Dean P. Evans
3320	George E. Evans
3350	Jay C. Evans
3334	Sewell O. ewhouse
2950	Hugh W. Ewing
3488	Charles A. Ten Eyck
3500	Bruce S. Eytinge
1162	Leander W. Faber
2043	Frederick Don Fagg
2999	George R. Fairbaun
2048	Richard H. Fairclough
826	Herbert G. Fales
629	Nugent Fallon
947	Tate L. Farnost
505	Arthur Farquhar
2642	John B. Farrell
1452	(Lt.) Murray Chas. Fartham
3079	Ivyn I. Farwell
2855	Henry Faurot, Jr.
1368	(1st. Lt.) Roscoe Fawcett

3169	Warren E. Faxon	1289	(Lt.) Harold J. Forshay	1391	A. Robertson Frye
642	Lee Quong Fay	2001	Jonathan Fortney	620	Earl B. Fuller
2578	George H. Fay	2567	DeWitt A. Forward	1020	Rosell H. Fuller
1068	Fred Feasel	2024	Esty Foster	450	Rutherford Fullerton
2860	William Feick	2433	Lee Wood Foster	2570	Emmet E. Furey
2726	Rutledge H. Feild	1963	Ralph E. Foster	820	George C. Furrow
1713	Jesse Keller Fenna	2956	William C. Foster	3525	Robert W. Fyan
3448	Paul E. Fenton	3300	Thad V. Foster	2528	Floyd Gahann
2608	Herbert F. Fenwick	3352	Lindsay B. Foster	1007	Edmund P. Gaines
530	Thomas F. Fergie	3289	Edwin B. Foster	1283	Chas. C. Gaines
761	Roderick C. Ferguson	1200	Albert Clark Foulk	269	A. B. Gaines, Jr.
2096	Leon D. Ferguson	140	(Lt.) Benjamin D. Foulois	356	Murray Bayne
3037	Philip M. Ferguson	2350	Edward H. Fowle		Galbraith
2565	Earl L. Ferguson	2267	Gordon Fowler	1479	Geo. Washington
1542	Aaron R. Ferneau	2070	Russell R. Fox		Galinger
2868	F. B. Fernhoff	2318	Arthur W. Fox	3506	Joseph J. Gallagher
3011	Homer V. Ferris	3129	Joseph W. Fox	32	Edson F. Gallaudet
594	(Lt. USA) Paul L.	3440	George B. Fox	2088	Louis E. Gallo
	Ferron	3260	Herbert F. Fox	672	Harold M. Gallop
2820	J. R. Ferry	3206	Roy D. Foxon	2818	Marvin Gallup
747	Oliver S. Ferson	1448	Olin C. Francis	364	John Galpin
1147	Roy R. Fetterhoff	2741	Paul R. Francis	921	Albert B. Galvin
1760	Lindsey D. Few	1570	Arthur S. Frandsen	2800	Robert L. Gandy
523	Louis E. Fideler	1628	Norman D. Frank	328	(Lt. USA) Harry Gantz
2616	John B. Field	1798	Frederick Frankfort	518	Harved H. Ganyau
3094	Ritner I. Fiester	2047	Lawrence W. Frankley	1231	John L. Garbright
203	Haldeman Figyelmessy	2443	Albert W. Franklin	2237	Leonard W. Garden
1662	Wm. H. Fillmore	3265	George T. Franklin	1484	Daryl Gardner
463	David D. Findlay	1871	Kenneth H. Franzheim	3063	Jo Francis Gardner
2899	Mathew E. Finn	2273	Walter Fraser	2919	Claude F. Garesche
803	Harry S. Firestone	2258	Dean B. Fraser	2211	Edmond A. Gareschem
85	F. T. Fish	2207	Henry A. Fratzer	764	L. H. De Garmo
291	Charles Eugene Fisher	306	William Fray	2309	Elmer C. de Garmo
3103	Randoph R. Fisher	3414	Karl A. Frederick	1363	Jos. H. Garnett
318	(Lt.) Shepler W.	1411	Byron B. Freeland	487	Frank G. Garratt
	Fitzgerald	84	Arch Freeman	3437	Harold C. Garratt
1944	Gordon P. Fitzgerald	2093	Charles M. Freeman	3002	William V. Garretson
2269	Walter T. Fitzpatrick	1258	Howard W. French	1731	Claude S. Garrett
3311	John E. Fladeland	1654	Roy A. French	2954	John W. Garrett
2649	Edmund J. Flaherty	775	Newt. Frey	2760	Kenneth Garrett
817	Reuben M. Fleet	875	Walter Frey	2529	Sterling M. Garwood
811	Hugh B. Fleming	1135	Paul E. Freydig	1635	Winder Gary
3312	Carl S. Fleming	471	Childs Frick	2405	Ellsworth F. Gaskell
2948	Ward B. Fletcher	1655	Max H. Friedman	2703	Alexander N. Gaston
436	Walter E. Flett	2910	Alfred E. Frieman	2814	Wentworth M. Gaston
1269	Harrison W. Flickinger	1499	(Lt.) Ernest C. Friesen	2537	William A. Gates
2627	Earle F. Flinn	24	J. J. Frisbie	3099	John B. Gault
3432	Wm. Spencer Flint	703	Patrick Frissell	2095	George E. Gause
1994	William R. Flowrnoy	213	Earl. V. Fritts	2688	Ernest H. Gay
2403	Peter E. Fluor	2436	Ralph V. Fritts	3215	Elmer J. Gaylord, Jr.
3112	Mortimer G. Flynn	1219	A. L. C. Fritz	739	Guy L. Gearhart
2359	Robert S. Fogg	498	John Frost	166	(Lt.) Harold Geiger
615	Royden Foley	1820	John W. Frost	1329	Louis C. Geisendort
2864	William B. Foley	1818	Edward P. Frost	2004	Leon P. Gendron
1972	Harold J. Folsom	2284	John A. Frost	2558	Benj. A. Gentry
3013	Francis M. Fonseca	1819	E. Rice Frost, Jr.	3105	Arthur L. Genung
462	Christopher W. Ford	2551	John O. Fry	1309	Henry F. George
2508	Harold R. Ford	1111	William A. Frye	2493	Walter H. Gerke
544	Joe R. Forkner	1073	George E. Frye	2564	Joseph M. Gerreta

1507	(Lt.) Wm. Winston Harrison	1893	Walter H. Helmrich, Jr.	633	Helen Hodge
1558	Landreth M. Harrison	2287	William S. Heltzen	1757	(Lt.) Alvin R. Hodge
2729	Elbert I. Harrison	2355	Laurence W. Helweg	733	James F. Hodges
1275	James E. Harrold	146	William H. Hemstrought	2505	Harold G. Hodgson
411	Gordon S. Harrower	1894	Paul R. Henderson	91	William Hoff
129	D. C. de Hart	2389	Denny E. Henderson	772	Edward L. Hoffman
3177	William C. Hart	1783	Jacob A. Heng	1394	Chas. R. Hoffman
3294	Jos. L. Hart, Jr.	2842	John E. Henn	1388	Verne W. Hoffman
1915	Claude E. Hartford	153	(Capt.) Fred'k B. Hennessy	1334	Chas. G. Hoffman
1550	William R. Hartline	2794	Chas. R. Henriques	2429	J. Frank Hoffman
2290	Clarence A. Hartmann	101	R. C. St. Henry	2679	Joseph K. Hoffman
1917	Fred. S.ff Hartmann	1069	W. Howard Henry	3255	Paul Hoffner
555	James Hartness	830	Edwin B. Henry	1650	(Lt.) Wm. A. Hogan
2072	Frank W. K. Hartshorne	2137	Kenneth M. Henry	1490	John R. Hogan
2368	Odber R. Hartt	1608	(Lt.) Percy C. Henry, Jr.	1319	Harry C. Hogan
1178	Cushman Hartwell	801	Harry C. Hequembourg	478	Robert W. Hogg
956	Earl M. Harvey	638	Theo. M. Hequembourg	2936	Mark G. Hogue
2199	Lloyd L. Harvey	103	(Ens. USN) V. D. Herbster	1208	Arne Hoishelt
2054	Harold M. Harvey			1744	Clarence E. Holborn
1152	Joseph F. Hasking	3383	Herbert W. Hereford	3263	Russell F. Holderman
3025	Reed H. Haslan	2120	Gerald F. Hermann	553	Dr. Chas. K. Holgate
2771	Chas. M. Hassi	979	Mark L. Herron	1446	Maurice Holland
1108	Philip E. Hassinger	2987	Siguard N. Hersloff	2341	Robert B. Hollender
1985	Morris O. Hastings	1684	Otto A. Hesse	542	Fred L. Hollin
147	Henry L. Hattemer	2908	John W. Hesser	843	Vincent P. Hollingsworth
3357	Cornlius J. Hauck	197	William A. Hetlick, Jr.	1453	Frank E. Hollingsworth
2074	K. M. Haugen	1290	Herbert C. Heubner	708	Chas. T. Holloway
127	Beckwith Havens	2228	James L. Hever	204	Harry Holmes
3417	Leland Hawkinson	399	Harold M. Hewitt	1695	Robert B. Holmes
3048	Malcolm Hay	2233	John B. Hiatt	2817	Elmer M. Holmes
2334	Thomas H. Hayden	503	Willis G. Hickman	63	L. E. Holt
2637	Benj. H. Hayes	2374	Cecil R. Hickman	677	Edward H. Holterman
3192	John R. Haylor	2305	John T. Hickmott	592	(Lt. USA) John D. von Holtzendorff
496	Arthur P. Hayood	2324	DeGarmo Hickmott		
1420	John M. Hayward	1959	Charles C. Higgins	3422	Lowell H. Holway
2840	Richard G. Hazeltine	2812	Stanley H. High	2798	Leiscester Hommingins
1276	Roy T. Hazzard	2234	Thomas H. Highley	2135	Gordon K. Hood
1264	Frank D. Healy	1383	Chas. D. Hightower	2327	Augustus S. Hooker
485	(Lt. USA) Jack W. Heard	216	Frederick C. Hild	1957	Harley L. Hooper
2536	Charles R. Heard	274	Thomas J. Hill	2243	James C. Hooper
815	Richard H. Hearn	234	James D. Hill	100	Frederick A. Hoover
2620	Thomas L. Heatson	1393	Thomas L. Hill	2379	Chester A. Hoover
2475	Chas. B. Hebbard	2458	Charles Hill	2188	Lionel P. Hopkins
1501	James L. Hebbards	3108	Hamilton L. Hill	796	Ernest H. Horigan
1634	Irving T. Hecht	2799	Ployer P. Hill	3038	David H. Van Horn
1773	(Lt.) Geo. L. Heck	2621	Hartwell C. Hill	3428	Norman E. Horn
1743	Lloyd E. Hederman	3370	Robert E. Hill	2124	Ernest G. Horne
671	Andrew H. Heermance	1458	(Lt.) A. Burt Hill, Jr.	301	Mrs. Richberg Hornsby
489	(Lt. USA) Leo G. Heffernan	2584	J. C. Hill, Jr.	2940	Camden R. Horrell
		2002	Geo. A. Himebaugh	2080	Thomas F. Horrigan
2097	Chester P. Hegan	1996	Nelson C. Hinckley	1172	Harry B. Hortman
2934	Adolph Hegge	625	Elliot P. Hinds	2028	Russell B. Horton
235	Alexander T. Heine	2356	David E. Hinman	2402	William O. Horton
277	Albert Sigmund Heinrich	3117	Charles L. Hirsch	3531	Elwood Horton
		2081	Ira W. Hirschfield	3393	Clarence F. Horton
933	Horace N. Heisen	1778	Thomas Hitchcock	3012	John H. Hosier
2810	Chas. L. Heisner	3339	J. H. Hoare	2982	Oakley W. Hosking
3399	Isaac H. Hellman	365	Basil Duncan Hobbs	231	Robert Y. Hoskino

262	Henry Sheehy Keating
1148	James A. Keating
873	Archie F. Keating
2103	James H. Keeley
2407	Ernest E. Keeling
1909	Lorenzo J. A. Keenan
1173	Charles W. Keene
2808	Frank L. Keever
2769	George M. Keightley
3244	William S. Keith
1029	Gordon H. Keller
1545	Frederick W. Keller
2597	Clarence R. Keller
3343	Dallas C. Keller
1154	Harold R. Kelley
874	William M. Kellie
856	Miles E. Kellin
490	Walter B. Kellogg
466	Lewis Kelly
1567	Philip John Kelly
1381	(Lt.) James N. Kelly
2431	Sherwin F. Kelly
3080	Joseph J. Kelly
3283	James O'R. Kelly
3477	Roland D. Kelly
3376	Fred. R. Kelly
3431	R. J. King Kelly
3529	John C. Kelso
1971	Philip G. Kemp
119	Frederick W. Kemper
383	Patrick S. Kennedy
97	Frank M. Kennedy
1171	Harold S. Kennedy
1844	David S. Kennedy
1732	Robert E. Kennedy
631	E. R. Kenneson
2895	Cornelius J. Kenney
1606	Raymond Kenny
950	Thomas F. Kent
2745	Arthur O. Kent
2949	Chester L. Kenworthy
1463	Johnson D. Kenyon
2487	William S. Kenyon
882	H. S. Kenyon, Jr.
2515	Wesley L. Keough
849	Vincent Kerens
2947	Edward E. Kermott
1809	Frederick M. Kern
3200	John T. Kern
2186	Henry H. Kerr
3436	William Lane Kerr
2512	Charles S. Keyes
1869	Nelson B. Keyes, Jr.
2435	H. C. Khruhlenberg
1288	Maurice McC. Kidd
1013	William A. Kidder
1753	(1st. Lt.) Ames M. Kidder
1048	Casper M. Kielland

1923	Daniel Kiely
2184	Thomas Kiernan
1828	Ed. W. Killgore
317	(Lt. USA) W. G. Kilner
3111	John H. Kiltgen
1792	Dan A. Kimball
1433	George H. Kimber
1440	August G. Kimmerle
1195	George J. Kinberg
2131	William O. Kinberg
3075	Robert L. Kincaid
1952	Roland H. Kinder
1024	Bertram T. King
1099	Paul B. King
1596	(Lt.) Wm. G. King
1594	Gelson T. King
1964	Paul E. King
2671	Olen King
3087	Cloize A. King
3345	Charles King
2511	Wm. Trott King, Jr.
2491	Burt H. Kinkley, Jr.
3489	Francis W. Kinney
529	(Lt. USA) Maxwell Kirby
2943	Marquis L. Kirby
3167	Harris C. Kirk
1509	Percy P. Kirkham
2603	James E. Kirkham
1481	Ralph R. Kirkland
2736	Everett L. Kirkpatrick
45	(Lt.) R. Carrington Kirtland
2346	Daniel Kiser
311	Frank Kitamura
2901	Charles C. Kittinger
1247	Edwin C. Klingman
125	John G. Klockler
2523	Carl P. Kloke
1387	Russell H. Klyver
992	Hugh J. Knerr
2052	James H. Knight
3530	James E. Knott, Jr.
780	Roland S. Knowlson
1126	Earl C. Koag
607	George U. Kobashi
1597	(Lt.) Alfred S. Koch
621	August Koerbling
905	Frank Kohent
2632	Hugo J. Kohr
120	M. Kondo
1970	Leonidas L. Koontz
117	Edard Korn
1437	Harold B. Koster
3344	Walter L. Kraeckmann
2611	Lester L. Kraft
2239	John Kramer
687	George W. Krapf
1872	Herman C. Krause

1620	(Lt.) Augustus H. Kriggler
704	Arnold M. Krogstad
644	Theo. de Kruijff
360	James S. Krull
2503	Howard E. Krum
752	Edmund A. Kruss
1349	Wm. B. Kuen
284	Carl T. Kuhl
1270	Wm. R. Kuhn
616	Luis Kwan
862	Henry F. La
1616	Andrew J. LaBoit
1873	Harry Lachmund
338	J. K. LaGrove
2	Frank P. Lahm
532	Emil M. Laird
2105	Walter R. Lalley
61	A. B. Lambert
896	Charles W. Lamborn
183	William A. Lamkey
1528	Wm. Lester Lamkin
626	Morton P. Lane
718	Franklin K. Lane, Jr.
2605	John T. Lanfall
3418	James J. Langin
842	Leon Lannoy
2858	Walter E. LaParle
1415	Edw. J. Larkin
1626	George R. Larkin
710	Edward P. Larrabee
1418	Earl Lathrup
1346	Douglas Lathrup
1324	Clayton C. Lavene
188	Ruth Bancroft Law
1230	Bernard A. Law
2540	Sidney F. Law
2977	Victor F. Lawler
2339	Nelson Lawnin
1063	R. Maurice Lawson
2792	Dudley B. Lawson
2751	John T. Lawson
2506	Edward T. Lawstuter
1714	Merritt L. Lawton
2393	Curry Lea
2983	William H. Lea
566	Oliver C. LeBoutillier
2687	Francis H. Ledbury
334	Robt. Edward Lee
2134	E. Hamilton Lee
2230	Theopilus Lee
2326	Zanna P. Lee
2019	John F. Lee, Jr.
2012	Leo J. Leeburn
1377	Horace W. Leeper
660	Walter E. Lees
1511	Claude Wm. S. Leffler
1301	W. Watson LeForce
1033	K. C. Leggett

2806	Alfred S. Mattson	2807	Raymond J. McGill	2008	Thomas Menke
1034	Russell L. Maughan	2516	Daniel J. McGity	2367	Sterlin R. Mensch
3285	Paul C. Maurer	1896	Edward T. McGovern	2441	Parrish D. Mercer
3369	George W. Maxim	1589	John E. McGovern	3001	Roert A. Mercer
1834	Elmer N. May	2750	George J. McGowan	1080	Joseph S. Meriott
959	Dudley B. Mayer	3015	Edward McGrady	1468	Edw. K. Merrill
1991	Walter W. Mayer	3375	Michael F. McGrath	3156	Cedric V. Merrill
3230	Herbert C. Mayer	255	N. M. McGuire	1183	Benj. M. Merton
2109	Theodore Maynz	1457	(Lt.) Arthur J. McHenry	3201	Joe P. Messinger
99	Albert Mayo	596	Jack R. McHugo	568	Harry H. Metcalf
2937	Thomas E. McAlister	2571	Donald W. McIlhiney	833	Manton B. Metcalf, Jr.
3378	Theo. A. McArn	3216	William D. McIlhinny	1852	John W. Metcalfe
2310	John K. McArthur	401	Alfred E. McKay	3303	Carlisle Metzger
1212	James T. McAtean	67	George W. McKay	1700	Bert P. Meyen
1205	Joel F. McavDid	1039	Ebgert McKean	176	Cord Meyer
3268	Wm. H. McAvoy	2496	Ralph Spencer McKee	1206	Lester L. Meyer
2148	Howard I. McBride	3073	James D. McKee	2815	Charles L. Meyer
2654	Roscoe E. McCabe	3390	Raymond F. McKenna	1866	Harold Meyers
3151	Charles D. McCabe	1347	George W. McKenzie	1575	George A. Meyler
2541	James A. McCaffrey	1588	(Lt.) Wesley R. McKenzie	3133	Paul Micelli
3254	Harry F. McCaffrey	1646	Geo. E. McKernon	3055	Berkeley S. Michael
2782	Lewis L. McCall	2742	A. Tremaine McKinstry	1942	Mortimer Middleton
94	J. B. McCalley	1128	Harold M. McKnight	2556	Ellis S. Middleton
2226	Harold C. McCarthney	1611	James A. McKnight	2971	Irvin B. Middleton
2325	Charles E. McCartney	1113	William B. McLaren	2915	Robert F. Midkiff
90	(Lt.) J. W. McClaskey	909	H. DeV. McLean	2039	George J. Milburn
2299	Arnold R. McClintock	210	(Lt.) Samuel H. McLeary	1358	(1st. Lt.) Wm. H. Miles
2582	Ralph A. McClintock	3382	Leland S. McLeod	1475	(Lt.) Niles E. Miles
1273	David M. McClure	3014	Daniel J. McLinden	845	Joseph H. Millard
2291	James G. McConkey	889	John B. McMartin	813	Henry R. Millard
1544	Murray McConnell	627	Robert R. McMath	1277	Jesse C. Millard
1624	Robt. E. McConnell	628	Neil C. McMath	538	James E. Miller
2193	William C. McConnell	451	Wallace H. McMillan	173	Bernetta A. Miller
622	Fletcher L. McCordic	111	R. E. McMillin	1251	Zenos R. Miller
3005	Robert D. McCorick	1328	Bryan McMullen	713	Hugh L. Miller
2062	Thomas H. McCormack	2125	Alexis B. McMullen	1025	E. J. F. Miller
2644	Clinton McCormick	2251	Harold R. McNabb	1012	Ray S. Miller
276	John Bernard McCue	3092	Silhas M. McNally	1602	(Lt.) Rolfe T. Miller
18	J. A. D. McCurdy	2847	L. J. McNamara	1326	John C. Miller
508	Curry A. McDaniel	657	Jos. T. McNarney	1339	George A. Miller
2206	Samuel F. McDonald	398	Charles McNicoll	2057	Max Miller
3044	Earl McDonald	1435	(Lt.) Norman B. McPeak	2190	Julian F. Miller
3442	John McDonald	2501	George S. McVay	1921	Galem Miller
3435	George C. McDonald	2263	Ray S. McWhorter	2444	Bennie A. Miller
3235	Frank W. McDonald, Jr.	1138	Asbury W. Meadows	1995	Charley Miller
477	John C. McDonnell	2159	Joseph E. Meagher	3018	Arthur J. Miller
1372	Harry L. McDonough	1717	Leland M. Means	2846	Royal McI. Miller
2510	Hubert B. McDonough	1827	Eugene B. Mechlin	2900	Edward A. Miller
2923	Alfred A. McDowell	3439	Theodore S. Meed	30	(Lt.) T. de Witt Milling
3491	L. A. McDowell	1855	Timothy E. Meehan	473	Peter C. Millman
2102	Bertrand J. McElin	2066	Nathaniel H. Meeker, Jr.	654	Benj. W. Mills
957	Jay W. McElroy			1758	(Lt.) D. W. Mills
2619	Paul E. McElroy	2050	Floyd B. Meisenheimer	2114	Charles H. Mills
1242	Clifford A. McElvain	983	Otto Melamet	2696	Harry H. Mills
2260	Edwin L. McFalls	1158	Lynn E. Melendy	2961	Ralph J. Minchan
1945	John J. McFarland	1756	Paul K. Melick	3243	Walter J. Ming
648	Donald R. McGee	1070	Vincent J. Meloy	1903	Henry V. Minges
1560	Abner F. McGehee	3284	Jesse I. Menefee	51	Louie Mitchell
987	Robert B. McGill	2504	Herman Mengel	1136	Horace W. Mitchell

2762	Fred. R. Older	2576	Franklin S. Payne	1021	Hugh M. Pierce
1055	James H. S. Olds	2560	Bryan W. Payne	2257	Leslie E. Pierce
1648	Harvey R. Olds	3308	John B. Payson	2906	Karl N. Pierce
1897	Rufus A. Oliphant	3371	Randolph Payson	1019	Norris E. Pierson
445	William S. Oliver	994	George H. Peabody	2569	Walter E. Pierson
2624	Herbert G. Oliver	1965	Dwight V. Peabody	2790	Owen H. Pinaire
226	Edward Olivier	416	Arthur H. Pearce	2335	Kyle J. Pinney
1794	Clarence A. Olsen	2450	Howard B. Pearce	2385	Raymond A. Piper
2040	Paul E. Olson	2787	William D. Pearson	977	Charles H. Pisbes
2989	William E. Olssen, Jr.	1274	Joseph R. Pearson, Jr.	2575	Chas. H. Platt
3479	John A. Orb, Jr.	3359	Jack J. Pease	3403	Edwafd H. Platz, Jr.
2966	Douglas C. Orbison	57	Paul Peck	2386	Leonard F. Plaut
2020	William F. Ordway	737	N. W. Peck	1492	Marll J. Plumb
1284	Horace Orlady	1762	(Lt.) Lee H. Peck	1296	Wm. Hazel Plyler
972	Edward Orr	2279	Theo. A. Peck	1083	Garland W. Poell
998	F. C. Osborn	738	William B. Peebles	3543	Francis Poindexter
623	(Lt.) B. R. Osborne	561	Dorothy Rice Peirce	1825	Edward J. Politoske
1032	Lenwood W. Ott	438	Harry L. Pell	2689	Thomas G. Pollard
404	Frank M. Ouge	1087	Thomas E. Pell	2044	Fred Don Pollard, Jr.
1305	Dudley M. Outcalb	2850	Geo. M. Pemerton	1860	Robert E. Pollock
1584	Maurice C. Owen	1553	Paul Penberthy	2566	Harold J. Polson
1491	Richard Owen, Jr.	1863	Ferris E. Pence	337	Chas McH. Pond
1281	(Lt.) John S. Owens	252	J. P. Pendhayn	1859	Richard E. Pond
2453	Celesta F. Owens	2181	Charles T. Pennebaker	3405	Albion W. Poole
823	Alan H. oynton	3463	Thomas Penney, Jr.	2264	Arnold Poppie
3373	Richard P. Ozier	2328	Jerome E. Pennington	1316	Kenneth L. Porter
3446	Walter Pack	387	Walter S. Penty	2201	Victor W. Porter
68	Phillips Ward Page	141	Cecil Peoli	2580	Lester L. Porter
96	Rutherford Page	2768	Charles E. Peoples	3486	John E. Porter
1690	Frank A. Page	2035	William H. Pepin	3253	Henry W. Porter
279	George A. Page, Jr.	3394	Paul G. Perdue	264	(Lt.) Henry B. Post
3331	Carl H. Panzer	3032	Alfred K. Perego	931	Leo F. Post
2554	George W. Parey	788	George H. Perkins	593	Edwin M. Post, Jr.
2718	Cheaney L. Parish	3338	Albert D. Perkins	955	Norman W. Potter
113	Harry Park	912	Arthur J. Perrault, Jr.	493	James E. Potvin
223	Joseph D. Park	1878	William L. Perry	1311	Howard H. Powal
640	Vitalis H. Park	1797	Marney D. Perry	2592	Daniel W. Powderly
734	Will D. Parker	2636	Pierce P. Perry	1408	Hugh C. Power
2430	Earle K. Parker	270	Chriss J. Petersen	2424	Herbert G. Pratt
2981	Harold W. Parker	1962	Vance C. Peterson	571	William F. Prentice
3512	Roy C. Parker	2175	Harold G. Peterson	1031	Harvey W. Presser
968	Walter F. Parkin, Jr.	2315	Roger F. Peterson	1638	Owen N. Price
25	P. O. Parmelee	3246	Jarrold A. Petraverg	2100	W. E. Price
2220	Arthur C. Parson	906	Harris E. Petres	2986	Edward F. Price
3199	Gustav A. Parsons	3367	Edward V. Pettis	2801	Chas. S. Price
3490	Claude P. Parsons	901	Harlan I. Peyton	2255	Walter E. Pride
925	Herbert G. Partridge	844	Glenn W. Peyzer	237	Maurice R. Priest
1718	Williiam H. Pascoe	2225	Merrill N. Pheatt	481	Frederick H. Prime
390	(Capt. USA) Wm. Lay Patterson	1000	Richard Phelan	281	Milton Winter Primm
		1410	Ralph M. Phelps	55	Norman Prince
504	David H. Patterson	3511	Raymond W. Phelps	754	Gordon C. Prince
576	Frank S. Patterson	1244	Charles T. Phillips	786	John C. Prince
762	LeLster A. Patterson	2000	Frank Phiscator	2600	Chester E. Pritchard
2973	James McK. Patterson	116	William Piceller	2525	Frank E. Pritchett
3	Louis Paulhan	1520	(Lt.) Sam. Pickard	562	John D. Probst
2089	Carl F. Paulson	2612	Elmo N. Pickeril	2303	W. Heath Proctor
2372	George P. Pawley	1806	Floyd M. Pickrell	159	Clifford B. Prodgers
902	David W. Paxson	1742	Christopher V. Pickup	619	Ira J. Proffitt
1478	Owen S. Payne	2662	Philip Pidgeon	3360	Thomas L. Puckett

3116	Ednor M. Rossiter	1763	(Lt.) Henry C. Sandusky	64	Jesse Seligman
2524	John H. Rothwell, Jr.	891	Harold M. Sanford	2390	Fred. E. Seller
1416	Edward F. Rough	2428	Louis C. Sanguinet	757	Cecil G. Sellers
2985	Frederick W. Rourke	353	K. F. Saunders	2130	Lamar Sellers
1600	Hiram H. Rowe	2881	Guy D. Saunders	1663	Wm. Laurie Seman
3119	Maurice B. Rowe, Jr.	3341	Edward R. Saunders	2486	John C. Semple
2179	Dudley E. Rowland	1979	Tmomas E. Saver	1221	Louis G. Senghas
393	(Lt.) Ralph Royce	3248	William G. Sawyer	260	Rudolph G. Sestak
1876	James A. Royer	591	(Lt. USA) Marton F.	3178	Thor J. Severson
220	Charles C. Roystone		Scanlon	1413	Robt. B. Sewell
1109	James G. Rray	2042	Eugene J. Scanlon	289	(Lt.) Fred Seydel
3190	Meyer C. Rubin	259	Cornelius Jackson	2209	Leland T. Seymour
1297	Richard M. Rubner		Schaap	791	George W. Sha
1240	Edward W. Rucker, Jr.	177	John S. Schaefer	3148	William L. Shaffer
2802	Lars Rue	3187	Julius E. Schaefer	3342	Edgar F. Shaner
2173	Joseph A. Ruegg	3196	Alfred G. Schafer	2667	H. V. Shank
182	Horacio Ruiz	1574	Rollin N. Schanck	2314	Clarence E. Shankle
2117	Jay A. Rummel	3380	Harry E. Schank	3095	Warren C. Shankle
935	Leslie J. Rummell	575	(Lt.) William G.	1115	Naple Deloe Shappell
1017	D. C. Rumsey		Schauffler, Jr.	2952	Graham P. Sharkey
1838	Frederick J. Rundbaken	3234	Leland S. Schech	1134	Maurice A. Sharp
3372	W. B. Rundle	819	Alfred R. Scheleen	1121	John W. Sharpnack
2293	Charles G. Runkle	756	Lewrence Schenk	1708	John B. Shaver
3209	Harry J. Runser	253	Maurice T.	382	James Alexander Shaw
132	R. B. Russell		Schermerhorn	1692	Donovan L. Shaw
533	(Lt. USA) Clinton W.	2033	Henry Schlachter	2733	George W. Shaw
	Russell	2676	Edgar C. Schmid	3127	Harold H. Shaw
1725	Ralph C. Russell	2410	John R. Schmitt	2672	Carleston C. Shay
1332	Donald C. Russell	2916	Herbert G. Schmitt	2272	Thomas F. Shea
1940	William M. Russell	1709	Fred. C. Schmocker	1787	John F. Sheehy
2217	Emerson C. Russell	1330	Leland D. Schock	1451	(Lt.) Frank H. Sheffield
2933	Lindsey G. Russell	3223	William O. Schock	2990	Lynn C. Shepard
3102	Franklin B. Russell	195	Erhard Scholovinck	1958	Floyd W. Shephard
3066	Charles P. Russell	9	Todd Schriver	2924	Ridgley G. Shepheard
3207	Foster Russell	2265	Rudy W. Schroeder	151	(Lt.) William C.
3461	Irwin B. Rutledge	1532	(Lt.) Clyde J.		Sherman
3081	Walter H. Rutterbusch		Schuemacher	374	Otokichi Shibaki
681	William Ord Ryan	3384	Dement Schuler	797	Emert Shields
3039	Robert E. Ryan	545	Edward G. Schultz	93	Charles W. Shoemaker
1867	Milton E. Ryniker	2337	Lloyd G. Schultz	2288	Lelie R. Shope
795	Henry G. Saal	143	Fred J. Schuman	2084	Harry C. Short
1854	Harry Saganas	2700	Herbert M. Sckick	2891	Myron R. Shrader
1369	Albert C. Sager	3067	Reuben B. Scobey	2362	Byrl H. Shrake
192	P. J. Sakamoto	3252	Hal A. Scoby	2416	Noble S. Shropshire
170	Alberto Salinas	3542	Richard W. Scofield	1353	Henry H. Sibley
172	Gustavo Salinas	309	Lyle H. Scott	3462	John W. Siegler
1502	Glenn C. Salisbury	1028	Thomas R. Scott	2876	Will. C. Sievert
1992	Henry W. Salisbury	2214	Neal J. Scott	3387	M. W. Silberman
2970	Earle E. Salisbury	2398	Ernest DeW. Scott	1919	Arthur E. Silcott
3218	Philip R. Sallee	3317	Harry E. Scouten	2791	Archie L. Sills
2601	George F. Samen	1271	Charles D. Seard	145	Oliver G. Simmons
2340	Herbert C. Sampter	2195	Hugh Sears	452	Robert Simon
225	S. F. Samura	1052	Arthur F. Seaver	945	Russell M. Simon
1150	Thomas P. Sandefur	2392	John L. Seawell	989	Herbert J. Simon
1279	Raymond F. Sanderhoff	458	Louis M. Seemann	1317	(Lt.) L. C. Simon, Jr.
2574	William P. Sanders	3515	Raymond P. Segurson	1303	Francis M. Simonds, Jr.
2962	Ralph L. Sanders	1202	George V. Seibold	1015	Arthur E. Simonin
2743	James H. Sandlin	258	Florence B. Seidell	567	Alan C. Simpson
890	Austin L. Sands	3191	Frank W. Seifert	359	John Clark Simpson

1313	Leonard Sullivan	378	August Thiele	2485	George A. Trozer
2231	Charles B. Sullivan	1843	Robert B. Thiewe	3233	Hold M. Trusler
2716	Edwin Sullivan	1582	Walter F. Thomas	278	Ritsugo Tsubota
3519	Pul Sullivan	1533	Harold B. Thomas	1726	Preston E. Tupper
1104	Marion B. Sulzberger	2292	Everett B. Thomas	510	George E. Turnbull
1978	Vernon D. Summerfield	3058	James R. Thomas	895	Frank B. Turner
2526	Ernest W. Sundberg	134	DeLloyd Thompson	818	Thomas Turner
358	Walter James Sussan	1751	Geo S. Thompson	1587	(Lt.) Wright E. Turner
1348	Robt Sutherland	2824	David E. Thompson	1637	(Lt.) F. C. Turner
3036	Edward A. Sutphen, Jr.	2691	John F. Thompson	1292	Charles F. Turner
316	Redondo B. Sutton	3353	Carl J. Thompson	22	J. C. Turpin
1140	Harry A. Sutton	3368	Gaugh W. Thompson	2029	Gardner S. Turrill
1810	Harry A. Sutton	3110	Henry Thomsen	419	Horace B. Tuttle
1374	Harold P. Sutton	112	Clarke Thomson	2330	George W. Tuttle
180	John S. Sverkerson	1423	(1st. Lt.) Walter A.	973	Ralph S. Twitchell
1018	Jacques M. Swaab		Thomson	149	W. Irving Twombly
1204	Charles H. Swan	2254	David W. Thornburg	982	Charles P. Tyrrel
3026	Charles V. Swan	1037	John E. Thorp, Jr.	3429	Theodore C. Uhler
2500	Ernest W. Swedberg	1705	Harold E. Thotter	104	C. E. Underood
1306	Wm. R. Sweeley	953	Chas. Thurlo, Jr.	300	C. E. Utter
3059	Hart T. Sweeney	2126	J. Peter Tiernan	1315	Emile J. Vadnais
3493	Ben A. Sweeney	1523	John Wm. Tierney	1417	Allen W. Valentine
1734	Florin F. Swerffeger	605	Carter Tiffany	1385	Ralph V. Valtier
3245	Arthur D. Swift	1340	Herbert C. Tiffany	789	Elmer R. Vanette
3257	Byron R. Switzer	1769	Milton Tilley	2079	Elling H. Veblen
3309	Ralph M. Syder	1218	Frank W. Tillman	1967	Theo. S. Van Veghten
569	George Sykes	2344	Andrew R. Tipton	2067	John MacF. VenderVoort
939	John S. Taber	1036	Henry P. Tithers	475	Lambert Vervoort
184	Glenn M. Tait	2951	Charles B. Titus	1799	Benton F. Vessey
219	Takayuki Takasaw	3333	Hubert J. Titus	2530	Cal V. Vickery
122	Koha Takeiski	3355	George G. Titzell, Jr.	2077	Merritt A. Vickery
3354	Elmer R. Talbot	1072	Van Wikle Todd	986	J. D. Vincent
250	(Lt.) Walter R. Taliaferro	784	Chauncey R. Todd	2779	Joseph E. Virgin
1295	Wm. W. Tanney	1790	Kirk W. Todd	3474	Fred. S. Van Vliet
3175	Elmer B. Tapley	62	(Lt.) J. H. Toers	1395	Karl C. Vogel
292	Sekiji Tateishi	1384	Benj. H. Tolbert	1060	Claude E. Vollmayer
517	Ralph L. Taylor	1999	Alexander Tolchan	3544	Howard Voshell
760	Moseley Taylor	618	Albert Fong Tom	156	Chauncey M. Vought
1096	Tonsend J. Taylor	2586	Frederick Tomkins	2136	Philip A. Wachtell
876	Berkeley H. Taylor	2383	Kenneth C. Tomlinson	1238	Leigh Wade
1676	Frederic H. Taylor	3085	James A. Tong	709	Harry Wagner
1694	Carroll G. Taylor	723	Allen S. Topping	712	Chas. Joseph Wagner
2440	Whitman Taylor	2482	Marshall G. Torrey	2085	Parker Wagner
2083	Harold L. Taylor	577	Joseph R. Torrey, 2nd	911	George A. Wagoner
2945	Richard F. Taylor	1400	Thomas L. Tousley	2562	Chester D. Wahle
2735	Alfred B. Taylor	2046	Robert R. Towers	2127	Harry W. Wait
2744	Bayard G. Taylor	2064	Bob G. Towner	186	H. Roy Waite
2563	George F. Taylor	715	Richard S. Townsend	1419	Marshall W. Waite
2825	Stewart J. Teaze	927	Edward M. Townsend, Jr.	271	William Walb
389	Roy Teernstra	2307	Ray P. Tracy	74	Henry W. Walden
1811	John W. Templeton	2426	Homer Trantham	832	Leonard A. Wales
930	Frank F. Tenney	1595	(Lt.) Verne E. Treat	883	Edward V. Wales
108	F. T. Terrill	461	Joe Graham Trees	2838	William C. Wales
869	Robert G. Thach	3176	Don Tresidder	554	(Lt. USA) John C. Walker
3146	Herbert von Thaden	1184	Vernon B. Trevellyan	368	W. Roy Walker
441	Alexander B. Thaw, 2nd	2590	Newland D. Trinler	892	Leslie L. Walker
924	Sigourney Thayer	1686	Manuel Trinta	880	Howe Walker
2585	Raymond H. Thayer	3086	Samuel P. Trother	926	Guy A. Walker
1918	William A. Thiel	1988	David K. Trotter	1754	(Lt.) Stephen P. Walker

2913	Edmand H. Wilson	2116	James A. Woodruff	907	Donald B. Wurzburg
546	Charles D. Wiman	635	Newton B. Woodville	3046	John A. Wyatt
2098	William B. Wimer	357	Arthur Gerald	664	Walter J. Wynne
130	(Lt. Col. USA) Charles		Woodward	2780	Toddie L. Wynne
	B. Winder	1257	Granville O. Woodward	194	C. Yamada
3520	Lyman A. Wine	1260	LeRoy G. Woodward	314	Tom T. Yamanaka
1009	William H. Wineapa	2412	William A. Woodward	3122	Chauncey DeT. Yeoman
2793	Burr H. Winslow	2920	Ernest W. Woodward	2320	Reuben J. Yocum
3239	Julian E. Winslow	2830	Irving J. Woodward	558	Alexander McB. Young
2266	George H. Wirth	1911	Douglas G. Woolf	600	Sen Yet Young
3114	Walter Wirz	2387	Clinton F. Woolsey	758	David H. Young
1228	Leslie W. Wishard	2016	Ralph H. Wooten	1057	Oscar Young
3033	Geroge H. Wiswall	76	John H. Worden	2467	Victor M. Young
3524	Robert R. Witbeck	3135	Paul Worth	3232	Leslie B. Young
53	Charles C. Witmer	1091	James R. Worthington	2457	Grover A. Youngs
2831	Frederick C. Witsell, Jr.	1576	Franklin Wortley	3250	Edwin F. Zacher
381	G. H. Witts	2169	Edward B. Wowry	1536	(2nd. Lt.) Wm. E. Zander
3120	Chester B. Wohler	661	Kaspar F. Wrede	2737	Herbert Zangler
484	Herbert Wolf	5	Wilbur Wright	1904	Frederick A. Zender
1512	Harry J. Wolf	254	R. M. Wright	2146	Raymond C. Zettel
1422	Gibson G. Wolfe	524	Frank W. Wright	1998	M. C. Ziebur
3356	Francis J. L. Wolfe	4	Orville Wright	1877	George F. Ziesmer
1143	Louis J. Wolfrod	1003	Chester E. Wright	472	Frederick W. Zimmer
1266	Claudius W. Womble	936	William E. Wright	296	Charles Lester
209	C. Murvin Wood	1842	Stanley V. Wright		Zimmerman
2783	Walter W. Wood	1993	C. A. Wright	846	Cyrus J. Zimmerman
1601	Horace W. Wood, Jr.	2484	Fred. C. Wright	2470	James L. Zimmerman
2495	James W. Woodard	2797	Bailey A. Wright	2661	Ernest L. Zingermann
3501	Philip J. Woodbury	2823	Joseph H. Wright	3184	Oscar R. Zipf
1153	Cony U. Woodman	2932	E. P. S. Wright, Jr.	1982	Edward Zogg
3502	Joseph E. Woodman	3299	George A. Wulp		

HYDROAEROPLANE AVIATOR

Military officers whose branch of service is not specified were probably U.S. Navy.

93	William H. Alexander	129	Frederick H. Becker	277	Lee H. Bristol
42	A. Livingston Allan	61	Earl F. Beers	37	Edward L. Britt
384	Dolph C. Allen	4	(Lt. Cmdr. USN) P. N. L.	23	(USN) Clarence K. Bronson
82	Charles L. Allen		Bellinger	177	William K. Bruckhauser
127	Donald E. Alvord	165	Louis J. Bergen	408	W Walter C. Bryan
106	Allen W. Ames	367	Walter H. Berghorn	136	John S. Buchanan, 2nd
293	Andrew Anderson	151	Thomas M. Bergin	372	Lester T. Bundt
198	Junius F. Andrews	54	Julien C. Biddle	157	Ellis J. Burchart
255	H. V. Andrews	382	Carl H. Biggs	360	George P. Burgess
73	Samuel W. Arnheim	156	G. J. T. Birdsall	206	J. Franklin Burke, Jr.
137	John W. Ashley	194	(Ens. USN) Horatio	196	(Ens. USN) Stuart M.
114	William B. Atwater		Blakeley		Butler
159	Raymond L. Atwood	352	Felix M. Blotuer	227	(Lt.) Richard E. Byrd, Jr.
228	Joseph W. Austin	342	Henry F. Blount	374	William H. Caldwell
188	Clinton D. Backus	155	Frederick Boger, Jr.	366	George C. Cannon
175	Morris H. Bailey	328	Henry Bomgarder	187	Robert C. Cantwell
180	George F. Baker	398	Charles A. Botzum	324	Francis J. Carlucci
282	William H. aBrd	65	Stanley Boxhall	85	Nathan B. Chase
39	(Lt. USN) H. T. Bartlett	70	Caleb S. Bragg	5	(Ens. USN) G. deC.
9	Ernest C. Bass	344	E. W. Brandenstein		Chevalier

124	(Lt. Cmdr. USN) Warren C. Child
370	Emile Chourre
303	Julius R. St. Clair
121	Kenneth H. Clapp
64	A. Rupert Clark
190	Henry Comyn Clayton
387	James O. Cobb
108	Dave Hennen Coddington
316	Edward H. Coffey, Jr.
81	Eugene A. Coffin
171	Wilson W. Coile
211	Anthony D. Colby
353	Delbert L. Conley
215	William Sinclair Cormack, Jr.
263	Arthur Corry
339	George E. Coughlin
184	W. E. Crosscup
2	(Lt. USN) Alfred A. Cunningham
392	Winsor H. Cushing
267	Albert M. Darby
281	Antonio J. DaSilva
166	Delozier Davidson
142	John H. Davidson
193	Joseph L. Dean
239	Robert F. Dibble
208	(Lt. Cmdr. USN) G. C. Dichman
88	Arthur F. Dietrich
100	Albert J. Ditman
75	Thomas Dixon, Jr.
7	William Ellwood Doherty
294	Bryant W. Donaldson
87	Thorne Donnelley
110	Gilgert W. Douglas
186	Thomas W. M. Draper
154	Wayne Duffett
307	Harry W. Dunlap, Jr.
52	Samuel B. Eckert
58	Blaiine Elkins
401	Norman E. Elsas
189	Fred T. Estabrook
59	J. Dickson Este
89	Jesse L. Esterwood
233	Ralph P. Evans
66	Francis T. Evans
99	George Ews
373	Earl M. Farmer
420	Guy H. Ferguson
383	Robert Fickinger
333	Louis J. Filley
31	Philip S. Fisher
46	Max C. Fleischmann
394	John C. Flood
119	John C. Foster

36	Robert G. Fowler
284	Stephan A. Freeman
400	Russell DeV. Friend
332	Samuel Frothingham
139	Arthur M. Gacdonald
176	Gibson Gardner
152	Joshua Garrison
236	Gordon D. Gates
56	John W. Geary
397	William J. Geddes
296	Horace F. Gibson
226	(Ens. USN) James R. Gillon
28	Robert Glendinning
279	Mario C. Godinho
261	Robb Gover
270	Justin D. Graves
130	Edwin R. Greenfield
343	James M. Grier
200	Rettig A. Griswold
128	Theodore P. Groavanor
144	Clarence H. Guyer
205	Paul J. Haaren
315	Brune P. Haas
314	Walter H. Hagy
38	E. Barton Hall
350	Ronald P. Hallett
235	S. S. Halliburton
311	Olean T. Hallum
147	Lloyd A. Hammer
390	Edward H. Hance, 3rd
41	Gerald T. Hanley
295	Hubert Harder
292	Wallace K. Harding
8	H. P. Harris
323	John W. Harris
49	(Ens. N.M., N.Y.) Lee H. Harris[1]
250	Francis Hartley, Jr.
20	B. R. Hassell
131	S. S. Hawkins
116	Clarence A. Hawkins
409	James H. Hawkins
385	Jojhn C. Herron
213	Frederick B. Hicks
149	Walter Hinton
245	Lyman A. Hodgdon
169	(Ens. USN) George S. Hodges
32	Geo. R. Hogsdon
290	John P. Holden
319	Emmert T. Holst
389	Allen D. Honeywell
232	Thomas T. Hoopes
305	Harry D. Horton
138	E. L. Van Houten
391	Walter M. Howlett
274	Henry W. Hoyt
288	Frank B. Hubacheck

168	Charles Edward Hubard
45	Edward Hubbard
318	Gerard L. Huiskamp
320	James H. Hulse
355	Richard P. Hummer
336	JoJhn G. W. Husted
173	Frank E. Hutcheon
120	Hurd Hutchins
377	Harold D. Hutchinson
327	Alfred F. Ingold
269	Eugene T. Izant
134	William Jackson
40	E. K. Jacquith
26	Roger W. Jannus
104	Alert R. Johnson
76	Stuart H. Johnson
368	Robert Jordan
312	John W. Judson
117	Kenneth B. Kees
340	Stephen F. Kelly
34	Beryl H. Kendrick
179	Stanley C. Kennedy
378	Stephen L. Kerr
79	Oliver P. Kilmer
304	Henry W. King
259	Frank M. Kinner
115	Joseph F. Knapp
283	Howard P. Knauer
371	George B. Kneass
244	Esten B. Koger
326	S. H. Krouse
346	Samuel H. Krouse
182	Harry W. Krumm, Jr.
153	Charles F. Kunkel
258	Edgar B. Laferty
376	William B. Lane, Jr.
122	J. William Laneto
251	Wayne L. Langley
103	George McC. Laughlin
21	Frank D. Laurence
402	Arthur Laverentz
403	William B. Lawrence, Jr.
141	Lewis H. Lee
68	Benjamin Lee
44	Walter E. Lees
163	Ralph A. Lehan
238	Henry P. Lewis
126	Dean E. Lochman, Jr.
291	John M. Lott
160	Alan J. Lowrey
306	Irving W. Lyon
421	Robert F. Lyon
135	Donald M. MacCaulay
10	Steve MacGordon
132	(Lt.) William Maeek
362	William A. Magee, Jr.
337	Daniel F. Maloney
310	Victor F. Marinelli
348	Richard A. Marschat

210	Lewis K. Marshall	212	Forrest C. Osgood	243	Paul E. Shumay
364	Matthew S. Martin	123	Charles W. Ostridge	84	Ricardo Fitz Simon
388	Horace C. Martin	91	George S. Ott	53	Eugene C. B. Simonin
71	(Lt.) C. P. Mason	276	John H. Oxley	72	Horatio N. Slater
220	Robert Matter	396	Alden L. Painter	347	Rallph E. Smith
225	George C. Mattison	92	Carlton D. Palmer	3	(Lt. USN) B. B. Smith
417	Frank A. Mauck	338	Kenneth S. Parker	413	Samuel A. Smith
25	(Lt. USN) L. H. Maxfield	416	Charles E. Parslow	51	Jay D. Smith
297	Frederick R. Maxwell	405	John D. Patterson	217	Earl B. Smith
224	Mark M. McChesney	29	Hugh A. Peck	357	Ralph N. Smith
275	William C. McConnell	113	L. S. Peck	254	Francis P. Smith
359	James S. McCormack	140	Lloyd A. Perry	172	Alvin W. Smith, Jr.
16	David H. McCulloch	308	F. Paul Peterman	162	(Ens. USN) William T.
406	John W. McCulloch, Jr.	379	Chester J. Peters		Snow
33	Edw. O. McDonnell	216	Carl O. Peterson	27	(USN) Earl W. Spencer
30	Frank S. McGill	102	Harman A. Peterson	11	Lawrence B. Sperry
358	John B. McGuire	300	Paul A. Philbin	164	(Ens. USN) John F. Staub
15	William Maitland	101	Anthony Pilser	375a	G. H. Stege, Jr.
	McIlvain	203	Lawson M. Pinkham	419	Robert G. Stephens
287	Earle P. McKellar	268	Russell P. Place	299	Allan W. Stephens
386	Horton A. McKin	77	Alfred E. Poor	112	Robert M. Stocker
80	Guy McLaughlin	301	George B. Post	341	Harold C. Stoker
167	Charles A. McLellan	97	G. Marcos Pouchan	19	(USN) Melvin L. Stolz
361	John W. McMurray	202	John E. Powell	109	Emery A. Stone
280	Colegate O. McShane	161	Ralph A. Powers	260	Harry E. Stovall
248	William Medusky	214	Hazen Curtis Pratt	302	Truman J. Strong
298	Edward J. Mershon	247	Paul Pryibil	111	Clarence A. Suer
286	George A. Midwood	237	Harold A. Pulliam	43	William F. Sullivan
317	Van Roy Miller	285	Irving M. Quiston	204	Herbert F. Sullivan
349	Howard A. Miller	262	Thatcher W. Rea	74	Marion B. Sulzberger
256	Charley Miller	86	(Lt. Cmdr. USN) A. C.	94	John T. Sunderman
218	John H. Miller, 3rd		Read	1	Adolph G. Sutro
60	Frank Mills	321	Clarence A. Reedell	170	Gilbert Nichols Swett
412	Sperry W. Mines	197	Albert F. Rice	98	Peter Talbot
246	Elmer L. Mitchell	313	Bayle M. Richardson	329	Robert A. Talbot
17	Walter D. La Mont	369	Isidor Richmond	222	James B. Taylor, Jr.
145	Lloyd R. Moore	230	James S. Robinson	221	Howard H. Tewksbury
12	Raymond V. Morris	354	Howard S. Robinson	57	George C. Thomas, Sr.
351	William R. E. Moss	242	A. Penrose Robinson	78	Philip A. Thompson
181	R. C. Mudge	375	Glen E. Robinson	345	Everet L. Thompson, Jr.
414	Alfred N. Munhall	309	George E. Rogers	240	Kirk W. Todd
63	Ector Orr Munn	50	George G. Ross	399	Trygve J. Tolnes
118	Thomas H. Murphy	335	Alfred L. Roulet	395	Frederick L. Tracy
252	John L. Murphy	289	Edgar H. Rust	183	Irving B. Tribken
410	William A. Murphy	95	John N. Rutherford	241	Ned Troutman
13	(Lt.) James M. Murray	107	Charles Edwin Ruttan	380	Gordon Tucker
14	(Lt. Cmdr. USN) Henry	83	James Salsman	322	William H. Van Tuyl
	Croskey Mustin	185	Anthony S. Santos	69	John H. Tweed
365	James F. Nash	278	Fileto F. DaS. Santos	325	Gerald T. Tyner
418	Guy W. Neel	174	Howard C. Sargent	90	Giochino Varim
178	Alan L. Nichols	18	(Lt. USN) Richard C.	47	Victor Vernon
148	James A. Nisbet		Saufley	35	J. B. R. Verplanck
199	James K. Noble	273	Herbert Schiff	6	L. A. Vilas
356	Sterling M. Nordhouse	253	Helmer Schmidt	404	Harold E. Waggoner
191	Harvey C. Norman	249	Otto W. Sclums	411	Ray B. Wallace
55	Dudley S. Norton	219	Winfield Scott Shannon	229	James H. Walsh
330	Thomas L. Nudd	231	Thomas R. Shearer	415	Francis B. Waterman
67	Clifton T. Oleson	264	Samuel D. W. Sheldon	265	Robert S. Waters
195	R. S. Ordway	271	William H. Sheppard	393	O. S. Waters

143	Stanley P. Waugh	105	Lawrence C. White	363	William J. Wolker
381	Russell Welles	24	(Lt. USN) K. Whiting	334	Edward P. Wright
266	Madison F. Welsh	158	James A. Whitted	146	Webster M. Wright
201	W. Malcolm West	22	Francis A. Wildman	257	Robert T. Young
272	Carlyle D. Weston	207	Chauncey K. Williams, Jr.	62	Sen Yet Young
125	Royal Wetherald	223	Richard L. Williamson	96	Marcos A. Zar
150	Oscar G. Wheeler	209	George Willman	48	Frederick W. Zimmer
192	Arthur C. Wheeler	133	David Wnedoza	331	(not assigned)
234	Harold D. Whitcomb	407	J. F. Wolfer, Jr.		

EXPERT AVIATOR

67	A. Livingston Allan	14	(Lt. USA) C. G. Chapman	182	(Lt. Cmdr. USN) G. C. Dichman
4	(Col. USA) Henry H. Arnold	32	(Lt. USN) Godfrey de C. Chevalier	233	(Lt. USA) S. H. Dicran
54	(Lt. USA) B. M. Atkinson	40	(Col. USA) Arthur R. Christie	23	(Lt. USA) Townsend Foster Dodd
173	Theodore S. Avery	199	E. W. Cleveland	122	Thorne Donnelly
176	Baron S. Barnes	204	(Lt. USA) Lloyd R. Clowes	218	(Lt. USA) Walker C. Dovsett
75	Walter V. Barney	77	Stewart W. Cogswell	121	(Lt. USA) Alonzo M. Drake
168	Horace H. Barse	82	John G. Colgan	213	(Lt. USA) E. E. Drehey
46	(Lt. USN) H. T. Bartlett	84	Carl W. Connell	
81	(Lt. USA) Carl T. Batts	214	(Lt. USA) Cecil H. Connoly	226	(Sgt. USA) St. J. Eaten
6	(Col. USA) Paul W. Beck	132	(Lt. USA) Lawrence E. Cook	125	(Lt. USA) D. E. Ellis
107	(Sgt. USA) Frank C. Behrend	114	Clarence B. Coombs	26	(Comdr. USN) Theodore G. Ellyson
29	(Lt. Comdr. USN) Patrick N. L. Bellinger	194	(Ens. USN) Arthur Corry	212	(Lt. USA) Jesse K. Fenne
120	(Lt. USA) Louis Bennett, Jr.	88	Stanley V. Coyle	124	(Maj. USA) Reuben Fleet
161	Richard B. Berry	116	Alfred Cram	236	(Lt. USA) Andrew H. Foote
86	(Sgt. USA) Ira O. Biffle	196	Harry B. Crewdson	
80	(Capt. USA) L. Phil Billard	74	Howard P. Culver	223	(Lt. USA) Harold R. Ford
240	(Lt. USA) Bert R. Blair	49	(Major USMC) Alfred A. Cunningham	7	(Brig. Gen. USA) B. D. Foulouis
63	Frederick T. Blakeman	51	(Lt. Col. USA) J. F. Curry	210	(Lt. USA) Joseph W. Fox
185	William H. Bleakley	170	Patrick S. Curtis	97	Albert B. Gaines
61	(Lt. Col. USA) R. C. Bolling	149	(Sgt. USA) Tobin S. Curtis	73	(Capt. USA) Harold M. Gallop
169	Frank L. Boyd	95	(Col. USA) H. J. Damm	43	(Lt. USA) Harry Gantz
13	(Lt. USA) Lewis Brereton	16	(Lt. Col. USA) Herbert A. Dargue	9	(Lt. Col. USA) Harold Geiger
35	(Lt. USN) Clarence K. Bronson	222	(Lt.) Alfred C. Daudt	205	(Lt. USA) John D. Gillett
55	(Lt. USA) John B. Brooks	128	(Lt. USA) Frederick Brock Daug	209	(Lt. USA) Ralph M. Gilmore
58	(Maj. USA) Roy S. Brown	172	(Lt. USA) John E. Davis	113	(Lt. USA) Paul Goldsborough
133	(Lt. USA) A. C. Burns	187	Curtiss LaQ Day	
17	(Lt. Col. USA) Joseph E. Carberry	203	(Capt. USA) Richard H. Depew	10	(Col. USA) L. E. Goodier, Jr.
76	Victor Carlstrom	147	(Lt. USA) William H. Derbyshire	39	(Col. USA) Edgar S. Gorrell
71	(Capt. USA) Norbert Carolin	109	(Maj. USA) Thorne Deuel	
206	(Lt. USA) Earl Carroll			
5	(Col. USA) Charles de F. Chandler			

141	(Sgt. USA) Wayman Haney
44	(Lt. Col. USA) Harry W. Harms
208	(Lt. USA) William R. Hartline
96	(Lt. Col. USA) Jack W. Heard
160	Horace N. Heiser
30	(Lt. Comdr. USN) Victor Herbster
228	(Lt. USA) Robert P. Hewitt
167	(Lt. USA) Earl S. Hoag
157	William H. Hoff
230	(Sgt. USA) Russell F. Holderman
91	E. H. Holterman
189	Gordon K. Hood
139	(Lt. USA) Henry S. Houghton
171	(Lt. USA) Gerard H. Hughes
119	George F. Hughes
179	Ira B. Humphreys
156	W. Jackson Hunt
224	(Lt. USA) Spencer S. Hunt
163	(Lt. USA) Henry A. Ilse
238	(Lt. USA) Frank L. Isbell
166	(Lt. USA) Walter P. Jacobs
78	James M. Johnson
215	Edward A. Johnson
126	Donald Johnston
83	Roderick H. Jones
11	(Lt. Col. USA) Roy C. Kirtland
193	Daniel Kiser
229	(Lt. USA) E. J. Klingaman
164	Ronald S. Knowlson
195	(Lt. USA) Alfred S. Koch
87	(Sgt. USA) James S. Krull
93	(Sgt. USA) E. A. Kruss
15	(Col. USA) Frank P. Lahm
117	(Lt. USA) D. I. Lamb
152	Charles W. Lamborn
85	(Sgt. USA) Frnklin H. Lane, Jr.
207	(Lt. USA) Walter E. LaParle
188	E. Hamilton Lee
79	Walter E. Lees

232	(Lt. USA) Richard H. Lees, Jr.
175	(Lt. USA) Thomas J. Lenihan
48	B. Blakeman Lewis
192	(Lt. USA) Joseph B. Lievre
1	Max T. Lillie
178	William Lindley
98	David B. Lindsay
186	(Lt. USA) David G. Logg
69	(Lt. USA) Seth Low, 2nd
20	Theodore C. MacCauley
137	Samuel P. Mandell
118	(Capt. USA) Robert Marsh, Jr.
52	(1st Lt. USA) H. S. Martin
2	Glenn L. Martin
112	(Lt. USN) C. P. Mason
42	(Lt. USN) L. H. Maxfield
53	(Lt. USN) Edward O. McDonnell
59	(Maj. USA) John C. McDonnell
34	(Major USMC) William M. McIlvain
158	William B. McLaren
136	Hubert DeV. McLean
12	(Lt. USA) Samuel H. McLeary
198	(Lt. USA) F. B. Meisenheimer
70	(Lt. USA) Cord Meyer
60	(Capt. USA) J. E. Miller
3	(Col. USA) T. DeWitt Milling
145	(Lt. USA) Emil H. Moltham
159	C. H. Monroe
154	John A. Morgan
47	Raymond V. Morris
25	(Col. USA) Joseph C. Morrow
89	Daniel P. Morse, Jr.
21	Hollis LeRoy Muller
197	(Lt. USA) Maurice H. Murphy
131	(Lt. USA) Samuel J. Mustain
28	(Capt. USN) Henry C. Mustin
41	(Lt. USA) Douglas B. Netherwood
134	(Capt. USA) R. L. Noggle
144	John S. North
90	Stephen H. Noyes
68	(Lt. USA) B. R. Osborne
231	(Lt. USA) Walter Pack
220	(Lt. USA) H. W. Parker
129	Herbert G. Partridge

180	Lester A. Patterson
100	(Maj. USA) William B. Peebles
200	E. N. Pickerill
143	(Lt. USA) Hugh M. Pierce
142	(Lt. USA) Norris E. Pierson
19	(Lt. USA) Henry B. Post
108	(Capt. USA) K. G. Puliam, Jr.
104	(Lt. USA) Herbert Pulitzer
190	(Ens. USN) Harold A. Pulliam[2]
201	Paul Pyribil
123	(Lt. Cmdr. USN) A. C. Read
56	Charles Reed
225	(Lt. USA) Harold J. Regan
65	(1st Lt. USA) G. E. A. Reinburg
115	(Maj. USA) Cushman A. Rice
191	(Capt. USA) Marcus H. Rice
37	(Lt. Comdr. USN) Holden C. Richardson
92	(Sgt. USA) Leon Richardson
50	Howard M. Rinehart
153	(Lt. USA) William D. Robbins
148	(Lt. USA) Harmon C. Rorison
140	(Maj. USA) D. C. Rumsey
150	(Lt. USN) C. E. Ruttan
94	(Capt. USA) William O. Ryan
33	(Lt. USN) Richard C. Saufley
72	William G. Schauffler, Jr.
110	(Lt. USA) Arthur A. A. Scheelen
216	(Lt. USA) Hugh Sears
24	(Lt. USA) Fred Seydel
217	(Lt. USA) William L. Shaffer
135	(Lt. USA) Arthur E. Simmon
138	Albert G. Simpson
227	(Lt. USA) Frank Simpson, Jr.
31	(Major USMC) Bernard L. Smith

211   (Lt. USA) Stanley Smith
174   (Lt. USA) Lottia A.
      Smith
151   (Lt. USA) Ralph C. J.
      Somers
45   (Lt. USN) Earl W.
      Spencer
64   (Ens. USN) Lawrence B.
      Sperry
165   Francis Stanton
234   (Lt. USA) F. H. Steil
103   (Sgt. USA) Felix Steinle
106   (Lt. USA) John B.
      Stetson
127   (Lt. USA) P. R. Stockton
221   (Capt. USA) Harry H.
      Sutton
38   (Col. USA) Redondo
      Sutton

146   John S. Taber
18   (Lt. USA) Walter R.
      Taliafero
66   (Capt. USA) R. L. Taylor
183   (Lt. USA) James B.
      Taylor, Jr.
219   (Lt. USA) Herbert Von
      Thaden
57   (Lt. USA) A. Blair Thaw
8   DeLloyd Thompson
162   (Capt. USA) J. N.
      Thorp, Jr.
130   (Lt. USA) Charles
      Thurlow, Jr.
239   (Lt. USA) Milton Tilley
105   Chauncey R. Todd
27   (Comdr. USN) John H.
      Towers
235   (Lt. USA) Don D. Wade

177   Rodman Wannamaker
155   Carrol F. Watson
202   Carl Weinstein
99   Ivan P. Wheaton
102   (Sgt. USA) Harry H.
      White
101   (Sgt. USA) Earl F. White
36   (Comdr. USN) Kenneth
      Whiting
62   (Sgt. USA) W. P. Willetts
22   (Lt. USA) R. H. Willis, Jr.
181   Henry P. Withers
184   Louis J. Wolford
111   (Capt. USA) Frank W.
      Wright
237   Not Indicated[3]

MEMBERS OF THE AERO CLUB OF AMERICA (AS OF 1919)

Honorary Members

The President of the United
    States
The Secretary of War
The Secretary of the Navy
The Governor of the State of
    New York
The Mayor of the City of
    New York
The Postmaster General,
    U.S.A.

Comte. Henri de La Vaulx
Col. Frank Purdy Lahm,
    U.S.A.
James Gordon Bennett
Wilbur Wright
Orville Wright
Glenn H. Curtiss
Brig. Gen. James Allen, U.S.A.
    (ret.)

Rear Admiral Robert B.
    Peary, U.S.N.
Hon. William G. Sharp
Alberto Santos-Dumont
Dr. Alexander Graham Bell
Lord Northcliffe
Gen. John J. Pershing, U.S.A.
Vice Admiral William S. Sims,
    U.S.N.

Life Members

"[of this Club, or former club of similar name, now members of this Club, with dates of earliest membership in either of them.]"[4]

Name	Date	Name	Date	Name	Date
Alger, Russell A.	1908	Dunscombe, George E.	1916	McCormick, Harold F.	1912
Astor, Vincent	1913	Edwards, Charles		McKee, J. Dalzell	1919
Baker, George F., Jr.	1906	Jerome	1905	McMillin, Emerson	1909
Bishop, Courtland F.	1905	Ferguson, Farquhar I.	1917	Miller, W.W.	1910
Blackton, J. Stuart	1909	Ferguson, Roderick		Ryan, Allan A.	1911
Blair, James A., Jr.	1910	Craig	1917	Ryan, Thomas F.	1919
Channing, J. Parke	1906	Green, Col. Edward		Schiff, Mortimer L.	1909
Clapp, Charles E.	1918	H.R.	———	Vanderbilt, W.K.	1912
Cochran, Alexander		Huntington, Archer M.	1908	Watson, Thomas L.	1905
Smith	1911	Kahn, Otto H.	1909	Wood, G.F. Campbell	1906
Collier, Robert J.	1909	Mayo, Virginius J.	1914	Wood, Henry A. Wise	1906
Cross, W. Redmond	1910	McCornick, Clarence K.	1910	Young, William Wallace	1910

Active Members

Abell, A.S., 3rd	1911	Berry, Walter	1917	Cahn, Jacob	1911
Abell, George William	1918	Biddle, Henry J	1916	Caldwell, R.J.	1918
Abell, Walter M., 2nd	1918	Bissell, Lebbeus F.	1917	Callan, John Lansing	1913
Abell, Edwin F., 2nd	1918	Black, Archibald	1916	Callender, Walter R.	1917
Ackerman, Albert H.	1916	Blair, J. Insley	1917	Camp, Walter	1911
Adamoli, Giuseppe	1917	Blair, Ralph K.	1918	Carpenter, J.H.	1917
Adams, Dr. Calvin Thayer	1905	Bliss, Wm. H.	1916	Carroll, Philip A.	1915
Adams, Frederick B.	1916	Blunt, Harrison Needham	1913	Carry, Edward F.	1916
Adams, William P.	1913	Boeing, W.E.	1915	Cartier, Pierre	1918
Adams, Porter H.	1915	Bole, Ben P.	1916	Castaldi, Awino	1916
Adams, Walter O.	1917	Bonney, W. Leonard	1913	Castle, William A.	1916
Albree, George Norman	1913	Borden, Howard S.	1916	Caswell, George F.	1916
Alger, Frederick M.	1908	Bossert, John	1914	Chandler, A.S.	1911
Allyne, Edmuund L.	1916	Bouldin, William, 3rd	1913	Chandler, Chas. de F., Capt. U.S.A.	1906
Arnold, Bion J.	1913	Bourne, B.F.	1916	Chapin, Chester W.	1916
Atwater, William B.	1914	Bovee, J. Wesley	1907	Chapin, Roy D.	1909
Atwood, Harry N.	1917	Bowman, John McE.	1915	Chenevert, Charles T.	1913
Babason, Roger W.	1917	Boyer, Philip	1916	Chester, Wm. Merrill	1916
Backus, Clinton D	1917	Brady, Nicholas F.	1915	Chubb, Percy	1911
Bacon, Roboert Low	1916	Bragg, Caleb S.	1910	Clapp, Charles E.	1918
Bacon, Wm. S.	1916	Branson, George R.	1916	Clark, Charles H., Jr.	1906
Bacot, John V.	1917	Brackenridge, George W.	1916	Clark, E.J.	1916
Bacot, John V., Jr.	1917	Breckenridge, John C.	1910	Clark, M. Jewell	1916
Baillie, F. W.	1917	Breese, Sidney S.	1916	Clark, Roswell D.	1918
Bailey, Charles L.	1916	Breuchaud, Jules	1916	Clarke, Lewis L.	1916
Baker, Guy Ellis	1911	Briggs, A. William	1917	Clarke, Thomas B.	1906
Baker, K.C.	1918	Brinegar, F.P.	1917	Cleland, W.B.	1917
Baldwin, Thomas S.	1906	Brinsmade, C.L.	1917	Close, Edward B.	1917
Baldwin, Wm. M.	1911	Brock, Walter L.	1916	Coffin, Howard E.	1909
Ballard, Edward H.	1916	Brokaw, Clifford	1910	Cogswell, Stewart W.	1916
Ballerini, Michele	1917	Brown, Franklin Q.	1911	Colby, Howard A.	1909
Bamberger, Clarence G.	1911	Brown, George McKesson	1907	Cole, Chas. K.	1916
Barber, Philip P.	1917	Brown, George W.	1916	Conner, C.H.	1916
Barnard, William H.	1909	Brown, Harold H.	1903[5]	Cook, Alfred A.	1911
Barney, J. Stewart	1910	Brown, Walston Hill	1918	Coolidge, T. Jefferson	1916
Barranco, Victor Hugo	1916	Brown, Warren D.	1917	Corbin, Arthur	1917
Barrett, G. Himman	1914	Brown, Wrisley	1917	Cordley, Frank R.	1907
Bartlett, Capt. Robert A.	1916	Brush, Chas. F.	1916	Coster, Edward L.	1918
Baruch, Bernard M.	1911	Buck, Fred W.	1916	Cowdin, Elliot C., 2nd	1917
Bass, Ernest C.	1916	Budd, Henry A.	1915	Cox, Chas. H.	1919
Batchelder, A.G.	1905	Budd, Hudson	1915	Crane, Richard	1917
Batchelder, Wallace	1916	Budlong, Milton J.	1905	Crimmins, Cyril	1910
Batts, John Thomas	1913	Buegeleisen, Elias	1918	Crisp, W. Benton	1911
Bean, F.A., Jr.	1916	Bullivant, Malcolm	1913	Cross, Eliot	1915
Beckwith, Edward P.	1909	Bumbaugh, G.L.	1906	Cullinan, J.S.	1916
Beckwith, Sidney F.	1914	Burden, I. Towsend, Jr.	1910	Curtis, Charles G.	1917
Belding, M.M., Jr.	1906	Burgess, W. Starling	1911	Curtis, Greely S.	1909
Belin, Chas. A.	1916	Burnham, Frederick K.	1910	Custer, Dr. L.E.	1911
Bell, Charles J.	1909	Burns, Sidney H.	1916	Custis, John Trevor	1911
Belmont, August	1909	Butler, George P.	1916	Cutler, James G.	1916
Bemis, James W.	1909	Butler, Wm. H.	1916	Cutting, Bronson M.	1916
Benedict, Howard G.	1917	Byrne, James	1911	Da Costa, Dr. Jose Simao	1916
Benet, Laurence	1917	Cabot, Godfrey	1915	Dalley, Henry Allen	1918
Berg, Hart O.	1909	Cabrera, Manuel Estrada	1914	Dallett, Frederic A.	1916
Berliner, Edgar M.	1914			Daniel, Paul	1915
Berliner, Emile	1906				

Hill, Richard J., Jr.	1916	La Guardia, F. H.	1916	Maxwell, Robt. C.	1916
Hipwell, Dr. A.L.	1917	Lahm, Frank S.	1906	Maxwell, William	1917
Hirschman, Jesse	1916	Lake, Christopher J.	1906	Mayer, F.R.	1917
Hoffman, C.		Lamb, Charles		McClellan, William	1917
Gouveneur	1908	Rollinson	1911	McComb, David J.	1908
Hogan, W.S.	1911	Lambert, A.B.	1908	McCoy, J.C.	1906
Hollaman, Rich G.	1916	La Montagne, R.M.	1911	McCulloch, David J.	1914
Hollander, Sumner R.	1914	Langdon, Woodbury	1916	McCurdy, John A.D.	1910
Holloway, Charles T.	1917	Lansden, John M.	1906	McCutcheon,	
Holmes, C.W.	1918	Larrabee, George L.	1916	William A.	1917
Holmes, R.C.	1918	Lascaris, Emanuel	1916	McGann, Robert G.	1911
Honeywell, H.E.	1916	Laurence, Charles L.	1906	McIntosh, J.H.	1917
Hopkins, Nelson S.	1917	Law, Frederick M.	1917	McKinley, J.C.	1918
Hopkins, Russell	1909	Lawrence, Dr. G. Alfred	1909	McQueen, G. Fred	1918
Hoppin, Francis L.V.	1906	Leavy, William A.	1917	Means, James	1908
Horwitz, M.	1910	Lehman, Felix L.	1918	Merrill, Chas. E.	1916
Hoyt, Colgate	1906	Leiter, Joseph	1906	Merrill, Thomas D.	1916
Hubbard, Charles W.	1916	Lemp, Louis	1909	Metz, Herman A.	1909
Hulbert, Murray	1916	Leopold, Joseph	1917	Metzger, William E.	1906
Hulst, E. Covert	1916	Lescarboura, Austin C.	1917	Meyer, Eugene, Jr.	1910
Humphreys,		Lewis, George	1916	Meyer, R.S.	1916
Frederick E.	1909	Lewis, Samuel C.	1916	Mickle, Joseph R.	1918
Humphreys, F. Landon	1913	Liebman, Adolph	1916	Milbank, Jeremiah	1913
Hunt, E. Norman	1912	Lilienthal, Philip N., Jr.	1911	Milburn, Devereux	1911
Huntington, Chester	1914	Lindley, Forrest P.	1917	Milhado, Allan L.	1918
Huntington, Howard	1910	Linn, Howard	1913	Miller, Arthur G.	1913
Hyde, James H.	1917	Litchfield, E. Hubert	1912	Miller, Charles E.	1905
Irwin, William T.	1918	Lockhart, Henry, Jr.	1916	Miller, C.J.S.	1906
Jack, R.K.	1916	Loening, Grover		Miller, Frank E.	1912
Jacob, Charles	1914	Cleveland	1911	Miller, George W.	1916
Jacobs, H.W.	1910	Loomis, Alfred L.	1908	Miller, J.B.	1916
Jeffrey, J.A.	1916	Lord, Warren A.	1916	Miller, John H.	1916
Jerwan, Shakir S.	1911	Lorillard, Pierre, Jr.	1906	Mills, W. McMaster	1905
Johnson, Charles A.	1916	Lounsberry, Richard	1915	Millward, Russell	
Johnson, James M.	1916	Lovett, R.A.	1916	Hastings	1917
Joy, Henry B.	1915	Lows, Edward, Jr.	1916	Mingle, Harry B.	1916
Judson, Albert L.	1916	Ludlow, Israel	1905	Mix, Melville W.	1916
Julliot, Henri	1917	Lundin, Capt. A.P.	1917	Moniz, Raymond T.	1915
Keech, Frank B.	1906	Lutz, Roger H.	1913	Moody, Harry A.	1916
Kelly, Thomas Hughes	1913	Luyties, Otto	1908	Moore, Charles J.	1917
Kelsey, C.W.	1906	Lyster, T.L.B.	1916	Morehead, William C.	1918
Kendrick, B.H.	1916	Macaulay, Theodore C.	1914	Morehouse, Samuel C.	1914
Kerens, Vincent	1917	Macdonald, Chas.		Morgan, A.H.	1907
Kettering, Charles F.	1917	Stuart	1917	Morrell, Robert Lee	1906
King, Charles C.	1917	Macdonald, K.B.	1916	Morris, Dave Hennen	1906
King, W.P.	1916	MacKusick,		Morris, Raymond V.	1913
Kingsbury, Jerome, M.D.	1913	Meredith H.	1918	Mortimer, Louis S.	1917
Kinsila, Edward B.	1908	Mackay, Clarence H.	1910	Moskovics, F.E.	1917
Kip, William Ruloff	1911	Macke, Gordon B.	1917	de Mossin, Borge	1916
Kirkner, George M.	1906	Male, Arthur E.	1916	Moulton, Arthur J.	1906
Kittridge, A.M.	1916	Manly, Charles M.	1905	Mudd, F.X.	1911
Knabenshue, A.R.	1917	Marcuse, Alexander J.	1918	Munn, Charles Allen	1907
Knapp, Joseph F.	1917	Marling, Alfred E.	1909	Munn, John P.	1914
Knerr, Harold H.	1913	Maroney, T.T.	1914	Munoz, S.C.	1917
Konta, Alex	1910	Martin, Glenn L.	1914	Musselmann, C.A.	1910
Kovarik, J.J.	1916	Matalene, Henry W.	1918	Myers, George M.	1911
Kraft, Henry P.	1916	Mauran, Max	1916	Myers, John Caldwell	1917
Kuntz, William J.	1917	Maxwell, Francis T.	1917	Nash, Lewis Halleck	1917
Kurz, C.A.	1917	Maxwell, Robert	1917	Niles, W.W.	1906

Suydam, Walter		Untermeyer, Alvin	1911	Weymann, Charles T.	1911
Lispenard, Jr.	1913	Upson, Ralph	1912	Wheeler, Schuyler	
Swan, Harry	1915	Von Utassy, G.	1911	Skaats	1917
Sweeney, Thomas B.	1914	Van Alen, J. Laurens	1910	Wheelwright, J.W.	1916
Sweet, Wm. L., Jr.	1916	Van Husen, Corwin	1917	White, Claude Graham	1911
Talbot, Richmond	1906	Vanderbilt, Cornelius	1911	White, Rollin Henry	1905
Talbott, Harold E., Jr.	1917	Van Siclen, Arthur	1916	Whitehouse, William	
Tappan, A.D.	1911	Veeder, C.H.	1906	Fitzhugh	1911
Tarbell, Gage E.	1909	Veit, Sidney B.	1913	Whiting, A.H.	1917
Taylor, Cecil Hamelin	1906	Verity, George M.	1916	Whitman, Roger B.	1916
Taylor, Henry R.	1906	Vernon, Victor	1916	Whitney, Harry Payne	1918
Taylor, Lloyd	1917	Verplanck, J.B.R.	1913	Whitney, Payne	1909
Terry, Dr. M.O.	1916	Vincent, Jesse Gurney	1916	Wiborg, Frank B.	1916
Testoni, Felice	1917	Vought, Chance M.	1916	Widener, George D.	1913
Tevis, Gordon	1915	Wade, J.H.	1916	Wight, Robert F.	1918
Tevis, Lansing K.	1915	Wade, J.H., Jr.	1907	Wild, Horace B.	1914
Thaw, Benjamin	1916	Wagner, Harry	1917	Willard, Charles F.	1916
Thaw, William	1913	Waldon, Sidney D.	1917	Williams, Harrison	1913
Thomas, William T.	1914	Walsh, Charles	1906	Williams, J. Newton	1918
Thompson, Everard	1914	Wanamaker, Rodman	1909	Williams, Wm. H.	1914
Thompson, Jefferson		Wanamaker,		Willis, Harvey A.	1911
DeMont	1911	Rodman, 2nd	1918	Willoughby, Hugh	
Thompson, John F.	1917	Warburg, Felix M.	1911	Laussat	1906
Thomson, Clarke	1912	Wardrop, G. Douglas	1915	Willys, John N.	1911
Thompson, Frederic	1908	Ware, Raymond	1916	Wilson, M. Orme	1909
Thompson, L.S.	1911	Waring, George Dudley	1916	Wilson, R. Thornton	1911
Thompson, M.W.	1911	Warner, A.P.	1908	Wise, Henry B.	1915
Thompson, Wm. B.	1915	Warner, Wm. Deshler	1918	Witmer, Charles C.	1914
Tindel, Harris E.	1916	Warren, Charles Elliot	1913	Wolf, Walter B.	1912
Todd, David	1906	Washburn, Thomas G.	1906	Wollam, C.K.	1911
Topping, W.	1916	Waterhouse, W.J.	1917	Wood, Otis F.	1918
Tower, A. Edward	1911	Watson, Paul	1917	Woodhouse, Henry	1911
Tracy, Joseph	1906	Weare, John	1917	Woodruff, Clarence C.	1916
Tudor, Harry E.	1918	Webster, C.W.	1915	Work, Bertram G.	1916
Truscott, Starr	1918	Webster, Hamilton Fish	1916	Wrightsman, C.B.	1917
Turner, K.M.	1909	Weil, Morton	1917	Wrightsman, Charles J.	1918
Turney, George W.	1914	Weiss, George L.	1918	Yeoell, Wm. J.	1916
Tuska, Benjamin	1911	Welch, A.M.	1906	Young, S. Marsh	1909
Twombly, W. Irving	1911	West, Charles L.	1917	Zahm, Albert Francis	1905
Ullman, Isaac M.	1914	Westerfield, J.R.	1916	Ziegler, Wm., Jr.	1916
Ulman, J. Stevens	1911	Weston, E.B.	1909	Zimmerman, P.G.	1916
Uppercu, Inglis M.	1909	Weston, Edward	1916		

Collegiate Members

Abell, Robert Louis		Coolidge, Hamilton	1916	Villard, Henry S.	1914
Woodbourne	1918	Sinclaire, Reginald	1914		

Navy and Army Members of the Aero Club of America as of 1919

Abernethy, Lt. Wilbur K.	Allen, Lt. Frederick H.	Anderson, Ens. Joseph B.
Abernethy, Lt. C.S.	Alvord, Lt. Donald B.	Anderson, Lt. Richard M.
Aehle, Lt. Truman H.	Alway, Lt. James D.	Anglin, Lt. Charles H.
Aeton, Lt. Gene W.	Ames, Ens. Alan W.	Appleman, Lt. Earle
Aldrich, Lt. Harry S.	Ames, Lt. Theodore G.	Arnold, Lt. Ivan T.
Allan, Lt. A. Livingston	Amis, Lt. Wm. N.	Arnold, Lt. Leslie P.
Allen, Lt. Paul V.	Ammel, Lt. Roy W.	Arnold, Col. Henry H.
Allen, Lt. Albert A.	Anderson, Lt. Werner	Atwater, Lt. Benj. L.

Atwell, Lt. William B.
Atwood, Ens. Raymond L.
Aubert, Lt. W. A.
Austin, Lt. William J.
Austin, Lt. Joseph W.
Austin, Lt. Eugene H.
Babcock, Lt. Howard C.
Backus, Lt. Chas. S., Jr.
Bailey, Lt. Cyrus W.
Bailey, Lt. Morris H.
Bailey, Lt. Louis C.
Bailey, Lt. Henry F.
Baker, Lt. Alfred B.
Baker, Lt. P.E.
Balderston, Lt. J.A.
Baldwin, Lt. Henry M.
Baldwin, Lt. Raymond P.
Bamberger, Major R. S.
Barber, Capt. Frank M.
Barber, Lt. N.C.
Bard, Ens. Wm. H.
Barker, Lt. Donald V.
Barker, Ens. G.S.
Barnes, Lt. Kenneth A.
Barre, Lt. Peter C.
Barrett, Lt. Vinta E.
Bartlett, Lt. Harold T.
Bass, Lt. Haskell H.
Bastian, Lt. Frederick R.
Batchelder, Lt. William W.
Bates, Lt. Lew A.
Batts, Lt. Carl T.
Beach, Lt. Merritt S.
Bealmear, Lt. Wm. C.
Bean, Lt. Lucas V.
Beattie, Lt. Theodore L.
Beau, Lt. Lucas V.
Beck, Lt. Col. Paul W.
Becker, Lt. Albert F., Jr.
Bedell, Lt. James W., Jr.
Beehler, Lt. Chas. H.
Behr, Lt. Kenneth P.
Bell, Ens. Colley W.
Bell, Lt. Robert W.
Bell, Lt. Chas. F.
Bellinger, Lt. Victor E.
Bellinger, Lt. Cmdr. P.N.L.
Bellman, Lt. Elliott
Belloni, Lt. C. Leopoldo
Benjamin, Ens. H.R.
Bennett, Lt. Fred C.
Bentley, Lt. Frank H.
Benton, Lt. George A.
Berkowitz, Lt. Ben.
Berrien, Cmdr. F.D.
Berry, Lt. Richard B.
Berry, Lt. Thornton A.
Best, Lt. Harvey G.
Bibb, Lt. John T.

Bible, Lt. Dana V.
Biddle, Lt. Eric
Bigelo, Lt. James L.
Bilheimer, Lt. Earl L.
Bingham, Gen. Theodore A.
Birklund, Lt. George R.
Bishop, Lt. James G.
Black, Lt. Bernard C.
Black, Lt. Robert O.
Blackmore, Lt. Wm. C.
Blake, Lt. John J.
Blakey, Ens. Robert K.
Blamer, Capt. DeWitt
Blanchard, Lt. Carleton W.
Blevins, Lt. Chas. E.
Bockxus, Lt. Harry N.
Bodenheimer, Cadet Bertram
Bogart, Lt. E.A.
Boggs, Lt. Willis
Bohen, Lt. Mark D.
Boldenweck, Lt. Louis C.
Bond, Lt. George C.
Bond, Lt. William L.
Bondurant, Lt. D.S.
Bone, Lt. Norflett G.
Bonn, Lt. Wesley C.
Bonnevelle, Lt. Richard W.
Boothe, Lt. William H.
Bottoms, Ens. Robert R.
Boudwin, Lt. J.E.
Bowden, Capt. H.
Bowen, Lt. J.B.
Bower, Lt. Claire A.
Bower, Lt. Paul E.
Bowyer, Lt. J.E.
Boxell, Lt. Earl F.
Braak, Lt. Gail V.
Bradford, Lt. Geo. E.
Bradford, Ens. Smith N.
Brandenburg, Lt. Walter O.
Brandt, Lt. Howard C.
Brant, Col. G.C.
Braun, Lt. Bruce E.
Breckon, Lt. Leslie S.
Brenneke, Lt. Augustus M.
Brew, Lt. Goerge J.
Brewer, Lt. Percy O.
Bristol, Capt. Mark L.
Bristol, Ens. Lee Hastings
Britton, Lt. Ralph R.
Brock, Lt. William A.
Broderick, Lt. W.J.H.
Brody, Lt. Alton A.
Brokemeyer, Lt. Albert F.
Bronson, Lt. Tyler C.
Brooke, Lt. Leon C.
Brooks, Lt. Roger E.
Brooks, Lt. Thomas
Brotherton, Lt. Wm. C.

Broun, Lt. W.J.
Brown, Lt. Ronald W.
Brown, Lt. Harold L.
Brown, Cadet Robert I.
Brown, Lt. Ernest L.
Bruch, Lt. Russell L.
Buchanan, Lt. Douglas R.
Budd, Lt. Denison M.
Buffum, Lt. Frederick Cyrus, Jr.
Bufkin, Lt. W.F.
Bumstead, Lt. John H.
Burger, Lt. Fairfax C.
Burgess, Lt. George P.
Burgess, Ens. W.E.
Burnet, Lt. Gilbert W.
Burns, Lt. Kenneth
Burns, Lt. Ruel F.
Burns, Lt. John V.
Burns, Ens. Arthur C.
Buser, Lt. Albert E.
Bush, Lt. Bradford S.
Cabot, Lt. James J.
Caldwell, Lt. F. Wyllys
Caldwell, Lt. Robert M.
Camblin, Lt. Roy W.
Cameron, Lt. Brinton M.
Camp, Capt. Walter, Jr.
Campbell, Lt. Don M.
Campuzanno, Lt. Santiago
Canby, Lt. John W.
Candlish, Lt. Robert H.
Caproni, Gianni, M.E.
Carberry, Col. Joseph E.
Cardoff, Lt. Earl F.
Carey, Lt. Homer F.
Carhart, Lt. Harold W.
Carlston, Lt. Arthur G.
Carmichael, A.W.
Carples, Lt. Bernard J.R.
Carr, Lt. Paul John
Carrier, Lt. Alfred C.
Carroll, Lt. Earl
Carroll, Lt. Thomas
Carson, Lt. W. Holmes
Carter, Lt. Roy C.
Catheart, Lt. Sewell C.
Cauthwell, Lt. Robert C., Jr.
Cavagnaro, Lt. James F.
Cavanagh, Cadet James F.
Cerreta, Lt. Joseph M.
Chalfant, Lt. H. O.
Chamberlin, Lt. Leo W.
Chambers, Capt. W. Irving
Chapin, Lt. C. Graham
Chapman, Lt. Leonard B.
Charroin, Lt. A.B.
Chaser, Lt. Philip B.
Chauchoin, Lt. C.

Chevalier, Lt. John B.
Child, Lt. Cmdr. Warren B.
Chirieleison, Lt. Frank
Christensen, Lt. Ezra A.
Christiansen, Lt. Charles E.
Christie, Maj. Arthur R.
Claar, Stewart B.
Clagett, Maj. Henry B.
Clapp, Ens. Kenneth H.
Clark, Lt. Ben H.
Clark, Lt. Charles
Clark, Lt. Hobart
Clark, Lt. Dana V.
Clark, Lt. John E.
Clark, Ens. Franklin S.
Clark, Lt. Earland F.
Clark, Lt. Gordon W.
Clark, Lt. Col. V.E.
Clark, Paymaster P.A.
Clark, Lt. Kenneth L.
Clarke, Lt. Frederic D.
Clawson, Harry O.
Clayton, Lt. John H.
Clearwater, Lt. James D.
Cliff, Lt. Nelson A.
Close, Ens. Eugene F.
Clowes, Lt. Randolph
Coffin, Lt. Eugene
Coffman, Lt. Lionel A.
Cogan, Lt. W.J.
Cohen, Lt. Cmdr. Albert M.
Coil, Lt. E.W.
Coleman, Lt. Leighton H.
Coles, Lt. Barry F.
Collier, Lt. David C.
Collier, Lt. Trezevant
Collins, Lt. Claude R.
Collins, Lt. Wendle L.
Comey, Lt. George M.
Cone, Frederick H.
Connolly, Maj. Maurice
Conway, Ens. Frank C.
Cook, Lt. Lawrence E.
Cook, Ens. Theodore K.
Cooper, Lt. Edwin Jonas
Cooper, Lt. Richard D.
Copeland, Lt. Jay Milton, Jr.
Corbett, Ens. Matt.
Corbett, Lt. Marsh M.
Corry, Ens. Arthur
Coster, Lt. Gerald H.
Cowan, Capt. Arthur S.
Craig, Lt. William C.
Craighead, Lt. Philip B.
Crawford, Lt. Frank H.
Crawford, Lt. William J.
Crehore, Lt. John D.
Crescentini, Lt. Luigi
Crisp, Lt. M.C.

Critz, Lt. Robert, Jr.
Crompton, Lt. George
Cronk, Lt. H.M.
Cross, Major Harry E.
Cross, Lt. John M.
Crosscup, Ens. W.E.
Crouse, Capt. J.L.
Crowdus, Lt. Walter C.
Crowell, Lt. Harold O.
Croxford, Lt. Frank D.
Culver, Lt. Col. C. C.
Cumming, Lt. Charles M.
Cummings, Lt. J.H.
Cummings, Lt. Frank J.
Cummings, Lt. Barnard
Cunningham, Lt. R.M.
Curry, Lt. Lea
Curtiss, Lt. Dwight W.
Cushing, Ens. Winsor H.
d'Annunzio, Maj. Gabriele
d'Annunzio, Capt. Ugo V.
da Silva, Ens. Antonio
Dade, Lt. A.L.
Daggett, Maj. Byron B.
Dahaman, Lt. Wallace W.
Dale, Lt. Russell R.
Dalton, Lt. Wilfred
Dargue, Maj. Herbert A.
Dauthitt, Lt. Laidley E.
Davidson, Lt. Wilbur L.
Davidson, Lt. Kenneth S.M.
Davidson, Lt. Rufus B.
Davies, Lt. Ward J.
Davis, Lt. Edwin K.
Davis, Lt. Homer H.
Davis, Lt. Clarence A.
Davis, Cmdr. Cleland
Dawson, Lt. John C., Jr.
Day, Lt. Curtiss L.
de Arce, L. Ponton
de Learie, Lt. George R.
De Shong, Lt. Lloyd M.
de Vore, Lt. Kenneth Lee
de Loo, Capt. Gar
de Roode, Lt. Clifford H.
De Garmo, Lt. Elmer C.
Dean, Lt. Alex R.
Decker, Lt. Kenneth N.
Deleplane, Lt. Edwin S., Jr.
Denny, Lt. Cary T.
Depew, Capt. Richard H.
Deuel, Maj. Thorne
Diamond, Lt. A.F.
Dichman, Lt. Ernest W.
Dick, Lt. Guy H.
Dickey, Lt. Lester J.
Dickinson, Lt. Charles E., Jr.
Dickinson, Lt. R. W.
Dicks, Lt. George E.

Dietrich, Lt. Richard H.
Diggins, Lt. Ralph C.
Dimmig, Lt. Howard
Dixon, Lt. T.D.
Dobbs, Lt. Silas A.
Dobson, Lt. Matt H.
Doehler, Lt. H.H.
Dolphin, Lt. William R.
Donahey, Lt. John W.
Donnohue, Sgt. John J.
Donovan, Lt. Edward
Doolin, Lt. Bernard M.
Dortch, Lt. Cmdr. I.F.
Douglas, Capt. Walter C.
Douglass, Lt. Norman J.
Dowdall, Lt. Joseph
Doyle, Milton D.
Dreher, Lt. Raymond
Drennon, Lt. Walter R.
Drescher, Lt. Herbert C.
Du Chemin, Ens. Nicholas M.
Dudley, Lt. William M.
Duell, Lt. Prentice Van W.
Dugas, Lt. Graham C.
Duke, Lt. William B.
Dunford, Lt. Samuel W.
Dunn, Lt. Charles A.
Dunn, Lt. Thomas F.
Durar, Lt. George H.
Durfee, Lt. Charles P.
Durnell, Lt. Ralph Milton
Duryea, Lt. Leslie N.
Dusossoit, Lt. F.J.
Dussean, Lt. Rudolph W.
Earl, Lt. Kenneth A.
Early, Lt. Lawrence
Eastman, Lt. Andrew J.
Ebert, Lt. Solomon Bernard
Eckstrom, Lt. Lawrence J.
Eddy, Lt. A.E.
Edlundh, Capt. R.A.
Edson, Lt. Albert L.
Ehlers, Lt. George W.
Ehrmanntrant, Ens.
  William R.
Eldridge, Ens. Carleton G.
Eldridge, Lt. Loyal A.
Eldridge, Lt. John R.
Elhart, Lt. Earl W.
Elliott, Clinton, Jr.
Ellison, Lt. James A.
Ely, Lt. Newell D.
Emden, Ens. Aaron L.
Engel, Lt. ORC, P.H.
English, Lt. Connell A.
English, Lt. Joseph P.F.
Ennis, Lt. Frank S.
Epler, Lt. Earl N.
Erdman, Lt. Charles R., Jr.

Erdman, Lt. Calvin P.
Erickson, Lt. Robert
Esterly, Ens. M.H.
Evans, Lt. Stephan G.
Evans, Lt. Arthur H.
Evans, Brig. Gen. Robert K.
Evans, Lt. Elisha E.
Evans, Lt. George E.
Ewan, Lt. Charles V.
Ewell, Capt. Arthur W.
Eytings, Lt. Bruce S.
Fairbairn, Lt. George R.
Farnum, Lt. Robert
Farre, Lt. Henri
Farrell, Lt. John B.
Faurot, Lt. Henry, Jr.
Fauxon, Lt. Warren E.
Fay, Lt. George H.
Feick, Lt. William
Feild, Lt. Rutledge H.
Felley, Lt. Louis Jay
Fenne, Lt. Jesse K.
Fenwick, Lt. Herbert F.
Fernhoff, Lt. F.B.
Ferry, Lt. J.R.
Fickinger, Lt. Robert
Field, Lt. John B.
Fiester, Lt. Ritner I.
Finn, Lt. Matthew E.
Fiske, Adm. Bradley A.
Fitzgerald, Lt. Gordon
Fitzpatrick, Lt. Walter T.
Flinn, Lt. Earle F.
Fluer, Lt. Peter E.
Flynn, Mortimer G.
Foley, Lt. William R.
Folsom, Lt. Harold J.
Ford, Lt. Harold R.
Forshay, Lt. Harold
Foster, Lt. L. Bruce
Foster, Lt. Esty
Foster, Ens. John C.
Fowler, Lt. Gordon
Fox, Lt. Russell
Francis, Lt. Paul Robertson
Frank, Lt. Norman D.
Fraser, Lt. Dean B.
Fraser, Lt. Walter
Fravel, Lt. Col. Ira F.
Freeman, Ens. Stephen A.
Frenzel, Lt. James F.
Friedman, Lt. Max H.
Fritts, Lt. Ralph Victor
Frost, Lt. Edward P.
Frost, Lt. E. Rice, Jr.
Fry, Lt. John
Frye, Lt. Abram R.
Fuller, Col. A.L.
Gahman, Lt. Floyd

Gallup, Lt. Marvin
Galvin, Lt. Albert E.
Gandy, Lt. Robert L.
Garlough, Lt. J.L.
Garrett, Lt. P.B.
Garrett, Lt. Kenneth
Gartz, Ens. Richard C.
Garver, Lt. J.B.
Garwood, Lt. Sterling M.
Gaskell, Lt. Elsworth
Gaston, Lt. Alexander N.
Gates, Lt. William A.
Gaton, Lt. W.M.
Gay, Lt. Ernest H.
Gaylord, Lt. E.J., Jr.
Geary, Lt. Harry O.
Gentry, Lt. Benj. A.
Genung, Lt. Arthur L.
Geyer, Ens. C.H.
Gheen, Ens. Joseph W.
Gheen, Lt. Raymond F.
Gibson, Ens. J.R.
Giffin, Lt. John L.
Gifford, Lt. Frank R.S.
Giles, Lt. Benjamin F.
Gillespie, Lt. Franklin S.
Gillespie, Lt. G.S.
Gilman, Lt. Charles
Gilson, Lt. Fred E.
Giroux, Lt. Victor L.
Girvin, Lt. Willard S.
Gleerup, Lt. William W.
Glogan, Lt. William E.
Goddard, Lt. Fred C.
Goddary, Lt. Fred C.
Goddary, Lt. Glenn
Godinho, Ens. Mario C.
Godwin, Lt. Grover
Goettel, Lt. Philip C.
Goodall, Lt. Thomas
Goode, Lt. Henry W.
Gooding, Lt. C.C.V.
Goodnough, Lt. Max H.
Gordon, Lt. Harry R.
Gore, Lt. Frank D.
Gorrell, Maj. E.S.
Goss, Lt. Lewis
Gover, Ens. Robb
Grady, Lt. Anthony J.
Grady, Lt. William A.
Graham, Sgt. H.J.
Graicunas, Lt. Vigtantas A.
Grant, Lt. Alfred A.
Grant, Lt. D.R.
Grant, Lt. William Wulfing
Grassi, Lt. Waldemar H.
Graves, Lt. J.D.
Gray, Lt. J.D.M.
Gray, Lt. R.M.

Grayson, Lt. Forrest
Green, Lt. Gerald R.
Greene, Lt. William
Greenfield, Ens. Edwin R.
Greenslade, Lt. Russell M.
Greenwood, Lt. Samuel A.
Gregg, Lt. Col. Harry W.
Greist, Lt. E.H.
Greotjen, Lt. Floyd L.
Griffin, Lt. Courtland B.
Griswold, Ens. Rettig A.
Gross, Lt. Edward
Grosvenor, Ens. Theodore P.
Guernsey, Lt. L.W.
Guidera, Lt. Albert M.
Guild, Lt. Paul Conrad
Gunderson, Lt. Leroy A.
Gwathney, Lt. Brooke
Haasl, Lt. Charles M.
Haddorff, Lt. Carl L.
Hagenbuck, Lt. Rea T.
 Rowland
Hagenbuck, Lt. H.J.
Haggerty, Lt. Truman H.
Hall, Lt. Oliver J.
Hall, Lt. George L.
Hall, Lt. James G.
Halliburton, Machinist S.S.
Hallum, Lt. O.T.
Halsey, Capt. Edward S.
Hamblet, Lt. Francis M.
Hamill, Lt. Howard E.
Hamilton, Lt. Edgar G.
Hamilton, Lt. Mark A.
Hammerstein, Lt. Clarence P.
Hammond, Lt. Fred R.
Hammond, Lt. William C.
Hancock, Lt. Royce D.
Hanlon, Lt. William J.
Harley, Lt. W.H.
Harmon, Lt. Ray W.
Harold, Lt. Eugene L.
Harper, Lt. Maitland C.
Harris, Ens. Harold C.
Harrison, Lt. Elbert I.
Harrison, Lt. William W.
Harshorne, Lt. Frank W.K.
Hart, Lt. Floyd H.
Hartford, Lt. Claude E.
Hartley, Lt. Francis, Jr.
Hartman, Col. C.F.
Hartman, Lt. Frederick
Hartman, Lt. Clarence A.
Hartman, Lt. Harry B.
Hartwell, Lt. C. Hill
Harvey, Earl M.
Harvey, Lt. Harold M.
Hasbrouck, Lt. Louis
Haslam, Lt. Reed H.

Hawkins, Ens. S.C.
Hay, Lt. Malcolm
Haylor, Lt. J.R.
Haynor, Lt. Norman A.
Hazeltine, Lt. Richard G.
Heard, Lt. Col. Jack W.
Heard, Lt. Charles B.
Hebbard, Lt. Charles B.
Heck, Lt. George L.
Hegan, Lt. Chester P.
Heisen, Lt. Horace N.
Heisner, Lt. Charles L.
Helweg, Lt. Laurence N.
Henderson, Lt. William A.
Henderson, Lt. Denny E.
Hendrick, Lt. George F.
Heng, Lt. Jacob Arthur
Henley, Lt. William C.
Henn, Lt. J. Erwin
Henriques, Lt. Charles R.
Herbster, Lt. V.D.
Herron, Lt. Mark L.
Hersey, Col. H.B.
Hever, Lt. James L.
Hiatt, Lt. John B.
Hickman, Lt. Cecil R.
Hickmott, Lt. DeGarmo
Hickmott, Lt. John T.
High, Lt. Stanley
Hill, Lt. Charles
Hill, Lt. J.C., Jr.
Hill, Lt. Ploya P.
Hill, Lt. Thomas L.
Hine, Lt. Harold M.
Hine, Lt. Virgil
Hinkle, Lt. Stacy C.
Hinma, Lt. Donald M.
Hinman, Lt. David E.
Hitchcock, Lt. William C.
Hoare, Lt. John L.
Hoatson, Lt. Thomas L.
Hobbs, Lt. John E.
Hodgdon, Ens. Lyman A.
Hodgson, Lt. Harold C.
Hoffman, Lt. Stoddard
Hoffman, Lt. Charles R.
Hogan, Lt. William A.
Hogan, Lt. John R.
Hogan, Lt. H.C.
Hogue, Lt. Mark C.
Holland, Lt. Maurice
Hollander, Lt. Robert B.
Hollborn, Lt. Clarence E.
Hollingsworth, Lt. Frank E.
Holmes, Lt. Elmer M.
Holst, Ens. E.T.
Hone, Lt. Charles
Hooker, Lt. Chas. J.
Hooper, Lt. Jas. C.

Hoover, Lt. Chester A.
Horgy, Ens. Walter W.
Horn, Lt. Norman E.
Horne, Lt. George W.
Horne, Lt. Ernest G.
Horton, Lt. Clarence F.
Horton, Lt. William O.
Hosier, Lt. J.H.
Hosking, Lt. Oakley W.
Houlihan, Lt. Daniel J.
House, Lt. William R.
Houston, Lt. Robert S.
Howe, Lt. Laurence L.
Hoyt, Lt. Henry W.
Hoyt, Lt. William K.
Hubbard, Lt. T.H.
Huber, Lt. Howard F.
Huebner, Lt. Herbert C.
Hughes, Cadet John E.
Hughes, Lt. Joseph V.
Hulbert, Lt. L. Gaylord
Hull, Lt. Justus M.
Hulse, Lt. James H.
Hunt, Lt. Spencer S.
Hunt, Lt. W. Jackson
Hunt, Lt. Jason S.
Hunt, Lt. John L.
Hunter, Lt. John Ackley
Huntington, Lt. R.O.
Hutcheon, Ens. Frank E.
Hutchins, Lt. H.
Hutchinson, Lt. A.H.
Hutchinson, Ens. L.B.
Hyde, Lt. Clarence E.
Hyland, Lt. George N.
Ilse, Lt. Henry A.
Ingold, Lt. Alfred F.
Innes, Lt. William W.
Innis, Lt. Cecil R.
Irving, Lt. Livingston G.
Jackson, Lt. Roger W.
Jacob, Lt. Walter P.
Jaeger, Lt. Otto
Jaenke, Lt. Wm. D.
Jagoe, Lt. W.M.
Jamison, Lt. Ross P.
Jenne, Lt. William K.
Jewett, Lt. E.H., Jr.
Johnson, Lt. George P.
Johnson, Lt. Clarence H.
Johnson, Lt. Geo. S.
Johnson, Lt. Cortland S.
Johnson, Lt. Everett B.
Johnson, Lt. J.L.
Johnson, Lt. Raymond C.
Johnston, Lt. Niel S.
Johnston, Lt. George E.
Johnstone, Lt. Clifford
Jolly, Lt. J.S.

Jones, Lt. Clifford E.
Jones, Lt. Brevard M.
Jones, Lt. Delbert
Jones, Lt. Elmer H.
Jones, Col. E. Lester
Jones, Lt. Howard H.
Jones, Lt. Roy L.
Jones, Lt. Almer Voss
Jones, Lt. Donald F.
Julian, Lt. Rupert
Kanitz, Lt. Edwin C.
Kann, Lt. E.A.
Kant, Ens. Edwin S.
Kaufman, Lt. Godfrey F.
Keating, Lt. Jas. Alfred
Keene, Lt. Chas. W.
Keever, Lt. Frank L.
Keightley, Lt. George M.
Keller, Lt. Clarence K.
Kelly, Lt. J.N.
Kelly, Lt. Sherwin F.
Kemp, Cmdr. C.S.
Kemp, Lt. Phillip
Kenly, Maj. Gen. W.L.
Kennedy, Lt. David S.
Kennedy, Lt. Harold S.
Kenney, Lt. Conelius J.
Kenny, Lt. Raymond
Kent, Lt. Arthur O.
Kenyon, Lt. Johnson
Keough, Lt. Wesley L.
Kermott, Lt. E.E.
Kern, Lt. John T.
Kerr, Lt. William L.
Kerr, Lt. Stephen L.
Kerr, Lt. Henry H., Jr.
Kesling, Lt. Ernest E.
Keyes, Ens. Kenneth B.
Kidd, Lt. Maurice M.
Kidder, Lt. C.J.
Kinberg, Lt. George
Kinder, Lt. Roland H.
King, Lt. Gelston T.
King, Lt. Cloize A.
King, Lt. H.C.
King, Lt. William T., Jr.
Kirchdorfer, Lt. Wm. F.
Kirk, Lt. John B.
Kirk, Lt. Harris C.
Kirkpatrick, Lt. James D., Jr.
Kirkpatrick, Lt. R.D.
Kirtland, Col. Roy C.
Klingman, Lt. Edwin C.
Kloke, Lt. Earl P.
Knauer, Lt. Howard P.
Kohr, Lt. Hugo J.
Koiner, Lt. Carl W.
Kratz, Cadet Henry A.
Krouse, Lt. Samuel H.

Krout, Lt. Ray W.
Kruesi, Capt. Walter E.
Krum, Lt. Howard E.
Kuiskamp, Ens. Gerard L.
La Parle, Lt. Walter E.
Lachmund, Lt. Harry G.
Lamax, Lt. Thornton G., Jr.
LaMont, Lt. W.D.
Lang, Lt. George H.
Lange, Ens. Karl S.
Laventhal, Lt. Ruby
Lawrence, Ens. J.B.
Lawson, Lt. John T.
Lawton, Lt. Merritt Lyon
Lazar, Maj. Eugene
LeClerg, Ens. Frederic
Ledbury, Lt. P.H.
Lee, Lt. Robert E.
Lee, Lt. Stanley B.
Leigh, Lt. Kenneth G.
Lenderking, Lt. Louis P., Jr.
Lennstrand, Lt. Guy S.
Lenox, Lt. William J.
Leonard, Lt. Cecil E.
Levitt, Lt. Morse D.
Lewis, Lt. Henry P.
Lewis, Ens. Harley B.
Lewis, Col. I.N.
Libby, Capt. Frederick
Liebmann, Lt. Col. Morris N.
Lievre, Lt. Joseph B.
Lindquist, Lt. Harry M.
Lindsay, Lt. Robert O.
Lindsay, Lt. P.K.
Lindsley, Lt. Dan L.
Lippencott, Lt. Wallace C.
Lipsner, Capt. B.B.
Little, Rear Adm. William N.
Livingston, Lt. E.P.
Lobdell, Lt. Jacob K.
Lochhead, Lt. Archie
Lochman, Ens. D.E.
Lockwood, Lt. Lyman B.
Lomery, Lt. Hugh
Loud, Lt. Lingard
Love, Lt. Ernest A.
Low, Lt. James B.
Lowell, Lt. Robert W.
Lowry, Lt. Edward B.
Lowsteeter, Lt. Edward T.
Luce, Lt. Robert F.
Luff, Lt. Frederic E.
Lyon, Lt. W.L.
Lyster, Lt. Arthur F.
Macaulay, Lt. Alexander V.
Mackenzie, Lt. William J.
MacKenzie, Lt. William J.
Maddox, Lt. G.J.
Magee, Lt. Christopher

Magruder, Lt. A.W.
Mahon, Lt. R.J.
Mahoney, Lt. Daniel F.
Mahr, Lt. Ralph E.
Mallers, Lt. John B.
Mallers, Lt. John B., 3rd
Malmgren, Lt. Carl E.
Maloney, Lt. John P.
Mapes, Capt. S. Herbert
Marschat, Ens. Richard A.
Marsh, Lt. Ralph A.
Marsh, Lt. Albert E.
Marshall, Lt. Lewis K.
Marshall, Lt. Chas. C.
Marshall, Lt. Richard H.
Martin, Lt. Harry J.
Martin, Lt. M. Rex
Martin, Lt. Richard C.
Masck, Lt. William
Mason, Lt. James M.
Mason, Lt. Clesson E.
Massey, Lt. Raymond R.
Massey, Lt. Bert V.
Mast, Lt. Walter E.
Mathews, Lt. Amos M.
Matthews, Lt. David R.
Mattson, Lt. Alfred S.
Maxfield, Lt. L.H.
McAlister, Lt. Thomas E.
McArn, Lt. Theodore A.
Mcaulay, Ens. Donald M.
McBride, Lt. Howard I.
McCaffrey, Lt. J. Aug.
McCall, Lt. Lewis L.
McCartney, Lt. Harold G.
McCartney, Lt. C.E.
McClaskey, Lt. J.W.
McCLintock, Lt. Ralph A.
McConkey, Lt. James G.
McCormack, Lt. Robt. D.
McCormack, Lt. J. Stanley
McCormak, Lt. THos. H.
McCutchen, Lt. Phillip T.
McDonald, Lt. Frank W., Jr.
McDonald, Lt. S. FLoyd
McDonough, Lt. H.B.
McDowell, Lt. ALfred A.
McElhinney, Lt. William D.
McElroy, Lt. J.W.
McElroy, Lt. Paul E.
McElvain, Lt. C.A.
McFalls, Lt. Edwin
McGehee, Lt. Abner F., Jr.
McGill, Lt. Raymond J.
McGinty, Lt. Daniel J.C.
McGovern, Lt. John E.R.
McGowace, Lt. G.J.
McIlvain, Lt. W.M.
McIntyre, Ens. Harry M.

McKee, Lt. J. Dalzell
McKenzie, Lt. Wesley R.
McKinstry, Lt. A.T.
McLaren, Lt. W.B.
McNabb, Lt. H.R.
McNally, Ens. Leo A.
McNamara, Lt. Lorimer J.
McVay, Lt. George E.
McWhorter, Lt. Ray S.
Means, Lt. Leland M.
Meany, Lt. John W.
Meehan, Lt. Timothy E.
Meeker, Lt. Nathaniel H., Jr.
Melamet, Lt. Otto
Meric, Lt. A.G.
Merril, Lt. C.W.
Merrit, Lt. Edward K.
Messinger, Lt. Joe P.
Metzger, Lt. Carlisle
Meyers, Lt. Chas. L.
Micelli, Lt. Paul
Middleton, Lt. Ellis S.
Midwood, Ens. George A.
Milburn, Lt. George J.
Miller, Col. Archie
Miller, Lt. Arthur J.
Miller, Lt. Julian F.
Miller, Lt. Zenos R.
Miller, Lt. Royall McI.
Millineaux, Lt. Lester R.
Milling, Col. T. DeWitt
Mills, Lt. D.W.
Mills, Lt. Chas. H.
Mills, Lt. Harry H.
Molthan, Lt. Emil H.
Monger, Lt. Walter V.
Monroe, Lt. C.H.
Montejth, Lt. Darrel M.
Montgomery, Lt. Roe F.
Moon, Lt. Lawrence B.
Moon, Lt. R.K.
Moor, Lt. Robert D.
Moore, Lt. Walter F.
Moore, Lt. Edwin C.
Moore, Lt. Maurice H.
Moore, Lt. Chas. R.
Moore, Lt. Marlin C.
Morange, Lt. Gronig S.
Morebach, Lt. Robert E.
Morehead, Lt. John L.
Morell, Commodore Henry
Morey, Lt. Philip J.
Morgan, Lt. Louie R.
Morgan, Lt. Stuart
Morgan, Lt. Stuart A.
Morison, Lt. James C.
Morris, Lt. Glenn D.
Morrisey, Lt. John F.
Morrow, Ens. Thomas I.

Morse, Ens. Alan A.
Mowry, Lt. Jared J.
Muir, Capt. Joe
Muirhead, Lt. B.R.
Munchhof, Lt. Theo. J.
Muncie, Lt. Floyd H.
Munford, Lt. Edmund S.
Murnen, Lt. George J.
Murphy, Lt. Harry C.
Murphy, Lt. Limus J.
Murphy, Ens. John L.
Murphy, Lt. Maurice
Murray, Lt. Harry E.
Murray, Lt. Kenneth M.
Mustain, Lt. Samuel J.
Mustard, Lt. Stanley P.
Mustin, Lt. Cmdr. Henry C.
Myers, Lt. George G.
Myers, Lt. Ray G.
Myers, Lt. Harold
Myers, Lt. Clarence G.
Myers, Lt. Maurice C.
Nash, Lt. Roland L.
Nassr, Lt. Anthony M.
Neber, Lt. Lawrence H.
Needham, Lt. Clarence E.
Neet, Lt. Lewis E.
Nelson, Lt. Luther
Netting, Lt. Charles L.
Newburg, Lt. Hwley D.
Newkirk, Lt. George H.
Newman, Lt. G. Barden
Nichols, Lt. Brayton
Nienhauser, Lt. Ralph P.
Noble, Lt. S. Shropshire
Noland, Ens. John L.
Noland, Lt. Raymond R.
Nordhouse, Lt. Sterling R.
Norfleet, Lt. J.P.
Norris, Lt. Howard D.
Norris, Lt. Leonard S.
Norton, Lt. Howard B.
Norton, Lt. Alwin W.
Nudd, Lt. Thomas L.
Nutt, Lt. Henry H.
O'Brien, Lt. Bernard J.
O'Brien, Lt. Thomas J.
O'Conner, Lt. Joseph P.
O'Gorman, Capt. W.D.
O'Laughlin, Lt. George
O'Leary, Lt. Dorman H.
O'Neil, Capt. Grover
O'Neil, Lt. Joseph H.
Oakleaf, Capt. H.B.
Ogden, Lt. James R.
Ogilvie, Lt. Alexander K.
Older, Lt. Fred R.
Olds, Lt. Harvey R.
Oliver, Lt. Herbert G.

Orb, Lt. John A., Jr.
Osborn, Lt. Frank C.
Outcalb, Lt. Dudley M.
Owen, Lt. Maurice C.
Owens, Lt. Celeste F.
Oxley, Ens. John H.
Packard, Ens. Edward B.
Page, Lt. Frank A.
Page, Lt. R.C.M.
Paine, Lt. R.B.
Palmer, Lt. Carlton M.
Pardy, Lt. G.W.
Parker, Lt. J. Brooks B.
Parkin, Lt. Walter F., Jr.
Parsons, Lt. Gistav A.
Partridge, Lt. Herbert G.
Parvis, Lt. Guiliano
Patterson, Lt. Robert E.
Patterson, Col. Wm. Lay
Pawley, Lt. George P.
Payne, Lt. Bryan W.
Peake, Lt. Junius B.
Pearce, Lt. Howard B.
Pearson, Lt. William D.
Peck, Ens. L.S.
Peck, Lt. Scott E.
Peck, Lt. Theodore A.
Peebles, Maj. Wm. B.
Pemberton, Lt. George H.
Penland, Lt. Paul W.
Pennebaker, Lt. Chas. T.
Pennington, Lt. Jerome E.
Pergeo, Lt. Alfred K.
Perkins, Lt. George
Perry, Lt. William L.
Pettengill, Lt. Raymond R.
Phelps, Lt. Ralph M.
Pickard, Lt. Samuel
Pickrell, Lt. Floyd M.
Pidgeon, Lt. Phillip
Pierce, Lt. Hugh M.
Pierce, Lt. Leslie E.
Pierson, Lt. Norris E.
Pierson, Lt. Walter E.
Piper, Lt. Raymond A.
Plant, Lt. Leonard F.
Platt, Lt. Harold L.
Platz, Lt. Edward H., Jr.
Plyler, Lt. W.H.
Pollock, Lt. Ganville
Pollock, Lt. Jacques J.
Pond, Lt. George K.
Pond, Richard E.
Pooke, Lt. H.M.
Porter, Lt. Victor W.
Porter, Lt. Kenneth L.
Porter, Capt. Harold E.
Porter, Lt. Lester K.
Porter, Henry W.

Porter, Lt. Lester L.
Post, Ens. Geo. B.
Post, Capt. F.A.
Powerly, Lt. Daniel W.
Powers, Lt. Edward W.
Pratt, Ens. H.C.
Pratt, Lt. Herbert G.
Prentice, Lt. Col. James
Price, Lt. Edward F.
Price, Lt. Owen N.
Pritchett, Lt. Frank E.
Proctors, Lt. W. Heath
Pruden, Russell G.
Pryibil, Ens. Paul
Pugh, Lt. Richard O.
Puliam, Capt. G.K., Jr.
Pulliam, Ens. H.A.
Purdy, Lt. Carroll F.
Quarnberg, Lt. Paul R.
Quin, Lt. Langdon C.
Quinn, Lt. J.J.
Raber, Lt. Oran L.
Radford, Lt. William A.
Ragatz, Lt. Edward G.
Raleigh, Lt. John F.
Randell, Lt. Hugh P.
Rankin, Lt. Allen
Ranney, Maj. A. Elliott
Rauh, Lt. Joseph A.
Ray, Cadet Lyle C.
Read, Maj. Norman H.
Readio, Lt. Roger F.
Ready, Lt. James B.
Reder, Lt. Louis D.
Redfield, Lt. A.W.
Redman, Lt. B. Ray
Reed, Lt. Carroll C.
Reed, Ens. Chas. R.
Reeve, Lt. Howard E.
Reid, Lt. Kenneth A.
Reid, Cmdr. James H.
Reilly, Lt. George C.
Reinhard, Lt. Henry A.
Reisz, Lt. George S.
Remey, Lt. John T.
Reynolds, Maj. John B.
Reynolds, Ens. Harry
Rice, Maj. Cushman A.
Rice, Lt. Franklin D.
Rice, Lt. George E.
Richards, Lt. Walter E.
Richman, Lt. G. Raymond
Richmond, Lt. Ira M.
Richmond, Lt. Isidor
Rickard, Lt. C.H.
Riddlesbarger, Lt. Rufus
Rider, Lt. William N.
Rieder, Lt. Louis D.
Rigg, Lt. D. Don

Riley, Lt. Joseph E.
Rinker, Lt. Harry M.
Ritter, Lt. Paul N.
Rivers, Lt. H.R.
Roach, Lt. Howard L.
Robbins, Lt. William Dudley
Robbins, Lt. Ralph B.
Roberts, Lt. William R.
Robertson, Lt. William B.
Robinson, Lt. Ward F.
Robinson, Lt. Charles McK.
Robson, Lt. William W.
Rockefeller, Ens. William
Rodger, Lt. Raymond J.
Roe, Lt. James A., Jr.
Rogenhurst, Lt. Edward
Rollins, Lt. M.E.
Ronan, Lt. John A.
Rorison, Lt. Harmon C.
Rosaire, Lt. Esme
Rose, Lt. Elmer J.
Rose, Lt. Waldo H.
Rothfeld, Lt. Tracy
Rothwell, Lt. John H., Jr.
Rouleau, Ens. Louis T.
Roulet, Ens. A.L.
Rucker, Ens. E.W., Jr.
Ruegg, Lt. Joseph A.
Ruiter, Lt. Raymond N.
Rummel, Lt. Leslie J.
Rundbaker, Lt. Frederick J.
Runkle, Lt. Charles G.
Runser, Lt. Harry J.
Russell, Lt. E.C.
Russell, Lt. Rober F.
Ruttan, Lt. Charles E.
Sadowsky, Cadet Jack P.
Salisbury, Lt. Earle E.
Salisbury, Lt. Henry W.
Sampter, Lt. Herbert C.
Sanders, Lt. Ralph L.
Sandlin, Lt. James H.
Sanford, Lt. H.M.
Santos, Ens. Fileto F.S.
Sapiro, Lt. Milton D.
Saunders, Lt. Guy D.
Scanlon, Lt. Eugene J.
Schadt, Lt. W.F.
Scheleen, Lt. Arthur
Schick, Lt. Herbert
Schiff, Ens. Herbert
Schiller, Lt. Carl J.
Schlums, Ens. O.W.
Schmitt, Lt. J.R.
Schmocker, Lt. Fred C.
Schock, Lt. Wm. O.
Schoeppe, Lt. Edward
Schroeder, Capt. R.W.
Schuch, Lt. Leland S.

Schuemacher, Lt. Clyde J.
Schultz, Lt. Harold S.
Schwabe, Lt. John C., Jr.
Scott, Lt. Ernest DeWolf
Scouton, Lt. Harry E.
Scully, Capt. William A.
Seaman, Lt. William Laurie
Sears, Lt. Hugh
Seawell, Lt. John L.
Seibold, Lt. George V.
Seitz, Lt. W.J.
Selden, Lt. Lynde
Sellers, Lt. Lamar
Severson, Lt. Thos. J.
Seymour, Lt. Leland S.
Shank, Lt. H.V.
Shank, Lt. William E.
Sharon, Lt. William F.
Shaw, Lt. George W.
Shaw, Ens. G.W.
Shea, Lt. Thomas F.
Sheeby, Lt. John F.
Shepard, Lt. Floyd W.
Shepherd, Lt. Rigby G.
Sheppard, Lt. William H.
Shidler, Lt. Horace
Shope, Lt. Leslie R.
Shoptaw, Lt. John W.
Shrader, Lt. M.R.
Shumway, Ens. Carl E.
Shumway, Ens. P.E.
Shutan, Maj. WIlliam H.
Siems, Lt. Charles
Silcott, Lt. Arthur E.
Silver, Lt. B.E.
Simon, Lt. L.C., Jr.
Simpson, Lt. Albert G.
Skelton, Lt. Edward W.
Skow, Lt. Charles T.
Slaven, Lt. Lant R.
Slimmon, Capt. James B.
Smith, Lt. Thomas J.
Smith, Lt. Samuel A.
Smith, Lt. Wesley L.
Smith, Ens. Alvin W., Jr.
Smith, Lt. Harrison P.
Smith, Lt. Henry C.
Smith, Lt. Lowell R.
Smith, Lt. Harold F.
Smith, Lt. Harold E.
Smith, Lt. Robert C.
Smith, Lt. Bernard L.
Smith, Lt. Charles H.
Smith, Lt. Paul P.
Smith, Lt. Arthur H.
Smith, Ens. Ralph E.
Smythe, Lt. Clifford E.
Snead, Lt. H. B.
Snedicor, Lt. H.T.

Snyder, Lt. Gerald S.
Somers, Lt. Ralph C.J.
Sota, Lt. Earle
South, Lt. Charles M.
South, Lt. J.C.
Southwick, Lt. Herman D.
Spangler, Lt. Earl O.
Spencer, Lt. Albert O.
Spencer, Lt. R.C.
Spier, Lt. James E.
Spitzer, Lt. Eugene R.
Sprague, Lt. Evan L.
Squier, Maj. Gen. George O.
Squiers, Lt. Bard M.
Stacy, Lt. Owen P.
Stalker, Lt. Willard
Stanley, Lt. John M.
Stanton, Lt. Louis G.
Starring, Lt. David S.
Stauffacher, Lt. E.M.
Steedman, Lt. Charles R.
Steel, Lt. John A.
Steele, Lt. Cyril H.
Steever, Maj. E.J.
Stege, Ens. E.H., Jr.
Steinberg, Lt. John C.
Steinert, Lt. Harold A.
Stenson, Lt. Irving C.
Stephens, Lt. Orville L.
Stephenson, Lt. MacCrea
Stevenot, Maj. J.E. Hamilton
Stevens, Lt. Horace S.
Stevenson, Lt. Frederic F.
Stewart, Lt. Kenneth M.
Stine, Lt. Harold B.
Stites, Lt. Francis B.
Stitt, Lt. Donald G.
Stocker, Ens. Robert
Stockett, Lt. Lewis O.
Stoker, Lt. Harold C.
Stone, Lt. John
Stone, Lt. H.D.
Stone, Lt. Milton A.
Stone, Ens. E.A.
Stoops, Lt. Robert C.
Stoppel, Ens. Fred H.
Stout, Lt. Shirley E.
Strahan, Lt. Donald P.
Street, Lt. Richard M.
Stroupe, Capt. Almon
Strum, Lt. Elmer A.
Stuart, Lt. George D.
Stuart, Lt. Percy C.
Sullivan, Lt. Charles B.
Sullivan, Ens. Herbert F.
Sullivan, Lt. Edwin
Sutton, Maj. Redondo B.
Sutton, Capt. Harry A.
Swaab, Lt. Jacques M.

Swedberg, Lt. Ernest W.
Sweet, Lt. Gilbert N.
Talcott, Lt. John
Tanney, Lt. William
Tapley, Lt. Elmer B.
Taylor, Lt. G.F.
Taylor, Ens. James B., Jr.
Taylor, Lt. Fredrick H.
Taylor, Lt. Bayard C.
Taylor, Lt. Alfred B.
Tease, Lt. Stewart J.
Ten Eyck, Lt. W. B.
Tenderking, Lt. Louis T., Jr.
Terry, Lt. J.R.
Thayer, Lt. Raymond H.
Thiel, Lt. William A.
Thomas, Lt. Alfred H.
Thomas, Lt. Walter F.
Thompson, Lt. Everett L., Jr.
Thompson, Lt. David E.
Thompson, Lt. George S.
Thompson, Lt. A.C.
Thompson, Lt. John F.
Thornburg, Lt. David W.
Thorp, Capt. J.N., Jr.
Tickell, Lt. Sam
Tierney, Lt. James V.
Tobin, Lt. William N.
Todd, Lt. H.M.
Tomkins, Lt. Frederick
Tong, Lt. James A.
Torrey, Capt. Hamilton R.
Towers, Lt. Cmdr. J.H.
Tracy, Lt. Ray P.
Train, Lt. R.L.
Trantham, Lt. Homer
Treat, Lt. H.W.
Trinler, Lt. N.D.
Tucker, Ens. Gordon
Tucker, Lt. M.A.
Tuckerman, Lt. Roger
Tupper, Lt. Preston E.
Turner, Lt. Wright E.
Turner, Lt. F.G.
Turner, Lt. Charles F.
Tuttle, Lt. Geo. W.
Tyner, Ens. Gerald K.
Tyrrel, Lt. Chas. P.
Van Dusen, Ens. Frederick
Van Eiff, Lt. Herman A.
Van Veghten, Lt. Theodore S.
Van Houten, Lt. E.L.
Vander Voot, Lt. J. MacE.
Vaughan, Lt. Guy O.
Vaughn, Lt. Grady M.
Veblen, Lt. Elling H.
Vickery, Lt. Carl V.
Virgin, Lt. Joseph E.
Vogel, Lt. Earl C.

Voshell, Lt. Howard
Wachtel, Lt. Morris F.
Wachtell, Lt. P.A.
Wade, Lt. Leigh
Wagner, Lt. Parker
Wagner, Lt. Ralph P.
Wahle, Lt. Chester D.
Wait, Lt. Harry W.
Walker, Lt. Lambert R., Jr.
Walker, Lt. Lloyd B.
Walker, Maj. J.C.
Walker, Lt. V.L.
Walker, Ens. William J.
Wallace, Lt. William, Jr.
Wallan, Lt. Alex Lee
Walls, Lt. William R.
Walter, Lt. William S.
Wann, Capt. R.B.
Wanser, Lt. Paul C.
Ward, Lt. John A.
Ward, Lt. Allen B.
Warde, Lt. Arthur
Ware, Lt. James G.
Warren, Lt. Jim C.
Washburn, Lt. Lawrence G.
Washburn, Lt. Wm. C.
Wasson, Lt. Roy J.
Watson, Lt. Philip W.
Watson, Lt. Col. Henry L.
Watson, Lt. Fred T.
Watson, Lt. Harold E.
Watt, Lt. Robert W.
Weaver, Lt. John H.
Webb, Lt. John E.
Weeden, Lt. Charles F.
Wehner, Lt. Joseph F.
Wehrle, Lt. Howard F.
Weidenbach, Lt. A.C.
Weiland, Lt. Stanley
Weinstein, Lt. Carl
Weisiger, Lt. Earle H.
Welsh, Lt. Floyd E.
Welsh, Lt. Wm. W.
Welty, Ens. Clair W.
Wentworth, Lt. R. Preston
Weston, Ens. W. Malcolm
Wheaton, Lt. Ivan P.
White, Lt. Harold A.
White, Lt. Lloyd K.
White, Lt. Edgar G.
White, Lt. Edgar W.
White, Ens. Dale
White, Lt. Wilbert W.
Whitehurst, Lt. Frank P.
Whitescarver, Lt. James F.
Whitfield, Lt. Raoul F.
Whitman, Lt. John B.
Whitman, Lt. M. Gilbert
Whitney, Ens. King

Wight, Lt. Stanley
Wightman, Lt. Norman H.
Wigman, Lt. John P.
Wilbourn, Lt. Frank W.
Wilbur, Lt. Jerry F.
Wilcox, Lt. Col. Cornelius
   DeW.
Wiley, Lt. Clarence D.
Wilkens, Lt. Charles H.
Wilkinson, Lt. James L.
Williams, Lt. Fred F.
Williams, Lt. John W.
Williams, Capt. Edward L.
Williams, Ens. Charles T., Jr.
Williams, Lt. Paul D.
Williams, Lt. Lloyd H.
Williams, Ens. Arthur S.
Williams, Lt. Warren L.
Williams, Lt. William A.
Williams, Capt. Theodore
Williams, Lt. Roger Q.
Williams, Lt. Richard G.
Williamson, Lt. Adrian
Williamson, Lt. Cleburne M.
Willrich, Lt. Edgar G.
Willson, Lt. Floyd A.
Wilson, Lt. Joseph V.
Wilson, Lt. Raymond
Wilson, Lt. Hobert LaD.
Wing, Ens. Herbert
Winslow, Lt. Julian E.
Wirgman, Lt. Steward L.
Wiser, Lt. G.B.
Wiswal, Lt. George H.
Witsell, Lt. Fred C., Jr.
Wolfe, Lt. Gibson G.
Womble, Lt. Claudius
Wood, Lt. Horace W.
Woodward, Lt. William A.
Woodward, Lt. Irving J.
Woodward, Lt. LeRoy
Woody, Lt. Kenyon
Woolsey, Lt. Clinton F.
Woolsey, Ens. William E.
Worthington, Lt. James R.
Wortley, Lt. Franklin
Wright, Lt. E.F., Jr.
Wright, Lt. Chester E.
Wright, Lt. C.A.
Wright, Lt. Joseph H.
Wynne, Lt. Teddie L.
Young, Lt. Victor M.
Young, Lt. Robert
Young, Lt. Leslie B.
Youngs, Lt. Grover A.
Zettel, Lt. Raymond C.
Ziesmer, Lt. George F.
Zimmerman, Lt. J.L.
Zingerman, Lt. Ernest L.

In Memoriam: Aero Club of America Members Who Died by 1918[6]

Paul Nocquet	1906	Frank M. Jacobs	1913	William H.	
Stuart Reid	1907	S. Osgood Pell	1913	Chesebrough	1917
John Franklin Cameron	1907	Charles W. Place	1913	A. H. Hall	1917
J. Henry Smith	1907	Lieut. Moss L. Love	1913	John J. Corning	1917
George H. Day	1908	Charles G. Gates	1913	Edgar B. Bronson	1917
Charles Oliver Jones	1908	George W. Bennett	1913	P. C. Millman	1917
O. H. P. Belmount	1908	Lieut. E. L. Ellington	1913	William Berri	1917
T. E. Selfridge	1908	Lieut. Hugh M. Kelly	1913	Victor Carlstrom	1917
Homer W. Hedge	1909	Lieut. James M. Murray	1914	W. G. Bee	1917
Percy F. Megargle	1909	Frederick T.	1914	Waldron Williams	1917
Raphael J. Moses	1909	Cyrus Mead	1914	Capt. R. L. Taylor	1917
Alden Sampson, 2nd	1909	L. D. Dozier	1914	Evert Jansen Wendell	1917
Thomas F. Walsh	1910	Harold Binney	1914	J. Dunbar Wright	1917
A. L. Pfitzner	1910	Frederick T. Leigh	1914	B. Blakeman Lewis	1917
Ferdinand D'Zuiba	1910	Johnson Sherrick	1914	William H. Cheney	1918
Octave Chanute	1910	Lee S. Burridge	1915	Joe Graham Trees	1918
Ralph Johnstone	1910	Melvin L. Stolz	1915	Lt. Louis Bennett, Jr.	1918
John B. Moisant	1910	Robert Pluym	1915	H. E. Tindel	1918
Arch Hoxsey	1910	Lt. W. R. Taliaferro,		Roger W. Jannus	1918
Paul Morton	1911	USA	1915	H. D. Babcock	1918
Edmund R. Gilman	1911	George I. Scott	1915	Maj. Clarence	
W. C. Greene	1911	Gen. George Moore		Fahnestock	1918
St. Croix Johnstone	1911	Smith	1915	James Gordon Bennett	1918
Eugene Ely	1911	S. T. Davis, Jr.	1915	E. B. Cresswell	1918
E. M. Mix	1911	Andrew Freedman	1915	James F. Miller	1918
John F. Carroll	1911	William S. Luckey	1915	Rayal C. Bolling	1918
David Wolfe Bishop	1911	Dr. H. L. E. Johnson	1916	Lloyd S. Allen	1918
Tod Schriver	1911	William Stanley	1916	Lt. A. Blair Thaw	1918
Winthrop E. Scarritt	1911	Stephenson		John W. Scott	1918
Armory S. Carhart	1912	MacGordon	1916	Samuel W. Arnheim	1918
Calbraith P. Rodgers	1912	J. Henry Carson	1916	Charles J. Follmer	1918
A. Lawrence Rotch	1912	Lt. R. C. Saufley	1916	Aldrich W. Green	1918
John Jacob Astor	1912	W. C. Robinson	1916	F. T. Chandler	1918
Edgar Meyer	1912	Samuel H. Valentine	1916	Robert P. Scott	1918
J. H. Loring	1912	Andrew C. Zabriskie	1916	Lt. Gino Gianfelice,	
Lieut. L. W. Hazelhurst	1912	Alexander Brown	1916	RIFC	1918
Alfred L. Seligman	1912	Silas Christofferson	1916	Capt. Silvio Resnati,	
Howard W. Gill	1912	Professor Percival		RIFC	1918
Percy S. Hudson	1912	Lowell	1916	J. G. Battele	1918
Ernestus Gulick	1913	Anthony H. Jannus	1916	Comdr. Robt. K.	
Luke J. Minahan	1913			Crank, USN	1918

SOARING PIONEERS: SOARING LICENSES ISSUED THROUGH 1936

American "D" Licenses

By 1936 100 "D" licenses had been issued internationally. Of these, eighty-six were held by Germans. Three were held by Americans. Wolf Hirth, of Germany, received "D" license number 1.

Jack O'Meara	Certificate number	12
Richard C. DuPont	Certificate number	32
Lewin B. Barringer	Certificate number	65

American "C" Licenses

The list below represents "C" licenses issued to Americans, and foreign nationals in America, by 1936. These are, presumably, listed in the order in which they were awarded, but the number shown is not necessarily the same as the number of the individual's "C" certificate.

1 Ralph S. Barnaby	50 Percy Pierce	99 Ernst Willer Spink
2 William Hawley Bowlus	51 Joseph Conrad Funk	100 Dana Levi Darling
3 William Van Dusen	52 Stanley W. Smith	101 Richard K. Koegler
4 J. Allison Moore	53 William Thomas Gunter	102 Julius Boone Schliemann
5 Earle Richard Mitchell	54 Frank O. Titus	103 Margaret Arnold Kimball
6 Albert E. Hastings	55 Elgin O. Marshall	104 Benjamin W. Badenoch
7 John C. Barstow	56 Alcide Santilli	105 Crozer Allaire du Pont
8 Roy H. Pemberton	57 Nathan Heath McDowell	106 Constantin Lhevinne
9 Charles A. Lindbergh	58 George Greene Slade	107 Lewin Bennitt Barringer
10 Anne Morrow	59 Walter Scott Snell	108 Emil A. Lehecka
Lindbergh	60 Bruce Leedy Helvie	109 Nelson N. Shapter
11 John Emerson Pratt	61 Charles J. Hochreiter	110 Gretchen Teighard
12 Ross Peacock	62 Ward C. Kecker	111 Dallas Wise
13 John Kelly O'Meara	63 Kenneth R. Stead	112 Clark Blanchard Millikan
14 Augustine C. Haller	64 Pratt Jones	113 Henry Nicoll Wightman
15 Warren E. Eaton	65 William R. Enyart	114 Arthur A. Ramer
16 Arrion P. Artran	66 Milton Wheller Thomas	115 William Placek
17 William L. Purcell	67 Helmuth William	116 George Fuller, Jr.
18 William A. Cocke, Jr.	Braendel	117 John Nowak
19 Roswell E. Franklin	68 H. Thorton Hildebrandt	118 Carl F. Hagemann
20 Burchard W. Wilson	69 Bazil Granville Reed	119 Arthur H. Bidlingmeyer
21 Franklin K. Iszard	70 George Joseph Malouin,	120 Henry D. Ellett, Jr.
22 Arthur B. Schultz	Jr.	121 E. Elliott Hood
23 Martin H. Schempp	71 Rudolph F. Setz	122 Earl Raymond Southee
24 James N. Wieberg	72 Robert F. Carey	123 Monroe H. Shoemaker
25 Edward T. Barton	73 Thomas C. Davey	124 Joseph A. Ober
26 Russell H. Holderman	74 Theodore C. Bonney	125 Leon Kubinski
27 Arthur L. Lawrence	75 Charles Hanson Gale	126 Ralph C. Newman
28 William J. Perfield	76 Emerson Mehlhose	127 Harry Rhinehart
29 Allen J. Rooke	77 Bernard F. von Bernewitz	128 William Hough Cook,
30 Wallace H. Franklin	78 Donald M. Hamilton	Jr.
31 James H. Stickler	79 Harold J. Bowen	129 Chester Joseph Decker
32 Joseph Lyman	80 John W. Andrews	130 Henry Charles Runkel
33 Thomas Phillips	81 Murry N. Fairbank	131 Barnard Leon Wade
34 Frederick A. Pippig	82 Wm. Washburn Moss, Jr.	132 Cleveland C. Hyde
35 Jacob S. Fassett, 3rd	83 Willis T. Sperry	133 Harold Willis Humber
36 Hattie M. Barnaby	84 Richard C. du Pont	134 James Ramage Thomson
37 Samuel N. Harmatuk	85 Henry B. Harris	135 William E. Bodenlos
38 Dorothy C. Holderman	86 Feliz Werner Braendel	136 Clarence Henry Baum,
39 Milton Farichild	87 Jack W. Laister, Jr.	Jr.
Stoughton	88 Frank Edmund Wickham	137 Theodore G. Bellak
40 George S. Stead	89 James Benjamin Kendrick	138 Elery D. Clark
41 Edward F. Andrews	90 Lyle Strub Lutton	139 Stephen duPont
42 Albert G. Sayre	91 Bert Baer Brooks	140 Charles Joseph Tubbs
43 Algred W. Smith	92 George Richards Bacon	141 Geroge W. Casey
44 Floyd J. Sweet	93 Richard W. Randolph	142 Philip Robert Eward
45 Donald W. Newsome	94 Joseph W. Conn	143 Christian B. Haas
46 Wolfgang B. Klemperer	95 Thomas C. Geroge	144 David Adams Mowrer
47 Youston Sekella	96 Warren Ellsworth Facey	145 Wm. Alvah Parks, Jr.
48 A. W. Roland Hirth	97 Clinton W. Barnard	146 Alfred H. Pepin
49 Martin A. Bystrom	98 Howard O. Funk	147 Delbert Andrew Reed

148 Paul A. Sanderson
149 Kurt K. Siemon
150 Dean Franklin Triplett
151 Louis A. Wollaeger
152 Clinton S. Janes
153 Harley M. Hedderly
154 Randall Chapman
155 Charles J. Csizmansky
156 Robert John Augurn
157 Thomas Greig
158 Donald Martin Alexander
159 Donald Walton Davis, Jr.
160 William Dolger

161 Ralph Rawlings Goodman
162 David C. Hill
163 Wm. Frederick Jenrick, Jr.
164 Marvin L. Michael
165 Paul E. Sandorff
166 Gustav Scheurer
167 Rudolph Lawrence Thoren
168 John J. Wallace
169 Felix E. A. Chardon
170 Warren John Merboth
171 Gerald John Urban Delay
172 Kenneth G. Findiesen

173 Hadley K. Wiard
174 Bruce Kilpartick Craig, Jr.
175 Maurice L. Waters
176 George F. Placek
177 Leon A. Donotaux
178 Herbet A. Arnold
179 Edward I. Ryder
180 Malcom Robert Schemot
181 Charles W. Fuller
182 Donald Webster Wheeler
183 E. Paul duPont, Jr.
184 Elmer Zook
185 Fred C. Barnes

PRESIDENTS OF THE AERO CLUB OF AMERICA (1905–1922)

1905–1906	Homer W. Hedge (charter president)
1906–1907	Courtland F. Bishop
1907–1908	Courtland F. Bishop
1908–1909	Maj. James C. McCoy (resigned)
	Courtland F. Bishop (succeeded)
1909–1910	Courtland F. Bishop
1910–1911	Allan A. Ryan
1911–1912	Robert J. Collier
1912–1913	Robert J. Collier (resigned)
	Alan R. Hawley (succeeded)
1913–1914	Alan R. Hawley
1914–1915	Alan R. Hawley
1915–1916	Alan R. Hawley
1916–1917	Alan R. Hawley
1917–1918	Alan R. Hawley
1918–1919	Alan R. Hawley
1919–1920	Alan R. Hawley (resigned July 1920)
	Charles J. Edwards (succeeded)
1920–1921	Charles J. Edwards
1921–1922	Charles J. Edwards

CERTIFICATE OF INCORPORATION OF THE AERO CLUB OF AMERICA I

We, the undersigned, all being persons of full age and at least two-thirds being citizens of the United States, and at least one of us a resident of the State of New York, desiring to form a stock corporation pursuant to the provisions of the Business Corporations Law of the State of New York, do hereby make, sign, acknowledge and file this certificate for that purpose, as follows:—

FIRST: The name of the proposed corporation is Aero Club of America.

SECOND: The purposes for which it is to be formed are:

To advance the development of the Science of Aeronautics and kindred sciences.

To encourage and organize aerial navigation and excursions, conferences, expositions, congresses and races.

To develop the breeding and training of carrier pigeons.

To hold, maintain and conduct games, meets, contests, exhibitions and shows of air-ships, balloons or other inventions or contrivances, designed to be propelled or travel through the air or otherwise.

To maintain a club house or club houses, aero garages and other houses, club grounds, electric and gas equipments and other accessories, aeronautic or otherwise, incidental to the business of the corporation upon such terms as the Board of Directors may from time to time provide.

To do everything necessary, suitable and proper for the accomplishment of any of the purposes or the furtherance of any of the powers hereinbefore set forth, and to do every other act or acts incidental or appurtenant to or connected with the aforesaid business, sports or powers or any part or parts thereof, provided the same be not inconsistent with the laws under which this corporation is organized.

THIRD: The amount of the capital stock is Five Hundred Dollars:

FOURTH: The number of shares of which the capital stock shall consist is one hundred, of the par value of Five Dollars each. The amount of capital with which said corporation will begin business is Five Hundred Dollars.

FIFTH: Its principal business office is to be located in the Borough of Manhattan County, City and State of New York, but the corporation shall have power to conduct its business in all its branches or any part thereof in any of the States or Territories of the United States, and in the District of Columbia.

SIXTH: Its duration is to be perpetual.

SEVENTH: The number of its directors is to be five, and it is hereby provided, pursuant to the law, that directors are not required to be stockholders.

EIGHTH: The names and post office addresses of the directors for the first year are:
[The names and addresses listed below are handwritten on the original.]

Dave H. Morris	68 Broad St., N.Y.
Augustus Post	31 Nassau St., N.Y.C.
Homer W. Hedge	120 Broadway, N.Y.C.
John F. O'Rourke	1 W. 34th St., N.Y.C.
Charles J. Glidden	10 P.O. Square, Boston

NINTH: The names and post office addresses of the subscribers to the certificates, and a statement of the number of shares of stock which each agrees to take in the corporation are as follows:

NAMES.	POST OFFICE ADDRESSES.	NUMBER OF SHARES

[The names and addresses listed below are handwritten on the original.]

Homer W. Hedge	120 Broadway, N.Y.C.	Twenty
David H. Morris	68 Broad Street, N.Y.	Twenty
Augustus Post	31 Nassau St., N.Y.C.	Twenty
John F. O'Rourke	1 W. 34th St N.Y.C.	Twenty
Charles J. Glidden	10 P.O. Square, Boston	Twenty

TENTH: Any increase in the number of directors shall be deemed to create vacancies in the board of Directors, and shall be filled in the manner provided in the by-laws for vacancies caused by death or resignation.

IN WITNESS WHEREOF we have made, signed, acknowledged and filed this certificate in duplicate.

Dated this 7th day or [sic] June, 1905.

[Signed]

> Augustus Post
> Homer W. Hedge
> David H. Morris
> John F. O'Rourke
> Charles J. Glidden

NATIONAL AERONAUTIC ASSOCIATION OFFICERS (1922-Present)

J

1922–1923
President—Howard E. Coffin
Vice President—B. H. Mulvihill
Treasurer—B. F. Castle
Secretary—H. W. Karr

1923–1924
President—Frederick B. Patterson
Vice President—Ralph W. Cram
Treasurer—B. F. Castle
Secretary—Dudley M. Outcolt
Governors-at-large: Orville Wright,
    William P. MacCracken, Jr., Elmer
    Sperry

1924–1925
President—Godfrey Cabot
Vice President—Maj. Ralph
    Schroeder
Treasurer—B. F. Castle
Secretary—Maj. Howard Wehrle
Editor—Ernest Jones

1925–1926
President—Godfrey Cabot
Vice President—Carl Wolfley
Treasurer—B. F. Castle
Secretary—Donald W. Douglas

Editor—Ernest Jones

1925–1927
President—Porter Adams
Vice President—Carl Wolfley
Treasurer—B. F. Castle
Secretary—Valentine Gephart
Editor—K. U. McGill

1927–1928
President—Porter Adams
Vice President—Elmer Sperry
Treasurer—B. F. Castle
Secretary—Valentine Gephart
Editor—K. U. McGill

1928–1929
President—Senator Hiram Bingham
Vice President—Roscoe Vaughn
Treasurer—B. F. Castle
Secretary—Valentine Gephart
Editor—K. U. McGill

1929–1930
President—Hiram Bingham
Vice President—Roscoe Vaughn
Treasurer—John F. Victory
Secretary—D. E. McDonald
Editor—Frederick Neeley

1930–1931
President—Hiram Bingham
Vice President—Robert J. Pritchard
Treasurer—John Victory
Secretary—H. Ralph Badger
Editor—William Enyart

1931–1932
President—Hiram Bingham
Vice President—Amelia Earhart
Treasurer—John Victory
Secretary—H. Ralph Badger
Editor—William Enyart

1932–1933
President—Hiram Bingham
Vice President—Amelia Earhart
    (resigned; succeeded by Richard E.
    Byrd)
Treasurer—John Victory
Secretary—H. Ralph Badger
Editor—William Enyart

1933–1934
President—Hiram Bingham
Vice President—F. Truebee Davison
Treasurer—John Victory
Secretary—Robert Garland
Editor—Hiram Bingham

1934–1935
President—Senator William McAdoo
Vice President—James Doolittle
Treasurer—John F. Victory
Secretary—Louise Thaden
Editor—Ray Cooper

1935–1936
President—Charles Horner
Vice President—Alford Williams
Treasurer—Benjamin King
Secretary—Louise Thaden
Editor—Wayne Parrish
General Counsel—Ruby Garrett

1936–1937
President—Charles Horner
Vice President—Fred Crawford
Treasurer—John Jouett
Secretary—H. J. Rand
Editor—Wayne Parrish
General Counsel—Ruby Garrett

1937–1938
President—Charles Horner
Vice President—E. E. Aldrin
Treasurer—Grove Webster
Secretary—William Enyart
Editor—Charles Horner
General Counsel—Ruby Garrett

1939
President—Charles Horner
Vice President—George Logan
Treasurer—John Jouett
Secretary—William Enyart
Editor—Charles Horner
General Counsel—Edward Knott

1940
President—Gill Rob Wilson
Vice President—Brig. Gen. Walter
    Kilner
Treasurer—William Reddy
Secretary—William Enyart
Editorial Committee selected
General Counsel—Frederick Lane, Sr.

1941
President—Gill Robb Wilson
Vice Presidents—Max Fleischman,
    William Enyart, Harry Coffey
Treasurer—William Reddy
Secretary and General Manager—
    G. deFreest Lanier
Chairman of the Editorial
    Committee—James Webb

1942
President—Gill Robb Wilson
Vice Presidents—Harry Coffey, Max
    Fleischman, William Enyart
Treasurer—William Reddy
Manager—Kendall K. Hoyt
Editor—S. C. Lechtman

1943
President—Gill Robb Wilson
Vice Presidents—Harry Coffey,
    William Enyart, Max Fleischman
Treasurer—William Reddy
Secretary—Wayne Parrish
General Counsel—William P.
    MacCracken

Editor—Swanee Taylor

1944
Presidents—Gill Robb Wilson, William Enyart
Vice Presidents—Harry Coffey, William Enyart, James Graham
Treasurer—William Reddy
Secretary—Richard Palmer
Editor—Gill Robb Wilson
General Counsel—William P. MacCracken
General Manager—Lowell Swenson

1945
President—William Enyart
Vice Presidents—Harry Coffey, James Graham, Glen Eastburn
Treasurer—William Reddy
Secretary—Richard Palmer
Editorial Board
General Manager—Lowell Swenson
General Counsel—William P. MacCracken

1946
President—William Enyart
Vice Presidents—Arthur Boreman, Sheldon Steers
Treasurer—William Reddy
Secretary—Mrs. James Doolittle
Editor—Lucille Thompson
General Manager—Lowell Swenson
General Counsel—William P. MacCracken

1947
President—L. Welch Pogue
Vice Presidents—Fred Crawford, Arthur Boreman
Treasurer—Gordon Brown
Secretary—Mrs. James Doolittle
Editors—Franklin Page, Ann Hecker
General Manager—Lowell Swenson
General Counsel—William P. MacCracken

1948
President—Arthur Boreman
Vice Presidents—Fred Crawford
Treasurer—Daniel Bell

Secretary—Mrs. James Doolittle
Editor—Clara Jo Hopkins
General Manager—Lowell Swenson
General Counsel—William P. MacCracken

1949
President—Louis Leverone
Vice Presidents—Edward Sweeney, Frederick Crawford
Treasurer—Horace Bromfield
Secretary—Mrs. William Brown
Editor—Clara Jo Hopkins
General Manager—R. M. Phelps
General Counsel—William P. MacCracken

1950
President—Louis Leverone
Vice Presidents—Edward B. Newill, Fred Crawford
Treasurer—Horace Bromfield
Secretary—Mrs. William Brown
Editor—Clara Jo Hopkins
General Counsel—William P. MacCracken

1951
President—Louis Leverone
Vice Presidents—Edward B. Newill, Fred Crawford
Treasurer—Horace Bromfield
Secretary—Mrs. William Brown
Editor—Kendall Hoyt
General Counsel—William P. MacCracken

1951–1952
President—Donald Webster
Acting Presidents—Joseph T. Geutling, Harry Coffey
Vice Presidents—Willis Brown, Jon Carsey, Adm. Luis De Florez, Adm. Emory S. Land, Edward Sweeney
Treasurer—Mae Simpson
Secretary—Mrs. William Brown
Editor—Keith Saunders
General Manager—Donald Webster
General Counsel—William P. MacCracken

1952–1953

President—Harry Coffey
Vice Presidents—Twelve elected
Treasurer—Edward Sweeny
Secretary—Mae Simpson
Editor—Keith Saunders
General Manager—Donald Webster
General Counsel—William P.
  MacCracken

1954

President—Thomas G. Lanphier, Jr.
Vice President—Jack Hughes
Treasurer—Edward Sweeney
Executive Secretary—Charles Logsden
Secretary—Arlene Davis
Editor—Keith Saunders
General Counsel—William P.
  MacCracken

1955–1959

President—Thomas G. Lanphier, Jr.
Vice President—Jacqueline Cochran
Treasurer—Edward Sweeney
Executive Secretary—Charles Logsden
Secretary—Arlene Davis
Editor—Keith Saunders
General Counsel—William P.
  MacCracken

1960

President—Jacqueline Cochran
Vice President—Martin Decker
Treasurer—Edward Sweeney
Executive Director—Ralph Whitener
Secretary—Arlene Davis
Editor—Keith Saunders
General Counsel—William P.
  MacCracken

1961

President—Jacqueline Cochran
Vice President—Martin Decker
Treasurer—Edward Sweeney
Executive Director—Ralph Whitener
Secretary—Arlene Davis
Editor—Keith Saunders
General Counsel—William P.
  MacCracken

1962

President—Martin Decker
Vice Presidents—Roger Fleming,
  William Ong
Treasurer—Edward Sweeney
Executive Director—Ralph Whitener
Secretary—Arlene Davis
Editor—Lou Davis
General Counsel—William P.
  MacCracken

1963–1965

President—William A. Ong
Vice President—Joseph P. Adams
Executive Director—Mitchell Giblo
Treasurer—Edward Sweeney
Secretary—Arlene Davis
Editor—William A. Ong
General Counsel—William P.
  MacCracken

1965–1966

President—Edward C. Sweeney
Senior Vice President—Robert B.
  Dillaway
Executive Vice President—Joseph P.
  Adams
Treasurer—E. Thomas Burnard
Secretary—Grace M. Harris
Editor—William A. Ong
General Counsel—William P.
  MacCracken

1966–1967

President—James F. Nields
Executive Vice President—Robert J.
  Murphy
Senior Vice President—Robert B.
  Dillaway
Treasurer—E. Thomas Burnard
Secretary—Grace M. Harris
General Counsel—William P.
  MacCracken
Honorary Life President—Jacqueline
  Cochran

1967–1968

President—James F. Nields
Executive Vice President—Robert J.
  Murphy

Senior Vice President—Robert B.
Dillaway
Treasurer—Joseph S. Murphy
Secretary—Ann Wood
General Counsel—William P.
MacCracken

1968–1969

President—Frederick B. Lee
Vice President—
Treasurer—Joseph S. Murphy
Executive Director—Brooke Allen
General Counsel—William P.
MacCracken

1970

President—Frederick B. Lee
Executive Director—Brooke Allen
Treasurer—Joseph S. Murphy

1971

Chairman of the Board—Frederick B.
Lee
President—A. S. (Mike) Monroney
Vice President—
Executive Director—Brooke Allen
Treasurer—Joseph S. Murphy

1972

Chairman of the Board—Frederick B.
Lee
President—A. S. (Mike) Monroney
Senior Vice President—Robert J.
Murphy, Jr.
Executive Vice President—J. B.
Montgomery
Treasurer—Joseph S. Murphy
Secretary—Ann Wood
General Counsel—Joel H. Fisher

1973

Chairman of the Board—Frederick B.
Lee
President—J. B. Montgomery
Executive Director—Maj. Gen.
Brooke E. Allen, USAF (Ret.)
Senior Vice President—John P.
Henebry
Executive Vice President—David
Cochran
Treasurer—J. Dawson Ransome

Secretary—Jean Ross Howard
Editor—William J. Winter
Advisory Editor—Col. M. A. Roth,
USAF (Ret.)
General Counsel—Joel H. Fisher
Honorary Chairman of the
Board—A. S. (Mike) Monroney

1974

Chairman of the Board—Frederick B.
Lee
President—J. B. Montgomery
Executive Director—Maj. Gen.
Brooke E. Allen, USAF (Ret.)
Senior Vice President—John P.
Henebry
Executive Vice President—David
Cochran
Treasurer—J. Dawson Ransome
Secretary—Jean Ross Howard
Editor—William J. Winter
Executive Editor—Col. M. A. Roth,
USAF (Ret.)
General Counsel—Joel H. Fisher
Honorary Chairman of the
Board—A. S. (Mike) Monroney

1975

President—John B. Montgomery
Senior Vice President—John P.
Henebry
Vice President—Finance—David
Cochran
Executive Vice President—Brooke E.
Allen
Assistant Executive Director—M. A.
Roth
Secretary—Jean Ross Howard
General Counsel—Joel Fisher

1976

Chairman of the Board—John B.
Montgomery
President—John P. Henebry
Senior Vice President—Secor D.
Browne
Executive Vice President—Robert
Hoover
Vice President—Finance—David
Cochran

Executive Director—Brooke E. Allen
Assistant Executive Director—M. A.
  Roth
Secretary—Jean Ross Howard
General Counsel—Joel Fisher

1977

Chairman of the Board—John B.
  Montgomery
President—John R. Alison
Senior Vice President—Secor Browne
Executive Vice President—Malcolm S.
  Forbes (resigned)
Assistant Executive Director—M. A.
  Roth
Executive Director—Brooke E. Allen
  (resigned to assume executive vice
  presidency)
Vice President—Finance—David
  Cochran
Deputy Executive Director—Vic
  Powell
Secretary—Jean Ross Howard
Secretary of Contest and Records
  Board—Everett Langworthy
Staff Secretary—Barbara Burnett
General Counsel—Joel H. Fisher

1978

Chairman of the Board—John B.
  Montgomery
President—John R. Alison
Executive Vice President—Brooke E.
  Allen
Senior Vice President—Secor Browne
Vice President—Finance—Robert H.
  Harris
Executive Director—Vic Powell
Secretary—Jean Ross Howard
Staff Secretary—Barbara Burnett
Secretary of Contest and Records
  Board—Everett Langworthy
General Counsel—Joel H. Fisher

1979

Chairman of the Board—John B.
  Montgomery
President—John R. Alison
Executive Vice President—Brooke E.
  Allen

Senior Vice President—Secor Browne
Vice President—Finance—Robert H.
  Harris
Secretary—Jean Ross Howard
Secretary of Contest and Records
  Board—Everett Langworthy
General Counsel—Joel H. Fisher

1980

President—John R. Alison
Senior Vice President—Clifton F. von
  Kann
Executive Vice President—Brooke E.
  Allen
Vice President—Finance—Robert H.
  Harris
Secretary of Contest and Records
  Board—Everett Langworthy
Secretary—Jean Ross Howard
General Counsel—Joel H. Fisher
  (Benjamin P. Lamberton, Acting
  General Counsel)

1981

Chairman of the Board—John R.
  Alison
President—Clifton F. von Kann
Senior Vice President—George C. Prill
Executive Director—Everett
  Langworthy
Executive Vice President—Brooke E.
  Allen
Vice President—Finance—Robert H.
  Harris
Secretary—Jean Ross Howard
General Counsel—Robert R. Gray

1982

Chairman of the Board—John R.
  Alison
President—Clifton F. von Kann
Senior Vice President—George C. Prill
Executive Vice President (Emeritus)—
  Brooke E. Allen
Executive Vice President—Everett
  Langworthy
Vice President—Finance—Ronald
  McWilliams
Secretary—Jean Ross Howard

Secretary of Contest and Records
Board—Milton M. Brown
General Counsel—Robert R. Gray

1983

Chairman of the Board—John R.
Alison
President—Clifton F. von Kann
Senior Vice President—George C.
Prill
Executive Vice President (Emeritus)—
Brooke E. Allen
Executive Vice President—Everett
Langworthy
Vice President—Finance—Malvern J.
Gross, Jr.
Secretary—Jean Ross Howard
Secretary of Contest and Records
Board—Milton M. Brown
General Counsel—Robert R. Gray

1984

Chairman of the Board—John R.
Alison
President—Clifton F. von Kann
Senior Vice President—George C.
Prill
Executive Vice President (Emeritus)—
Brooke E. Allen
Executive Vice President—Everett
Langworthy
Vice President—Finance—Malvern J.
Gross, Jr.
Secretary—Jean Ross Howard
Secretary of Contest and Records
Board—Milton M. Brown
General Counsel—George N. Carneal
Editor—A. J. Rankin

1985

Chairman of the Board—John R.
Alison
President—Clifton F. von Kann
Senior Vice President—George C.
Prill
Executive Vice President—Everett
Langworthy
Vice President—Finance—Malvern J.
Gross, Jr.
Secretary—Easter Russell French

Secretary of Contest and Records
Board—Milton M. Brown
General Counsel—George U.
Carneal
Editor—A. J. Rankin

1986

Chairman of the Board—John R.
Alison
President—Clifton F. von Kann
Senior Vice President—George C.
Prill
Executive Vice President—Everett
Langworthy
Vice President—Finance—Malvern J.
Gross, Jr.
Secretary—Easter Russell French
General Counsel—George U. Carneal

1987

Chairman of the Board—John R.
Alison
President—Clifton F. von Kann
Senior Vice President—George C.
Prill
Executive Vice President—Everett W.
Langworthy
Vice President—Finance—Malvern J.
Gross, Jr.
Vice President, Contest and
Records—Milton M. Brown
Corporate Secretary—Tracie L. Gates
General Counsel—George U. Carneal

1988

Chairman of the Board—John R.
Alison
President—Clifton F. von Kann
Senior Vice President—George C.
Prill
Executive Vice President—Everett W.
Langworthy
Vice President—Finance—Malvern J.
Gross, Jr.
Vice President, Contest and
Records—Milton M. Brown
Corporate Secretary—Tracie L. Gates
Editor—Edward Pinto
General Counsel—George U. Carneal

1989

Chairman of the Board—John R. Alison

President—Clifton F. von Kann

Senior Vice President—Raymond J. Johnson

Executive Vice President—Everett W. Langworthy

Vice President—Finance—Malvern J. Gross, Jr.

Secretary, Contest and Records—Wanda D. Odom

Corporate Secretary—Tracie L. Gates

General Counsel—George U. Carneal

1990

Chairman of the Board (Emeritus)—John R. Alison

Chairman of the Board—Clifton F. von Kann

President—Malvern J. Gross, Jr.

Senior Vice President—Ray Johnson

Executive Vice President—Everett Langworthy

Vice President—Finance—William R. Edgar

Contest and Records—Arthur Greenfield

General Counsel—George U. Carneal

1991

Chairman of the Board—Wesley L. McDonald

President—Malvern J. Gross, Jr.

Senior Vice President—George W. Putnam, Jr.

Vice President—Finance—William R. Edgar

Corporate Secretary—M. E. Dullum

Contest and Records—Arthur Greenfield

General Counsel—George U. Carneal

1992

Chairman of the Board—Wesley L. McDonald

Chairman of the Board (Emeritus)—Clifton F. von Kann

President—Malvern J. Gross, Jr.

Senior Vice President—George W. Putnam, Jr.

Vice President—Finance—William R. Edgar

Corporate Secretary—M. E. Dullum

Contest and Records—Arthur Greenfield

General Counsel—George U. Carneal

MISSION STATEMENT OF THE NAA

The following is the NAA's mission statement as of January 1992:

The National Aeronautic Association is the National Aero Club of the Untied States. Its primary mission is the advancement of the art, sport, and science of aviation and space flight by fostering opportunities to participate fully in aviation activities, and by promoting public understanding of the importance of aviation and space flight to the United States. In carrying out this mission, NAA, as the National Aero Club of the United States will:

Develop opportunities to strengthen the mutual objectives of NAA and its corporate members, sport aviation organizations, aero clubs and other aviation affiliates, including the formation of affiliated aero clubs in U.S. cities where such organizations do not now exist;

Represent United States aviation throughout the world as a member of the Federation Aeronautique Internationale;

Encourage, coordinate, document and promote competition and record making aviation and space events in accordance with the rules prescribed by the Federation Aeronautique Internationale, of which NAA is the official U.S. representative;

Recognize and reward those who make outstanding contributions to the achievement of aviation and space flight through presentations of awards and other honors;

Endorse sound national programs and other efforts designed to help the United States remain a leader in aviation and space flight;

Support and encourage aviation and space education programs;

Promote and encourage public participation in, and appreciation of, U.S. aviation and space activities.

ARTICLES OF ASSOCIATION OF THE NATIONAL AERONAUTIC ASSOCIATION

L

WE, the undersigned, being the original corporators hereinafter named, for the purpose of forming a corporation to do business and carry on its operations, both within and without the State of Connecticut without capital stock and not for profit, pursuant to the General Corporation Law of the State of Connecticut and the acts amendatory thereof and supplemental thereto, do hereby make, sign, acknowledge and file this certificate for that purpose, as follows:

FIRST: The name of this corporation is : "NATIONAL AERONAUTIC ASSOCIATION OF U.S.A., (INCORPORATED.)"

SECOND: The purposes or objects for which said corporation is formed are:

1. To foster, encourage and advance the science of aeronautics and all kindred and allied sciences.

2. To encourage and promote the study and advancement of the science of aerial navigation of every kind and to hold and conduct conferences and congresses for the purpose of such study.

3. To kindle and keep alive a general interest in the art of flying and to lend its aid and encouragement to any person, organization or institution which is engaged or interested in advancing this art.

4. To advise and encourage those engaged in the trade and business of manufacturing and/or operating any and all types of aircraft, aeronautic machinery and parts and general equipment and supplies used in aeronautics and in various systems of aerial navigation by supplying general or scientific knowledge of such subjects or by lending financial encouragement therein.

5. To establish, maintain and conduct, and also to lend its support and financial aid to scientific societies, clubs, classes, schools, colleges, corporations and other institutions,

engaged in whole or in part in promoting the study or advancing the science of aviation or allied and kindred sciences.

6. To gather, compile and disseminate general and scientific data of every kind having to do with the science of aviation or any of the allied and kindred sciences and to edit and publish the same in the form of bulletins, pamphlets, magazines and books and to generally distribute the same.

7. To aid and encourage the establishment and maintenance of a uniform and stable system of laws relating to the science of aeronautics and the art of aerial navigation and all allied and kindred sciences and arts.

8. To encourage the study, establishment and promulgation of uniform customs, ground rules, flying rules, plans and routes for aviation.

9. To collect, edit and disseminate general and scientific knowledge of flying fields, flying routes, interstate and foreign aerial postal routes, atmospheric conditions and other kindred knowledge, to foster progress in the science of manufacturing, improving, and/or operating any and all kinds of aircraft, to encourage inventions and improvements having to do or connected with aerial navigation.

10. To encourage, promote, arrange for and carry on aerial expositions, exhibits and contests in order that the general interest in aviation may be developed and sustained to sanction contests and formulate rules, administer such rules, certify records, and to grant or contribute toward the granting of awards, prizes and distinctions for the improvement, encouragement and advancement of any and all branches of aviation.

11. To co-operate with the executive departments, commissions and other agencies of State or Federal Governments in their investigations of and legislation pertaining to aviation and at the request or suggestion of such departments, commissions or agencies, to furnish such information as may be possessed by this corporation.

12. To borrow money to use for any of the purposes or objects for which this corporation is organized as herein-before specified and to issue the notes of this corporation therefor or to secure the same by any lawful means and to take, receive, own and use monies, notes, bonds, mortgages or other securities or evidences of indebtedness for the uses and purposes for which this corporation is organized.

13. To lease, hold, own or sell, or otherwise dispose of any real or personal property or other property necessary for or incidental to the purposes and objects for which this corporation is organized, and to display therein selected aviation and travel related memorabilia.

14. To do all and everything necessary, suitable and proper for the accomplishment of any of the purposes or for the attainment of any of the objects or for the furtherance of any of the powers hereinbefore set forth either alone or in association with other corporations, firms, individuals, governmental agencies, schools, colleges or institutions and to do every other act or acts, thing or things incidental or appertaining to or growing out of or connected with the aforesaid purposes or powers or any part or parts thereof, provided the same be not inconsistent with the Laws of the State of Connecticut under which this corporation is organized.

15. To collect, collate, catalogue and display aviation memorabilia in furtherance of the above purposes.

THIRD: This corporation is to have perpetual existence.

FOURTH: The initial number of Governors shall be not less than three and not more than thirty. The number of Governors thereafter shall be established by the Board of Governors.

FIFTH: In furtherance, and not in limitation of the powers conferrred [sic] by statute the Board of Governors is expressly authorized:

(a) To make and alter the By-laws of this corporation;

(b) To make and alter the rules, customs and regulations relating to and governing the conduct of the operation and use of the facilities and properties of the corporation;

(c) To carry on all operations and activities of the Corporation;

(d) To authorize and enter into contracts and to execute the same and to execute and to enter into all other legal instruments necessary and proper in the carrying out of all purposes for which this corporation is organized;

(e) To elect not less than three nor more than nine of its members as an Executive Committee as provided by the By-laws, which Executive Committee, when so designated, shall have the exercise any and all powers which the Board of Governors in the management and conduct of the business and the affairs of this corporation might exercise and with the same force and effect.

SIXTH: The principal office or place of business of the corporation in the State of Connecticut shall be located in the City of Hartford, County of Hartford. The corporation shall have an office in Washington, D.C. (to be known as national headquarters) and shall keep the books of this corporation (subject to the provisions of the statute of this state) at said office, and shall have branch offices, if the by-laws so provide, at such other places as the Board of Governors may determine.

SEVENTH: The annual meetings of this corporation, if the by-laws so provide, shall be held at such places and on such dates as shall be determined by the Board of Governors, from time to time, in its discretion.

EIGHTH: The members shall not be liable for any of the obligations of the corporation, nor shall the private property of the members be subject to the payment of corporate debts to any extent whatever.

NINTH: The names and places of residence of each of the original corporators of this corporation are:

NAME	PLACE OF RESIDENCE
Glenn L. Martin	16800 St. Clair Ave., Cleveland Ohio
Van H. Burgin	409-4th Nat'l Bk. Bldg., Atlanta, Ga.
Charles S. Rieman	22 W. Monroe St., Chicago, Ill.
Ralph W. Cram	Davenport, Iowa
Porter H. Adams	2 Commonwealth Ave., Boston, Mass.
C. H. Messer	1803 W. Third Ave., Spokane, Wash.
Wm. D. Tipton	c/o Flying Club of Baltimore, 7 Keyser Bldg., Baltimore, Md.
Edgar G. Tobin	207 Augusta St., San Antonio, Texas
Bernard H. Mulvihill	B. F. Jones Bldg., Pittsburgh, Pa.

TENTH: The corporators do hereby declare and certify that the facts herein stated are true and accordingly have hereunto set their hands and seals the thirteenth day of October, 1922.

In the Presence of:
Harold E. Hartney   Glenn L. Martin
E. C. Thompson   Van H. Burgin
                              Ralph W. Cram
                              Charles S. Rieman
                              Porter H. Adams
                              Claude H. Messer
                              William D. Tipton
                              Edgar Gardner Tobin
                              Bernard H. Mulvihill

NOTES

CHAPTER 1

1. "Autoists Must Behave, Says Judge Crane," *New York Times*, December 14, 1904, 6:3 (hereafter referred to as NYT).
2. "Automobile Club Elects New Officers," NYT, November 22, 1904, 7:4.
3. "More Balloon Flights Over Central Park," NYT, November 15, 1905, 12:5.
4. "Colonel C. J. Glidden, Phone Pioneer, Dies," NYT, September 12, 1927, 23:3.
5. Jean Paul Blanchard, *Journal of my Forty-Fifth Ascension, Being the First Performed in America, On the Ninth of January, 1793* (Philadelphia: Charles Cist, 1793) 14.
6. He was identified only as "The French philosopher, Reinser the 2d." Origen Bacheler, ed., in The Family Magazine—or—Weekly Abstract of General Knowledge, May 11, 1833, 30–31.
7. Bacheler, in *Family Magazine*, May 18, 1833, 35.
8. Tom Crouch, *The Eagle Aloft* (Washington, D.C.: Smithsonian Institution Press, 1983) 417–63. Crouch's definitive work on the history of ballooning in America contains numerous accounts of gimmicks employed by professional balloonists to draw crowds.
9. Edgar Beecher Bronson, "An Aerial Bivouac," *American Magazine*, October 1907, 623. Quoted in Frank Oppel, ed., *Early Flight: From Balloons to Biplanes* (Secaucus, N.J.: Castle, 1987) 187–96.
10. Ibid.
11. Roy Knabenshue, son of the editor of a Toledo newspaper, first began his aeronautical career as a balloon operator named "Professor Don Carlos" because his father disapproved of the occupation. Later, when aviation became fashionable, he resumed use of his real name and his father's newspaper proudly published accounts of his accomplishments. Harold Morehouse, "Roy Knabenshue," *Flying Pioneers Biographies*. Typewritten manuscript, NASM archives.

12. Frederick Jackson Turner, "The Significance of the Frontier in American History" [1893]. Quoted by Richard Current, John A. Garraty, and Julius Weinberg, eds., *Words That Made American History*, Vol. II (Glenview, Ill.: Scott, Foresman, 1978) 182–205.

13. Irwin Unger, *These United States*, combined edition (Englewood Cliffs, N.J.: Prentice Hall, 1992) 591.

CHAPTER 2

1. "Aero Club Invites Foreign Balloonists," NYT, October 24, 1905, 11:5. "To Study Ballooning, New Aero Club Plans," NYT, November 13, 1905, 7:2. Bishop, who succeeded Hedge, later claimed to have been the first president of the Aero Club of America. Many of the articles in later years, especially those written after World War I, list Bishop as the first president of the organization.

2. "Aero Club Invites Foreign Balloonists." "To Study Ballooning, New Aero Club Plans." Godfrey L. Cabot, "The Federation Aeronautique Internationale," *The National Aeronautic Magazine*, September 1934, 9–14.

3. "Toured Africa in Auto," NYT, September 16, 1905, 1:6.

4. Cabot, "The Federation Aeronautique Internationale."

5. Aero Club of America articles of incorporation. New York Department of State, Division of Corporations, Albany, New York.

6. "To Study Ballooning, New Aero Club Plans."

7. "More Balloon Flights Over Central Park," NYT, November 15, 1905, 12:5.

8. Augustus Post, "Aero Club of America," *Fly*, November 1908, 10.

9. "More Balloon Flights Over Central Park." This article reported that the total number of members had risen to ninety-six, and that the first general meeting for the Aero Club would be scheduled whenever a total of one hundred members had been secured. Anticipating that they would soon have the four additional members, the members were arranging a "smoker" for the following month.

10. Post, "Aero Club of America," 10. "The preliminaries," it would later appear, consisted of setting up a corporation in which the "few who had previously thought of a club" were the exclusive stockholders. This organizational structure would result in rather severe internal problems during 1909, and led to an apparent reforming of the Aero Club in 1910 (see Chapter 7).

11. "Promising to Give Us Wings," NYT, November 16, 1905, 10:5.

12. Advertisement, NYT, January 13, 1906, 10:4.

13. One of these photographs was specifically mentioned in the January 27, 1906, *Scientific American*. The article stated: "A single blurred photograph of a large birdlike machine propelled by compressed air, and which was constructed by Whitehead in 1901, was the only other photograph besides that of Langley's machines of a motor-driven airplane in successful flight." This quote has been cited as proof that inventor Gustave Whitehead predated the Wright Brothers in building a practical airplane. Whitehead's controversial claim is still being pressed by proponents from Bridgeport, Connecticut (where Whitehead conducted most of his experiments), but there are convincing arguments against his claim.

14. "Prof. Bell Favors Kites," NYT, January 19, 1906, 2:6.

15. "Big Balloon Damaged in Armory Auto Show," NYT, January 15, 1906, 7:3.
16. "The Aero Club of America's Exhibit of Aeronautical Apparatus," 93–94.
17. Ibid.
18. "Another Attempt to Solve Aerial Navigation Problem," NYT, January 7, 1906, pt. III, 2:1.
19. "The Aero Club of America's Exhibit of Aeronautical Apparatus," 93–94.

CHAPTER 3

1. Daniel Caulkins, M.D., *Aerial Navigation* (Toledo, Ohio: Blade Printing and Paper, 1895) 42–49. Although Dr. Caulkins's theory of propulsion could not be borne out, he did accurately forecast the use of flying machines carrying hundreds of people from one continent to another. Another of his proposals, to build strong, lightweight structures using thin sheets of aluminum in a honeycomb configuration, was likewise far ahead of its time.
2. Pioneer aviator Charles Foster Willard, in a letter to aviation historian E. D. Weeks, of Des Moines, Iowa, stated, "... the U.S. patent office did not issue patents on flying machines, ie aeroplanes ... 'No vehicle having left the surface of the earth to navigate the air without a balloon, no patent can be granted' which was the standard 'treatment.'" Willard to Weeks (undated), Charles F. Willard file, NASM archives, Washington, D.C. "I recall clearly how Prof. Simon Newcombe [a colleague of Samuel Langley at the Naval Observatory] in 1902 'proved beyond question' that it would be impossible for a heavier-than-air machine to rise from the ground." Statement of Henry Woodhouse, "Aircraft Production," transcript of the U.S. Senate Subcommittee of the Committee on Military Affairs, Washington, D.C., July 11, 1918, 661. The US Patent Office turned down one pre-Wright (1900) application for an airplane patent by saying, "No successful effort has yet been made to rise from the earth's surface by means of an aerial vessel unprovided with a balloon. The practicability of the apparatus is so problematical that actual demonstration of operativeness will be required before the grant of a patent." When the Wrights first applied for their airplane patent they had in fact not yet publicly demonstrated the operativeness of their flying machine. "Airship Patents Affected," NYT, April 2, 1912, 11:5.
3. "Aero Club Honors the Wright Brothers," NYT, March 18, 1906, 8:5.
4. Ibid.
5. Sir Hiram S. Maxim, *Artificial and Natural Flight* (New York: Macmillan and London: Whittaker, 1908) 109. In reference to the European opinion of the early Wright claims, a newspaper article quoted Lt. Frank P. Lahm as saying, "A pretty universal impression seems to exist in Europe that they are sheer advertisers without any real merit back of their mystifying unwillingness to show what they have got." "Our Army To Have an Airship Fleet," NYT, December 15, 1907, 3:1.
6. Fred C. Kelly, *The Wright Brothers: A Biography Authorized by Orville Wright* (New York: Ballantine, 1950) 107–13.
7. "The New Flying Machine," NYT, March 2, 1906, 8:4. The figure appears to have actually been $200,000. Included in the Wrights' deal with the French was delivery of a prototype and instructions on how to fly it.

8. Victor Lougheed, *Vehicles of the Air* (Chicago: Reilly and Britton, 1909) 150–52.

9. Kelly, *Wright Brothers*, 43–44, 178.

10. Ibid., 61–65.

11. Ibid., 74–75.

12. "The Wright Airship Again," *Scientific American*, June 11, 1904, 458.

13. Kelly, *Wright Brothers*, 81.

14. Tom Crouch, *The Bishop's Boys: A Life of Wilbur and Orville Wright* (New York: W. W. Norton, 1989) 301–5.

15. Gertrude Bacon, *Balloons, Airships and Flying Machines* (New York: Dodd, Mead, 1905) 116.

16. Sir Hiram Maxim, *Artificial and Natural Flight*, 109, 160.

CHAPTER 4

1. "Ballooning as a Sport Receives Big Impetus," NYT, January 22, 1906, 5:3. Augustus M. Herring, the man mentioned as the builder of a glider that was sold at the exhibition, was one of the more interesting characters in American aviation history. As the assistant to Octave Chanute, in whom the Wrights had confided during the early years of their experiments, Herring had access to many of the brothers' secrets. He later formed a short-lived partnership with Glenn Curtiss: the Herring-Curtis Company, against which the Wrights would later file patent infringement suits.

2. Columbia University and the Aero Club established an early working relationship. Columbia founded the first University Aero Club in the United States, and later established the first aeronautical engineering curriculum in this country as part of its physics and pure sciences departments. In December 1908, the Aero Club extended use of their club rooms to faculty and students at Columbia. One of the founding student members, First Vice President Grover Cleveland Loening, went on to become one of the most highly respected designers of amphibious aircraft in the world, and a winner of the Collier Trophy.

3. "Ballooning as a Sport Receives Big Impetus."

4. "The Balloon Came Back to Aero Club's House," NYT, February 6, 1906, 7:3. There was no follow-up article telling what happened to the other two balloons.

5. The gas used was commonly described as "coal gas," and was a flammable by-product of burning coal. The Aero Club was aware that hydrogen gas, or "water gas," might provide more lift and sought commercial sources for it as well.

6. "Aeronaut in Flight Over Hudson River," NYT, February 12, 1906, 1:1.

7. Ibid.

8. Augustus Post, "Something About Aero Clubs," *Fly*, November 1908, 10–11.

9. "No Word of Balloon That Made Its Escape," NYT, March 12, 1906, 7:1.

10. In addition, the rules of the FAI required a prospective license holder to make a certain number of ascensions with a license holder and to receive the endorsement of two licensed pilots before he or she could be certified. Levee and de la Vaulx were probably intended to perform this service since, at that time, Frank S. Lahm and Frank P. Lahm were the only two licensed American balloonists, having been accredited by the Aero Club of France. The senior Lahm was in Paris and the ju-

nior was undoubtedly too involved with his military responsibilities to give flight instruction.

11. "French Aeronaut Here with Three Balloons," NYT, March 25, 1906, 10:1. James Gordon Bennett was a wealthy publisher who promoted competition by offering trophies and cash prizes for automobile, balloon, and airplane racing. Tom Crouch, *The Eagle Aloft* (Washington, D.C.: Smithsonian Institution Press, 1983) 542–43. Competitors and the press commonly referred to each of these interchangeably as the Gordon Bennett Trophy, the Gordon Bennett Prize, and, more correctly, the Gordon Bennett International Cup (even though the trophy was not a cup). When Bennett later offered a prize for airplane competition, it was properly called the Gordon Bennett Aviation Cup, but, again, this distinction was seldom made. The criteria for winning the airplane competition varied from year to year, and were determined by the aero club sponsoring the event.

12. "Aeronaut's Close Call in Balloon Ascension," NYT, April 1, 1906, 5:1.

13. "Balloon Sails Over River," NYT, April 3, 1906, 2:6.

14. "Mrs. J. P. Thomas Rises 5,000 Feet in Balloon," NYT, April 12, 1906, 1:5.

15. "De La Vaulx Refused to Make Balloon Trip," NYT, April 15, 1906, 9:1. This same article mentions that Dr. J. P. Thomas, one of the more enthusiastic members of the club, had recently split with the officials of the Aero Club. The reason for this split is not stated, but Thomas's reported exploits with balloons over the next few years suggest an excess of daring and a lack of good judgment.

16. "Balloon Travels 35 Miles," NYT, April 19, 1906, 15:3.

17. Post, "Something About Aero Clubs," 10.

CHAPTER 5

1. Although this competition was frequently called a race, it was in fact a distance, rather than a speed, event.

2. "Race of 16 Balloons Is Started At Paris," NYT, October 1, 1906, 1:3.

3. L. T. C. Rolt, *The Aeronauts* (New York: Walker, 1966) 241.

4. Cleveland Moffett, "Winning the First International Balloon Race," *McClure*, October 1907, 637–48.

5. The two Lahms were the only Americans qualified to pilot an entry in the race, since competitors had to hold a balloon pilot's license. Both were Aero Club of France license holders.

6. Henry Blanchard Hersey, "Experiences in the Sky," *The Century Magazine*, March 1908, 643–55.

7. "Great Balloon Race Won By An American," NYT, October 2, 1906, 4:1.

8. The Hon. Charles S. Rolls was an avid aviation enthusiast and a co-founder of the Rolls-Royce automobile company. His achievements in automobiling and flying were numerous, but he also earned the unfortunate distinction of becoming England's first airplane fatality.

9. Rolt, *Aeronauts*, 241. "Great Balloon Race Won by an American." "Missing Balloon Safe: Lahm is the Winner," NYT, October 3, 1906, 6:1.

10. "Aero Club Will Give Trophy to Lieut. Lahm," NYT, October 28, 1906, 10:7.

11. Tom Crouch, *The Eagle Aloft* (Washington: Smithsonian Institution Press, 1983) 546. "Aeronauts Are Eager for Big Balloon Race," NYT, November 27, 1906, 10:4.
12. It was in response to the scheduling of this event that automobile manufacturers began the now standard practice of "rolling out" the coming year's models in the fall.
13. "Novel Balloon Exhibits," NYT, December 2, 1906, 15:3.
14. "The Second Annual Exhibition of the Aero Club of America," *Scientific American,* December 15, 1906, 447–49.
15. "Novel Balloon Exhibits," 15:3. In his biography of the Wright Brothers, Fred Howard says that this was actually a thirty-horsepower engine, and that it was the brothers' first attempt at constructing an engine that could be mounted vertically. Fred Howard, *Wilbur and Orville: A Biography of the Wright Brothers* (New York: Alfred A. Knopf, 1987) 206.
16. The *Scientific American* writer who covered the exhibition (probably S. Y. Beach) stated that the Langley engine developed 52.4 horsepower at a weight of 125 pounds, yielding 1 horsepower per 2.4 pounds (although the writer calculated it at 1 horsepower per 2.2 pounds). "The Second Annual Exhibition of the Aero Club of America," 447–49.
17. "Aeronauts in Session Arrange Big Contest," NYT, January 14, 1907, 11:1.
18. "St. Louis Now Has An Aero 300," NYT, March 31, 1907, pt. III, 7:1.
19. Ibid.
20. Crouch, *Eagle Aloft,* 546–47.
21. "Austrian May Compete in Big Balloon Race," NYT, February 10, 1907, pt. II, 10:1.
22. Of those Aero Club members who flew at St. Louis, Capt. Charles de Forest Chandler—license number 8—held the most recent Aero Club license. Only those licensed by an FAI-affiliated club could pilot a balloon in the competition.
23. "Chandler and McCoy Test Yellow War Balloon of U.S. Army Signal Corps," NYT, September 22, 1907, 2:1.
24. Crouch, *Eagle Aloft,* 546–48.
25. He was later criticized for this "illegal" use by Judge Advocate General Davis. "Judge Advocate of U.S. Army Declares Pres. Roosevelt's Use of Troops for Bennett Trophy Race Was Illegal," NYT, November 26, 1907, 1:2.
26. Crouch, *Eagle Aloft,* 546–48.
27. "Aeroplane's Fine Flight," NYT, November 8, 1907, 1:4. "Try for Aeroplane Prize," NYT, November 10, 1907, pt. V, 4:1. "May Ask Congress for Army Airship," NYT, November 11, 1907, 16:1. "Getting Ready for Airship of War," NYT, November 15, 1907, 16:1. "To Spend $25,000 for Army Airship," NYT, November 20, 1907, 8:7. "Two War Balloons for U.S.," NYT, November 25, 1907, 16:4. "Army to Buy Aeroplane," NYT, November 26, 1907, 5:2. "Army Wants Aeroplane," NYT, December 10, 1907, 8:6 "Our Army to Have an Airship Fleet," NYT, December 15, 1907, pt. III, 3:1. "Government Asks Bids for Airships," NYT, December 24, 1907, 1:5. "Farman's Record Flight," NYT, December 31, 1:2.
28. Fred C. Kelly, *The Wright Brothers: A Biography Authorized by Orville Wright* (New York: Ballantine, 1950) 85–127.
29. "Shots Hit Glidden Balloon," NYT, June 21, 1908, 1:2.

30. "Shot at Balloon, Jailed," NYT, July 4, 1908, 1:1.
31. In an Aero Club notice to members dated June 30, 1908. Aero Club of America files, National Air & Space Museum archives, Washington, D.C. (hereafter referred to as NASM archives).
32. "Balloon Makes New Endurance Record," NYT, June 8, 1909, 3:2.
33. "Gunning for Ballons," NYT, June 9, 1909, 6:4.
34. Augustus Post, "A Fall From the Sky," *The Century Magazine,* October 1910, 935–47.
35. Frank S. Lahm, whose son had won the first Bennett competition in 1906, was to have accompanied McCoy, but did not.
36. Post, "A Fall From the Sky," 935–47.

CHAPTER 6

1. From an article (probably written by editor Alfred W. Lawson) titled "Captain Homer W. Hedge: The Organizer of the Aero Club of America," *Fly,* June 1909, 5.
2. Some sources list Farman's father as a Scotsman.
3. "$10,000 Earned by Farman in Airship," NYT, January 14, 1908, 3:5.
4. "Study the Birds for Aerial Flight," NYT, March 10, 1908, 8:3.
5. The claims that Gustave Whitehead, later associated with Beach, predated the Wrights in powered flight gained much of their appearance of legitimacy through Albert F. Zahm's 1945 book *Early Powerplane Fathers* (Notre Dame, Ind.: University Press, 1945). Zahm was a member of the "Langley Society," an informal group of aviators and aeronautical authorities who, like Beach, refuted the Wrights' entitlement to a patent on the airplane.
6. "Drop Balloons for Airships," NYT, April 8, 1908, 1:5.
7. "Aero Club takes Wing on a 'Glider'," NYT, April 13, 1908, 16:5.
8. Undated notice on the letterhead of the Aero Club of America, 12 East 42d Street, New York. Aero Club of America file, NASM archives.
9. Letter from Albert C. Triaca to Aero Club members, October 29, 1909. Aero Club of America file, NASM archives. These members did not (at that time) resign from the Aero Club, but rather formed a new organization of a more commercial nature to develop and fly airplanes. See Chapter 7 for more on Triaca's initiative.
10. Letter from the Aero Club to members, dated June 30, 1908. Aero Club of America file, NASM archives.
11. Louis S. Casey, *Curtiss: The Hammonsport Era 1907–1915* (New York: Crown, 1981) 2.
12. Casey, *Curtiss,* 4–25.
13. Tom Crouch, *The Bishop's Boys: A Life of Wilbur and Orville Wright* (New York: W. W. Norton, 1989), 362–63.
14. Casey, *Curtiss,* 17.
15. President Bishop was in Europe on a prolonged cross-country automobile tour. He suffered paralysis during the trip and was unable to attend to the affairs of the club during his lengthy hospital stay in France.
16. "Farman May Fly Here," NYT, July 10, 1908, 14:2. It seems likely that the original negotiations with Farman were initiated by some of those who later broke

away to form the Aeronautic Society of New York. Hawley, acting as president of the club, readily allowed the St. Louis men to undertake the financial backing of Farman's tour. Whatever the reason, it turned out to be a wise move on behalf of the club.

17. "Farman, Who Flies, Is Welcomed Here," NYT, July 27, 1908, 14:3.

18. The design was "a triangle of red with the United States shield in the center." "Farman, Who Flies, Is Welcomed Here."

19. "Farman's Airship Arrives," NYT, July 29, 1908, 7:2.

20. "Farman, Who Flies, Is Welcomed Here."

21. "Farman's Airship Like a Huge Bird," NYT, July 31, 1908, 12:1.

22. "Two Test Flights Made by Farman," NYT, August 1, 1908, 1:1.

23. "First Public Flight Made by Farman," NYT, August 3, 1908, 3:3.

24. "Farman Races an Auto," NYT, August 5, 1908, 2:4.

25. MacMechen's genuine effort to salvage the fiasco earned him the respect of aviation enthusiasts. He later published many aviation articles in popular magazines.

26. "Farman Shy $17,000 and a Backer, Too," NYT, August 10, 1908, 2:4.

27. "Press Agents Haunt Farman," NYT, August 11, 1908, 1:1. On February 12, 1923 (Edison's seventh-sixth birthday), "The Wizard" was honored by the NAA with the conferral of an honorary membership. "Honorary Membership to Mr. Edison." *Aerial Age,* March 1923, 103.

28. "Farman Machine Attached," NYT, August 12, 1908, 1:3.

29. "Farman's Aeroplane Saved in Night Raid," NYT, August 15, 1908, 4:3.

30. "French Praise Wrights," NYT, August 10, 1908, 2:4.

31. "Farman Bears No Malice," NYT, August 16, 1908, pt. II, 3:1. "Farman's Aeroplane Saved in Night Raid."

32. "Wright Aeroplane Flies at Capital," NYT, September 4, 1908, 1:6.

33. "Wright Flies Over an Hour," NYT, September 10, 1908, 1:7.

34. "Wright Ship Up Over 70 Minutes," NYT, September 12, 1908, 1:1. "Wright Breaks His Airship Record," NYT, September 13, 1908, 1:3.

35. Eric Hodgins and F. Alexander Magoun, *Sky High* (Boston: Brown, Little, 1935) 190–91.

36. Henry Serrano Villard, *Blue Ribbon of the Air* (Washington, D.C.: Smithsonian Institution Press, 1987) 16.

37. Letter from Orville Wright to Courtland F. Bishop, President of the Aero Club. "Wrights Won't Fly in French Air Race," NYT, March 23, 1909, 5:3.

38. "Herring May Enter International Race," NYT, April 16, 1909, 18:3.

39. Alden Hatch, *Glenn Curtiss, Pioneer of Naval Aviation* (New York: Julian Messner, 1942) 143.

40. Casey, *Curtiss,* 55.

41. "Curtiss's Aeroplane Ready," NYT, June 11, 1909, 3:6. The official name of this plane was the *Golden Flyer,* but the press labeled it the "Gold Bug," because of the yellow color of its bamboo outriggers and the yellow silk used to cover the wings. The plane that Curtiss took to the Rheims meet was very similar in construction (but with an eight-cylinder engine and slightly shorter wings), and was known as the "Rheims Machine," or the "Rheims Racer." The names of these planes were commonly interchanged by the press of the day.

42. "15,000 See Airships Put Through Their Paces," NYT, August 21, 1909, 1:1.

43. In one of the many letters Charles F. Willard was later to write to his friend "Hud" Weeks, Willard described the heroes of aviation as "two sour-faced, stiff-necked batchelors with an old-maid sister." Willard to Weeks (undated), Charles F. Willard file, NASM archives.

CHAPTER 7

1. W. H. Phipps, "The Junior Aero Club of America," *Fly,* March 1909, 15.
2. Claudia M. Oakes, *United States Women in Aviation through World War I* (Washington, D.C.: Smithsonian Institution Press, 1978) 10–12. "Woman Has New Aeroplane," NYT, July 31, 1908, 12:1.
3. "Novel Balloon Exhibits," NYT, December 2, 1906, 15:3. Phipps, "The Junior Aero Club of America," 15. "Women Talk of Flying," NYT, March 28, 1909, 2:1.
4. Edward Durant, "Junior Aero Club of America Bulletin No. 3," *Fly,* August 1909, 23. "Flying Machines in the Big Garden," NYT, September 26, 1909, 2:11. "Aeroplane for a Woman," NYT, September 29, 1909, 4:2. Oakes, *United States Women in Aviation through World War I,* 10–12.
5. "Model Airplane Awards," NYT, August 6, 1912, 7:3.
6. The original Aeronca C-2 has been beautifully restored and now resides in the collection of the National Air & Space Museum. For more information about Roche and the Aeronca, see Jay P. Spenser, *Aeronca C-2—The Story of the Flying Bathtub* (Washington, D.C.: Smithsonian Institution Press, 1978).
7. Harold Morehouse, "George A. Page," *Flying Pioneers Biographies.* Typewritten manuscript, NASM archives.
8. "For Forts, $10,000,000 More," NYT, January 19, 1909, 1:6. "Want Airships for Army," NYT, January 20, 1909, 1:6.
9. "$500,000 is Voted for Army Airships," NYT, January 31, 1909, 1:4.
10. "House Votes Down Airships," NYT, February 3, 1909, 3:2. Letter to Members of the Aero Club (probably from president Courtland Bishop), February 20, 1909. Aero Club of America file, NASM archives.
11. "Balloon Rates Come High," NYT, December 16, 1908, 5:3.
12. Minutes of the Aero Club meeting, February 1, 1909. Aero Club of America file, NASM archives.
13. Letter from A. Holland Forbes to Aero Club members, September 24, 1909. Aero Club of America file, NASM archives. The original request from a certain group of members (of which Orrel A. Parker, Wilbur R. Kimball, and Stanley Y. Beach were the leaders) was for the number of directors to increase from five to eleven, with the additional six directors being elected by the general membership. This would have given a majority vote to elected directors. "Important Facts," an undated flyer apparently distributed by Parker, Kimball, and Beach, on or about October 9, 1909. Aero Club of America file, NASM archives.
14. Letter from Orrel A. Parker, Wilbur R. Kimball, and Stanley Y. Beach to Aero Club members, October 9, 1909. Aero Club of America file, NASM archives. "Row Starts Anew in the Aero Club," NYT, October 17, 1909, 7:3.
15. The directors at the time were J. C. McCoy, Courtland F. Bishop, A. Holland Forbes, Samuel H. Valentine, and Charles J. Edwards. Minutes of the Aero Club meeting, November 5, 1908. Aero Club of America file, NASM archives.

16. Letter from Orrel A. Parker, Wilbur R. Kimball, and Stanley Y. Beach to other Aero Club members, October 9, 1909. Aero Club of America file, NASM archives.
17. "Faction in the Aero Club," *New York Herald,* October 26, 1909.
18. Letter from Albert C. Triaca to Aero Club members, October 29, 1909. Aero Club of America file, NASM archives.
19. "Aero Club Fight Taken to Court," NYT, October 31, 1909, 20:5. "Aero Club of America Bulletin No. 2," November 30, 1909. Aero Club of America file, NASM archives.
20. Letter from Courtland F. Bishop to James Means, November 4, 1909. Letter from William Hawley to James Means, February 17, 1909. Aero Club of America file, NASM archives.
21. This 1910 merger may explain why some later sources sometimes call Bishop (instead of Homer Hedge) the first president of the Aero Club of America. The functions of the Aero Club were taken over by the National Aeronautic Association in 1922, but the actual corporation survived, on paper, until 1926, when the State of New York dissolved it for nonpayment of franchise tax. Courtland F. Bishop, President, and Augustus Post, Secretary, "Articles of Incorporation, Aero Corporation, Limited." New York Department of State, Division of Corporations, February 16, 1910.

    The author was, unfortunately, unable to locate any bylaws that might have been written for Aero Corporation, Limited. In the absence of these, or a similar source of information, it would be impossible to state conclusively why Bishop and Post merged the Aero Club into a new corporation. It seems reasonable to assume that the move was intended to appease members who might have been in agreement with Parker, Kimball, and Beach by expanding the board from five to six members (rather than the eleven board members sought by the three named dissenters), and creating a new slate of twelve governors. Likewise, it would be reasonable to assume that the new structure was designed to protect the organization's officials against further assaults such as the one mounted by Parker, Kimball, and Beach. How the organization was able to continue calling itself the Aero Club of America, even after its legal merger into Aero Corporation, Limited, remains a puzzle.
22. "Balloon Spy [*sic*] on Autoists," NYT, May 24, 1909, 1:4.
23. The *Golden Flyer,* the Herring-Curtiss machine built for the Aeronautic Society, was bought by Charles Strobel at the January 1910 Dominguez exhibition, the first international air meet to be held in America (see Chapter 8). He sent it to Tampa, Florida, where people paid twenty-five cents apiece to see it sitting in a tent. Later, it was displayed in the furniture department of Tiedke's Department Store in Toledo, Ohio.
24. Out of many hundreds of members of the Aero Club and affiliated clubs, less than fifty spherical balloon pilot's licenses had been issued when the club's 1914 membership roster was published.
25. A book that captures much of the spirit of the exhibition days is Sherwood Harris's *The First to Fly: Aviation's Pioneer Days* (New York: Simon & Schuster, 1970). Perhaps the most comprehensive collection of information about individual exhibition pilots is *Flying Pioneers Biographies.* This collection of more than three hundred biographical sketches was compiled by the late Harold Morehouse, a noted aeronautical engineer, who knew many of the early pilots personally. Although the collection is not always accurate and, unfortunately, lacks citations for

the author's sources of information, the Morehouse biographies contain a
wealth of information about America's pioneering aviators. Copies of the unpublished collection are in the NASM archives, but selected biographies have
appeared in various issues of the American Aviation Historical Society's *AAHS
Journal*.

26. Louis S. Casey, *Curtiss: The Hammondsport Era 1907–1915* (New York: Crown,
    1981), 1–3. George Hardie, Experimental Aircraft Association Historian, with
    Stanley I. Vaughn, pioneer aviator. Audiotaped interview, September 12, 1962.
    Experimental Aircraft Association archives, Oshkosh, Wisconsin. "Novel Balloon
    Exhibits."

27. Advertisement for Virginia College for Young Ladies, Roanoke, Virginia. *Fly*, No-
    vember 1908, 18. "Three Immortals," *Fly*, November 1908, 5.

28. President's report to the Aero Club, Fall 1908. Aero Club of America file, NASM
    archives.

29. By February 1909, the Aero Club had signed articles of affiliation with the
    Aero Club of Ohio and the Aero Club of New England. Letter to members of
    the Aero Club, February 1, 1909, NASM archives. Throughout the year 1909,
    Fly magazine regularly reported news of new and existing aero clubs.

30. "Balloons to Race," NYT, August 10, 1908, 2:4.

31. "Bid for Balloon Race," NYT, December 29, 1908, 10:4.

32. "Want Aeronauts Licensed," NYT, September 13, 1908, pt. II, 3:2.

33. "Wants Ballooning Regulated," NYT, April 3, 1909, 7:3.

34. The first federal aviation licensing requirements were passed on December 31,
    1926, but aviators were given until July 1, 1927, to comply. Nick Komons,
    Bonfires to Beacons (Washington, D.C.: Smithsonian Institution Press, 1989) 92–
    99.

35. "To License Pilots," NYT, November 27, 1909, 10:6.

36. It seems that the actual documents were not issued until 1911, as that is the date
    appearing on Curtiss's number 1 license at on display in the National Air & Space
    Museum.

37. H. H. Arnold, "The First Ten," *Flying Sportsman and Skyways*, August 1947, 18–50;
    "The Second Ten," September 1947, 24–61; "The Third Ten," October 1947,
    29–54.

38. Paulhan came to America late in 1909 for the Dominguez meet held in January
    1910 (see Chapter 8). Newspaper articles show that he was at Aero Club head-
    quarters during March of that year, and club records indicate he applied for an
    American license at that time. "Inspect Aviation Sites," NYT, March 7, 1910,
    10:6.

39. *Grand Rapids News*, reprinted in "In the Slip Stream," *Aero and Hydro*, June 6,
    1914, 125.

40. "Biplane Strikes Cow," NYT, May 30, 1911, 3:11.

41. "Jefferson City, Mo.," *Aero*, January 28, 1911, 72.

42. Lt. Lester J. Maitland, *Knights of the Air* (New York: Doubleday, Doran, 1929)
    121–22.

43. "Aviators Arrested." *NYT*, February 20, 1911, 1:2.

44. *New York Sun*, *Litchfield* (Illinois) *Herald* and *Detroit News-Tribune*, untitled articles
    reprinted in "In the Slip Stream."

CHAPTER 8

1. Letter from Augustus Post to James Means, on Aero Club of America letterhead, November 23, 1908. Minutes of the Aero Club meeting, November 5, 1908. Aero Club of America file, NASM archives.
2. "Topics of the Times—Art and the Aeroplane," NYT, December 28, 1908, 8:4.
3. Letters from the Aero Club to members, February 1 and February 20, 1909. Aero Club of America file, NASM archives. "Taft to Give Aero Medals," NYT, April 1, 1909, 6:6.
4. "Success Well Won, Taft Tells Wrights," NYT, June 11, 1909, 2:2.
5. The complicated issues and long-running disputes that underlie the Wrights' legal battles have been thoroughly investigated by scholars and popular writers alike, and the reader is referred to a number of excellent accounts for a detailed discussion. Two of the best are *The Bishop's Boys* by Crouch and *The Wright Brothers* by Kelly.
6. "Wrights Start Suit on Curtiss Airship: Action Brought Against Aeronautic Society Which Owns Machine Used by Willard," NYT, August 20, 1909, 2:4. "15,000 See Airship Put Through Its Paces," NYT, August 20, 1909, 2:2.
7. "Wrights to Fight Foreign Aeroplanes," NYT, September 25, 1909, 1:4.
8. "Big Men of Finance Back of the Wrights," NYT, November 23, 1909, 1:1.
9. Obituary of Captain Homer W. Hedge. NYT, September 11, 1909, 9:4.
10. "28 Balloons Start in Races at Zurich," NYT, October 2, 1909, 1:4.
11. On December 31, 1908, Wilbur Wright made this record-setting flight at Auvours, France. The flight lasted two hours, twenty minutes, and twenty-three and a half seconds. *The Motor* editorial staff, *The Aero Manual,* 1910 (London: Temple Press, 1910) 206.
12. Henry Serrano Villard, *Blue Ribbon of the Air* (Washington, D.C.: Smithsonian Institution Press, 1987) 53–58.
13. "Big Aviation Meet for Los Angeles," NYT, December 23, 1909, 11:1.
14. "Aero Club Defied," NYT, December 24, 1909, 2:6.
15. Samuel T. Clover, "First Meet of the Man-Birds in America." *The Outing Magazine,* February 1910, 750–63.
16. "Paulhan in Flight, Headed for France," NYT, March 22, 1910, 6:2.
17. "Would Own Wright Patents," NYT, March 25, 1910, 11:2.
18. Fred C. Kelly, *The Wright Brothers: A Biography Authorized by Orville Wright* (New York: Ballantine, 1950) 175–76.
19. "Are the Wrights Justified?" *Aeronautics,* April 1910, 141.
20. "Aviation Meet is Now Assured," NYT, April 10, 1910, pt. IV, 1:7.
21. "Protest From Aero Club Members," NYT, April 19, 1910, 11:1.
22. "Aviators Organize to Oppose Wrights," NYT, May 24, 1910, 8:7.
23. Ibid. "Aero Federation Formed," NYT, June 3, 1910, 2:1.
24. "Aero Convention Here," NYT, June 18, 1910, 9:2.
25. "Aero Club Free to Act," NYT, June 21, 1910, 2:5.
26. "Tarbell Won't Run Big Aviation Meet," NYT, August 4, 1910, 1:5.
27. "Aviators Can Fly Despite Wrights," NYT, June 15, 1910, 2:6. "Aero Club and the Wrights," NYT, June 18, 1910, 9:2. "National Aero Body Formed After Fight," NYT, June 23, 1910, 2:1. "National Body Organizes," NYT, June 24, 1910, 9:2.

28. Harold Morehouse, "Roy Knabenshue," *Flying Pioneers Biographies.* Typewritten manuscript, NASM archives.
29. "Hamilton Files Protests," NYT, July 27, 1910, 4:1.
30. "Harvard Aero Meet Loses Its Sanction," NYT, August 2, 1910, pt. III, 2:3.
31. Elsbeth E. Freudenthal, *Flight Into History* (Norman: University of Oklahoma Press, 1949) 230–31.
32. Fanciulli's abstention from the committee meeting and subsequent resignation from the Aero Club were conspicuous examples of how Aero Club members tried to remain fair and impartial in their dealings with various members of the flying community. Because those men who were the Aero Club's officers were also among the most likely to become involved in various aspects of the fledgling aviation industry, this was not always easy. Robert Collier, for example, was one of the Wright Brothers' most ardent supporters (and purchaser of two of their earliest commercially produced airplanes), yet the first recipient of the Collier Trophy was Glenn Curtiss, the Wrights' staunch adversary in a highly volatile lawsuit.
33. "Tarbell Won't Run Big Aviation Meet," NYT, August 4, 1910, 1:5.
34. "Making New Plans for Aviation Meet," NYT, August 5, 1910, 3:3.
35. Victor Lougheed, *Vehicles of the Air* (Chicago: Reilly and Britton, 1909).
36. *Cyclopedia of Automobile Engineering,* Vol. 4 (Chicago: American School of Correspondence), 1912.
37. E. B. Heath Aerial Vehicle Company (Chicago, Illinois) catalog F. This catalog is not dated, but was probably published in 1911. The cover states that the company was established in 1909. Collection of the author.
38. Correspondence of the Roberts Motor Manufacturing Company, Sandusky, Ohio. Rheinhardt Ausmus Collection, Rutherford B. Hayes Presidential Center Library, Freemont, Ohio.

CHAPTER 9

1. "Curtiss Will Try to Fly From Albany," NYT, May 25, 1910, 1:5. "$55,000 Prizes in Aero Flights," NYT, June 1, 1910, 1:5. "Water Flight for Curtiss," NYT, August 29, 1910, 16:2. "Chicago Aero Meet," NYT, May 28, 1911, pt. IV, 12:7. "Another 1,000-Mile Flight Proposed," NYT, June 18, 1911, pt. IV, 10:5.
2. Fred Howard. *Wilbur and Orville: A Biography of the Wright Brothers* (New York: Alfred A. Knopf, 1987) 357–61.
   The undisputed stars of the Wright exhibition team were Arch Hoxsey and Ralph Johnstone. The two often appeared together at aviation exhibitions (accompanied by Wright pilots Walter Brookins and Phil Parmelee), each trying to outdo the other with feats of aerial daring. The press soon took a keen interest in this rivalry and dubbed the two pilots "The Heavenly Twins," reporting every new maneuver and smashed flying record to eager readers. There are conflicting reports as to the Wrights' reaction to Hoxsey and Johnstone's flying antics. Morehouse claims that Orville Wright appeared, unannounced, at one of their flying performances and later scolded the two for taking needless chances. But, in an interview printed by *Aero* magazine, Johnstone stated, "the Wrights did not agree with us when we said ... that there was nothing to be gained for aviation by sensational 'stunts' in

the air . . . [they said] that these things were important because they showed what an aeroplane can do." Yet the two continued to explore the limits to which their airplanes could be flown.

On November 17, 1910, in Denver, Colorado, the wings of Johnstone's plane collapsed as he was making a spiral dive, plunging the aviator to his death. Before his crew could reach the wreckage, the crowd surged from the grandstands and pillaged the remains of the plane and pilot for souvenirs. Hardly more than a month later, on December 31, 1910, at Los Angeles, Hoxsey met a similar fate as his plane rolled, inverted, and fell to the earth.

Ralph Johnstone, quoted in "The King of the Air," *Aero,* November 26, 1910, 12. "The Johnstone Fatality," *Aero,* November 26, 1910, 10. Morehouse, *Flying Pioneers Biographies.*

3. Fred T. Jane, ed., *Jane's All the World's Aircraft* (London: Sampson Low, Marston, 1914) 189. The source of this list is not given, but it appears to have been gleaned from American flying journals. It has some conspicuous flaws. For example, only a small percentage of those licensed by 1914 are mentioned, and some of those listed as unlicensed pilots may simply have flown with another pilot operating the controls. Still, the point that a large number of American pilots—probably the majority—were not licensed is valid.

4. Interview by the author with Glen Messer, pioneer aviator, at the March 1989 meeting of the Early Birds' Association, Long Beach, California.

5. Since many of the "Curtiss" airplanes were actually copies or derivatives more correctly labeled "Curtiss-type" airplanes, rather than true Curtiss factory-built planes, the measurements and construction methods varied from builder to builder. Some used individual wing panels with segmented spars and others built the wings in complete units with solid spars.

6. An excellent example of an original Curtiss-type exhibition airplane, complete with transportation crating system, spare parts, and tools, is in the collection of the Albuquerque Museum, Albuquerque, New Mexico. This particular plane was packed away about 1916 and remained in storage undisturbed until 1985.

7. The author's study drew data primarily from information in the *Flying Pioneers Biographies* of Harold Morehouse (typewritten manuscript, NASM archives). The data were converted into a format suitable for analysis using the computerized statistical package SPSSX. Although data were not available for every pilot of the period, the analysis represents a sufficiently large number of them to reveal accurately general trends in early American aviation. The Curtiss and Wright machines were by far the two most common designs indicated in the study. Of the airplanes that made up the remaining 35%, many were identified by the name of the builder rather than the design. A "Greenwell," for example, may have actually been a Curtiss-type plane built by someone named Greenwell. Few amateur builders tried to make copies of the Wright plane for fear of lawsuits, but some other companies made Wright-type aircraft under license.

8. Messer interview. Interview by the author with Virginia State Supreme Court Justice William E. Spain, June 1983, Richmond, Virginia. Judge Spain's father was the mayor of Richmond when Willard flew there.

9. The first pilot to receive acclaim for looping an airplane was the Frenchman Adolphe Pegoud. A young Russian military officer named Nesterov was probably the first to actually accomplish the maneuver, but, instead of receiving acclaim for his

feat, he was punished by Russian military authorities for endangering a military aircraft. Curtis Prendergast and the Editors of Time-Life Books. *The First Aviators* (Alexandria, Va.: Time-Life Books, 1980) 144.

10. Aero Club of America pilot's license information cards, NASM archives.
11. "To Restrain Aviators," NYT, June 12, 1913, 2:6. Claudia M. Oakes, *United States Women in Aviation through World War I* (Washington, D.C.: Smithsonian Institution Press, 1978) 30.
12. "Beachey Will Fly No More," NYT, May 13, 1913, 6:2.
13. Jane, *Jane's All the World's Aircraft,* 189–90.
14. "Beachey to Quit Flying," NYT, March 9, 1913, pt. IV, 6:2.
15. "Beachey Will Fly No More."
16. Morehouse, *Flying Pioneers Biographies.*
17. "Urges Aerial Licenses," NYT, March 31, 1913, 7:6.
18. "Licenses for Aviators," NYT, May 18, 1913, 8:4.
19. Undated transcript of talk delivered by Rheinhardt Ausmus. Rheinhardt Ausmus Collection, Rutherford B. Hayes Presidential Center Library, Freemont, Ohio.
20. "Independent Auto Makers to Fight," NYT, January 6, 1911, 12:3.
21. "Aero Club Bars Her Out," NYT, January 30, 1911, 3:7.
22. "Three Women Venture in Biplane," *Detroit Free Press,* June 20, 1911, 1:7.
23. The first woman aviator issued a license was Baroness Raymonde de la Roche. She earned her certificate from the Aero Club of France in 1910.
24. Oakes, *United States Women in Aviation through World War I,* 26.
25. Ibid., 33–38.

CHAPTER 10

1. R. P. Hearne, *Aerial Warfare,* quoted in his "Strategy and Tactics of a Flying Machine Campaign," *Current Literature,* October 1909, 449–52.
2. The Japanese originally planned to launch the attack approximately twenty minutes after they had formally issued a declaration of war. The attack actually came before the declaration was communicated to U.S. officials.
3. David W. Noble, *The Progressive Mind: 1890–1917* (Minneapolis: Burgess, 1981) 40–43.
4. Daniel Caulkins, M.D., *Aerial Navigation* (Toledo, Ohio: Blade Printing and Paper, 1895) 10–11.
5. "Aeronauts Form National Defense," NYT, January 22, 1911, pt. IV, 5:4. The original Aeronautical Reserve was short-lived, but was revived two years later under the names First Aviation Corps and Provisional Aviation Battalion. Much to the displeasure of the Aero Club, Mortimer Delano, the man who attempted this revival, tried to use the club's reputation and that of the National Aeroplane Fund to promote his own position as "Chief of Staff."
6. Sherwood Harris, *The First to Fly: Aviation's Pioneer Days* (New York: Simon & Schuster, 1970) 229–31.
7. Glenn Curtiss, as quoted ibid., 231.
8. D. Layman, *To Ascend from a Floating Base* (Cranbury, N.J.: Associated University Presses, 1979) 126–28.

9. Harold Morehouse, "Hugh A. Robinson," *Flying Pioneers Biographies.* Typewritten manuscript, NASM archives.

10. Circus performers may have directly and indirectly contributed a great deal to early aviation development. Aside from their daring and familiarity with working high above the ground, many knew that acrobatics could be performed with machinery. "Looping" cars and bicycles in jumps off ramps was a common circus act. In another act, the "Globe of Death," motorcycle riders would use centrifugal force to hold themselves to the inside surface of a wire mesh sphere while riding in consecutive loops. Knowledge of such techniques later translated into aerobatic flying skills.

11. "Army Post to Train Aviators," NYT, March 30, 1911, 12:1.

12. "Aeroplanes for Life Savers," NYT, May 7, 1911, pt. IV, 8:1.

13. Collier lost an eye in a 1906 polo scrimmage with H. P. Whitney, E. W. Roby, Reginald Brooks, and others. Ironically, Whitney, whose mallet accidentally injured Collier, was later named as one of the primary beneficiaries of Collier's estate. Interestingly enough, all of the beneficiaries of Collier's will refused their inheritances, so that Collier's widow would inherit the entire estate.

14. The change in officers went as follows: president, Robert J. Collier replaced Allan A. Ryan; first vice president, James A. Blair, Jr., replaced Courtland F. Bishop; second vice president, Maj. Samuel Reber replaced Dave Hennen Morris; third vice president, Harold F. McCormick replaced James A. Blair, Jr. Henry A. Wise Wood was elected "additional Vice President."

15. "Aero Club Will Help Aeronautics," NYT, November 19, 1911, pt. IV, 8:7.

16. "The Robert J. Collier Trophy," *National Aeronautics,* July 1961, 4. The unidentified author of this article cites Frederick R. Neeley as the source of much of the information contained therein, from an article in the December 1950 issue of *Pegasus* (the magazine of the Fairchild Engine and Aircraft Corporation). Another good article on Collier and his trophy is William Kroger, "For Greatest Achievement: The Story Behind American Aviation's Most Prized Award," *National Aeronautics,* December 1944, 15–18.

17. Bulletin of the Aero Club of America, 1912. Aero Club of America file, NASM archives. At different times the term "preceding year" seems to have been interpreted as the twelve calendar months preceding the date of the presentation ceremony (which has varied greatly over the years from midsummer to late fall to early spring), or, as has been the case in more recent years, as the calendar year preceding the year in which the awards ceremony takes place. For this reason, the Collier Trophy for a given year may have been given for an event that occurred during that year or the preceding year, depending on the committee's interpretation at the time.

18. Keyser's other works included statues at the Maryland State House and the Parliament Building in Ottawa, Canada. In his lifetime he won several international awards for his portraits, public memorials, and mortuary sculpture. Obituary, the *Baltimore Sun,* September 27, 1959, 23:2.

19. Frederick R. Neeley, "The Robert J. Collier Trophy," *National Aeronautics,* June 1961, 4.

20. "Visits a Warship in 'Aerial Taxicab,'" NYT, May 10, 1912, 7:1.

21. "Callier [*sic*] Flies Alone," NYT, May 24, 1912, 7:1.

22. William Kroger, "For Greatest Achievement," *National Aeronautics,* December 1944, 15–18.

23. Morehouse, *Flying Pioneers Biogrpahies.*
24. Robert J. Collier, "R. J. Collier No Transatlantic Flier." Letter to the editor of the NYT, June 24, 1913, 10:5.
25. "An Offer for the America," NYT, September 2, 1914, 9:5.
26. "R. J. Collier Dies at Dinner Table," NYT, November 9, 1918, 13:1.
27. "Col. Vanderbilt Up in Aerial Flight," NYT, October 6, 1912, pt. III, 10:1.
28. "Will Fly for the Navy," NYT, July 22, 1913, 6:7.
29. Reportedly, the flying boat was sold to England for use by the military, but on an early flight it was landed at too high a speed, run entirely aground, and severely damaged. The engines were removed and no attempt was made to salvage the rest of the plane.
30. Dr. Jerome C. Hunsacker, *Some Lessons of History,* originally delivered as the Second Wings Club "Sight" Lecture (New York: Wings Club, 1966) 8–9.
31. "Belmont At Head of Aviation Corps," NYT, May 28, 1915, 5:5.
32. "Aeroplane Service," NYT, May 22, 1915, 10:4.
33. "Cabrera Contributes $200," NYT, July 2, 1915, 13:1.
34. "Navy to Lend Aeroplanes," NYT, June 25, 1915, 12:2.
35. Information sheet sent by the Aero Club of America to the Roberts Motor Company, February 24, 1916. Rheinhardt Ausmus Collection, Rutherford B. Hayes Presidential Center Library, Freemont, Ohio.
36. "Favor Enlarging Our Air Defenses, NYT, September 26, 1915, pt. II, 13:3.
37. "Funston Sends Reassuring Reports," NYT, March 26, 1916, pt. I, 2:3.
38. "Voted by Congress," NYT, March 29, 1916, 2:5.
39. "Aviators to Train for War at Once," NYT, June 25, 1916, 4:1.
40. "Our Aero Beginning to Outstrip Europe's," NYT, October 29, 1916, pt. I, 21:1.
41. "Harvard Leads in Air Preparedness," NYT, July 16, 1916, pt. I, 13:5.
42. "Our Aero Beginning to Outstrip Europe's."
43. "Army Paves Way for Volunteers," NYT, February 3, 1917, 5:2. "Relations with Germany are Broken Off . . . ," NYT, February 4, 1917, pt. I, 10:6. "Colleges Lay Plans for Service in War," NYT, February 5, 1917, 11:5. "Yale Men Organize Second Air Corps," NYT, March 12, 1917, 10:8.

CHAPTER 11

1. Archibald D. Turnbull and Clifford L. Lord, *History of United States Naval Aviation* (New Haven, Conn.: Yale University Press, 1949) 32–95.
2. "'Fight Hard!' Is Cry at Aero Club Feast," NYT, March 31, 1917, 2:4.
3. "Two Tickets in Aero Club," NYT, October 31, 1918, 11:3.
4. "Aero Club Offers Services to Army," NYT, February 4, 1917, pt. I, 10:6.
5. "Need 10,000 Airmen to Cripple Germany," NYT, May 27, 1917, pt. I, 8:1.
6. "Plan to Aid Aero Work," NYT, January 14, 1918, 11:2.
7. "Ask Increase for Airmen," NYT, January 30, 1918, 4:4.
8. Howard Mingos, *The Birth of an Industry* (New York: W. B. Conkey, 1930) 16–20.
9. Ibid., 17–39.
10. Ibid., 27–39.

11. Although the Curtiss and Wright companies were the major recipients of these payoffs, they were not the only ones to receive money for outstanding patent claims.

12. Mingos, *Birth of an Industry,* 14–26.

13. Ibid., 27–39. Throughout Mingos's book, which was written eleven years after the end of World War I (and eight years after the demise of the Aero Club), there are references to actions by unnamed officials of the "Aeronautic Society." Even though an organization with a similar name, the Aeronautical Society of New York, was still in existence during the years in question, when Mingos's comments are viewed in the context of events involving the leaders of the Aero Club, especially Woodhouse, it seems almost certain that he is referring to the Aero Club.

14. In 1918, Woodhouse testified at length before the U.S. Senate's Subcommittee on Military Affairs, stating that aircraft production (under the charge of the Aircraft Production Board, and carried out by the MAA) was grossly inadequate. In another hearing, conducted after the end of the war, he blamed the MAA for keeping affordable airplanes out of the hands of American aviators by opposing efforts to sell European-made surplus planes in the United States. "Aircraft Production," transcript of the U.S. Senate Subcommittee of the Committee on Military Affairs, Washington, D.C., July 11, 1918, Vol. I, 651–708. "Importation of Surplus Aircraft," transcript of the hearings before the House Committee on Ways and Means, Washington, D.C., June 1, 1920, part 1, 61–63, 76–84. Mingos, *Birth of an Industry,* 27–44.

15. "Aero Club Row Compromised," NYT, November 2, 1918, 11:3.

16. "Wood Replies to Critic," NYT, November 11, 1918, 9:5.

17. "Importation of Surplus Aircraft," 29.

18. In 1917 the Aero Club of America recognized outstanding achievement by a woman pilot for the first time by awarding a gold medal to Ruth Law for a record cross-country flight on November 19, 1916.

19. "Maynard Wins Transcontinental Race," NYT, October 19, 1919, 1:1.

20. Letter from George B. Weller, Rawlins, Wyoming, to NAA president Malvern J. Gross, Jr., July 18, 1990. NAA files.

21. "Seeks to Oust Aero Club," NYT, January 6, 1920, 14:7. "Flying Club Grants Altitude Record," NYT, November 2, 1919, 14:4.

22. "Fliers [*sic*] Party Causes Stir," NYT, April 26, 1919, 15:4.

23. "Officers Uphold Aero Club Fund," NYT, June 9, 1920, 32:2.

24. "Henry Woodhouse Seeks Injunction," NYT, July 22, 1920, 11:4.

25. "Aero Club's Answer Assails Woodhouse," NYT, August 8, 1920, pt. II, 1:5.

26. "Flying Clubs Join in One Organization," NYT, August 17, 1920, 18:1.

27. Aeronautical Chamber of Commerce, *Aircraft Yearbook for 1922* (New York: Aeronautical Chamber of Commerce of America, 1922) 239 (hereafter referred to as *Aircraft Yearbook for. . .*).

28. A memorandum to Howard Coffin dated July 15, 1921, outlines plans for such a move. Aero Club of America file, NASM archives.

29. Although the event was originally called the National Airplane Races, they were being commonly referred to as the National Air Races, the name by which they are called today, as early as 1928. "Events Sanctioned for the Year," *National Aeronautics,* May 1928, 80.

30. Memorandum to Howard Coffin dated July 15, 1921.

31. A resolution to sell all Aero Club property to trustees Harry B. Thayer, W. F. Fullam, and Charles Thaddeus Terry was made by Howard E. Coffin, and seconded by Philip J. Roosevelt. It carried unanimously among the following members and officers in attendance: "Chas. Jerome Edwards; Courtlandt [*sic*] Field Bishop; Richard F. Hoyt; Howard E. Coffin; Caleb S. Bragg; Maurice G. Cleary; Philip A. Carroll; Philip J. Roosevelt; Lorillard Spencer; Mr. Anderson; Mr. Crawford; Mr. Robertson; Augustus Post." Augustus Post, recording secretary, "Minutes of a Regular Meeting of the Board of Governors of the Aero Club of America," Aero Club club house, 11 East 38th Street, New York, February 1, 1922, NASM archives.

32. "Woodhouse Sues Aero Board Again," NYT, September 7, 1922, 10:1.

33. "Woodhouse Called Ex-Convict in Court," NYT, September 26, 1922, 4:2.

CHAPTER 12

1. Program of the 1922 National Airplane Races (Detroit: Detroit Aviation Society, 1922). Collection of the author.

2. From a score sheet attached to a program for the 1922 National Airplane Races. Collection of the author.

3. Nick Komons, *Bonfires to Beacons* (Washington, D.C.: Smithsonian Institution Press, 1989) 54–55.

4. C. V. Glines, "Fifty Years Ago with the NAA," *National Aeronautics,* Spring 1973. Glines attributes this objective to Orville Wright.

5. Extract from the NAA charter. NAA file, NASM archives.

6. "Army Airmen Race Despite High Winds," NYT, October 14, 1922, 7:1.

7. "To Incorporate National Association," NYT, October 14, 1922, 7:1.

8. The district vice presidents and governors were, respectively: First District, Porter H. Adams/Godfrey L. Cabot; Second District, John D. Larkin, Jr./Maurice G. Cleary; Third District, L. F. Sevier/R. J. Walters; Fourth District, L. Sevier/Van H. Burgin; Fifth District, Glenn L. Martin/D. M. Outcalt; Sixth District, Charles S. Rieman/S. D. Waldon; Seventh District, Ralph Cram/Howard F. Wehrle; Eighth District, Edgar Tobin/William F. Long; Ninth District, P. G. Johnson/C. H. Messer. The governors-at-large were: William P. MacCracken, Jr., Newton D. Baker, Leonard Wood, Gould Dietz, and W. F. Roberts.

9. Federal Aviation Administration (FAA) historian Nick Komons has constructed a compelling, if not totally convincing, argument that the NAA's detractors, those who perceived the officers to be operating out of self-interest, were acting under "mere impression." *Bonfires to Beacons,* 59–60.

10. Ibid., 55–67.

11. "Aircraft Production," transcript of the U.S. Senate Subcommittee of the Committee on Military Affairs, Washington, D.C., July 11, 1918, Vol. I, 674–76.

12. Komons, *Bonfires to Beacons,* 68–93.

13. "Harold Evans Hartney," in Writers' Program of the Works Projects Administration, *Who's Who in Aviation: 1942–1943* (Chicago: Ziff-Davis, 1942) 187.

14. Howard Mingos, *The Birth of an Industry* (New York: W. B. Conkey, 1930) 52–53.

15. Ibid., 48–49.

16. Ibid., 37–55.

17. Ibid., 54.

18. Komons, *Bonfires to Beacons,* 12, 29, 58.

19. The Canuck was the Canadian version of the famous Curtiss JN-4 trainer, called the Jenny in the United States. There were only minor differences between the two models.

20. Interview by the author with Raymond Vaughn, April 1981, Toledo, Ohio.

21. Roger E. Bilstein, *Flight in America* (Baltimore, Md.: The Johns Hopkins University Press, 1984) 61.

22. Komons, *Bonfires to Beacons,* 28–29.

23. Mail carrying dated back as far as the first balloon flight in America and letters were frequently carried by the early pioneer airplane pilots. Regular airmail flights conducted entirely by the United States Postal Service, however, did not begin until 1918.

24. Komons, *Bonfires to Beacons,* 25.

25. Ibid., 22–25.

26. "Would Teach 1,000 to Fly," NYT, July 26, 1923, 12:8. This cash bonus seems ridiculously small by today's standards, but would have purchased nearly one hundred gallons of fuel in 1923.

27. *NAA Review,* Vol. 1, No. 1, December 1, 1923, 3.

28. Paul Edward Garber, *Building and Flying Model Aircraft* (New York: Ronald Press, 1928) 2.

29. Ibid., 21–22.

30. NAA news releases dated May 14 and April 23, 1923, NAA file, NASM archives.

31. "Passage of Winslow Bill will be step toward 'America First in the Air,'" *National Aeronautics,* December 1923, 3. The title of the official magazine for the National Aeronautic Association changed periodically. Throughout this book the NAA magazine will be cited as *National Aeronautics,* even though it appeared at various times as *The National Aeronautic Association Review, NAA Review, Aeronautic Review, The Aeronautic Review, The National Aeronautic Magazine,* and *National Aeronautics.* At the present time the NAA publishes a newsletter called *For the Record.*

32. Komons, *Bonfires to Beacons,* 59.

33. "Backs Up Aviation Bill," NYT, January 10, 1923, 22:8.

34. "Schwab Urges Law to Control Flying," NYT, January 28, 1933, 14:1.

35. "Aviation Films To Be Available For Chapter Meetings," *National Aeronautics,* July 1924, 4. "Express Interest in Aviation Measure," *National Aeronautics,* March 1924, 1.

36. Komons, *Bonfires to Beacons,* 59.

37. Proceedings of the Eleventh Annual NAA Convention, August 18–19, 1932. NAA file, NASM library. The proceedings note that there were no figures available for membership before 1925.

38. Komons points out that few of the gypsy fliers were involved in the NAA in the first place. Although his observations are correct, the independent fliers had the sympathy and support of a surprising number of rank and file NAA members. *Bonfires to Beacons,* 58–59.

39. Ibid., 59–61.

40. "The Airways Marking System," *National Aeronautics,* June 1927, 8.

41. "Awards 15 Records to Navy Seaplanes," NYT, November 4, 1923, 5:1.

42. "Says We Lead World in Aircraft Advance," NYT, March 9, 1925, 3:2.

43. Komons, *Bonfires to Beacons,* 80–84.

44. Ibid., 83–88. The story of how the Air Commerce Act came to be is rather lengthy and complex. Persons interested in a far more complete account of the passage of this legislation are urged to read Komons's excellent book.
45. "Says We Lead World in Aircraft Advance."
46. "Mitchell Attacks Byrd," NYT, August 13, 1926, 2:6.
47. "Mitchell is Proposed as Head of Aero Body," NYT, Augut 27, 1926, 17:2.
48. Komons, *Bonfires to Beacons,* 43.
49. "Mitchell Opens New Aviation Fight," NYT, August 28, 1926, 10:8.
50. Komons, *Bonfires to Beacons,* 43.
51. "Wants an Airport for Every City," NYT, September 8, 1926, 12:2.
52. Interview by the author with Nell MacCracken, daughter of William MacCracken, March 1990, Washington, D.C.

CHAPTER 13

1. John T. McCutcheon, "Crossing the Atlantic Ocean by Flying Boat" [cartoon], *Aero and Hydro,* February 28, 1914, 274.
2. "Mail Pilot Flies Entry for Paris Flight; C. A. Lindbergh Will Fly a Ryan Monoplane," NYT, March 1, 1927, 16:3.
3. "Cannot Waive Flight Notice," NYT, April 10, 1927, pt. II, 7:4.
4. Joseph Hamlen, *Flight Fever* (New York: Doubleday, 1971) 69–70.
5. Stephan Wilkinson, "The Search for L'Oiseau Blanc," *Air & Space/Smithsonian,* February/March 1987, 86.
6. Hamlen, *Flight Fever,* 78–82
7. Charles A. Lindbergh, "Leap Fog at Night," *National Aeronautics,* October 1926, 162. Charles A. Lindbergh, "He Does it Again," *National Aeronautics,* November 1926, 174.
8. Collier trophy list of recipients, NAA files.
9. Throughout World War I the U.S. government contracted for the manufacture of only 714 parachutes. Of these, only 448 were actually delivered to the field. All of these were used by the Signal Corps in observation balloons, and most were of the variety known as "basket parachutes," which lowered the entire balloon basket, including the records and maps aboard, as well as the observer. Report of Benedict Crowell, Assistant Secretary of War, in *America's Munitions 1917–1918* (Washington, D.C.: U.S. Government Printing Office, 1919) 341.
10. *Aircraft Yearbook for 1927,* 242–244.
11. *Aircraft Yearbook for 1928,* 18–25.
12. Eaton Manufacturing Company, *A Chronicle of the Aviation Industry in America: 1903–1947* (Cleveland: Eaton Manufacturing Company, 1948) 45.
13. *Aircraft Yearbook for 1928,* 108–111.
14. "French Reluctantly Return Lindbergh Flight Barograph," NYT, January 21, 1928, 3:2.
15. The original date was to have been August 12, but pilots entered in the competition voted for a postponement when several accidents, some fatal, were caused by competitors rushing to ready their planes in time for the deadline.
16. Hamlen, *Flight Fever,* 213.
17. Ibid., 214.

18. "Aeronautic Body for Check," NYT, August 24, 1927, 4:4.

19. "Bar Association for Flight Control," NYT, September 3, 1927, 2:6.

20. "Scouts Lindbergh's 'Luck,'" NYT, February 17, 1928, 10:6.

21. Quoted from a magazine article in Muriel Earhart Morrissey and Carol L. Osborne, *Amelia, My Courageous Sister* (Santa Clara, Calif.: Osborne, 1987) 124.

22. Procedings of the Eleventh Annual NAA Convention, August 18–19, 1932. NAA file, NASM archives.

23. "Plans Clubs to Cut the High Cost of Flying," NYT, June 12, 1929, 16:2.

24. Lester D. Gardner, *Who's Who in American Aeronautics,* Third Edition (New York: Aviation Publishing, 1928). The book had been originally published in 1925 and the 1928 edition was a greatly expanded version of the first two editions, the original of which was called *The Blue Book of American Airmen.*

25. Edith Dodd Culver, *Tailspins* (Santa Fe, N.M.: Sunstone Press, 1986). Edith Dodd Culver is the widow of Paul Culver, pioneer civilian, military, and airmail pilot. The book is a collection of her memories of life as the young wife of an early aviator.

26. The original plaque is now in the Southern Museum of Flight at Birmingham, Alabama. Although the effect was certainly not intentional, these plaques created some confusion for the descendants of other early flying pioneers. They list (with the exception of the Wright Brothers) only those persons who were still living at the time the organization was formed, who were able clearly to prove eligibility, and who knew of the organization's existence and expressed a desire to join. Omission of an early flier's name from the plaque does not necessarily indicate that doubts exist about his or her flying status. Indeed, by the end of 1916 there had been over one hundred more licenses issued by the Aero Club than there were members in the Early Birds. Because flying licenses were not required, more than two thousand pilots in all might have met the eligibility requirements of the Early Birds of America.

27. Telephone interview by the author with Eldon Cessna, son of Early Bird charter member Clyde Cessna, founder of Cessna Aircraft Company, April 1991.

28. For years the organization sought to establish a fitting official repository for its early aviation memorabilia. At one time Henry Ford's Greenfield Village Museum was considered, and some materials were reportedly turned over to them. More recently, the National Air & Space Museum was chosen—largely owing to the influence of Early Bird member Paul Garber—but significant amounts of Early Bird materials have also been turned over to the Air Force Museum at Wright-Patterson Air Force Base, Dayton, Ohio; the Curtiss Museum, Hammondsport, New York; the Southern Museum of Flight, Birmingham, Alabama; and the Naval Aviation Museum, San Diego, California.

29. Undated list entitled "Some Items of Service Rendered to the National Aeronautic Association By John F. Victory 1926–1935." NAA files.

30. "Honor the Wrights at Kitty Hawk Site," NYT, December 18, 1928, 18:2. In keeping with the hospitality shown the Wrights on their initial voyage to North Carolina, the farmers of Dare County joined together to build a road from the ferry landing to what is now known simply as Kill Devil Hill. The origin of the landmark's name is uncertain. Some have speculated that the shape of the sand dunes resemble the horns of a devil. The author submits a new possibility: two old North Carolina folk names for a certain hand tool, a sort of cross between an axe

and a sledgehammer that is used to split firewood, are "go-devil" and "kill-devil." The origin of this name, too, is obscure, but the author can attest from experience that prolonged use of the tool will exorcise the devil—or any other form of energy—from the user. Perhaps the curved shape of the dune reminded some early Kitty Hawker of the wide, curved, dull blade of this tool.

CHAPTER 14

1. This expression, now in common use, was originally a bastardization of the term "affixed wing."
2. Frank A. Tichenor, "Air—Hot and Otherwise: The NAA—That's Enough," *Aero Digest,* July 1930, 2.
3. Coffin reportedly contributed $120,000, Patterson gave $50,000, and Cabot contributed unspecified, but significant, sums to keep the organization afloat. Nick Komons, *Bonfires to Beacons* (Washington, D.C.: Smithsonian Institution Press, 1989) 59.
4. "Bingham is Slated for Air Post Again," NYT, July 19, 1931, pt. II, 3:2.
5. "Christopher Quits Aeronautic Body," NYT, April 3, 1931, 8:6.
6. Treasurer's report for 1932 and membership records for 1932. NAA file, NASM archives.
7. Ibid.
8. Letter from Glenn Martin to William MacCracken, April 20, 1933. NAA file, NASM archives.
9. Ibid.
10. Ibid.
11. "Amelia Earhart Quits National Air Group; Opposes Policies of Bingham Association," NYT, May 8, 1933, 17:2.
12. Ibid.
13. Letter from Dudley Steele to William MacCracken, May 9, 1933. NAA file, NASM archives.
14. "Airmen Face Ban for Chicago Race," NYT, July 13, 1933, 8:6. William R. Enyart, "Chronology of Los Angeles–Chicago Impasse." Typewritten summary of events prepared by Enyart at the request of Hiram Bingham on August 12, 1933. NASM archives.
15. Enyart, "Chronology of Los Angeles–Chicago Impasse."
16. Ibid.
17. Ibid.
18. Claudia M. Oakes, *United States Women in Aviation: 1930–1939* (Washington, D.C.: Smithsonian Institution Press, 1985). Donna Veca and Skip Mazzio, *Just Plane Crazy: Biography of Bobbi Trout* (Santa Clara: Osborne, 1987). Jacqueline Cochran and Maryann Bucknum Brinley, *Jackie Cochran: An Autobiography* (New York: Bantam, 1987).
19. The founders of the organization mailed letters to all 117 of the female pilots then licensed in the United States, inviting them to join. The club's name is derived from the number who responded.
20. Muriel Earhart Morrissey and Carol L. Osborne, in *Amelia, My Courageous Sister* (Santa Clara, Calif.: Osborne, 1987), credit humorist Will Rogers with this term.

21. Oakes, *United States Women in Aviation: 1930–1939*, 31. All the Gee Bees eventually crashed.

22. Ibid., 37.

23. John Alison quoted from interview by the author with John Alison and Gen. Brooke Allen (Ret.), April 1991, Washington, D.C.

24. Cochran and Brinley, *Jackie Cochran*, 116–26, 312.

25. John Tegler, *Gentlemen, You Have a Race* (Severna Park, Md.: Wings, 1984) 8.

26. This story was told to the author by one of the few participants still living, under the condition that he not be identified. When asked who else, other than those listed, had been involved, he responded that he could not recall any others, but added, "When word got around what was up, there was no shortage of men wanting to be next in line. Jackie was a strong-willed woman and people either liked her or disliked her—there was no in between."

27. Cochran and Brinley, *Jackie Cochran*, 353.

28. William Stephen Grooch, *Skyway to Asia* (New York: Longmans, Green, 1936). In this book, Grooch tells the impressive story of laying the groundwork for a transoceanic airway from his vantage point as operations manager of the installation crew.

29. "AMA's 50th Anniversary," *Model Aviation*, June 1986, 95–102. Most of the information herein on the early days of the AMA is drawn from this article.

30. "Story of AMA," *National Aeronautics*, March 1951, 3.

31. "AMA's 50th Anniversary."

32. Jay P. Spenser, *Aeronca C-2—The Story of the Flying Bathtub* (Washington, D.C.: Smithsonian Institution Press, 1978) 23.

33. Paul A. Schweizer, *Wings Like Eagles* (Washington, D.C.: Smithsonian Institution Press, 1988) 7.

34. In the course of doing research on the early glider movement in the United States, the author frequently encountered the names of German immigrants who came to America to work (usually in the engineering field) for large companies. Conspicuous among these were Goodyear and General Electric, and some of the early gliding clubs were founded by employees of such companies.

35. Schweizer, *Wings Like Eagles*, 14.

36. Ibid., 18–19.

37. Interview by the author with Willis Sperry, younger brother of Jack Sperry, June 1985, Akron, Ohio.

38. Although the roman numeral II is often omitted from modern discussions of this sailplane, it does appear to have been preceded by one or more traditional German primary gliders, manufactured at Baker-McMillen under the direction of Klemperer. There are references to Klemperer flying such a primary plane of his own construction, presumably the *Cadet I*.

39. Schweizer, *Wings Like Eagles*, 23–25.

40. Ibid., 32.

41. Telephone interview by the author with Paul A. Schweizer, Sr., January 6, 1991.

42. Chauncey E. Spencer, *Who Is Chauncey Spencer?* (Detroit: Broadside Press, 1975) 29–35.

CHAPTER 15

1. Page Shamburger, *Tracks Across the Sky* (Philadelphia: J. B. Lippincott, 1964) 152–53.

2. "When in the middle 1930's the airmail contracts were suddenly canceled, American aviation suffered a body blow. Repercussions from the punitive Congressional investigations sponsored by Senators Gerald P. Nye and Hugo Black—now Mr. Justice Black of the United States Supreme Court—interfered with both military and commercial development and halted progress. While American aviation was being kicked around as a political football, Messrs. Hitler, Mussolini, Hirohito and Stalin seized the favorable opportunity, so unexpectedly handed them, to inaugurate their bids for world dominion under the Douhet doctrine of victory through air force." Eugene E. Wilson, *Slipstream: The Autobiography of an Aircraftsman* (Palm Beach, Fla.: Literary Investment Guild, 1967) xiii.

3. Interview by the author with Nell MacCracken, daughter of William MacCracken, July 1990, Washington, D.C.

4. Roger E. Bilstein, *Flight in America* (Baltimore, Md.: The Johns Hopkins University Press, 1984) 96–100.

5. Ibid., 96–100.

6. Gill Robb Wilson, "The New NAA," *National Aeronautics*, June 1940, 19–26.

7. *Aircraft Yearbook for 1939,* 157–60.

8. Wilson, "The New NAA."

9. Robert A. Searles, "AOPA: 50 Years of Service," *Business & Commercial Aviation,* April 1989, 94.

10. Wilson, "The New NAA," 19.

11. At the time he was elected president the key debate raging within the NAA was whether aviation would be best promoted by encouraging new aircraft production or encouraging new runway construction.

12. Wilson, "The New NAA," 19–26.

13. The full-page ad featured a photograph of an attractive young woman standing seminude above the London skyline. It was, to say the least, an unusual feature for an aviation magazine (coming some fifteen years before the publication of the first issue of *Playboy*), but one that seems to have met with some resistance. The advertisement was not repeated in subsequent issues.

14. "Public Subsidies," *National Aeronautics*, January 1946, 7.

15. General Frank M. Andrews to G. deFreest Larner, general manager of *National Aeronautics*, published in the January 1941 issue, page 46.

16. "Air Reserve Association Affiliates with NAA," *National Aeronautics*, January 1941, 24. "ARA Objectives for 1941," *National Aeronautics*, April 1941, 54.

17. Caption beneath photograph of the forty-eight "Cub" training planes, *National Aeronautics*, June 1941, 34.

18. "NC 26641—Heading South," *National Aeronautics*, March 1941, 9.

19. "Up From Harris Hill," *National Aeronautics*, August 1941, 9.

20. Thilbert H. Pearce, "First to Jump," *The State* (Raleigh, N.C.), January 1975.

21. Gill Robb Wilson, "Civil Aviation Requests Clearance," *National Aeronautics*, August 1941, 21.

22. Gill Robb Wilson, "The Civil Side of Air Power," *National Aeronautics*, December 1941, 9. "Civil Air Patrol," *National Aeronautics*, January 1942, 12.

23. "The Civil Air Patrol," *National Aeronautics,* January 1946, 7.
24. "CAP Future," *National Aeronautics,* January 1946, 23.
25. "NAA Moves," *National Aeronautics,* March 1942, 17. The author confesses that he found little humor in this particular cartoon.
26. Mary O. Merck, "'Bye Baby Bunting . . . Mama's Gone A-Riveting," *National Aeronautics,* January 1943, 31.
27. *The Life and Times of Rosie the Riveter* [documentary film] (Los Angeles: Clarity Educational/Direct Cinema, 1980).
28. "In There Pitching," *National Aeronautics,* March 1943, 29.
29. The 99s later proved to be just as dedicated to accomplishing the objectives of peace. In 1963 they came to the assistance of a young Korean woman who was studying at an American university. The woman, Kyung Kim, dreamed of returning to her native country and helping teach women there how to fly airplanes. But the dream was clouded by the seemingly impossible task of financing an airplane to take back with her. The 99s, however, believed in making such dreams come true. They organized a national drive, collecting S&H Green Stamps from women across America. The Sperry and Hutchinson Company agreed to redeem three million of their premiums, usually earned with grocery store purchases, for a Piper Colt training airplane. By April of that year the airplane, christened *Miju-Ki,* Korean for *USA Flight,* was en route to Korea to fulfill its mission of teaching thirty Korean women, screened from over two thousand applicants, to become pilots. "Miss Kim Gets Wings for Teaching," *National Aeronautics,* April 1963, 3. The contributions this woman made to aviation in her country over the next twenty-nine years were recognized internationally in 1992, when she was awarded the prestigious Gold Medal of the FAI for outstanding contributions to aeronautics.
30. Louis R. Purnell, "The Flight of the Bumblebee," *Air & Space/Smithsonian,* October/November 1989.
31. Theodore W. Robinson, "The Tuskegee Experience," sidebar to Purnell's "The Flight of the Bumblebee."
32. "Two Prominent NAAers Missing," *National Aeronautics,* February 1943, 52.
33. Paul A. Schweizer, *Wings Like Eagles* (Washington, D.C.: Smithsonian Institution Press, 1988) 85–86.
34. "Besides the Aces," *National Aeronautics,* February 1944, 20. On September 7, 1976, Masajiro (Mike) Kawato, who, as an eighteen-year-old Japanese Imperial Navy seaman had shot Boyington down in 1944, flew a Piper Comanche nonstop from Tokyo, Japan, to Crescent City, California. In 1991 he was recognized for this flight by the NAA.
35. "Air Youth Trophy Announced," *National Aeronautics,* June 1943, 15.
36. "Air Youth Program," *National Aeronautics,* May 1942, 21.
37. "Smithsonian to Receive Brewer Trophy Duplicate," *National Aeronautics,* March 1950, 4.
38. "The Fortieth Anniversary: The World Honors the Wright Brothers; NAA Awards Collier Trophy to Arnold," *National Aeronautics,* January 1944, 12–13.
39. John Goldstrom, *A Narrative History of Aviation* (New York: Macmillan, 1930) 46–64.
40. "Charlie McCarthy Becomes Junior Air Reserve Cadet," *National Aeronautics,* February 1943, 23.

41. "Believe-It-Or-Not Ripley Visits Omaha for Youth Fairs," *National Aeronautics,* February 1943, 22. "Ripley Rambles," *National Aeronautics,* February 1943, 38. "Report on Ripley," *National Aeronautics,* March 1943, 21.
42. Oliver Stewart, *First Flights* (New York: Pittman, 1958) 184–90. Robert M. Bartlett, *Sky Pioneer: The Story of Igor Sikorsky* (New York: Scribner's, 1947) 100–24. Samuel C. Williams, *Report on the Helicopter* (New York: Brundage, Story, and Rose, 1955) 17–19.
43. "Aviation's Rope Trick," *National Aeronautics,* April 1943, 16.
44. Bartlett, *Sky Pioneer,* 129.
45. Ibid., 145–46.
46. Igor Sikorsky, "The Coming Air Age," *Atlantic Monthly,* September 1942, 33–39.

CHAPTER 16

1. "Restrictions," *National Aeronautics,* October 1945, 30. "Private Flying Ban," *National Aeronautics,* September 1944, 9. "Flight Restrictions," *National Aeronautics,* September 1944, 32.
2. John P. V. Heinmuller, "New Records Needed," *National Aeronautics,* July 1944, 12. "The Record Race," *National Aeronautics,* January 1946, 11. "Timing is Intricate," *National Aeronautics,* January 1946, 12.
3. "Timing is Intricate." "Jet Establishes New Speed Range," *National Aeronautics,* January 1946, 13. "B-29 is Distance King," *National Aeronautics,* January 1946, 14.
4. "FAI and Advancing Speeds," *National Aeronautics,* January 1946, 1.
5. This was a popular topic for the Enyart administration in a regularly featured section of the postwar *National Aeronautics* called "Private Flying."
6. "Air Meets Re-Open," *National Aeronautics,* March 1946, 9.
7. "CAA Examiners," *National Aeronautics,* October 1945, 29. "Flying Boom," *National Aeronautics,* October 1945, 29.
8. "Planes," *National Aeronautics,* October 1945, 29.
9. Telephone interview by the author with Paul A. Schweizer, Sr., January 6, 1991.
10. Known affectionately as "grasshoppers," these were light aircraft adapted for military use from prewar civilian designs. They served numerous roles, generally as couriers and short-haul transport planes, but also functioned at times as spotter planes, and even as air ambulances.
11. "The Industry: It's Still Unsure About Purchases, Research, and Surplus Sales," *National Aeronautics,* October 1945, 45. "Surplus Disposal," *National Aeronautics,* August 1944, 43. "Surplus Disposition," *National Aeronautics,* July 1944, 47.
12. "Surplus," *National Aeronautics,* January 1946, 30.
13. More than thirty thousand military surplus airplanes eventually were sold to civilians. A great many of these were planes like the C-47 (the military version of the DC-3), which were converted for use by airlines and wealthy individuals wanting luxurious personal aircraft.
14. "New Gasoline," *National Aeronautics,* October 1945, 32.
15. In the 1980s most aircraft fuel distributors finally discontinued 80-octane gasoline in favor of a "standardized" low-lead 100-octane fuel. The producers felt that their operations would become more efficient if they were able to store and distribute

only one grade of fuel, which, they claimed, met the majority of general aviation's needs. Owners of planes designed to run on the lower-octane, unleaded gas turned to automotive fuels that were more compatible with their engines. The Experimental Aircraft Association, an air sports organization of the NAA, demonstrated to the Federal Aviation Administration that certain applications of automobile fuels, or "mogas," were safe for aircraft. They obtained permission to issue supplemental type certificates, or STCs (amendments to the original airworthiness certificates issued to manufacturers by the FAA) for use of the automobile fuels in airplane engines. Many aircraft owners, especially those operating antique and classic planes, feel that the EAA certificate has done much to reduce maintenance and extend the life of aircraft engines originally designed to operate on unleaded fuel.

16. Howard Mingos, ed., *The Aircraft Yearbook for 1947* (New York: Lanciar, 1947) 408.

17. "Award," *National Aeronautics,* October 1945, 45.

18. Howard's devotion to excellence was also manifested in his flying. His aerobatic routine earned him the respect of thousands of pilots and nonfliers who saw him perform at more than 1500 air shows during the 1940s, 1950s, and 1960s, and won him a place of leadership on early aerobatic teams that represented the United States in international competition. Howard died while flying a German Bücker Jungmeister biplane, which had first been shipped to America aboard the dirigible *Hindenburg.* His family and former employees subsequently rebuilt the aircraft and donated it to the National Air & Space Museum, where it remains today as a memorial to Howard.

19. "Joint Project: Boy Scouts and NAA Agree to Pool Air Youth Efforts," *National Aeronautics,* October 1945, 53.

20. G. Harvey Ralphson, *Boy Scouts in an Airship* (Chicago: M. A. Donohue, 1915). It is interesting to note that advertisements in this same book also offered four books by Margaret Burnham under the heading The Girl Aviator Series. Although early flight was clearly male-dominated in practice, it seems evident that young women were equally interested in flying, even though they were restricted, for the most part, to experiencing it vicariously.

21. "Cub Plane Donated to Girl Scouts Awarded Yearly to Best Flight," *National Aeronautics,* September 1945, 55.

22. "Truman Becomes Member," *National Aeronautics,* November 1945, 59.

23. "Veterans & Employment," *National Aeronautics,* January 1946, 28.

24. "Driv-Ur-Self," *National Aeronautics,* March 1951, 6.

25. Daniel R. Zuck, *An Airplane in Every Garage* (Washington, D.C.: Vantage Press, 1958) 122–25.

26. "NAA Role in Air Policy, Chapter Stimulation Plans Are Key Points Approved by Convention in Akron," *National Aeronautics,* July 1949, 3.

27. "Industry and Research," *National Aeronautics,* January 1946, 29.

28. Devon Francis, *Mr. Piper and His Cubs* (Ames: Iowa State University Press, 1973) 134–35. Production numbers for 1946 vary, depending on the source. *The Aircraft Yearbook for 1947* cites 32,882 civilian and 1217 military planes manufactured in the first eleven months of that year. The Bureau of the Census of the U.S. Department of Commerce claimed that 34,874 civilian and 1330 military aircraft were turned out the same year.

29. Zuck, *An Airplane in Every Garage,* 29.

30. "NAA Staff Report Suggests Local Activities," *National Aeronautics,* July 1948, 10–11.
31. "Resolutions Passed by 26th National Convention," *National Aeronautics,* July 1948, 5–6.
32. "NAA Role in Air Policy . . .," 3–5.
33. "National Aviation Meeting is Being Planned by NAA for December 15–17 in Washington," *National Aeronautics,* October 1949, 3.
34. "National Aviation Forum Cites Need of Unity to Support Advancement of Air Power for Peace," *National Aeronautics,* January 1950, 3.
35. "Wilson Attacks Air Policy, Urges NAA Lead in Inquiry," *National Aeronautics,* November 1949, 7.
36. "No Time to Play Cowboy," *National Aeronautics,* July 1950, 1.
37. Kendall K. Hoyt, "Civil Air Mobilization," *National Aeronautics,* July 1950, 3. In fairness to Leverone and Hoyt, they were not the only ones who espoused such beliefs. Zuck's *An Airplane in Every Garage,* published in the late 1950s, contained detailed maps of areas that would be most likely to suffer from nuclear fallout and showed would-be plane owners how they could fly from major cities to "safe" areas in case of such a Russian attack. It is possible that the Leverone/Hoyt philosophy helped inspire Zuck's thinking on this matter.
38. "Box-top Colonels," *National Aeronautics,* November 1950, 1.

CHAPTER 17

1. Interview by the author with Francis M. Rogallo, March 1991, Kitty Hawk, North Carolina.
2. "Five International Model Records, First for US, Being Sent to FAI," *National Aeronautics,* October 1949, 2.
3. Ibid.
4. "The National Air Races Must Be Perpetuated," *Southern Flight,* October 1949, reprinted in *National Aeronautics,* October 1949, 6. John Tegler, *Gentlemen, You Have a Race* (Severna Park, Md.: Wings, 1984) 16. "The Air Races and the Press," *National Aeronautics,* October 1949, 1. Air Force General H. H. Arnold later stated that "Lindbergh gave me the most accurate picture of the Luftwaffe, its equipment, leaders, apparent plans, training methods, and present defects that I have so far received." Presentation of Wright Trophy to Lindbergh Will Highlight Aviation Anniversary Dec. 17," *National Aeronautics,* December 1949, 3.
5. "National Air Races in Future to Feature Jets, Midgets; Management Bans Racing of All Surplus Military Planes," *National Aeronautics,* April 1950, 4.
6. Don Berliner, "Pylon Racing's on the Rise," *National Aeronautics,* March 1963, 14–15.
7. When an aircraft is accelerated, either linearly or rotationally, inertial forces are imposed on the control surfaces. These inertial forces are transmitted to the control column and felt by the pilot. During rapid acceleration, such as that encountered in aerobatics or pylon racing, these forces can become significant enough to overpower the pilot's input. Dynamic balancing of the control surfaces seeks to minimize these inertial forces by careful selection of the position of the hinge line and

the shape and mass distribution of the control surface. However, the complete elimination of these forces is generally not practical. Internet correspondence with Professor David Rogers, professor of aerospace engineering, U.S. Naval Academy, Annapolis, Maryland.

8. Many of these blueprints still remain as part of the NAA material held by the NASM archives.

9. "In the Wind," *National Aeronautics*, March 1963, 15.

10. "Jackie Cochran Sets New Record," *National Aeronautics*, January 1950, 7. The record flight was hardly Cochran's first. In 1948 she flew a P-51 to a new women's international record for the one-hundred-kilometer closed course. On that flight she averaged 469 miles per hour. "Cochran Sets New Records With a P-51," *National Aeronautics*, January 1948, 16.

11. "Midget Race, Aerobatics Highlight Miami Maneuvers," *National Aeronautics*, February 1950, 2.

12. "Interest Reported Shows Chapters Still Real Foundation of NAA," *National Aeronautics*, April 1950, 6–7.

13. "Chapters NOT to Be Dropped" [sidebar to "Convention in St. Louis June 10–13 Will Chart Course for NAA's Future"], *National Aeronautics*, May 1950, 3.

14. Coffey, an Aero Club member since 1914, a World War I veteran, and a founder of the CAP, was killed in the crash of his private plane near Hood River, Oregon, in June 1954.

15. "W. P. McCracken [sic], Jr., Honored For 29 Years Service to NAA," *National Aeronautics*, November 1951, 2.

16. "The Men Behind NAA," *National Aeronautics*, September 1964, 22.

17. Keith Saunders, "The Hour Is Late," *National Aeronautics*, January 1955, 5.

18. Keith Saunders, "This Trend Must Be Halted," *National Aeronautics*, May 1956, 3.

19. Clyde P. Barnett, "A Timely Self Inspection," *National Aeronautics*, June 1962, 2–3.

20. "U.S. Parachutists May Go to Moscow," *National Aeronautics*, May 1956, 2.

21. "Parachute Meet Hurt by Weather," *National Aeronautics*, June 1958, 9.

22. "Parachuting Laws Surveyed by NPJRI," *National Aeronautics*, March 1955, 4. The 1960s television series *Ripcord* and the 1969 Burt Lancaster movie *The Gypsy Moths* would give the sport an added impetus. Both featured exciting aerial footage, but also exaggerated the perils of parachuting. Many of the impressionable young men and women in the audience kept secret their desires to jump from an airplane until they were old enough to risk parental disapproval and live out their own dreams of unencumbered human flight. The author was one of those young people. When, about 1960, his Boy Scout troop leader (a Marine Corps gunnery sergeant and skydiver named Davis) took the troop to see an exhibition by the U.S. Army's Golden Knights precision parachute team, he knew that he must someday emulate the larger-than-life heroes who landed only feet from the spot where he and his friends sat. In 1972 he made the first of several parachute jumps, becoming firmly enamored with the air.

23. George Hardie, Jr., and John C. Burton, "The Long Road Back: Founding the Experimental Aircraft Association," *Sport Aviation*, July 1986, 57–59.

24. "National Security and NAA's New Look," *National Aeronautics*, January 1961, 2–3.

25. Lanphier had served as president from 1954 to 1959. He was one of the most distinguished U.S. military pilots in the Pacific Theater in World War II, having flown

over one hundred combat missions. On April 18, 1943, Lanphier made history by downing the Japanese bomber carrying Admiral Isoroku Yamamoto, commander of the Japanese Imperial Navy. This was the same Admiral Yamamoto who had planned and executed the infamous attack on Pearl Harbor. When Cochran became president, Lanphier assumed the chair of the NAA's board of directors.

26. John Alison quoted from interview by the author with John Alison and Gen. Brooke Allen (Ret.), April 1991, Washington, D.C.

27. Robert H. Dillaway, "High, Hot and Hazardous," *National Aeronautics,* September 1964, 8.

28. The current record is 216.84 miles per hour, set in 1970 at Windsor Locks by Byron Graham, flying a Sikorsky S-67.

29. Telephone interview by the author with Beverly Witherspoon, March 4, 1991, Durham, North Carolina.

30. Much later it was discovered that the Soviet method of returning space capsules to their target areas—which were located on land, within Soviet borders, rather than in the open ocean—was so unrefined that the cosmonaut bailed out of the descending capsule, coming down under his own parachute, rather than enduring a dangerously hard landing inside the spacecraft. In order to circumnavigate the FAI rule that pilots must land in their aircraft for a flight to be certified as a record, Soviet premier Nikita Krushchev himself insisted that Gagarin had returned to earth inside *Vostok I.* Walter A. McDougall, . . . *The Heavens and the Earth: A Political History of the Space Age* (New York: Basic Books, 1985) 246.

31. G. Harry Stine, "Model Rocketry Comes Of Age," *National Aeronautics,* January 1963, 8.

32. Ralph V. Whitener, "Where Is Our Welcome Mat?" *National Aeronautics,* January 1962, 3.

33. "U.S. Army Parachute Team International Records Claimed," *National Aeronautics,* May 1962, 21.

34. "Massachussettes Spreads Welcome Mat for World Parachute Teams," *National Aeronautics,* September 1962, 22–23. M/Sgt. Allen G. Mainard, USMC, "It's a Long, Short Way from Pond's Hay Patch," *National Aeronautics,* October 1962, 4–5.

35. "Wuffos" is the traditional name skydivers apply to the nonparachuting masses who flock to drop zones, sometimes hoping to witness tragedy but usually just intensely curious about the sport. The term apparently came out of questions asked by southern onlookers (probably near Ft. Bragg, North Carolina, or Ft. Benning, Georgia) who seemed to begin all questions with a dialectically slurred "What for . . ."—as in "Whuffo you wanna jump outta a perfeckly good airplane?"

36. The photographs appeared in numerous aviation and popular magazines, including *National Aeronautics* and *Parachutist,* as well as several books, including Andy Keech, *Skies Call* (Edinburgh: Morris & Gibb, 1974).

37. "An Old Art Reborn," *National Aeronautics,* December 1962, 10–11.

38. It was Nance, a Piedmont Airlines pilot from Winston-Salem, North Carolina, who loaned his Great Lakes biplane to the team.

39. Ralph V. Whitener, "We Lost, But We Won!" *National Aeronautics,* September 1962, 20–21.

40. Nicholas King, "Viet Nam [*sic*] Risks and Problems," *New York Herald Tribune.* Reprinted in *National Aeronautics,* April 1962, 11.

41. "A Rose Garden Affair," *National Aeronautics,* September 1962, 12–13.

42. William P. MacCracken, "What 'Flight Plan '63' Meant to Me," *National Aeronautics,* January 1963, 3.
43. Don Berliner, "Ray Rawlings Wants to Fly—The Big Question Is How?" *National Aeronautics,* November 1962, 30–31.
44. William Strohmeier, "Pilot's Licenses Can Benefit Career Opportunities for Youth," *National Aeronautics,* November 1962, 30. Strohmeier worked for Taylorcraft and Piper Aircraft Corporation.
45. The Timers Aero Club was a unique chapter of the NAA in that it was dedicated to the cause of recruiting and training timing stewards: persons who authenticated record attempts. The Timers Aero Club served as an adjunct to the NAA Contest Board. "Behind U.S. World Records—The NAA Contest Board," *National Aeronautics,* June 1964, 10–11, 24.
46. "Kitty Hawk—Mission Accomplished," *National Aeronautics,* March 1964, 8.
47. William A. Ong, "What Is NAA—What Does It Do?" *National Aeronautics,* June 1964, 2.
48. Interview by the author with Floyd Sweet, April 1991, McLean, Virginia.
49. Quoted by William L. O'Neill in *Coming Apart* (New York: Times Books, 1971) 137.
50. "Losses," *National Aeronautics,* December 1964, 2.

POSTSCRIPT

1. Edward C. Sweeney, "A Message from the President," *National Aeronautics,* December 1965, 3.
2. "The Men Behind NAA ...," *National Aeronautics,* September 1964, 22.
3. Michael J. H. Taylor, ed., *Jane's Encyclopedia of Aviation* (New York: Portland House, 1989) 189.
4. Roger E. Bilstein, *Flight in America* (Baltimore, Md.: The Johns Hopkins Press, 1984) 303–4.
5. Telephone interview by the author with Lawrence Wilson, archivist, National Air & Space Museum, August 1992.
6. John Alison quoted from interview by the author with John Alison and Gen. Brooke Allen (Ret.), April 1991, Washington, D.C.
7. It was for the most part solitary pioneers who experimented with homemade Rogallo wings in the early and mid-1960s. In 1961, Tom Purcell of Raleigh, North Carolina, built a Rogallo wing device that was towed behind an automobile at the Raleigh-Durham airport. NASA was, at the same time, constructing its own Rogallo wing glider on the west coast, and sent Milt Thompson, a test pilot and future astronaut, to Raleigh to learn how to fly on Purcell's homebuilt machine. Purcell later put the wing onto pontoons, and it was with this device that Rogallo himself first flew. Francis M. Rogallo, address delivered at a celebration marking the 42d anniversary of the Rogallo wing, August 15, 1990, Kitty Hawk, North Carolina.
8. Interview by the author with John Harris of Kitty Hawk Kites, March 1991, Nag's Head, North Carolina.
9. Vic Powell, "From *Ground Skimmer* and Bamboo Bombers—How Our Sport Got Where It Is Today," *Hang Gliding,* January 1981, 19–21.

10. About half of the sixteen thousand active pilots are members of the USHGA. Telephone interview by Arthur W. Greenfield, Jr., NAA secretary, Contest and Records Board, with Gregg Lawless, USHGA president, August 1992.

11. "300 Mile Hang Glider Record," *For the Record,* September/October 1990, 5.

12. Both Barry Palmer and Bill Bennett experimented with powered hang gliders in the 1960s—Bennett by attaching an engine to his own back like a knapsack. Daniel F. Poynter, *Hang Gliding: The Basic Handbook of Skysurfing* (North Quincy, Massachusetts: Daniel F. Poynter, 1973) 202. John Lake mounted an engine on a Wills Wing hang glider to make early powered flights. Telephone interview by the author with John Ballantyne, president of the United States Ultralight Association, March 1991. In March 1966, Peter F. Girard and Fred Landgraf applied for a patent on a "Demountable Aircraft with Flexible Wing" that employed a Rogallo wing attached to a light framework, powered by a "pusher" gasoline engine and propeller (patent number 3,361,388 was issued to them on January 2, 1968). But it is John Moody who is usually credited with being the father of the modern American ultralight movement because, beginning in the 1970s, he first offered a kit for sale that combined Larry Morrow's Easy Riser ultralight with an engine and propeller. Ballantyne interview.

13. Although it is not certain what the weight of the Demoiselle actually was (the weight would have varied somewhat from plane to plane), had it been built of aluminum and dacron, rather than bamboo and silk, it certainly would have fallen into the same category as modern ultralights.

14. Arthur E. Joerin and A. Cross, "How to Build the Famous 'Demoiselle,' Santos-Dumont's Monoplane," *Popular Mechanics,* June 1910, 775–81.

15. The Quicksilver was just one of many fine ultralight designs manufactured in this country. It was chosen as an example because it was among the first commercially manufactured machines and has an evolutionary history that is representative of the entire industry.

16. Bob Lovejoy, "Evolution of the Quicksilver," *Ground Skimmer,* July–September 1974, 10–12.

17. Telephone interview by the author with John Lasko, former employee of Eipper-Formance, Inc., April 1991.

18. In many European countries the light airplane movement is relatively new and no such tradition has been established. There, two-seat light planes in the "microlight" category using Rogallo wings are quite popular.

19. Ballantyne interview.

20. Telephone interview by the author with John Lasko, former employee of Eipper-Formance, Inc., April 1991.

21. Luis Marden, "The Bird Men," *National Geographic,* August 1983, 198–217.

22. "Ultralights—Flying or Dying?" segment of *20/20* originally broadcast on ABC, December 8, 1983.

23. The author was one of a group of ultralight instructors and fliers who performed a review of the videotape of the *20/20* segment, played in slow motion, shortly after it aired. As seen on the tape, the pilot reached forward, grabbed a down tube (structural member), and appeared to be pulling himself forward as if trying to stand up. This movement appeared to cause the down tube to crumple and the forward motion of the pilot continued, as he proceeded to fall away from the plane. Although his motivations in those critical seconds will never be known, he may have felt that

he was out of control, panicked, and decided that he would be better off jumping out before the plane climbed higher.

24. Ballantyne interview.

25. Letter from former SSA president William Ivans, San Diego, California, to NAA president Malvern J. Gross, Jr., August 24, 1992. NAA files.

26. John Alison quoted from interview by the author with John Alison and Gen. Brooke Allen (Ret.), April 1991, Washington, D.C.

27. Brooke Allen quoted from interview by the author with John Alison and Gen. Brooke Allen (Ret.), April 1991, Washington, D.C.

28. From the mission statement of the *NAA Association Development Plan* (undated: probably early 1982), NAA files.

29. NAA files.

30. Agendas for *Aerospace I* and *Aerospace II,* NAA files.

31. Mode C transponders are radio devices that allow air traffic controllers to identify readily a given airplane, its position, and its altitude. Although many pilots agree that such devices are beneficial for aircraft operating in areas where air traffic is dense (generally around major airports), the proposal would have required the devices to be installed on many aircraft that did not operate in high-traffic environments—like gliders and hot air balloons—or that were not designed to accommodate such modern electrical devices. In 1986 the estimated cost of installing Mode C transponders was between $700 and $800 for planes equipped with electrical systems, but much higher for the numerous aircraft without electricity-generating capability. The installation of Mode C in some of the airplanes originally built as postwar training aircraft, for example, could result in an expense equal to the value of the plane.

32. "Aviation Tort Bill Introduced In Congress," *For the Record,* Fall 1987, 5.

33. Kirk S. Thomas, director of the Soukup & Thomas International Balloon and Airship Museum (Mitchell, S.D.) and founder of the Virgin Islands Balloon and Airship Association, letter to NAA president Malvern J. Gross, Jr., July 1992. NAA files.

34. Telephone interview by the author with Karl H. Stefan, August 28, 1992.

35. Kirk S. Thomas, letter to NAA president Malvern J. Gross, Jr., April 8, 1991. NAA files.

36. Tom Crouch, *The Eagle Aloft* (Washington, D.C.: Smithsonian Institution Press, 1983) 662.

37. Ibid.

38. Ibid. National Aeronautic Association. *World and United States Aviation and Space Records & Annual Report* (Washington, D.C.: National Aeronautic Association, 1990) 13.

39. Thomas letter, April 8, 1991.

40. Telephone interview by the author with Mike Wallace, 1992 U.S. representative to the Gordon Bennett competition, August 1992. Thomas letter, April 8, 1991.

41. Fax letter from Kirk Thomas and Jacques Soukup to NAA president Malvern J. Gross, Jr., September 27, 1992. NAA files.

42. Telephone interview by the author with John Burton, EAA director of corporate communications, August 1992. Oshkosh, it has been said, is to the aviation enthusiast what all the theme parks in the world, transplanted to one location, would be to the child. If

so, a new counterpart to Disney World is quickly developing in the form of the springtime EAA gathering in Lakeland, Florida. In a few short years the "Sun 'n Fun" fly-in has grown from a friendly gathering of local pilots to the first big aviation event of the year, anxiously awaited by southern and northern pilots alike. There, pilots can thaw out from the winter freeze among an array of aircraft ranging from jets to ultralights.

43. In this manner Thomas Pratt, an Ohio pilot, won the microlight "distance in a straight line" record. On September 30, 1987, Pratt covered 639.34 miles in his Mitchell Silver Eagle, breaking the existing record (set the previous year by an Australian) by a shade under 150 miles. Another American microlight pilot did not need to compete against anyone but himself when he took to the air, because his flights were made to establish the performance records for flights in amphibians weighing less than 661 pounds. Matthew Naylor, of San Antonio, took his Quicksilver GT 400 over the three kilometer course at a speed of 58.31 miles per hour on June 5, 1984. The next day he flew the same plane over a fifteen- and then a twenty-five-kilometer course, establishing a speed record for amphibians of 75.10 miles per hour. National Aeronautic Association, *World and United States Aviation and Space Records* (Arlington, Va.: National Aeronautic Association, 1992) 153.

44. During the 1989 international competition at Chantilly, France, the first-place crew of Jon Iseminger and Rudy Hobbs scored an unheard-of 796 points out of a possible total of 800. This near-perfect accomplishment by the crew from Fort Rucker, Alabama, will be difficult to beat. At the same competition the U.S. team, consisting of three crews, scored 2373 of 2400 possible points, beating the second-place Soviet team by 171 points and showing that the Army pilots were consistent in their excellent performance. "U.S. Helicopter Team Sweeps World Championships," *For the Record,* November/December 1989, 1–3.

45. Telephone interviews by the author with George W. Putnam, past president of the Helicopter Club of America and head of the U.S. delegation at the 1989 competition, April 1991, and Jean K. Tinsley, president of the Helicoper Club of America, August 1992.

46. "U.S. Captures World Title in Model Helicopter Championships," *For the Record,* November/December 1987, 2.

47. B. J. Worth, a USPA national director and the organizer of the incredible Olympic effort, summed up the jump in this way: "The skydiving exhibition performed during the opening ceremonies of the Seoul Olympics was a unique opportunity to showcase one of the most exciting forms of aviation to the world. The seventy-nine men and women involved, twenty-four of whom were American, clearly possess the highest levels of skill. They demonstrated how far the modern sport of skydiving has come in a few brief decades." Telephone interview by the author with Worth, May 1991.

48. Taylor, *Jane's Encyclopedia of Aviation,* 241–251.

AFTERWORD

1. Paragliding involves a nonrigid wing that develops its shape from ram air entering its envelope, and which then creates lift. The wing is made of cloth and can

be packed in a backpack and easily carried from one launch site to another. A paraglider can function much as a hang glider in thermal conditions. For the time being paragliding activities are centered in a new organization, the American Paragliding Association, which is affiliated with the U.S. Hang Gliding Association.

APPENDIX F

1. Edwards's position as first treasurer is mentioned in *Fly,* Vol. 1, No. 1, November 1908.
2. Augustus Post, "Something About Areo [*sic*] Clubs," *Fly,* November 1908, 10.
3. Crouch, *Eagle Aloft,* 533.
4. A *New York Times* article dated November 13, 1905, lists these men as founding members of the Aero Club of America. Membership rosters published by the Aero Club nine or more years later show several enrollment dates that conflict with these.
5. These men were mentioned in a *New York Times* article dated November 15, 1905. They were in a group that included several known members of the Aero Club, and were mentioned in a context that suggested (but did not specifically state) that they, too, were members. Most are mentioned in other sources as being members, but the exact date each joined may be uncertain.
6. These men were listed on the Aero Club of America membership roster of 1914 as having joined in the fall of 1905.
7. Stockholders listed in Aero Club of America certificate of incorporation, June 7, 1905, book 144, page 524, State of New York, Office of the Secretary of State.

APPENDIX G

1. Believed to be "Naval Militia of New York."
2. The original document showed Pulliam to be an ensign in the U.S. Army. This obviously should have read "USN."
3. In place of license number 237, 227 was repeated.
4. Statement accompanying this list in the Aero Club of America Handbook, 1919. This apparently refers to the reorganization of February 1910 (see Chapter 7).
5. Obviously a typographical error. Possibly 1913.
6. Many, but not all, of those listed died from aviation-related causes.

BIBLIOGRAPHY

ARCHIVAL MATERIALS

Albany, New York: New York Department of State, Division of Corporations

Aero Club of America articles of incorporation, June 28, 1905.

Fremont, Ohio: Rheinhardt Ausmus Collection, Rutherford B. Hayes Presidential Center Library

Correspondence of the Roberts Motor Manufacturing, Sandusky, Ohio.
Undated transcript of talk delivered by Rheinhardt Ausmus.

Arlington, Virginia: National Aeronautic Association files

Letter from George B. Weller, Rawlins, Wyoming, to NAA president Malvern J.
   Gross, Jr., July 18, 1990.
"Some Items of Service Rendered to the National Aeronautic Association by John F.
   Victory 1926–1935" (undated list).
Mission statement, *NAA Association Development Plan* (undated: probably early 1982).
Letters from Kirk S. Thomas of the Soukup & Thomas International Balloon and
   Airship Museum (Mitchell, South Dakota) and the Virgin Islands Balloon and

Airship Association to NAA president Malvern J. Gross, Jr., April 8, 1991 and
July 1992.

Letter from William Ivans, San Diego, California, to NAA president Malvern J. Gross,
Jr., August 24, 1992.

Suitland, Maryland: National Air & Space Museum (NASM) archives at the Paul E. Garber facility

National Aeronautic Association Collection
Treasurer's Report for the NAA, 1932.
Letter from Glenn Martin to William MacCracken, April 20, 1933.
Letter from Dudley Steele to William MacCracken, May 9, 1933.
"Chronology of Los Angeles–Chicago Impasse." Enyart's typewritten summary of
events, dated August 12, 1933.

Washington, D.C.: National Air & Space Museum (NASM) archives

The Aero Club of America and National Aeronautic Association files contain miscella-
neous correspondence, publications, minutes, pamphlets, news clippings, etc., of the
Aero Club from 1906 to 1921, and the NAA from 1922 to the present.

Aero Club of America File
Aero Club notice to members, June 30, 1908.
Notice to members (undated) on Aero Club letterhead.
Letter from Albert C. Triaca to Aero Club members, October 29, 1909.
Letter from the Aero Club to members, June 30, 1908.
Letter from the Aero Club to members, February 20, 1909.
Minutes of the Aero Club meeting, February 1, 1909.
Letter from A. Holland Forbes to Aero Club members, September 24, 1909.
"Important Facts." An undated flyer distributed to Aero Club members (apparently
by Parker, Kimball, and Beach), c. October 9, 1909.
Letter from Orrel A. Parker, Wilbur R. Kimball, and Stanley Y. Beach to Aero Club
members, October 9, 1909.
President's report to the Aero Club, Fall 1908.
Minutes of the Aero Club meeting, November 5, 1908.
"Aero Club of America Bulletin No. 2." November 30, 1909.
Letter from Courtland F. Bishop to James Means, November 4, 1909.
Letter from William Hawley to James Means, February 17, 1909.
Letter to Aero Club members, February 1, 1909.
Letter from Augustus Post to James Means, November 23, 1908.
Bulletin of the Aero Club of America, 1912.
Memorandum to Howard Coffin, July 15, 1921.
"Minutes of a Regular Meeting of the Board of Governors . . .," February 1,
1922.

Bibliography 363

Charles F. Willard file
NAA File
Copy of the NAA charter, 1922.
NAA news releases, May 14 and April 23, 1923.
Proceedings of the Eleventh Annual NAA Convention, August 18–19, 1932.
Harold Morehouse. *Flying Pioneers Biographies* (typewritten, unpublished).
Aero Club of America pilot's license information cards.

BOOKS

Aeronautical Chamber of Commerce, *Aircraft Yearbook for 1922, 1927, 1928,* and
    1939. New York: Aeronautical Chamber of Commerce of America, 1927, 1928,
    and 1939.
America's Munitions 1917–1918. Washington, D.C.: U.S. Government Printing Office,
    1919.
Bartlett, Robert M. *Sky Pioneer: The Story of Igor Sikorsky.* New York: Scribner's, 1947.
Bacon, Gertrude. *Balloons, Airships and Flying Machines.* New York: Dodd, Mead, 1905.
Bilstein, Roger E. *Flight in America.* Baltimore, Md.: The Johns Hopkins University
    Press, 1984.
Blanchard, Jean Pierre. *Journal of my Forty-Fifth Ascension, Being the First Performed in America, On the Ninth of January, 1793.* Philadelphia: Charles Cist, 1793.
Casey, Louis S. *Curtiss: The Hammondsport Era 1907–1915.* New York: Crown, 1981.
Caulkins, Daniel, M.D. *Aerial Navigation.* Toledo, Ohio: Blade Printing and Paper, 1895.
Cochran, Jacqueline, and Brinley, Maryann Bucknum. *Jackie Cochran: An Autobiography.*
    New York: Bantam, 1987.
Crouch, Tom. *The Bishop's Boys: A Life of Wilbur and Orville Wright.* New York: W.W.
    Norton, 1989.
———. *The Eagle Aloft.* Washington, D.C.: Smithsonian Institution Press, 1983.
Culver, Edith Dodd. *Tailspins.* Santa Fe, N.M.: Sunstone Press, 1986.
Current, Richard, Garraty, John A., and Weinberg, Julius, eds., *Words That Made American
    History,* Vol. II. Glenview, Ill.: Scott, Foresman, 1978.
Cyclopedia of Automobile Engineering, Vol. 4. Chicago: American School of Correspondence, 1912.
Eaton Manufacturing Company, *A Chronicle of the Aviation Industry in America: 1903–
    1947* (Cleveland: Eaton Manufacturing Company, 1948) 45.
Francis, Devon. *Mr. Piper and His Cubs.* Ames: Iowa State University Press, 1973.
Freudenthal, Elsbeth E. *Flight Into History.* Norman: University of Oklahoma Press,
    1949.
Garber, Paul Edward. *Building and Flying Model Aircraft.* New York: Ronald Press, 1928.
Gardner, Lester D. *Who's Who in American Aeronautics,* Third Edition. New York: Aviation
    Publishing, 1928.
Goldstrom, John. *A Narrative History of Aviation.* New York: Macmillan, 1930.
Grooch, William Stephen. *Skyway to Asia.* New York: Longmans, Green, 1936.
Hamlen, Joseph. *Flight Fever.* New York: Doubleday, 1971.
Harris, Sherwood. *The First to Fly: Aviation's Pioneer Days.* New York: Simon & Schuster,
    1970.

Hatch, Alden. *Glenn Curtiss, Pioneer of Naval Aviation.* New York: Julian Messner, 1942.

Hodgins, Eric, and Magoun, F. Alexander. *Sky High.* Boston: Brown, Little, and Company, 1935.

Howard, Fred. *Wilbur and Orville: A Biography of the Wright Brothers.* New York: Alfred A. Knopf, 1987.

Hunsacker, Dr. Jerome C. *Some Lessons of History.* New York: Wings Club, 1966 (originally delivered as the Second Wings Club "Sight" Lecture).

Jane, Fred T., ed. *Jane's All the World's Aircraft.* London: Sampson Low, Marston, 1914.

Keech, Andy. *Skies Call.* Edinburgh: Morriss & Gibb, 1974.

Kelly, Fred C. *The Wright Brothers: A Biography Authorized by Orville Wright.* New York: Ballantine, 1950.

Komons, Nick. *Bonfires to Beacons.* Washington, D.C.: Smithsonian Institution Press, 1989.

Layman, D. *To Ascend from a Floating Base.* Cranbury, N.J.: Associated University Presses, 1979.

Lougheed, Victor. *Vehicles of the Air.* Chicago: Reilly and Britton, 1909.

McDougall, Walter A. . . . *The Heavens and the Earth: A Political History of the Space Age.* New York: Basic Books, 1985.

Maitland, Lt. Lester J. *Knights of the Air.* New York: Doubleday, Doran, 1929.

Maxim, Sir Hiram S. *Artificial and Natural Flight.* New York: Macmillan and London: Whittaker, 1908.

Mingos, Howard. *The Birth of an Industry.* New York: W. B. Conkey, 1930.

———. *The Aircraft Yearbook for 1947.* New York: Lanciar, 1947.

Morrissey, Muriel Earhart, and Osborne, Carol L. *Amelia, My Courageous Sister.* Santa Clara, Calif.: Osborne, 1987.

The Motor editorial staff. *The Aero Manual, 1910.* London: Temple Press, 1910.

National Aeronautic Association. *World and United States Aviation and Space Records & Annual Report.* Washington, D.C.: National Aeronautic Association, 1990.

———. *World and United States Aviation and Space Records.* Arlington, Va.: National Aeronautic Association, 1992.

Noble, David W. *The Progressive Mind: 1890–1917.* Minneapolis: Burgess, 1981.

Oakes, Claudia M. *United States Women in Aviation through World War I.* Washington, D.C.: Smithsonian Institution Press, 1978.

———. *United States Women in Aviation: 1930–1939.* Wahington, D.C.: Smithsonian Institution Press, 1985.

O'Neill, William L. *Coming Apart.* New York: Times Books, 1971.

Oppel, Frank, ed. *Early Flight: From Balloons to Biplanes.* Secaucus, N.J.: Castle, 1987.

Prendergast, Curtis, and the Editors of Time-Life Books. *The First Aviators.* Alexandria, Va.: Time-Life Books, 1980.

Poynter, Daniel F. *Hang Gliding: The Basic Handbook of Skysurfing.* North Quincy, Mass.: Daniel F. Poynter, 1973.

Ralphson, G. Harvey. *Boy Scouts in an Airship.* Chicago: M.A. Donohue, 1915.

Rolt, L. T. C. *The Aeronauts.* New York: Walker, 1966.

Schweizer, Paul A. *Wings Like Eagles.* Washington, D.C.: Smithsonian Institution Press, 1988.

Shamburger, Page. *Tracks Across the Sky.* Philadelphia: J. B. Lippincott, 1964.

Spencer, Chauncey E. *Who Is Chauncey Spencer?* Detroit: Broadside Press, 1975.

Spenser, Jay P. *Aeronca C-2—The Story of the Flying Bathtub.* Washington, D.C.: Smithsonian Institution Press, 1978.

Stewart, Oliver. *First Flights*. New York: Pittman, 1958.

Taylor, Michael J. H., ed. *Jane's Encyclopedia of Aviation*. New York: Portland House, 1989.

Tegler, John. *Gentlemen, You Have a Race*. Severna Park, Md.: Wings, 1984.

Turnbull, Archibald D., and Lord, Clifford L. *History of United States Naval Aviation*. New Haven, Conn.: Yale University Press, 1949.

Unger, Irwin. *These United States,* combined edition. Englewood Cliffs, N.J.: Prentice Hall, 1992.

Veca, Donna, and Mazzio, Skip. *Just Plane Crazy: Biography of Bobbi Trout*. Santa Clara, Calif.: Osborne, 1987.

Villard, Henry Serrano. *Blue Ribbon of the Air.* Washington, D.C.: Smithsonian Institution Press, 1987.

Williams, Samuel C. *Report on the Helicopter.* New York: Brundage, Story, and Rose, 1955.

Wilson, Eugene E. *Slipstream: The Autobiography of an Aircraftsman.* Palm Beach, Fla.: Literary Investment Guild, 1967.

Writers' Program of the Works Projects Administration. *Who's Who in Aviation: 1942–1943*. Chicago: Ziff-Davis, 1942.

Zahm, Albert F. Early Powerplane Fathers. Notre Dame, Ind.: University Press, 1945.

Zuck, Daniel R. *An Airplane in Every Garage*. Washington, D.C.: Vantage Press, 1958.

CATALOGS AND PROGRAMS

E. B. Heath Aerial Vehicle Company. Catalog F. Chicago: E. B. Heath Aerial Vehicle Company, c. 1911 (collection of the author).

Program and score sheet of the 1922 National Airplane Races. Detroit: Detroit Aviation Air Society, 1922 (collection of the author).

FILMS AND TELEVISION PROGRAMS

The Life and Times of Rosie the Riveter. Los Angeles: Clarity Educational/Direct Cinema, 1980.

"Ultralights—Flying or Dying?" Segment of *20/20* originally broadcast on ABC, December 8, 1983.

INTERVIEWS

By the Author

Alison, John, and Allen, Gen. Brooke (Ret.), Washington, D.C., April 1991.

Ballantyne, John, telephone interview, March 1991.

Burton, John, telephone interview, August 1992.

Cessna, Eldon W., telephone interview, April 1991.

Harris, John, Nag's Head, North Carolina, March 1991.

Lasko, John, telephone interview, April 1991.

MacCracken, Nell, Washington, D.C., July 1990 and March 1990.
Messer, Glen, Early Birds Association meeting, Long Beach, California, March 1989.
Putnam, George W., telephone interview, April 1991.
Rogallo, Francis M., Kitty Hawk, North Carolina, March 1991.
Rogers, David, Internet correspondence, August 1992.
Schweizer, Paul A., Sr., telephone interview, January 6, 1991.
Spain, Justice William E., Richmond, Virginia, June 1983.
Sperry, Willis, Akron, Ohio, June 1985.
Stefan, Karl H., telephone interview, August 28, 1992.
Sweet, Floyd, McLean, Virginia, April 1991.
Tinsley, Jean K., telephone interview, August 1992.
Vaughn, Raymond, Toledo, Ohio, April 1981.
Wallace, Mike, telephone interview, August 1992.
Wilson, Lawrence, telephone interview, August 1992.
Witherspoon, Beverly, telephone interview, March 4, 1991.
Worth, B. J., telephone interview, May 1991.

By Others

Lawless, Gregg, by Arthur W. Greenfield, Jr., NAA secretary, Contest and Records Board.
    Telephone interview, August 1992.
Vaughn, Stanley I., by George Hardie, Jr., Experimental Aircraft Association historian.
    Audiotaped interview, September 12, 1962. Experimental Aircraft Association Archives, Oshkosh, Wisconsin.

MAGAZINE AND JOURNAL ARTICLES

Anonymous. "Are the Wrights Justified?" *Aeronautics,* April 1910, p. 141.
Anonymous. "The Johnstone Fatality," *Aero,* November 26, 1910, 10.
Anonymous. "The King of the Air," *Aero,* November 26, 1910, 12.
Anonymous. "Honorary Membership to Mr. Edison," *Aerial Age,* March 1923.
Anonymous. "AMA's 50th Anniversary," *Model Aviation,* June 1986, 95–102.
Arnold, H. H. "The First Ten," *Flying Sportsman and Skyways,* August 1947, 18–19, 48,
    50; "The Second Ten," September 1947, 24–25, 45, 52, 55, 61; "The Third
    Ten," October 1947, 29–30, 52, 54.
Bacheler, Origen, ed., in *The Family Magazine—or—Weekly Abstract of General Knowledge,* May 11, 1833, 30–31; May 18, 1833, 35.
Bronson, Edgar Beecher. "An Aerial Bivouac," *American Magazine,* October 1907, 623.
    Quoted in Oppel, *Early Flight.*
Clover, Samuel T. "First Meet of the Man-Birds in America," *The Outing Magazine,* February 1910, 750–63.
Hardie, George, Jr., and Burton, John C. "The Long Road Back: Founding the Experimental Aircraft Association," *Sport Aviation,* July 1986, 57–59.
Hearne, R. P. "Strategy and Tactics of a Flying Machine Campaign," *Current Literature,*
    October 1909, 449–52 (extracted from the author's book *Aerial Warfare*).

Hersey, Henry Blanchard. "Experiences in the Sky," *The Century Magazine*, March 1908, 643–55.

Joerin, Arthur E., and Cross, A. "How to Build the Famous 'Demoiselle,' Santos-Dumont's Monoplane," *Popular Mechanics*, June-July 1910, 775–81.

Lovejoy, Bob. "Evolution of the Quicksilver," *Ground Skimmer*, July-September 1974, 10–12.

McCutcheon, John T. "Crossing the Atlantic Ocean by Flying Boat [cartoon]," *Aero and Hydro*, February 28, 1914, 724.

Marden, Luis. "The Bird Men," *National Geographic*, August 1983, 198–217.

Moffett, Cleveland. "Winning the First International Balloon Race," *McClure*, October 1907, 637–48.

Neely, Frederick R. "The Robert J. Collier Trophy," *Pegasus* (magazine of the Fairchild Engine and Aircraft Corporation), December 1950, reproduced in *National Aeronautics*, June 1961, 4–12.

Pierce, Thilbert H. "First to Jump," *The State* (Raleigh, N.C.), January 1975, 8–12.

Post, Augustus. "A Fall From the Sky," *The Century Magazine*, October 1910, 935–47.

Powell, Vic. "From *Ground Skimmer* and Bamboo Bombers—How Our Sport Got Where It Is Today," *Hang Gliding*, January 1981, 18–21.

Purnell, Louis R. "The Flight of the Bumblebee," *Air & Space/Smithsonian*, October/November 1989, 32–40 (also contains "The Tuskeegee Experience," sidebar by Theodore W. Robinson).

Searles, Robert A. "AOPA: 50 Years of Service," *Business & Commercial Aviation*, April 1989, 94.

Sikorsky, Igor. "The Coming Air Age," *Atlantic Monthly*, September 1942, 33–39.

Tichenor, Frank A. "Air—Hot and Otherwise: The NAA—That's Enough," *Aero Digest*, July 1930, 2.

Wilkinson, Stephan. "The Search for L'Oiseau Blanc," *Air & Space/Smithsonian*, February/March 1987, 86.

PROCEEDINGS AND ADDRESSES

"Aircraft Production," transcript of the U.S. Senate Subcommittee of the Committee on Military Affairs, Washington, D.C., July 11, 1918, Vol. I.

"Importation of Surplus Aircraft," transcript of the House Committee on Ways and Means, Washington, D.C., May 28, 1920, part 1.

Rogallo, Francis M. Address delivered at a celebration marking the 42d anniversary of the Rogallo wing. Kitty Hawk, North Carolina, August 15, 1990.

NEWSPAPERS

Baltimore Sun, September 27, 1959.

Detroit Free Press, June 20, 1911.

New York Times, various issues, 1904–1937.

New York Herald, October 26, 1909.

MAGAZINES

Fly, various issues, 1908–1909.
For the Record, various issues, 1986–1987.
National Aeronautics Magazine (published under various titles), various issues from 1922 onward.
Scientific American, various issues from 1904 onward.

INDEX

This index includes entries corresponding to, among others, the names of persons, organizations, key places, and aircraft of various types mentioned in the main text, the notes, and Appendixes A and C–E. Entries corresponding to citations in the notes are suffixed with an n; those corresponding to citations in the sidebars, with an s. The reader is reminded that additional lists of key persons may be found in Appendix B (Gordon Bennett Cup winners), Appendix F (founding members of the Aero Club of America), Appendix G (Aero Club license holders), Appendix H (presidents of the Aero Club), and Appendix J (officers of the NAA).

ABA, *See* American Bar Association

Abruzzo, Ben, 212–13

Academy of Model Aeronautics (AMA), 139, 153, 174–75, 214, 221

Adams, Elsie W., 246

Adams, Joe, 255

Adams, Porter, 116, 120, 124, 125, 126

Addems, Walter J., 256

Aerial Age magazine, 100

Aerial Coast Patrol Unit Number One, 91

Aerial Experiment Association, 39, 40, 43, 44

Aero and Hydro magazine, 119

Aerobatic Club of America, 188

Aero Cavalcade, 148

Aero Club No. 1, 11, 22, 23

Aero Club No. 3, 12

Aero Club No. 9, 12

Aero Club of Belgium, 9

Aero Club of France, 9, 22, 29, 42, 57, 77, 121, 328n

Aero Club of Illinois, 71

Aero Club of Kansas City, 191, 194

Aero Club of Russia, 185

Aero Club of Spain, 9

Aero Club of St. Louis, 30, 31

Aero Club of Switzerland, 9

Aero Club of the United Kingdom, 9, 77

Aero Club of Washington, 240

Aero Digest, 129

Aerodrome, 12, 30, 153

Aero magazine, 68

Aeronautical Digest, 112

Aeronautic Federation of America, 65

Aeronautics Branch, Department of Commerce, 56, 111–12, 116, 124–25, 126s, 230

Aeronautic Society of New York, 39, 44, 45, 51, 65, 66

Aeronca aircraft manufacturer, 165

Aeronca C-2, 48, 139, 333n

Aeronca C-3, 139

Aerospace Industries Association, 240

AH-64 Apache helicopter, 199s, 235

Aiken, William S., Jr., 256

Air Commerce Bureau, Department of Commerce, 144

Air Coordinating Committee, 180

Aircraft Owners and Pilots Association (AOPA), 146, 149, 203, 205

Aircraft Production Board, 94, 95, 96, 105, 342n

Air Force, 176s, 199s, 218s,, 233, 234, 235, 236

Air Force Museum, 346n

Air Force One, 163

Air Mail Service, U. S., 110s, 230

Air Power magazine, 100

Air Reserve Association, 147

Air Transport Association, 240

Akron Condor, 141

Albuquerque, New Mexico, 212

Aldrin, Edwin E., Jr., 193s, 234

Alison, John, 184, 197, 200, 206, 209

Allen, Brooke, 197, 200, 206, 208–9

Allen, Bryan, 173

Allen, James, 32, 33, 49, 55, 81